A Biblical Case for the Premillennial, Post-Tribulational Rapture of the Church

Randall Monroe

1

Table of Contents

Introduction

The Purpose

The purpose for this paper is threefold. **First,** it is my intention to reveal the historical facts surrounding the origin and development of the pretribulation rapture teaching. **Second**, to describe the interpretative methods used to support the doctrine of the pretribulation rapture. **Third**, to explain the theological contradictions that the pretribulation rapture doctrine produces.

The Starting Position

First, it is believed that the Bible, in its entirety, is the authoritative, inerrant, inspired Word of God. **Second**, that a consistent literal method of interpretation of the Biblical text naturally results in a premillennial understanding of Scripture. **Third**, that a literal interpretation of the Scriptures reveals that the Second Coming of the Lord Jesus Christ and the rapture of His Church will occur *after* the Tribulation and *not* before. **Fourth**, that the pretribulation rapture teaching rests solely and completely upon speculation, assumption and inference - *not* the literal statements of the Scriptures.

The Methodology

The key arguments used by Dispensationalists[1] in support of the pretribulation rapture theory[2] are presented in the words of the movements most able proponents. Only

---

[1] Dispensationalists maintain that the Church will be removed from the earth **before** the beginning of the future tribulation period described in Matthew 24 and Revelation 6-18. The primary tenant of Dispensational theology is the doctrine of the pretribulation rapture. Virtually every interpretative decision is designed to advance and protect the concept of the pretribulation rapture. Note that the word "rapture" does not occur in the Scriptures. It is derived from the English word "rapt" which means "to transport." *Rapt* comes from the Latin *raptus* and means "to seize." The term "rapture" is universally used by Dispensationalists in place of the Greek word **harpazo**, which is translated "will be caught up" in 1Thess.4:17. Additionally, Dispensationalists divide the Scriptures into different "dispensations" or periods of time, in which God is dealing with mankind in a specific manner, while testing mankind's obedience to specific revelations of His will. Most Dispensationalists see seven different "dispensations." They are Innocence (Gn.1:28-3:13); Conscience (Gn.3:23); Human Government (Gn.8:20); Promise (Gn.12:1); Law (Ex.19:8); Grace (Jn.1:17); Kingdom (Eph.1:10).

[2] Dwight Pentecost, a leading Dispensational scholar, begins a discussion of the pretribulational rapture under the chapter heading "The Pretribulation Rapture Theory." *Things To Come* - Zondervan Publishing House, 1964, p.193.

recognized mainstream Dispensational leaders, teachers and scholars are quoted. All emboldened and italicized words or phrases contained within these quotations are added for emphasis unless otherwise noted. All quotations are fully footnoted. Abbreviations such as *Ibid., Idem, Op. cit., Loc. cit.*, have been intentionally avoided in order to make the sources for all quotations easily and readily available to the reader. Every effort has been made to fairly and accurately present all quotations in their original context. In order to better acquaint the reader with the authors quoted, brief biographical sketches of these authors appear either in the footnotes or in **Appendix A**. Furthermore, the honesty, integrity, sincerity and spirituality of these authors is in no way questioned. They are all regarded to be good and godly men, who have endeavored to faithfully teach the Word of God. I call into question only the validity of their interpretative methods and the aptness of their conclusions - *not* their sincerity, motives or spirituality.

The Assumptions of Historicity and Orthodoxy

The supreme doctrine of modern Dispensationalism is the pretribulation rapture of the Church. The overwhelming majority of American evangelical Christians accept this doctrine because they are convinced that it is based upon a literal premillennial[3] interpretation of the Scriptures. They are convinced that the Dispensational method of interpretation is synonymous with a literal premillennialism and that the doctrine of the pretribulation rapture is the natural result. Furthermore, they are persuaded that a truly literal interpretation of the Scriptures cannot be achieved unless the Dispensational method is employed. Therefore, for many evangelical denominations, the acceptance of the Dispensational method and the pretribulation rapture doctrine has become the acid test of Christian orthodoxy. To deny either is often viewed as tantamount to the denial of the faith that has once and for all been delivered unto the saints.[4] But most of these

---

[3] **Pre-millennialism** teaches that Christ will return *before* the millennium and establish a thousand year reign on earth, as opposed to **a-millennialism**, which sees *no* literal millennium on earth and **post-millennialism** which sees Christ return to the earth *after* the millennium.

[4] George Eldon Ladd has observed that Dispensationalism, "...has come to be exclusively identified with premillennialism in the minds of masses of American evangelicals. Thousands of devout Christians know of no sort of Premillennialism other than the dispensational view." And again, "...many Christians have never heard any sound Bible teachers who held a different position and therefore have naturally concluded that pretribulationalism is essential to premillennialism. This is not true historically, and it is not true theologically or Biblically." *Crucial Questions About the Kingdom of God* - George Eldon Ladd, Wm.B. Eerdmans Publishing Co., 1977, p.49, and *The Blessed Hope* - George Eldon Ladd, Wm.B. Eerdmans Publishing Company, 1980, p.52.

well-intentioned believers are completely unaware that the premillennial interpretation of the Scriptures existed long **before** the development of Dispensationalism and its pretribulation rapture theory. Unknown to millions of evangelical Christians is the fact that the early Church, which clearly held to a premillennial interpretation of the Scriptures, also held to a **post**-tribulational rapture of the Church.[5] It is therefore my intention to demonstrate to the reader, contrary to commonly held opinion, that the Dispensational doctrine of a pretribulation rapture; (a) is **not** based upon a literal interpretation of the Biblical text as is frequently claimed; (b) is **not** synonymous with premillennialism, as is regularly assumed; and (c) is in fact a new and novel doctrine that lacks both theological validity and historical legitimacy.

Randall Monroe
2019

---

[5] See **Appendix B** for a detailed discussion of the **post-tribulational** views of the early Church.

Chapter One
A Brief Overview of Dispensational Teaching

Chapter One Outline:
1. Dispensationalism Defined.
2. The Dispensational Distinction Between Israel and the Church.
3. The Pretribulational Rapture of the Church.

1. Dispensationalism Defined.

The word "Dispensationalism" is derived from the Greek noun *oikonomia.* It is a compound word comprised of *oikos* - *house*, and *nomos* - *law*. It thus refers to the rule, oversight or management of household affairs, and in the New Testament is translated "stewardship," "dispensation," or "administration."[6] The English word "economy" is derived from the Greek word *oikonomia*. An "economy" is generally understood to refer to the organization, administration and management of the affairs of an organized system. It is in this sense, that Dispensationalists have adopted the word *oikonomia* (dispensation) to represent their theological system of Bible interpretation. For example, **H.A. Ironside**, the well-known and highly respected Bible teacher and evangelist asks, "What is meant by a 'dispensation?'...We find that the original word has been brought over into English; it is our word 'economy.'...What is an economy? An economy is an ordered condition of things...A dispensation, an economy, then, is that particular order or condition of things prevailing in one special age which does not necessarily prevail in another."[7] Following the same train of thought, **Charles Ryrie**, states that, "Dispensationalism views the world as a household run by God. In this house-hold world God is dispensing or administering its affairs according to His own will...These various stages mark off the distinguishably different economies in the outworking of His total purpose, and these economies are the dispensations."[8] And **Renald Showers** writes, "...the term dispensation as it relates to Dispensational Theology could be defined as a particular way of God's administrating His rule over the world as He progressively works out His purpose for world history."[9]

---

[6] In the New Testament, the word *oikonomia* is found in, Lk.16:2,3,4; 1Cor.9:17; Eph.1:10; 3:2; Col.1:25.
[7] *In the Heavenlies* - H.A. Ironside, Loizeaux Brothers, 1937, p.66-67.
[8] *Dispensationalism Today* - Charles Caldwell Ryrie, Moody Press, 1970, p.31.
[9] *There Really Is A Difference* - Renald E. Showers, The Friends of Israel Gospel Ministry, Inc., 2002 p.30.

While these definitions may be helpful in revealing the Dispensationalist's presuppositional approach to the Scriptures, they fail to clearly state what the distinctive elements of Dispensational teaching really are. In fact, the defining elements of Dispensational teaching are much more than simply recognizing God's different methods of administering His rule over the nations as He works out His plan and purpose in history. It is important to understand that the recognition of different dispensations or historical periods of Divine administration does **not** make one a Dispensationalist. Admitting this fact, **Charles Ryrie** states, "...a man can believe in dispensations, and even see them in relation to progressive revelation, without being a dispensationalist."[10] Thus, the recognition of different "dispensations" is **not** the defining element of modern Dispensationalism. Rather, the two crucial and distinctive elements that distinguish Dispensational teaching are: first, a rigid distinction between Israel and the Church, and second; the secret, imminent, pretribulational rapture of the Church.

2. The Dispensational Distinction Between Israel and the Church.

Dispensationalism is characterized by a theological system of interpretation that makes a sharp distinction between Israel and the Church. Dispensationalists strenuously argue that, Israel is **not** a part of the Church. It is important to understand that Dispensationalists use the term "Israel" to refer to both the *nation* collectively and to *saved individuals* within that nation. This dual application of the term "Israel" can often be misleading and confusing. For example, **Renald Showers** argues that "...Israel is a nation... but the church is not...the nation of Israel and the Church are separate, distinct entities."[11] Few would object to this statement. Obviously, national Israel is no more a part of the Church than any other nation. However, this is not the real issue. The real question is, "Are the *redeemed individuals* of Old Testament Israel a part of the Church?" To this question, Dispensationalists respond with a resounding "No!" Again, **Renald Showers** maintains that, "There is a distinction between the saved Jews of the Church and the saved Jews of Old Testament Israel; the term 'the church of God' can be applied legitimately only to the church but **not** to Old Testament Israel; and Old Testament Israel and the church are **not** essentially the same."[12]

---

[10] *Dispensationalism Today* - Charles Caldwell Ryrie, Moody Press, 1970, p.44.
[11] *Maranatha* - Renald Showers, The Friends of Israel Gospel Ministry, Inc., 1995, pp.230, 231.
[12] *Maranatha* - Renald Showers, The Friends of Israel Gospel Ministry, Inc., 1995, p.231.

Clearly, Showers maintains that the "saved Jews" of the Old Testament period are **not** a part of the Church. However, he attempts to support this assertion by equating the "saved Jews" of the Old Testament period with "Old Testament Israel." This confuses and confounds the issue. These terms are **not** synonymous. It is obvious from Scripture that many Jews who were a part of "Old Testament Israel" were **not** saved - and no one is claiming that "Old Testament Israel" is a part of the Church. Rather, the real question is "Are the saved Jews of the Old Testament period a part of the Church?"

Dispensationalists categorically reject the traditional premillennial belief that the New Testament Church is a continuation of God's one redemptive plan for mankind. Dispensationalism uniformly denies the unity between Old and New Testament believers and thus the historical continuity of God's redemptive work. For example, **Lewis Sperry Chafer** chides those who, "...cannot recognize that the Church is a new, heavenly purpose of God, absolutely disassociated from both Jew and Gentile (Gal.3:28; Col.3:11), but sees the Church only as an ever increasing company of redeemed people gathered alike from all ages of human history..."[13] Likewise, **John Walvoord**, asserts that, "The church as the body of Christ is therefore a new entity, and the term *ecclesia* [i.e., Church] when used in this sense refers **only** to saints of the present dispensation."[14] And **Charles Ryrie** maintains that, "The church stands distinct from Israel and did not begin until the Day of Pentecost, and thus did not exist in the Old Testament...The church...is distinct to this present time period."[15]

Thus, Dispensationalists deny that God has one company of redeemed people, comprising both Old and New Testament believers. They maintain that the Old Testament believers are a separate and distinct group that must be distinguished from New Testament believers. As a result of this distinction, Dispensationalists uniformly teach that Israel or "the Jews" represent God's "earthly people," while the "Church" is composed of God's "heavenly people." **A. C. Gaebelein** explains that, "Israel's calling is earthly; theirs is an earthly kingdom, ours [i.e. the Church] is altogether heavenly."[16] **C.H. Mackintosh** asserts that, "...the church forms no part of the ways of God with

---

[13] *Systematic Theology* - Lewis Sperry Chafer, Dallas Seminary Press, Vol.IV, p.34.
[14] *The Rapture Question* - John F. Walvoord, Zondervan Books, 1981, p.25.
[15] *Basic Theology* - Charles C. Ryrie, Victor Books, 1986, p.399.
[16] *The Gospel of Matthew* - A.C. Gaebelein, Loizeaux Brothers, Inc., 1910, 1982, p.110.

9

Israel and the earth. The church does not belong to time, but to eternity. She is not earthly, but heavenly."[17] And **Lewis Sperry Chafer** likewise affirms that, "The dispensationalist believes that throughout the ages God is pursuing *two distinct purposes:* one related to the earth with earthly people and earthly objectives involved which is Judaism; while the other is related to heaven with heavenly people and heavenly objectives involved which is Christianity."[18] **Dwight Pentecost** underscores this dichotomy that Dispensationalism creates between Old and New Testament believers when he states that, "There is a distinction between the true church and true or spiritual Israel. Prior to Pentecost there were saved individuals, but there was no church, and they were a part of spiritual Israel, not the church."[19] **Pentecost** further asserts that, "The church and Israel are two distinct groups..."[20] and that "...the distinction between Israel and the church, make it impossible to identify the two in one program."[21] Dispensationalists therefore conclude that God has two separate and distinct redemptive programs - one for Israel and one for the Church. And these two different programs must, in the words of **Pentecost,** "...be distinguished as two separate entities with whom God is dealing in a *special program...*"[22]

Dispensationalists further maintain that the "special program" for Israel ceased when the Jews rejected Jesus as their King, and the special program for the Church then promptly began. The special program for the Church is described as a "parenthetical period" that is located between the 69th and the 70th weeks of Daniel's prophecy contained in chapter 9:25-27. Dispensationalists claim that the Church exists exclusively within this "parenthesis." **H.A. Ironside** refers to this parenthetical period as, "...one of the great and important truths of the Word." He then explains that, "Between the sixty-ninth and seventieth weeks we have a Great Parenthesis which has now lasted over nineteen hundred years. The seventieth week[23] has been postponed by God Himself who changes the times and the seasons because of the transgression of the people...the moment Messiah died on the cross, the prophetic clock stopped. There has not been a tick upon that clock for nineteen centuries. It will not begin to go again until

[17] *Papers on the Lord's Coming* - C.H.M., Loizeaux Brothers Publishers, n.d., p.104.
[18] *Dispensationalism* - Lewis Sperry Chafer, Dallas Seminary Press, 1936, p.107.
[19] *Things To Come* – J. Dwight Pentecost, Zondervan Publishing House, 1964, p.199.
[20] *Things To Come* – J. Dwight Pentecost, Zondervan Publishing House, 1964, p.193
[21] *Things To Come* – J. Dwight Pentecost, Zondervan Publishing House, 1964, p.202.
[22] *Things To Come* – J. Dwight Pentecost, Zondervan Publishing House, 1964, p.201.
[23] The phrase, "the seventieth week" is commonly used by Dispensationalists to refer to the Tribulation period.

the entire present age has come to an end, and Israel will once more be taken up by God."[24] Thus, Dispensationalists teach that since the death of Christ, God has ceased all dealings with national Israel, and that He will not resume His dealings with national Israel again until after the rapture of the Church. Following Ironside, **John Walvoord** teaches that, "...the Scriptures indicate that the church of the present age is a distinct body of believers, but there is good evidence that the age itself is a *parenthesis* in the divine program of God... Those who believe that the present age is a *parenthesis* regard it as the extended period of time between the close of the sixty-ninth week of Daniel and the beginning of the seventieth week." **Walvoord** then goes on to say that, "As the church is a distinct body with special promises and privileges, it may be expected that God will fulfill His program for the church by translating the church out of the earth *before* resuming His program for dealing with Israel and the Gentiles in the period of the Tribulation."[25] Thus, Dispensationalists maintain that the Church began at the end of the 69th week (when Israel rejected Jesus) and that the Church will be removed from the earth before the beginning of the 70th week (the Great Tribulation). The period of time between the 69th and 70th weeks is termed the "Great Parenthesis," and is referred to as the "Church Age."

Furthermore, Dispensationalists claim that God's dealings with national Israel immediately and completely ceased at the 69th week, when that nation rejected Jesus' offer to establish the earthly Davidic Kingdom for Israel. They insist that Jesus Christ offered Himself to Israel as their theocratic King and fully intended to establish the earthly Davidic Kingdom promised to Israel in the Old Testament. **Lewis Sperry Chafer** writes, "The evidence is complete respecting the fact that Israel's kingdom was offered to that nation by Christ at His first advent."[26] However, Dispensationalists also contend that because Israel rejected Jesus as their King, the promise of the earthly theocratic kingdom was "postponed" and the "parenthesis" or "Church Age" was begun. **C.H. Mackintosh** declares that, "Messiah was rejected, cut off, and had nothing. What then? God signified His sense of this act, by suspending for a time His dispensational dealings with Israel. The course of time is interrupted. There is a great gap."[27] **Mackintosh** goes on to say, that it is within this "gap" that the Church, "...is called into

[24] *The Great Parenthesis* - H.A. Ironside, Zondervan Publishing House, 1953, p.23.
[25] *The Rapture Question*, John F. Walvoord, Zondervan Books, 1981, pp.25,37.
[26] *Systematic Theology* - Lewis Sperry Chafer, Dallas Seminary Press, Vol.IV, p.266.
[27] *Papers on the Lord's Coming* - C.H.M., Loizeaux Brothers Publishers, n.d., p.102.

existence during an unnoticed interval - a break or parenthesis consequent upon the cutting off of the Messiah."[28] **A.C. Gaebelein**, also commenting on Israel's rejection of Jesus' kingdom offer, declares that, "It is the great turning point in this Gospel [i.e., the Gospel of Matthew] and with it the offer of our Lord to Israel as their King, as well as the offer of the Kingdom ceases."[29] Dispensationalists contend that because Israel rejected Jesus Christ as their theocratic King (as well as the earthly kingdom that He offered), God has postponed His plan for Israel and is now dealing exclusively with the Church, and will not again resume His dealings with Israel until *after* the Church is raptured and the tribulation commences. For example, **W.E. Blackstone** asserts that, "...God begins to deal with Israel again *after* He has taken the church away."[30] Likewise, **C.H. Mackintosh** states, "Then when the church has gone to be with her Lord in the heavenly home, God will resume His public actings with Israel. They will be brought into great tribulation, during the week already referred to [i.e., the seventieth week of Daniel, which is also referred to as the Great Tribulation period]."[31]

Dispensationalists therefore, view the future Tribulation as a period that pertains specifically to Israel and *not* the Church. For example, **Lewis Sperry Chafer** declares that the coming tribulation, "...is the time of Jacob's trouble;[32] that it is unrelated to the church; and it is terminated by the glorious appearing of Christ."[33] Likewise, **John Walvoord**, in a discussion about the future tribulation insists that, "The Tribulation deals with the Jewish people primarily." **Walvoord** therefore concludes that, "...the church is in no way involved in this time of future trouble."[34] **Gerald Stanton** tersely declares that, "The emphasis of the Tribulation is primarily Jewish."[35] And **Dwight Pentecost** insists that, "...every passage dealing with the tribulation relates it to God's program for Israel..."[36]

[28] *Papers on the Lord's Coming* - C.H.M., Loizeaux Brothers Publishers, n.d., p.104.
[29] *The Gospel According to Matthew* - A.C. Gaebelein, Loizeaux Brothers, Inc.,1982, p.233.
[30] *Jesus Is Coming* - William E. Blackstone, Kregel Publications, 1989, p.99.
[31] *Papers on the Lord's Coming* - C.H.M., Loizeaux Brothers Publishers, n.d., p.105.
[32] The phrase, "the time of Jacob's trouble" occurs in Jer.30:7 and is commonly used by Dispensationalists to refer to the future Great Tribulation.
[33] *Systematic Theology* - Lewis Sperry Chafer, Dallas Seminary Press, Vol.IV, p.360.
[34] *The Rapture Question* - John F. Walvoord, Zondervan Books, 1981, pp.43,46.
[35] *Kept From the Hour* – Gerald B. Stanton, Zondervan Publishing House, 1956, p.35.
[36] *Things To Come* - J. Dwight Pentecost, Zondervan Publishing House, 1964, p.196.

Because the future tribulation is seen as distinctively "Jewish," it is not surprising that it is also viewed as a Divine punishment upon Israel. For example, **W.E. Blackstone**, under the chapter title, "The Day of Jacobs Trouble," declares, "Surely Israel will be restored but there is an awful time of trouble awaiting her. Israel's sins are mountain high. The guilt of innocent blood is on the Israelite's - the precious blood of Jesus Christ (Matthew 27:25)."[37] **Clarence Larkin** asserts that, "The Tribulation is not for the perfecting of the Saints. It has nothing to do with the Church. It is the time of Jacob's Trouble (Jer.30:7), and is the Judgment of Israel, and it is God's purpose to keep the Church out of it."[38] **Lewis Sperry Chafer** explains that, "At the end of this age, Israel must pass through the great tribulation, which is specifically characterized as 'the time of Jacob's trouble'...and before entering her kingdom, she must come before her King in judgment."[39] **Louis Talbot** rhetorically asks, "Who will go through the tribulation?... The nation of Israel, still rejecting Christ as her Messiah, will pass through this time of sorrow, described as the time of Jacob's trouble."[40] Likewise, **Dwight Pentecost** also contends that one of the primary reasons for the future Tribulation is to punish the Jews for their rejection of Jesus and the Theocratic Kingdom He sought to establish. While referring to Israel, **Pentecost** asserts that, "The nation willfully and knowingly rejected Jesus Christ as their Saviour and Sovereign, and the nation so blessed of God must experience chastening by God because of the national sin of rejecting Christ."[41]

Dispensationalists consistently deny the essential unity between Old Testament and New Testament believers. They adamantly reject the proposition that God has one continuous redemptive plan for all of humanity. Instead, they strenuously argue that God has two separate and distinct redemptive "programs" - the one being "earthly," which concerns Israel, and the other being "heavenly," which concerns the Church. Dispensationalists thereby exclude all Old Testament believers from membership in the Body of Christ by isolating the Church in "...an unexpected and unpredicted parenthesis..."[42] located between the 69th and 70th weeks of Daniel 9:26-27. And it is this ***dispensational distinction***, which leads Dispensationalists to conclude that the

---

[37] *Jesus Is Coming* - William E. Blackstone, Kregel Publications, 1989, p.173.
[38] *Dispensational Truth* - Clarence Larkin, published by Rev. Clarence Larkin, 1920, p.14.
[39] *Dispensationalism* - Lewis Sperry Chafer, Dallas Seminary Press, 1936, p.31.
[40] *God's Plan for the Ages* - Louis T. Talbot, published by Louis T. Talbot, 1936, 1943, p.137.
[41] *Will Man Survive?* - J. Dwight Pentecost, Zondervan Publishing House, 1980, pp.75-76.
[42] *The Rapture Question* - John F. Walvoord, Zondervan Publishing House, 1981, p.25.

Church *cannot* go through the future Tribulation. They reason that since Israel is "an earthly people," she *must* remain on earth during the Tribulation. And whereas the Church is composed of "a heavenly people," she *must* be caught up to heaven *before* the beginning of the Tribulation. Thus, it is this dispensational dichotomy between Israel and the Church that provides the stimulus for the pretribulational rapture theory. Dispensationalists recognize and admit this cause and effect relationship. For example, **Charles Ryrie** states that, "The distinction between Israel and the Church leads to the belief that the Church will be taken from the earth before the beginning of the Tribulation (which in one major sense concerns Israel.)"[43] And **John Walvoord** declares that, "A proper distinction between the church and Israel naturally leads to pretribulationalism..."[44] Thus, the pretribulational rapture theory is dependent upon the separation of Old Testament and New Testament believers. **John Walvoord** underscores the necessity of this dichotomy when he states, "If the term church includes saints of all ages, then it is self-evident that the church will go through the Tribulation...If, however, the term church applies only to a certain body of saints, namely the saints of this dispensation, then the possibility of the translation of the church before the Tribulation is possible, even probable."[45]

3. The Pretribulational Rapture of the Church.

The second distinctive element of Dispensationalism is the pretribulational rapture of the Church. Dispensationalists uniformly maintain that the rapture of the Church will occur *before* the beginning of the Great Tribulation referred to in Matthew 24 and in Revelation 6-18.

For example, **W.E. Blackstone** insists that, "...the church...will be taken out of the world to escape the Tribulation."[46] **Clarence Larkin** likewise affirms that, "The typical teaching of the Scriptures demand that the Church be caught out 'before' the Tribulation."[47] **Charles Ryrie** declares that, "Pretribulationalism teaches that the rapture of the church (both dead and living saints) will occur before the seven-year

---

[43] *Dispensationalism Today* - Charles Caldwell Ryrie, Moody Press, 1970, p.159.
[44] *The Rapture Question* - John F. Walvoord, Zondervan Publishing House, 1981, p.20.
[45] *The Rapture Question* - John F. Walvoord, Zondervan Publishing House, 1981, pp.21-22.
[46] *Jesus Is Coming* - William E. Blackstone, Kregel Publications, 1989, p.209.
[47] *Dispensational Truth* - Clarence Larkin, published by Rev. Clarence Larkin, 1920, p.14.

tribulation period that is, before the seventieth week of Daniel 9:24-27."[48] **Dwight Pentecost** maintains that, "...the church, the body of Christ, in its entirety, will, by resurrection and translation,[49] be removed from the earth before any part of the seventieth week of Daniel begins...A number of arguments may be presented in support of the pretribulation rapture position."[50] And **John Walvoord** confidently promises that, "...it may be expected that God will fulfill His program for the church by translating the church out of the earth before resuming His program with Israel and with the Gentiles in the period of Tribulation."[51]

Dispensationalists also teach that the pretribulational Coming of Christ will be a "secret" event that is unobserved by the world. **William Blackstone** maintains that, "Jesus is the Morning Star, and He is also the Sun of Righteousness. Only those who are up early and watching see the morning star. So it will be *only the true and faithful church that will see Christ at the Rapture* as the Bright and Morning Star."[52] While referring to the coming of Christ to rapture His Church, **C.I. Scofield** declares that the rapture, "...is *visible only to those who are caught up* to meet the Lord in the air." **Scofield** goes on to say that, "the other coming" at the end of the Tribulation, "...will be witnessed by all tongues and nations, and will for them be an awful event."[53] The secrecy of the pretribulational rapture has always been an important element of Dispensational teaching. For example, the renowned educator and commentator, **Charles L. Feinberg** emphasizes the element of secrecy when he states that, "...the coming of the Lord for His own is *not seen by the world*, whereas His visible appearing will be seen by all when He comes in power and great glory with His holy angels."[54] The well-known radio Bible teacher, **M.R. De Hann** explains that the rapture of the Church, "...will be so sudden, so *secret*, that the unsaved who remain will be utterly confused, non-plussed and mystified by the unexplainable, sudden, dramatic disappearance of millions of believers...it is a mystery because...only those who have been born again and washed in the blood, will hear the shout when it occurs...The rest of the inhabitants of the earth may realize that something has happened, but they will

---

[48] *Basic Theology* - Charles C. Ryrie, Victor Books, 1986, p.482.
[49] Dispensationalists frequently use the word "translation" as a synonym for the word "rapture."
[50] *Things To Come* - J. Dwight Pentecost, Zondervan Publishing House, 1964, p.193.
[51] *The Rapture Question* - John F. Walvoord, Zondervan Books, 1979, p.37.
[52] *Jesus Is Coming* - William E. Blackstone, Kregel Publications, 1989, p.216.
[53] *Prophecy Made Plain* - C.I. Scofield, The Gospel Hour, 1967, pp.138-139.
[54] *Premillennialism or Amillennialism?* - Charles Feinberg, Zondervan Publishing House, 1936, p.207.

not know what it was."[55] **Louis Talbot**, a highly respected pastor and educator has written, "The church will be *secretly translated*. The world will *not see* the Lord when He meets the church in the air (1Thess.4:17)...only the church will see Him when He comes for His saints...As a thief in the night, He will come; and only the ears of the redeemed will be tuned to hear, the voice of the archangel and the trump of God." [56] And **Lehman Strauss**, the well-known and highly respected Bible teacher, author and conference speaker states that, "The Lord's coming for His Church will be sudden, selective, *secret* and startling."[57] And while contrasting the inconspicuousness of the pretribulation rapture with the high visibility of the Second Coming of Christ, **John Walvoord** explains that, "...the rapture of the church...will probably *not be seen* by the world, the second coming of Christ will be seen by the entire world."[58]

It should be noted that many modern Dispensationalists consciously refrain from referring to the secrecy of the pretribulational rapture. Some, like **Tim LaHaye**, engage in semantical arguments. However, while denying a secret rapture, **LaHaye** unintentionally describes a secret rapture. For example, **LaHaye** asserts that, "Through the years some have tried to discredit the pre-Trib Rapture theory by calling it the secret rapture. Of course, nowhere in Scripture is the term secret applied to this event. However, anyone who does not participate in the Rapture will *not actually see it*...The occurrence would much better be labeled the sudden rapture...I expect the Rapture to be electrifyingly sudden but *not secret*...millions of people will suddenly vanish from the earth...Unexpected, yes! *Unseen, yes*! But *not secret*."[59] **Dr. LaHaye** has evidently overlooked the fact that an event that is "unseen" is by definition "secret." The word "secret" refers to that which goes unnoticed, is unobserved or is hidden from others. And this is precisely how Dispensationalists describe the pretribulation rapture. Others, like **Gerald Stanton,** attempt to sidestep the secrecy issue altogether. For example, **Stanton** explains that, "The important point is that the rapture will be sudden, unexpected, an event which will take the world by surprise, and is not whether it will or will not be secret. Pretribulationalism does not need this term, and many do not use

---

[55] *The Secret Rapture* - M.R. De Hann, M.D., The Radio Bible Class, Grand Rapids, Mich., n.d., pp.2-3.
[56] *God's Plan of the Ages* - Louis T. Talbot, 1936, 1943, pp.139-140.
[57] *God's Plan for the Future* - Lehman Strauss, Zondervan Publishing House, 1965, p.92.
[58] *Major Bible Prophecies* - John F. Walvoord, Harper Paperbacks, Zondervan Publishing House, 1994, p.308.
[59] *No Fear of the Storm* - Tim LaHaye, Multnomah Press Books, 1992, pp.32-35

it."[60] However, **Stanton** is apparently unaware of just how important the concept of secrecy is to pretribulationalism. The teaching that Christ will come unannounced and unobserved is essential to the feasibility of the pretribulation rapture theory. This is due to the fact that the Scriptures only describe one visible coming of Christ at the end this age *after* the Tribulation period. The early proponents of Dispensationalism clearly understood, that if they were to successfully argue that the Lord will also come for the Church *before* the beginning of the Tribulation, that coming of necessity must be unobserved by the world, and therefore by definition, "secret."

In addition to secrecy, Dispensationalists also teach that the pretribulational rapture will be "imminent." **Lewis Sperry Chafer** declares that, "The imminent return of Christ to receive His Church is held before every believer as a blessed hope."[61] When Dispensationalists use the word "imminent" they mean that the rapture of the Church is to be expected at any-moment and without any preceding prophetic signs or indications.[62] **Clarence Larkin** succinctly defines the Dispensational use of the word "imminent" when he states that, "By 'Imminency' we mean 'may happen at any time.'"[63] **W.E. Blackstone**, commenting on the imminent appearing of Christ states, "...not daring to say that He will come tomorrow, nor a thousand years from now, but only this are we sure of - He may come now."[64] Likewise, **C.H. Mackintosh** maintains that, "The Thessalonian Christians...were converted to the hope of the Lord's return. They were taught to look out for it daily."[65] **Lehman Strauss** declares that, "...the rapture is the next major event in God's prophetic program. The Translation of the Church to heaven is imminent. It can take place at any time."[66] And **John Walvoord** likewise affirms that, "...the rapture passages seem to indicate an imminent rapture...the rapture could occur at any moment."[67] And again, while referring to the pretribulational rapture, **Walvoord** stresses that, "Most important is the fact that this event, as described, is presented as an imminent event with no preceding order of events..."[68]

---

[60] *Kept From the Hour* – Gerald B. Stanton, Zondervan Publishing House, 1956, p.24.
[61] *Systematic Theology* - Lewis Sperry Chafer, Dallas Seminary Press, 1948, Vol.IV, p.367.
[62] The word "imminent" literally means, "Threatening to occur immediately." *Webster's Collegiate Dictionary*, Fifth Edition, G. & C. Merriam Co., 1941. This is precisely how Dispensationalists use the word.
[63] *Dispensational Truth* - Clarence Larkin, published by Rev. Clarence Larkin, 1920, p.15.
[64] *Jesus Is Coming* - William E. Blackstone, Kregel Publications, 1989, p.70.
[65] *Papers on the Lord's Coming* - C.H.M., Loizeaux Brothers Publishers, n.d., p.22.
[66] *God's Plan for the Future* - Lehman Strauss, Zondervan Publishing House, 1965, pp.83-84.
[67] *The Blessed Hope and the Tribulation* - John F. Walvoord, Zondervan Publishing House, 1976, p.149.
[68] *The Rapture Question* - John F. Walvoord, Zondervan Books, 1981, p.202.

Summary

There are two essential teachings that characterize the Dispensational interpretation of Scripture.

First, Dispensationalists make an absolute, razor-sharp distinction between Old Testament believers (Israel) and the New Testament Church. **Lewis Sperry Chafer** declares that, "Dispensationalism has its foundation in and is understood in the distinction between Judaism and Christianity."[69] **Dwight Pentecost** maintains that, "There is a distinction between the true church and true or spiritual Israel."[70] And **Charles Ryrie** explains that, "The essence of dispensationalism, then, is the distinction between Israel and the Church." **Ryrie** goes on to say that, "...the clear distinction between Israel and the Church...is a vital part of dispensationalism."[71]

Second, Dispensationalists emphasize the pretribulational rapture of the Church. They assert that the rapture will be an "imminent" event. This means that the Coming of Christ for His Church will be a secret, unannounced, any-moment event that will occur *before* the onset of the Tribulation period. **Arno C. Gaebelein** reveals just how important this doctrine of imminence is when he declares, "...the most important and vital doctrine...in the New Testament, [is] the imminency of the coming of the Lord."[72] And **John Walvoord** emphasizes the centrality of the any-moment rapture teaching when he describes the doctrine of imminency as, "...the central feature of pretribulationism..." declaring that, "...the doctrine of imminency, which is the heart of pretribulationism..."[73]

---

[69] *Dispensationalism* - Lewis Sperry Chafer, Dallas Seminary Press, 1936, 1951, p.41.
[70] *Things To Come* - J. Dwight Pentecost, Zondervan Publishing House, 1964, p.199.
[71] *Dispensationalism Today* - Charles C. Ryrie, Moody Press, 1970, pp.47, 159.
[72] *The Rapture: Pre-Mid-Post-Tribulational?* - Richard R. Reiter, Zondervan Publishing House, 1984, p.23.
[73] *The Rapture Question*, John F. Walvoord, Zondervan Books, 1981, pp.51,53.

Chapter Two
The Historical Development of the Pretribulation Rapture Teaching

Chapter Two Outline:
1. John Nelson Darby.
2. Darby's Personality and Character.
3. The Conditions and Circumstances that Gave Rise to the Pretribulation Rapture Teaching.
4. The Albury and Powerscourt Prophetic Conferences.
5. The Development of the Pretribulation Rapture Doctrine.
6. The First Major Schism Within the Brethren Movement.
7. The Spread of Darby's Dispensationalism to America.
   (a) The Acceptance of Darby's Prophetic Scheme by Influential American Clergymen.
   (b) The Circulation of Dispensational Books and Tracts.
   (c) The American Prophetic Conference Movement.
   (d) The Bible Institute Movement.
   (e) Publishing.
   (f) The Emotional Appeal of the Secret Rapture Doctrine.
8. The American Controversy Over the Secret Rapture Teaching.

1. John Nelson Darby.

How did this immensely popular doctrine of a secret, any-moment pretribulational rapture of the Church become so ingrained into the theology of modern evangelicalism?[74] The answer to this important question centers around a man named **John Nelson Darby**.

John Darby was born November 18, 1800 in London, England. His early education began at Westminster School. At fifteen years of age Darby entered Trinity College in Dublin. He graduated in 1819 with honors and spent the next three years studying law. In 1822, he was admitted to the Irish Chancery Bar, but never actually practiced law.[75]

---

[74] See **Appendix D** for a detailed discussion of who first suggested a pretribulation rapture of the Church.
[75] *John Nelson Darby* - W.G. Turner, C.A. Hammond, London, 1944, p.13.

In 1825 Darby "was admitted to Deacon's Orders in the Irish Church."[76] Then in 1826, he was ordained as a priest and made curate of the church at Calary. At this point in his life, Darby was described as, "...a rich, well-placed young man...brilliant, gifted, talented, well connected, in a circle possessing great influence..."[77] However, by 1827, Darby had become disillusioned with the Church of Ireland. He became convinced that the established church was a spiritually corrupt and apostate organization. The complete corruption and ruin of all organized Christian religion became a recurring theme in Darby's writings. He was persuaded that, "The church itself as a system, trusted to man's responsibility, has been all a failure."[78] He therefore admonished his followers to, "Keep in mind that it is by false doctrines that Satan has corrupted all the church."[79] He frequently warned his followers that, "...judgment is coming upon the professing church."[80] His solution to this perceived apostasy was complete and total separation from the organized Church.

Darby soon attached himself to a group of Christians who referred to themselves simply as "Brethren." These were like-minded individuals, who had withdrawn from the organized Church and formed small, informal fellowship groups of "Brethren" throughout Ireland and England. They soon became known as the "Plymouth Brethren," because one of the larger and more active groups was located at Plymouth, England. In an attempt to reclaim a more scriptural form of Christianity, the Brethren would gather in the name of Christ, relying solely on the leading and guidance of the Holy Spirit. Their objective was to regain the apostolic simplicity and zeal of the early Church. Coupled with their enthusiasm was an excited expectancy of the nearness of the Second Advent of Christ. The Brethren were opposed to all forms of denominationalism; they subscribed to no creeds or confessions of faith; they rejected church membership and formal church names as unscriptural; and they made no provision for the office of pastor because they contended that all believers were to be recognized as priests, and therefore were authorized and empowered to minister. John Darby soon became a

---

[76] *John Nelson Darby* -W.G. Turner, C.A. Hammond, London, 1944, p.15.
[77] *John Nelson Darby* -W.G. Turner, C.A. Hammond, London, 1944, p.15.
[78] *The Collected Writings of J.N. Darby* - Edited by William Kelly, Stow Hill and Tract Depot, Prophetic No.4, Vol.11, n.d., p.280.
[79] *The Collected Writings of J.N. Darby* - Edited by William Kelly, Stow Hill and Tract Depot, Prophetic No.4, Vol.11, n.d., p.290.
[80] *The Collected Writings of J.N. Darby* - Edited by William Kelly, Stow Hill and Tract Depot, Prophetic No.4, Vol.11, n.d., p.302.

dominant force within this movement and is recognized as one of its principal founders, and most important theologian. Historian **William Neatby** observes that, "...the maker of Brethrenism as a system, its guiding and energizing spirit throughout, was John Nelson Darby."[81]

2. Darby's Personality and Character.

Although John Darby had no formal theological training, he was well versed in Hebrew, Greek and Latin. Darby believed that he was called, "...to rescue plain Scripture statements from the garbage of theology."[82] Brethren historian, **Roy Coad** (himself a fourth generation Brethren) has observed that Darby's, "...approach to truth was subjective, and a matter of insight rather than logic." And that he "...seems perpetually to be imposing on Scripture a pre-conceived system of interpretation."[83] Darby was also a prolific writer. His *Collected Writings*, which were compiled and edited by William Kelly,[84] fill 34 volumes, and are divided topically into nine sections - apologetic, critical, doctrinal, ecclesiastical, evangelic, expository, miscellaneous, practical and prophetic. The Brethren regard this work as "the cream of the brethren writings."[85] Darby's *Synopsis of the Books of the Bible* fill another five volumes and his *Letters* another three volumes. Darby also wrote devotionally, composed poetry and hymns and translated the Bible into French, German and English.[86]

As an author, Darby's style can only be described as extremely complicated, and convoluted. At times he is almost incomprehensible. Darby frequently constructed long, complex and intricate sentences, which are virtually impossible to understand. **William**

---

[81] *A History of the Plymouth Brethren* - William Blair Neatby, Hodder and Stoughton, London, 1902, p.44.

[82] *The Collected Writings of J.N. Darby* - edited by William Kelly, Stow Hill and Tract Depot, Prophetic No.4, Vol.11, n.d., p.353.

[83] *A History of the Brethren Movement* - F. Roy Coad, Regent College Publishing, 2001, pp.110, 123.

[84] W.G. Turner comments, "The greatest of Darby's friends in every way was the late Mr. William Kelly of Blackheath, London...They were singularly like-minded, truly taught of God in the same school. They had their differences, but not in doctrine, or fundamentals, for everything that was best in John Nelson Darby's teaching and practice found its ablest exponent and advocate in William Kelly." *John Nelson Darby* - W.G. Turner, C.A. Hammond, London, 1944, p.51.

[85] *The History of the Brethren* - Napoleon Noel, edited by William F. Knapp, 1936, p.30.

[86] C.H. Spurgeon's *The Sword And The Trowel* (1874, p.18) made the following observation regarding John Darby's English translation of the Bible: "Suffice it to say, that some renderings are good, and some of the notes are good; but taken as a whole, with a great display of learning, the ignorance of the results of modern criticism is almost incredible. And the fatal upsetting of vital doctrines condemns the work as more calculated to promote skepticism than true religion - the most sacred subjects being handled with irreverent familiarity."

Neatby refers to Darby's "written and spoken composition" as "half ludicrous and half disgusting."[87] Historian **Roy Coad** describes Darby's writing style as "...slovenly, tortuous and obscure, and his thought was rarely systematized...Darby was a mystic: he felt rather than thought his way through a problem."[88] **W.G. Turner**, in his biography of Darby states, "John Nelson Darby was a singularly voluminous author, whose works are well worth reading, and yet little likely to be read...Mr. Darby's expression no doubt was difficult to the uninitiated..."[89] And historian **Earnest Sandeen** has observed, that, "He left a massive set of *Collected Writings* which are almost uniformly unintelligible."[90] Unquestionably, Darby lacked the ability to communicate his thoughts in a clear and concise manner.[91]

Francis William Newman (1805-1897), Professor of Latin at University College, London and Professor of Political Economy at Oxford, was at one time a very close friend of John Darby. He offers some interesting and significant firsthand insights into Darby's personality and character in his book entitled, *Phases of Faith*, first published in 1850.

Shortly after **Francis Newman's** graduation from Balliol College, he traveled to Ireland (circa 1827) where he first became acquainted with John Darby. As a young man, **Newman** recollects that he found Darby, whom he refers to as "the Irish clergyman," to be "a most remarkable man, who rapidly gained an immense sway over me... His bodily presence was indeed weak! A fallen cheek, a bloodshot eye...a seldom shaven beard, a shabby suit of clothes and a generally neglected person...In spite of the strong revulsion which I felt against some of the peculiarities of this remarkable man, I for the first time in my life found myself under the dominion of a superior...I cease to wonder in the retrospect, that he riveted me in such bondage. Henceforth I began to ask: What will *he* say to this or that? In *his* reply I always expected to find a higher portion of God's Spirit than I could frame for myself. In order to learn Divine truth, it became to me a surer

---

[87] *A History of the Plymouth Brethren* - William Blair Neatby, Hodder and Stoughton, London, 1902, p.49.
[88] *A History of the Brethren Movement* - F. Roy Coad, Regent College Publishing, 2001, p.106.
[89] *John Nelson Darby* - W.G. Turner, C.A. Hammond, London, 1944, pp.53,55.
[90] *The Roots of Fundamentalism* - Earnest R. Sandeen, The University of Chicago Press, 1970, p.31.
[91] C.H. Spurgeon, commenting on Darby's *Practical Reflections* on the Psalms, stated, "Too mystical for ordinary minds. If the author would write in plain English his readers would probably discover that there is nothing very valuable in his remarks." *Commenting On Commentaries* - C.H. Spurgeon, Kregel Publications, 1954, p.84.

process to consult him, than to search for myself and wait upon God...I could have accepted him as an apostle commissioned to reveal the mind of God."[92]

However, over time, Newman's fascination with Darby abated and he regained his senses and began to recognize that Darby, "...displayed a wonderful power of bending other minds to his own, and even stamping upon them the tones of his voice and all sorts of slavish imitation. Over the general results of his action I have deeply mourned...dwarfing men's understandings, contracting their hearts, crushing their moral sensibilities, and setting those at variance who ought to love: yet oh! how specious was it in the beginning! He only wanted men to 'submit their understanding to God,' that is, to the Bible, that is, to his interpretation!"[93]

John Darby would tolerate no questioning of his authority or disagreement with his teachings. Commenting on this serious character flaw, **Professor Clarence Bass**[94] has observed that, "The principle of unity and tolerance...was replaced by a principle of caustic examination of every theological difference, however minor, until absolute agreement and allegiance to one man was demanded. That man was J.N. Darby."[95] Likewise, historian **Earnest Sandeen** describes Darby as, "...a man with magnetic, electric personal qualities combined with a tyrant's will to lead and intolerance of criticism. Perhaps he should be described as a petty tyrant, for he was most tyrannical about petty things." **Sandeen** then goes on to describe Darby as a man with a "preoccupation with prophecy" who had, "...little patience or respect for other students of prophecy."[96] And **Roy Coad**, an authority on Brethren history has observed, that Darby, was convinced that, "...anything which opposed his own work was *ipso facto* born of evil."[97] **Professor Bass** provides a very balanced assessment of Darby's complicated personality and character when he observes that, "He was neither perfectly good nor utterly bad, though he often displayed the characteristics of both...Simple in taste, benevolent in disposition, kind in temperament, considerate in his awareness of others, humble in spirit, sympathetic in nature, he was at the same time ruthless in

---

[92] *Phases of Faith* - Francis William Newman, 1860, Humanities Press, Leicester Press, 1970, pp.17, 20-21.
[93] *Phases of Faith* - Francis William Newman, 1860, Humanities Press, Leicester Press, 1970, p.21.
[94] Clarence B. Bass was Associate Professor of Systematic Theology at Bethel Theological Seminary in St. Paul, Minnesota. He holds degrees from Wheaton College (BA, MA) and the University of Edinburgh (PhD).
[95] *Backgrounds to Dispensationalism* - Clarence B. Bass, Wm. B. Eerdmans Publishing Co., 1960, p.91.
[96] *The Roots of Fundamentalism* - Earnest R. Sandeen, The University of Chicago Press, 1970, p.67.
[97] *A History of the Brethren Movement* - F. Roy Coad, Regent College Publishing, p.134.

controversy, belligerent to those who opposed him, jealous of his position of authority, and exacting in his demands."[98]

3. The Conditions and Circumstances that Gave Rise to the Pretribulation Rapture Teaching.

The predominant eschatological view of the 18th century was post-millennialism. **Daniel Whitby** was the first to advocate this interpretative approach to Scripture.[99] Whitby's, post-millennialism postulated that the world would be converted to Christ through the preaching of the Gospel, and that world conditions would therefore continually improve, ultimately ushering in the Millennial Age. However, the late 1700s and the early 1800s were filled with uncertainty and apprehension for most people living in Europe. Instead of world conditions improving, it seemed to most people that the very foundations of European civilization were crumbling. Feelings of uncertainty and despair prevailed. Rapid social, economic and political changes within England, accompanied by European political tensions, the French Revolution and the subsequent Napoleonic Wars, helped give rise to the feeling that the end of the world was drawing near. By 1830, Great Britain was in the midst of a resurgence of interest in unfulfilled Bible prophecy that focused upon the Second Coming Christ. Many prophetic periodicals were being circulated and scores of books dealing with Biblical prophecy were being published.[100] Accompanying this resurgence was a renewed interest in the futurist premillennial interpretation of prophecy. Ministers began to question the tenants of both post-millennialism and pre-millennial historicism[101] and

---

[98] *Backgrounds to Dispensationalism* - Clarence B. Bass, Wm. B. Eerdmans Publishing Co., 1960 pp.57,51.

[99] Daniel Whitby (1638-1726) was educated at Trinity College, Oxford. He was the first to advance a systematic Post-Millennialism that taught that the Millennium would be ushered in as a result of the spread of the Gospel and the conversion of the Gentile nations, **before** the Second Coming of Christ. In later life he embraced Arianism, thus rejecting both the doctrine of the Trinity and the Deity of the Lord Jesus Christ. John K. Henshaw (1792-1852), bishop of the Protestant Episcopal Church in Rhode Island, declared, "The commonly received opinion of a Spiritual Millennium, consisting in a universal triumph of the Gospel, and the conversion of all nations, for a thousand years before the coming of Christ, is a novel doctrine, unknown to the Church for the space of sixteen hundred years. So far as we have been able to investigate its history, it was first advanced by Rev. Dr. Whitby, the Commentator." *An Inquiry Concerning the Second Advent*, as quoted in *Maranatha* - James H. Brookes, Fleming H. Revell Company, n.d., p.323.

[100] *The Origins of the Brethren* - Harold H. Rowdon, Pickering & Inglis Ltd., 1967, pp.12-14.

[101] The early premillennial historicism of this period adopted "the day-year theory," which held that the 1260 prophetic days of Daniel and Revelation (Dan.7:25; 12:7 and Rv.11:2-3; 13:5) were to be interpreted as 1260 years, and not 1260 literal days. Additionally, they believed that the prophecies of the Book of Revelation had for the most part been fulfilled in European history. The system was soon completely discredited and discarded as spurious.

24

began to consider the validity of the futurist premillennial interpretation of the Scripture.[102] This resurgence of interest in unfulfilled Bible prophecy sparked a series of prophetic conferences that were convened to study and discuss a variety of prophetic subjects.

4. The Albury and Powerscourt Prophetic Conferences.

The first of these prophetic conferences was held in 1826 at the estate of **Mr. Henry Drummond**, located at Albury Park, England. They continued annually for five consecutive years. Drummond was a successful banker and member of the House of Commons. He was also an evangelical Christian who held to the historicist premillennialism that was popular at that time. His keen interest in unfulfilled Bible prophecy prompted him to invite leading millenarians to come together to discuss the end-time prophecies. Drummond sought to provide a forum that facilitated an open discussion of Bible prophecies pertaining to the Second Advent of Christ. The participants arrived at a general consensus, having determined that, (1) the Second Coming of Christ was very near; (2) that the established churches were in a state of terrible unbelief and apostasy; and (3) that Divine judgment was about to fall upon all of Christendom (which was equated with the world).

Lady Theodosia Powerscourt,[103] who was also extremely interested in the study of unfulfilled Bible prophecy, attended some of the Albury conferences. She was so impressed with the proceedings that she determined to duplicate them at her home at Powerscourt House, in County Wicklow, Ireland. The Countess was the widow of Lord Powerscourt. She has been described as "a remarkable woman, pious, and warm-hearted with more than a touch of mystic."[104] The Powerscourt conferences were held for three consecutive years beginning in 1831 through 1833. Like Albury, the most notable millenarians from England, Scotland and Ireland were invited to participate. The meetings normally lasted for a week and addressed a wide range of prophetic

---

[102] The futuristic interpretation maintains that the prophecies of the book of Revelation will be fulfilled in the future, at the end of the present age.

[103] Lady Powerscourt (Theodosia Howard) was the daughter of Col. & Mrs. Howard. She married Lord Powerscourt in 1823. Lady Powerscourt died on December 30, 1836 at 36 years of age. *The Origins of the Brethren* - Harold H. Rowdon, Pickering & Inglis Ltd., 1967, p.86.

[104] *The Origins of the Brethren* - Harold H. Rowdon, Pickering & Inglis Ltd., 1967, p.86.

subjects dealing with the end of the age and the Coming of Christ. John Darby attended all three of these conferences, and was apparently quite taken with Lady Powerscourt, whom he planned to marry. However, because well-intentioned friends counseled Darby that his marriage would impede his itinerant preaching ministry, he was dissuaded and further thoughts of marriage were abandoned. It was at the third conference that Darby introduced his conviction that there was a clear dispensational difference between God's dealings with the Jews and the Church. This distinction between Old and New Testament saints then provided the basis upon which Darby introduced the idea of the pretribulational rapture to the conference.[105]

5. The Development of the Pretribulation Rapture Doctrine.

Darby maintained that dispensational distinctions must be made between Israel and the Church (i.e., between Old Testament believers and New Testament believers). According to Darby, God was dealing differently with Israel and the Church because He had different plans and purposes for them. It seems that the seminal idea for making these dispensational distinctions between Old and New Testament saints came to Darby from his study of Isaiah 32. Within several of his personal letters **Darby** explained that;

"The coming of the Lord was the other truth which was brought to my mind from the word...Isaiah xxxii. brought me the earthly consequences of the same truth, though other passages might seem perhaps more striking to me now: *but I saw an evident change of dispensation in that chapter,* when the Spirit would be poured out on the Jewish nation, and a king reign in righteousness...[106] and again,

---

[105] Brethren historian **Harold Rowdon** observes that it was at the third Powerscourt conference in 1833, that J.N. Darby introduced his belief that, "...the era of the Christian Church is to be distinguished from all that has gone before and all that will follow. The Christian dispensation (i.e., the administration of God's purposes during the Christian era) was therefore distinguished from the Jewish dispensation on the one hand and the future dispensation on the other." Rowdon then states that; "This distinction was the means by which Darby related the idea of the rapture of the Church to the unfulfilled prophecies of Scripture." *The Origins of the Brethren* - Harold H. Rowdon, Pickering & Inglis Ltd., 1967, p.97. Also, historian **Ernest Sandeen**, says that, "Darby introduced into discussion at Powerscourt the ideas of a secret rapture of the church and a parenthesis in prophetic fulfillment between the sixty-ninth and seventieth weeks of Daniel. These two concepts constituted the basic tenets of the system of theology since referred to as dispensationalism." *The Roots of Fundamentalism* - Earnet R. Sandeen, University of Chicago Press, 1970, p.38. It is highly likely, that it is this 1833 Powerscourt conference that H.A. Ironside is referring to when he mused that, "It was in these meetings that the precious truth of the rapture of the Church was brought to light; that is, the coming of the Lord in the air to take away the church before the great tribulation should begin on earth. The views brought out at Powerscourt castle not only largely formed the views of Brethren elsewhere, but as years went on obtained wide publication in denominational circles..." *A Historical Sketch of the Brethren Movement* - H.A. Ironside, Loizeaux Brothers, 1985, p.23.

[106] *Letters of J.N.D. - Volume One, 1832-1868*, Stow Hill Bible and Tract Depot, London, n.d., pp.515-516.

"...I saw that the Christian, having his place in Christ in heaven, has nothing to wait for save the coming of the Saviour...the 32nd chapter of Isaiah taught me clearly, on God's behalf, that there was still an economy to come...this chapter clearly sets forth the corresponding earthly part."[107]

It was this idea of a change in the dispensations that led Darby to two momentous conclusions. First, he reasoned that the coming tribulation period pertained to Israel and *not* to the Church. **Darby** declared;

"Thus these four passages [i.e., Jer.30:7; Dan.12:1; Mat.24:21; Mk.13:19], which speak of the unequalled tribulation, apply it distinctly to Jacob, Jerusalem, and Judea, and the Jews, *not* the church."[108]

And second, Darby reasoned that since the future tribulation pertained to Israel and *not* the Church, the Church must necessarily be removed from the earth *before* the tribulation commenced. Commenting on Revelation 3:10, **Darby** remarked;

"...when the church is addressed, it is with a declaration that she will be kept from that hour which shall come to try others. So that thus far the testimonies of Scripture declare that the unequalled tribulation is for Jacob, and that, when the time of temptation is spoken of in addressing the church, it is to declare that the faithful shall be kept out of it." **Darby** then concluded, "We have found that the passages which speak of the tribulation first apply it directly to the Jews on one side, and then exclude the church from it on the other."[109]

Darby claimed to have arrived at his pretribulational rapture theory as early as 1830. Writing in 1850, **Darby** declared that he discovered the pretribulation rapture while studying Second Thessalonians 2. He stated that;

"Here then is the passage in its true force: 'Now we beg you, brethren, by the coming of our Lord Jesus Christ and our gathering together to him, that ye be not soon shaken in mind, nor be troubled, neither by spirit, nor by word, nor by letter as [if it were] by us, as that the day of the Lord is present. Let not any one deceive you in any manner, because [it will not be] unless the apostasy have first come and the man of sin have been revealed,' etc. That is, the apostle gives two reasons why they should not believe that the day of the Lord was come: first, the rapture of the saints is not yet; and

---

[107] *Letters of J.N.D. - Volume Three, 1879-1882*, Stow Hill Bible and Tract Depot, n.d., pp. 298-299.

[108] *The Collected Writings of J.N. Darby* - Edited by William Kelly, Stow Hill and Tract Depot, Prophetic No.4, Vol.11, n.d., p.111.

[109] *The Collected Writings of J.N. Darby* - Edited by William Kelly, Stow Hill and Tract Depot, Prophetic No.4, Vol.11, n.d., pp.112,113.

secondly, the object of the judgment is not revealed. It is this passage which, twenty years ago, made me understand the rapture of the saints before - perhaps a considerable time before - the day of the Lord (that is, before the judgment of the living)."[110]

What Darby failed to mention was that a Mr. T. Tweedy, an Irish ex-clergyman who had joined the Brethren movement, initially made the suggestion that Second Thessalonians 2, provided "decisive" textual support for the concept of a secret pretribulation rapture. William Kelly, Darby's close associate, visited B.W. Newton at Plymouth in 1845. It was at this time that Newton told Kelley about a letter he had received from Darby that acknowledged Mr. Tweedy's help in resolving a "difficulty" regarding the secret rapture theory. According to Newton, Darby stated that it was Mr. Tweedy who helped solve his "difficulty" by directing his attention to Second Thessalonians 2:1-2. In his pamphlet, *The Rapture of the Saints: Who Suggested It, Or Rather on What Scripture?* **William Kelly** relates; "Now it so happens that, during a visit to Plymouth in the summer of 1845, Mr. B. W. Newton told me that, many years before, Mr. Darby wrote to him a letter in which he said that a suggestion was made to him by Mr. Tweedy (a spiritual man and most devoted ex-clergyman among the Irish Brethren), which to his mind quite cleared up the "difficulty" previously felt on this very question [i.e., the pretribulation rapture]."[111] **Kelly** goes on to explain that, "It was new however to hear that Mr. Tweedy, who died full of blessed labours in Demerara, was the one who first suggested, as decisive proof from Scripture, 2 Thess.ii.1,2. I so implicitly believed in his [i.e., Newton's] telling me the truth as conveyed in Mr. D.'s [i.e., Darby's] letter to himself, that it did not occur to me to question Mr. D. [i.e., Darby] about it."[112] Note that Brethren historian **Harold Rowdon** states that, "Newton related the same story in his reminiscences where he dated the letter **1832** or **1833**."[113]

While Kelly does not specifically describe the nature of Darby's difficulty or the solution proposed by Mr. Tweedy, B.W. Newton does. In his unpublished reminiscences, Newton refers specifically to Darby's letter. Newton and Darby were at odds over Darby's new secret rapture theory. In his letter, Darby attempted to answer

---

[110] *The Collected Writings of J.N. Darby* - Edited by William Kelly, Stow Hill and Tract Depot, Prophetic No.4, Vol.11, n.d., p.67.

[111] *The Rapture of the Saints: Who Suggested It, Or Rather on What Scripture?* - William Kelly, T. Weston, 1905, p.6.

[112] *The Rapture of the Saints: Who Suggested It, Or Rather on What Scripture?* - William Kelly, T. Weston, 1905, p.8.

[113] *The Origins of the Brethren* - Harold H. Rowdon, Pickering & Inglis Ltd., 1967, p.97, fn.84, p.107 per the *Fry MS*, pp.238-239.

the objections that Newton had raised and thereby heal the rift that had arisen between them. **Newton** states that, "At last Darby wrote from Cork, saying he had discovered a method of reconciling the whole dispute, and would tell me when he came. When he did, it turned out to be the 'Jewish Interpretation.' The Gospel of Matthew was not teaching Church Truth, but Kingdom Truth, and so on. He explained it to me and I said, 'Darby, if you admit that distinction you virtually give up Christianity.' Well, they kept on at that until they worked out the result, as we know it. The Secret Rapture was bad enough, but this was worse."[114]

Robert Cameron,[115] who was personally acquainted with both B.W. Newton and John Darby[116] also sheds some additional light upon the nature of Darby's "difficulty" and Mr. Tweedy's proposed solution. **Cameron** explains that Darby's teaching of a secret pretribulation rapture, "...ran up against an insuperable difficulty. Matthew 24:29-30 says: *Immediately after the Tribulation...shall appear the sign of the Son of Man in heaven.*' For three years they [i.e., Darby and his Brethren followers] were hung up on this horn. The Tribulation had not come, nor had the 'abomination' that preceded it been seen; therefore, the Advent was not historically imminent, however imminent it might be to the heart."[117] In other words, according to Cameron, Darby realized that his pretribulational rapture teaching which he discovered in Second Thessalonians, did not harmonize with the prophetic sequence of events described in Matthew 24.[118] **Cameron**

---

[114] *Prophetic Developments with a Particular Reference to the Early Brethren Movement* - F. Roy Coad, C.B.R.F. Occasional Paper Number 2 (Pinner, Middlesex, 1966), p.24, as quoted from the *Fry Manuscripts* located in the Christian Brethren Archive at John Rylands University Library at Manchester, England.

[115] Robert Cameron (1839-1927) was a Baptist pastor at Brantford, Ontario Canada. He edited the prophetic periodical *Watchword and Truth.*

[116] **Robert Cameron** states that he, "...went to England and met many godly men of the brethren, and amongst them Mr. Muller, Mr. Newton and Mr. Darby. Mr. Muller and Mr. Darby were often met in America afterwards, and both were dearly loved." *Watchword and Truth* - Vol. XXIV, No.5, May 1902, p.136. With respect to John Darby, **Robert Cameron** states, "We knew him well. Our first acquaintance with him personally was in New York City, nearly thirty years ago." *Watchword and Truth* - Vol. XXIV, No.11, November, 1902, p.327.

[117] *Scriptural Truth About the Lord's Return* - Robert Cameron, Fleming H. Revell Company, 1922, p.71.

[118] Historian **William Neatby** states that, "...Darby insisted that the whole Christian Church would be removed to heaven by a rapture unobserved by the world, shortly before the outbreak of the Tribulation...It is clear that the doctrine of the secret rapture is inconsistent with the description given of the Second Advent in the prophetic passages of the Gospels. Darby therefore taught that these descriptions were given to the apostles, not as the founders of the Christian Church, but as the representatives of a faithful remnant in the midst of apostate Judaism...This involved a different view of the Gospels from that which had previously obtained among Christians...A tendency accordingly grew up to treat large portions of the Gospels as 'Jewish.'" *A History of the Plymouth Brethren* - William Blair Neatby, Hodder and Stoughton, London, 1902, p.105.

goes on to explain that, "At this juncture, a godly clergyman, by the name of Tweedy, who afterwards died in Demerara, came to England and solved the problem by teaching that this discourse of our Lord [i.e., The Olivet Discourse of Matthew 24] was for Jews, that the Church would be caught up, secretly, before the Tribulation, and that this present evil Age would *not* end at the resurrection and translation of the Church to be with the Lord. The whole company caught at this solution, cried 'eureka' - handed over the Olivet Discourse to a Jewish Remnant, and proclaimed the new dogma to the world."[119]

Thus, with Mr. Tweedy's help, the theological tension was relieved. Second Thessalonians 2, provided "decisive proof" of a pretribulation rapture, and any Biblical prophecies that presented chronological problems for the secret pretribulation rapture could now be "dispensationally" interpreted away (i.e., selectively applied to a future Jewish remnant and not to the Church).[120] Darby now felt free to continue to develop and refine his new secret pretribulation rapture teaching. Darby soon drew a definite and clear distinction between the "coming" of Christ "for" His Church *before* the tribulation and the "appearing" of Christ in judgment *after* the tribulation. **Darby** claimed that, "...we must be caught up to meet Him, and that before He appears to all...our hope of Christ's coming for us is not properly His appearing...His coming...is the rapture of the saints, preceding their and Christ's appearing...So that at their rapture He has not appeared yet...This rapture before the appearing of Christ is a matter of express revelation...At the appearing comes the judgment of this world."[121]

---

[119] *Scriptural Truth About the Lord's Return* - Robert Cameron, Fleming H. Revell Company, 1922, p.71.

[120] Brethren historian **Roy Coad** observes that, "Darby was sorely concerned over the differences [i.e., that had arisen between himself and B.W. Newton]...Darby's solution was to project considerable sections of the New Testament away from the Church, as applicable only to a future dispensation of the restored Jewish remnant, which the Secret Rapture adherents envisaged. This would remove all the difficulties, and those Scriptures in the Gospels and elsewhere which presented such difficulty to adherents of the new teaching were thus simply explained: they referred not to the Church at all, but to the future Jewish remnant." *Prophetic Developments* - Roy Coad, C.B.R.F. Occasional Paper Number 2 (Pinner, Middlesex, 1966), pp.23-24. **Ernest Sandeen** states, "Darby attempted a resolution of his exegetical dilemma by distinguishing between Scripture intended for the church and Scripture intended for Israel...Darby's difficulty was solved by assuming that the Gospels were addressed partly to Jews and partly to Christians." *The Roots of Fundamentalism* - Ernest R. Sandeen, The University of Chicago Press, 1970, p.66.

[121] *The Collected Writings of J.N. Darby* -Edited by William Kelly, Stow Hill and Tract Depot, Prophetic No.4, Vol.11, n.d., pp.154-155.

Darby further maintained that the pretribulational "coming" of Christ to rapture the Church would be a "secret" event that would be *unheard* and *unseen* by the world. For example, while commenting on First Thessalonians 4:13-18, **Darby** asserted that, "The shout, the voice of the archangel, and the trump of God, are *not to be taken as the voice of God to all the world*...But the only persons who hear it are 'the dead in Christ,'... Then we which are alive and remain shall be caught up together with them in the clouds, to meet the Lord in the air...at the proper time the Lord comes (it is not said appears) and calls us up to be forever with the Lord..."[122] Again, while criticizing certain individuals who questioned the propriety of his Dispensational distinctions between Israel and the Church, **Darby** charged that these, "...adversaries of the truth, ...obscure the great and vital truth of the rapture of the church - I mean the *secrecy of the rapture*."[123]

The secrecy of the pretribulational rapture became a major element within Darby's teaching, and the early proponents of Darbyism openly advocated it. For example, **William Kelly**, the close friend and associate of Darby, while referring to Colossians 3:4, argues, "Where is the least hint that the world and the Church shall behold Christ at the same time? That the first moment of seeing Christ will be the same for an unbeliever as for a believer? The very reverse is true."[124] And again, while referring to the "shout" of 1Thessalonians 4:16, **Kelly** declares, "...it is mere and ignorant unbelief to press the fact that the Lord so shouts, and then to conclude that all the world must hear Him at that epoch. It is contrary to every analogy, that the world will be witnesses of the Lord's coming to take away the believers... Of course the world may be alarmed and astonished for a while by the fact of the disappearance of so many."[125] **Charles H. Mackintosh**, an early proponent of Darby's pretribulational rapture teaching declared, "When our Lord shall come to receive His people to Himself no eye shall see Him, no ear shall hear His voice, save His own redeemed and beloved people." And again, "He will come as a bridegroom to receive the bride; and when He thus comes none but His own shall hear His voice or see His face."[126]

---

[122] *The Collected Writings of J.N. Darby* - Edited by William Kelly, Stow Hill and Tract Depot Prophetic No.4, Vol.11, n.d., p.235.

[123] *The Collected Writings of J.N. Darby* - Edited by William Kelly, Stow Hill and Tract Depot Prophetic No.4, Vol.11, n.d., p.120.

[124] *Lectures on the Second Coming* and Kingdom - W. Kelly, Believer's Bookshelf, 1970, p.207.

[125] *Lectures on the Second Coming* and Kingdom - W. Kelly, Believer's Bookshelf, 1970, p.208.

[126] *Papers on the Lord's Coming* - C.H.M., Loizeaux Brothers Publishers, n.d., pp.24,27-28.

The Rev. Thomas Croskery was a contemporary critic of John Darby. He was thoroughly familiar with the doctrines of early Brethrenism. **Rev. Croskery** observed that, "The Brethren hold that Jesus Christ will come a second time *secretly* to take away all His saints, living and dead from the earth; and that He will come a third time *publicly*, along with the same saints, to judge the world. An interval of years…will intervene between His coming *for* His saints and His coming *with* His saints. The first coming [i.e., *for* His saints] is to be so *secret* that the rest of mankind will know nothing of it, or of the removal of the saints, who are thus to be spared from the tribulation of the last days."[127] Likewise, historian **William Blair Neatby**, has affirmed that, "With regard… to the dispensational and prophetic views of the Brethren…With very few exceptions…they all held the doctrine of the *secret rapture of the Church*; and it would scarcely be possible to exaggerate the extent to which all their ministry and worship, and not less their ordinary life and conversation, have been molded and coloured by this belief."[128]

Darby also asserted that the secret, pretribulational rapture was to be expected at any moment, or as modern Dispensationalist assert - the rapture is "imminent." **Darby** rhetorically asked, "When is the Christian to expect the Lord? I answer, always." Again, with reference to the secret, pretribulational rapture, **Darby** confidently asserted that, "…there is no event, I repeat, between us and heaven."[129] And again, **Darby** expectantly proclaimed, "He might come tomorrow, or tonight, or now."[130]

Darby also flatly rejected the traditional premillennial view that the Church represented a continuation of God's one redemptive plan for humanity. The historic position of the Church has always been that the entire company of the redeemed is a part of the assembly now termed "the Church." **Darby** emphatically denounced this belief as, "totally unscriptural." He declared, "I deny that saints before Christ's first coming, or after His second, are part of the church." **Darby** could therefore insist that, "The church

---

[127] *Plymouth-Brethrenism: A Refutation of its Principles and Doctrines* - Rev. Thomas Croskery, William Mullan & Son, 1879, p.138.
[128] *A History of the Plymouth Brethren* - William Blair Neatby, Hodder and Stoughton, London, 1902, pp.227-228.
[129] *The Collected Writings of J.N. Darby* - edited by William Kelly, Stow Hill and Tract Depot, Prophetic No.4, Vol.11, n.d., pp.156-157.
[130] *The Collected Writings of J.N. Darby* - edited by William Kelly, Stow Hill and Tract Depot, Prophetic No.4, Vol.11, n.d., p.207.

is the center after Christ of the heavenly system, the Jews of the earthly."[131] Thus, **Darby** isolated the Church within a "parenthesis" that effectively disassociated it from the Old Testament saints of the past, and the future saints of the Great Tribulation and Millennium. **Darby** stressed the critical importance of understanding this parenthetical concept when he declared, "This lapse of time, this parenthesis in the ways of God...and I refer to it because we should never understand God's dealings with mankind, unless we get hold of this. At the end of Daniel 9 you find the Spirit of God shewing a certain period... the parenthesis, or lapse of time, during which the Jews were all set aside... We have the sixty-nine weeks, and then there is a lapse. Messiah comes, is rejected, and gets cutoff, does not get the kingdom at all, gets nothing...the Jews are set aside, and the times of the Gentiles are running on, and nothing is fulfilled or brought to an accomplishment, because what He is doing is gathering the heavenly saints."[132] **Darby** concluded that, "...the Jews being set aside as a nation, the church was formed."[133] And thus, "The Church is a heavenly timeless gap in the world's history."[134] **Darby** maintained that the Church alone represented God's "heavenly" people. He declared, "...the church, a heavenly people..."[135] He also maintained that the Jews are God's "earthly" people, who will display "...God's righteousness on the earth."[136] Thus, by virtue of his "parenthesis theory," Darby isolated the Church from Old Testament saints, thereby creating a dichotomy between Old and New Testament believers. This then reinforced his conclusion that the "earthly" Tribulation pertained to God's earthly people, the Jews, and *not* to the Church, who are God's heavenly people. **Darby** rhetorically asks, "Now who are in the tribulation in the passages which speak of it in Scripture?...the Jews are in it - the church *not*."[137] Thus, Darby taught that the church, as God's heavenly people, were exempt from the coming Tribulation, whereas, the

---

[131] *The Collected Writings of J.N. Darby* - edited by William Kelly, Stow Hill and Tract Depot, Prophetic No.4, Vol.11, n.d., pp.345, 334.

[132] *The Collected Writings of J.N. Darby* - edited by William Kelly, Stow Hill and Tract Depot, Prophetic No.4, Vol.11, n.d., pp.241, 242, 243.

[133] *The Collected Writings of J.N. Darby* - edited by William Kelly, Stow Hill and Tract Depot, Prophetic No.4, Vol.11, n.d., p.326.

[134] *The Collected Writings of J.N. Darby* - edited by William Kelly, Stow Hill and Tract Depot, Prophetic No.4, Vol.11, n.d., pp.243-245, 344.

[135] *The Collected Writings of J.N. Darby* - edited by William Kelly, Stow Hill and Tract Depot, Prophetic No.4, Vol.11, n.d., p.77.

[136] *The Collected Writings of J.N. Darby* - edited by William Kelly, Stow Hill and Tract Depot, Prophetic No.4, Vol.11, n.d., p.47.

[137] *The Collected Writings of J.N. Darby* - edited by William Kelly, Stow Hill and Tract Depot, Prophetic No.4, Vol.11, n.d., p.164.

Jews, as God's earthly people, were destined to endure the sufferings of the Tribulation as punishment for their rejection of Jesus Christ. It is important to understand that Darby's novel interpretative approach to the prophetic Scriptures represents a radical departure from the traditional teachings of historic premillennialism.

Dispensationalists are extremely sensitive to the criticism that their Dispensational interpretation of the Scriptures is of very recent origin and therefore devoid of any legitimate historical basis. For example, in an attempt to defend pretribulationalism against the charge that it lacks historical legitimacy, **John Walvoord**, explains that, "The charge that the doctrine of imminency is a new and novel doctrine is false, but the charge that pretribulationism has been developed and defined to a large extent in recent centuries is true."[138] In an attempt to blunt the criticism of "novelty," many modern Dispensationalists claim that Darby did not actually originate Dispensationalism; rather, they maintain that he simply "rediscovered" dispensational truths that were previously taught in the early Church but subsequently "lost." For example, **Napoleon Noel**, in his very sympathetic history of the early Brethren movement, insists that, "No one can honestly dispute the fact that Mr. Darby was used of God in the *recovery* for the church of a vast amount of most precious and important truth that had been *lost and forgotten* almost from the time of the apostles...it can be said of him [Darby] as it could of no other of his time, that the Lord used him to bring cosmos [i.e., order] out of chaos for the church of God."[139] **H.A. Ironside** claims that, "The Napoleonic wars had directed attention to the prophetic scriptures as never before, and the truth of the Lord's imminent return was *rediscovered* after it had been seemingly *lost for centuries*." **Ironside** goes to claim that Dispensational teaching was, "...the special work of the Holy Spirit in *recovering precious truth long lost* through the church's declension and partial apostasy."[140] **Gerald Stanton** asserts that, "The Brethren and other godly men of that period were used by the Lord to *restore* to the Church the *whole truth* of the second coming of Christ, and when that truth was *restored* it was pretribulational!"[141] **John Walvoord**, argues that, "The statement...that pretribulationalism was unknown until the nineteenth century is a half-truth. Pretribulationalism as it is known today is comparatively recent, but the *concept of imminency* of the Lord's return - which is the

---

[138] *The Rapture Question* - John F. Walvoord, Zondervan Publishing House, 1981, p.53.
[139] *The History of the Brethren* – Napoleon Noel, edited by William F. Knapp, 1936, p.54.
[140] *A Historical Sketch of the Brethren Movement* - H.A. Ironside, Loizeaux Brothers, 1985, pp.8,32.
[141] *Kept From the Hour* - Gerald Stanton, Zondervan Publishing House, 1956, p.223.

important point - clearly dates to the early church."[142] And **Dwight Pentecost** maintains that, "This doctrine of imminence, or 'at any moment coming,' is ***not a new doctrine*** with Darby, as is sometimes charged, although he did clarify, systematize, and popularize it."[143] And **Charles Ryrie** explains that, "Informed dispensationalists... recognize that as a system dispensationalism was largely formulated by Darby, but that outlines of a dispensationalist approach to the Scriptures are found much earlier. They only maintain that certain features of the dispensational system are found in the teaching of the early church...It is granted that as a system of theology dispensationalism is recent in origin. But there are historical references to that which eventually was systematized into dispensationalism."[144] **Ryrie** goes on to say, "There is no question that the Plymouth Brethren, of which John Nelson Darby (1800-1882) was a leader, had much to do with the systematizing and promoting of dispensationalism."[145]

Thus, Dispensationalists admit that the modern system of Dispensational theology is the work of John Darby and therefore of very recent origin. However, in the very next breath, Dispensationalists attempt to diminish the serious implications of this admission by asserting that Dispensationalism is not really new because "certain features" of Dispensationalism were taught in the early Church. These features are purported to be the doctrine of "imminence," and the sharp distinction between Israel and the Church, which were inexplicably "lost," and after 1,800 years, rediscovered, refined and systematized by John Darby. All of these assertions however, are historically false.

In the first place, the early Church[146] taught ***none*** of the distinctive Dispensational doctrines advanced by John Darby and popularized by his followers. More specifically, the early Church made ***no*** Dispensational distinction between the redeemed saints of the Old Testament and New Testament and they knew absolutely nothing about an imminent, any-moment, secret, pretribulational rapture of the Church.[147]

---

[142] *The Blessed Hope and the Tribulation* - John F. Walvoord, Zondervan Publishing House, 1976, p.42.
[143] *Things To Come* - J. Dwight Pentecost, Zondervan Publishing House, 1958, p.203.
[144] *Dispensationalism Today* - Charles Caldwell Ryrie, Moody Press, 1965, pp.66-67.
[145] *Dispensationalism Today* - Charles Caldwell Ryrie, Moody Press, 1965, p.74.
[146] i.e., the Ante-Nicene Period (ca. A.D.100-A.D.325). This is the historical period that immediately followed the New Testament Apostolic Period.
[147] See **Appendix B** and **Appendix C** for detailed discussions about the early Church's teachings and the claims of Dispensationalism.

In the second place, Darby's own account of the development of his Dispensational system totally refutes the claims of historicity by its modern day proponents. John Darby's teaching was *not* the "rediscovery" of "lost" truth buried and forgotten within the writings of the Ante-Nicene Fathers as Dispensationalists claim. Darby himself has testified that his Dispensational distinctions were *not* based upon the teachings of men, but rather, that the Lord revealed them to him as he studied Isaiah 32. **Darby** declared, "But I must, though without comment, direct attention to chapter xxxii of the same prophet [Isaiah]; which I do the rather, because in this it was the Lord was pleased, *without man's teaching,* first to open my eyes on this subject, that I might learn His will concerning it throughout - not by the first blessed truths stated in it, but the latter part, when there shall be a complete *change in the dispensation*, the wilderness becoming the fruitful field of God's fruit and glory, and...pride be utterly abased."[148]

In the third place, John Darby has personally testified that the origin of the doctrine of a secret, imminent, pretribulational rapture of the Church, resulted from his study of Second Thessalonians 2:1-3. **Darby** states that, "It is this passage which, twenty years ago,[149] made me understand the rapture of the saints before - perhaps a considerable time before - the day of the Lord (that is, before the judgment of the living.)"[150] Thus, Darby clearly states that he did *not* ascertain his secret rapture teaching by "rediscovering" ancient truths that were buried and forgotten within the writings of the early Church. On the contrary, he testifies that the secret, any-moment rapture teaching was the direct result of his personal study of Second Thessalonians.

And in the fourth place, Darby strenuously maintained that the Dispensational distinction, which he made between the Jews and the Church was the "essential key" to correctly understand and interpret the Scriptures. **Darby** claimed that, "Those who believe in the rapture of the church before the appearing of Christ hold that the church has a special and peculiar character and connection with Christ...But above all, the question of the church and its privileges, as formed by the Holy Ghost sent down from

---

[148] *The Rapture of the Saints: Who Suggested It, or Rather on What Scripture?* - William Kelly, T. Weston, 1905, p.5. William Kelly uses this quote to prove that Darby deduced his Dispensational system from the Scriptures and *not* from the teachings of men or demons, as had been charged.
[149] Darby penned this statement circa 1850, thus 20 years prior would be approximately 1830.
[150] *The Collected Writings of J.N. Darby* - edited by William Kelly, Stow Hill and Tract Depot, Prophetic No.4, Vol.11, n.d., p.67.

heaven, is *important and essential* in this matter, and a right understanding of it *a key to the interpretation of the word of God*."[151] It is hard to imagine that the Dispensational system, which Darby claimed was "essential" to the "right understanding" of the Scriptures could have possibly gone completely unnoticed for 1,800 years of Church history! This historical fact alone should give every Dispensationalist serious pause!

6. The First Major Schism Within the Brethren Movement.

Not all of the early Brethren accepted Darby's new Dispensational teachings. In fact, the first divisive controversy in the Brethren movement was sparked by Darby's prophetic teachings. His insistence on making a sharp distinction between Old and New Testament believers and his teaching of a secret, any-moment pretribulational rapture of the Church soon polarized the Brethren. The most notable Brethren leaders who took issue with Darby's new teachings were George Muller[152] and Henry Craik[153] of Bristol, and Benjamin Wills Newton and Samuel P. Tregelles of Plymouth.

It was B.W. Newton and Samuel P. Tregelles who assumed the forefront in opposing Darby's new teachings. Newton was initially very good friends with Darby, and worked closely with him. However, Darby's new Dispensational teachings, which he introduced at the third Powerscourt conference, strained the relationship to the breaking point. **H.A. Ironside** describes Newton's reaction to Darby's new teaching in the following words: "He [i.e., Newton] considered Mr. Darby's dispensational teaching as the height of speculative nonsense. He was vehemently opposed to the idea of the church being a special company of whose calling and destiny the Old Testament knows nothing, a line of things emphasized by Mr. Darby, Mr. Bellett and other intimates. When at the Powerscourt meetings the idea of the cancelled seventieth week of Daniel, beginning

---

[151] *The Collected Writings of J.N. Darby* - edited by William Kelly, Stow Hill and Tract Depot, Prophetic No.4, Vol.11, n.d., p.119.
[152] George Muller (1806-1898) is remembered as a great man of faith who built numerous orphan houses and selflessly cared for hundreds of orphans. Muller never made his financial needs known, nor did he ever solicit monetary funds. Rather, he simply prayed and depended upon God to meet their needs.
[153] Henry Craik (1805-1866) met George Muller at Devonshire and soon partnered with him in a ministry that lasted 44 years. He co-pastored with George Muller at the Bethesda Chapel in Bristol.

after the rapture of the church, was suggested by Sir Edward Denny and Mr. Darby...It was, however, utterly rejected by Mr. Newton..."[154]

Newton, an accomplished Biblical scholar, rejected Darby's new teachings because he was convinced that they lacked adequate Scriptural support. As early as 1840, in a series of handwritten letters that were circulated among the Brethren, **Newton** stated that, "...the *secret return* of the Lord Jesus is, I believe, a *doctrine altogether new*. There has been nothing in which the Church of God has through every age been more unanimously agreed, than in expecting the next return of the Lord Jesus to be in manifested glory...yet I think it will be admitted that a *new doctrine* upon such a subject, advanced for the *first time within the last few years,* requires most plain and decisive evidence from Scripture before it should receive any countenance. But I have searched in vain for such evidence."[155] In his opposition to Darby's new teaching, **Newton** raised a vitally important question when he asked, "Will the Second Advent of our Lord and Savior for which we wait, be *secret*, or in manifest glory? Will it terminate the age of human evil, or will evil still reign and triumph after it? Until the 19th century there had been in the true Church of God a happy unanimity in answering these questions...They have all with one voice affirmed that when our High Priest returns 'without sin, unto salvation,' He will return in manifested glory...Nevertheless, a doctrine so *truly new* as the *secret coming* of the Lord, and the *secret removal of His saints*, must, by its very novelty, awake suspicion, and should therefore be jealously tested by the Scripture of Truth." **Newton** was adamant that, "We have no test of Truth except the Scripture." [156] It was his conviction of the absolute and final authority of the Scripture that convinced Newton that Darby's new Dispensational scheme was untenable. Newton's considered opinion was that, "...the whole testimony of Scripture is against it."[157]

Samuel P. Tregelles, who was one of the most accomplished Biblical scholars of his day, agreed with Newton's assessment of Darby's secret rapture teaching. Tregelles declared that, "...the doctrine of the *secret coming* of Christ, which many now preach as

---

[154] *A Historical Sketch of the Brethren Movement* - H.A. Ironside, Loizeaux Brothers Publishers, 1985, p.32.
[155] *Five Letters* - Benjamin Wills Newton, Houlston and Sons, London, 1877, *Fifth Letter*, pp.72,73.
[156] *The Second Advent Not Secret But In Manifested Glory* - Benjamin Wills Newton, Sovereign Grace Advent Testimony, n.d., p.1.
[157] *Five Letters* - Benjamin Wills Newton, Houlston and Sons, London, 1877, *Fifth Letter*, p.72.

if it were the acknowledged truth of God, instead of being (as is really the case) that which at every point would require proof from Scripture. But not only is this doctrine of the coming of Christ not taught in the Word of God... it is refuted by whatever speaks of the Lord's coming in the clouds of heaven when every eye shall see Him... It is likewise contradicted by specific and individual Scriptures, which, in simple testimony or in legitimate deduction, would be conclusive to a mind subject to God's Word."[158]

Both Newton and Tregelles strenuously objected to Darby's secret, any-moment rapture theory on the grounds that the Scriptures clearly spoke of a visible, glorious return of Christ **after** specific intervening events. **Newton** argued that, "...to speak of intervening events antecedent to the coming of the Lord is not contrary to, but accordant with, the teaching of the Apostles... Surely then it behooves us to be very jealous of the introduction of a principle which condemns the practice of the Apostles, and even of the blessed Lord Himself."[159] Likewise, **Tregelles** observed that, "The Church is called to 'patience of hope,' and not to mere excitement of speculative expectancy... they knew that the Lord's coming could not take place until certain things had occurred, and until certain moral features of opposition between the Church and the world had displayed themselves."[160]

However, Darby disposed of these objections by asserting that the prophetic portions of the Gospels, which clearly predict intervening events, were **not** addressed to the Church, but to a future Jewish remnant. Thus, Darby effectively "**dispensationalized**"[161] large portions of the Gospels, declaring that they rested upon "**Jewish ground**"[162] and therefore had **no application** to the Church. For example, **Darby** asserted that, "I still believe that Matthew 24... is addressed to the disciples as Jews...and *I do not think it addressed to the church* as the church...The standing, therefore, of Peter and his companions on the Mount of Olives was clearly not our standing at all... On which side of the cross were the disciples? Did they trust in the blood of Jesus?... One thing is clear

---

[158] *The Hope of Christ's Second Coming* - S.P. Tregelles, The Sovereign Grace Advent Testimony, n.d., pp.32-33.
[159] *Five Letters* - Benjamin Wills Newton, Houlston and Sons, London, 1877, *First Letter*, pp.6-7.
[160] *The Hope of Christ's Second Coming* - S.P. Tregelles, The Sovereign Grace Advent Testimony, n.d., pp.20-21.
[161] The term "dispensationalize" refers to the Dispensational practice of dividing the New Testament Scriptures into Jewish and Christian portions.
[162] The phrase "Jewish ground" was coined by John Darby and was subsequently adopted by Dispensationalists to obliquely refer to those portions of the New Testament Scriptures that they contend apply to a future Jewish remnant and **not** to the Church.

- they did *not* trust in the blood of Jesus, and they had therefore *no* communion with the things unto which faith in Jesus now introduces. And thus they were clearly to be dealt with *not upon the ground of the church*... They were on the dark side of the pillar of testimony, so they ought to have been addressed, if at all, as a *Jewish remnant*."[163]

Newton and Tregelles reacted strongly to Darby's reasoning, arguing that the Gospels were in fact Christian Scriptures and were therefore to be applied directly to the Church, and not to a future, non-Christian Jewish remnant.[164] Referring to the Olivet Discourse in Matthew 24, which warns of tribulation and suffering just prior to the Second Advent of Christ, **Newton** observed that, "...these words, so plain and so solemn, have of late been rejected as having no proper application to ourselves on the ground of the Apostles being Jews, and therefore representatives of Jews and not of Christians...and the principle is that where there is anything characteristically Jewish in place or circumstance, there is that which is not properly Christian: *a principle so fatal to Truth that I cannot believe that godly, thoughtful minds would ever have sanctioned it*, had it not been _assumed_*, that no events antecedent to the Lord's return are made known to the Church...*"[165] **Newton** then rhetorically asks, "Are then the prophetic instructions of the Lord in the Gospels addressed to the Apostles as representatives of Christians or Jews? Of those who believed in Christ, or those who knew not or rejected His name?" He then concludes that, "They are addressed to persons who believe in and obey Jesus risen; who suffer for His name's sake during the time of His personal absence, and during the time of Israel's unbelief."[166]

Tregelles pointedly explains Darby's practice of casually dismissing all Scriptures that contradicted his Dispensational scheme, when he observed, "Thus the doctrine held and taught by many is, that believers are concerned not with a public and manifested coming of Christ in the clouds of heaven with power and great glory...but with a *secret* or private coming...But if things are so, to whom would the Scriptures apply which give

---

[163] *The Collected Writings of J.N. Darby* - edited by William Kelly, Stow Hill and Tract Depot, Prophetic No.4, Vol.11, n.d., pp.3,14,15,17,18.
[164] Brethren historian **Roy Coad** has observed that, "When Darby's followers proceeded to develop the distinction between Jewish and Christian hopes, dividing the Scriptures of both Testaments between them, and making numerous deductions which fundamentally changed traditional interpretations and doctrines, Newton concluded that he was faced with a full-blown heresy." *A History of the Brethren Movement* - F. Roy Coad, Regent College Publishing, 2001, p.130.
[165] *Five Letters* - Benjamin Wills Newton, Houlston and Sons, London, 1877, *First Letter*, pp.11-13.
[166] *Five Letters* - Benjamin Wills Newton, Houlston and Sons, London, 1877, *First Letter*, pp.13-14.

warning of perilous times? To whom could signs be given? This consideration has led to the ***Jewish interpretation of Scripture. Whatever has been felt to be a difficulty has been set aside by saying that it is 'Jewish'; and that one word has been deemed to be quite enough to show that it has nothing to do with the Church. On this principle the application of very much of the New Testament has been avoided***...An undefined term becomes an easy mode of explaining away distinct statements, which cannot be reconciled to a theory; because in this manner no meaning whatever is assigned to the passages whose testimony has to be avoided. This has been the case with the word 'Jewish' in connection with the Scriptures, which teach the manifest appearing of the Lord in glory. ***In this manner the first three Gospels have been called Jewish, whenever any portion of their teaching was felt as a difficulty.***"[167] Thus, Darby effectively nullified any statement of Scripture that seemed to conflict with his Dispensational scheme, by simply declaring it to be upon "Jewish ground." This was Darby's euphemistic way of saying that those portions of the Scripture had no direct application to, or for, the Church.

Newton and Tregelles argued strenuously against Darby's secret rapture; his distinction between Old and New Testament believers; and his division of the New Testament Scriptures into "Jewish" and "Christian" sections. Instead, they advocated a traditional premillennial interpretation of the Scripture, which taught a glorious Second Advent of Christ to raise the righteous dead and rapture the Church *after* the Tribulation. They argued that the Gospels were inspired Christian Scriptures, written by Christians for Christians. They also contended that the Scriptures revealed a single redemptive program that included all true believers who comprised one redeemed people of God.[168] However, despite the well-reasoned, Biblical objections of Newton and Tregelles, Darby's new Dispensational teachings continued to spread throughout Great Britain and the European continent, gaining wide approval and acceptance among millenarians.

---

[167] *The Hope of Christ's Second Coming* - S.P. Tregelles, The Sovereign Grace Advent Testimony, n.d., pp.36-38. Likewise, Josiah Teulon, vice-principal of The Theological College at Chichester has observed, "...the Brethren, when pressed with passages from our Lord's discourses which mitigate against their theories as to the Rapture and the Appearing, are wont to declare that such passages have nothing to do with the Church, but are intended for the Jewish remnant in the latter day, and are addressed to the Apostles, not as representing the Church, but as representing that remnant." *The History of the Plymouth Brethren* - J. S. Teulon, Society for Promoting Christian Knowledge, London, 1883, pp.199-200.

[168] **William Neatby** relates that, "Newton strenuously upheld that Abraham and the rest of the faithful of old would form in heaven an integral part of the Church, the Bride of Christ. Darby resisted this as a view derogatory from the Church's special glory, and roused against Newton a great enthusiasm on behalf of her invaded prerogatives." *A History of the Plymouth Brethren* - William Blair Neatby, Hodder and Stoughton, London, 1902, p.106.

7. The Spread of Darby's Dispensationalism to America.

The late 1800s was a time of tremendous social, economic, political and religious change in America. The rapid scientific, industrial and social advances tended to undermine confidence in the trustworthiness of the Bible. Scientific theories in particular called into question the reliability of the Biblical text. For example, the theories of Darwinian evolution[169] and geologic Uniformitarianism[170] served to cast doubt on the accuracy of Scripture. Many within the established churches concluded that modern science had disproved the supernatural claims of Scripture. A religious movement known as "Modernism" began to gain widespread acceptance within the mainline Christian denominations of America. Modernism, also known as "Liberalism" embraced the theology of the "higher critics," which boldly denied the truthfulness of the Bible. Essential doctrines, such as the Incarnation, the Trinity, the Deity of Jesus Christ and His bodily Resurrection were openly rejected. Mankind was no longer viewed as destitute fallen sinners in need of Divine salvation. The doctrines of the depravity of man, the necessity of individual regeneration, the reality of heaven and hell were exchanged for a new, modern gospel that advocated the "Fatherhood of God and the Brotherhood of Man." Thus, the true Gospel was replaced with a new "social gospel" that sought to correct the perceived social injustices of American society. Many churches and seminaries were infected with these critical liberal views and quickly abandoned a belief in the trustworthiness, authority and reliability of the Biblical text.[171]

The dominant eschatological view in America at this time was the *post*-millennialism of Daniel Whitby. But by the late 1800s, many conservative Christians had become increasingly uncomfortable with Whitby's *post*-millennialism and the growing liberalism that was associated with it. In an attempt to reclaim a literal interpretation of Scripture, many Christians began turning to a *pre*-millennial interpretation of the Bible. It was precisely at this moment in history that John Darby's premillennial Dispensationalism was introduced into America. Between the years of 1862 and 1877,

---

[169] Charles Darwin (1809-1882) originated the theory of evolution, which attributes the origin of life to naturalistic causes and processes, thereby eliminating Divine supernatural intervention.

[170] Sir Charles Lyell (1797-1875) is the originator of the theory of Uniformitarianism, which declares that the geologic formations of the earth are the result of observable natural processes that are in operation at the present, and not cataclysmic events as described in the Bible, such as the Flood.

[171] For an excellent discussion of "Modernism," see the article entitled, *Liberalism* in the *Dictionary of Theological Terms* - Alan Cairns, Ambassador Emerald International, 2002, p.263.

John Darby made seven trips to the United States and Canada.[172] During this time period Darby diligently labored to spread his new Dispensational teachings. His greatest successes were experienced in the larger metropolitan cities - especially in New York, Boston, Chicago and St. Louis.[173] The most significant and important converts to his system were the theologically conservative ministers within the mainline Christian denominations. Many urban pastors readily embraced much of Darby's Dispensational teachings in their move away from a liberal *post*-millennialism and towards a conservative *pre*-millennialism, and as would be expected, they were soon teaching it to their respective congregations. As **George Ladd** has aptly observed, Darby's teachings, "...came with a freshness and vitality which quite captured American Christians...His system of prophetic interpretation was eagerly adopted...because its basic futurism seemed to be a recovery of a sound Biblical prophetic interpretation - which it was - and to give to the doctrine of the Lord's return the importance it deserved."[174]

7a. The Acceptance of Darby's Prophetic Scheme by Influential American Clergyman.

Many American clergymen enthusiastically adopted Darby's prophetic teachings. For example, one of the earliest and most important converts to Darbyism was James Hall Brookes (1830-1897), the pastor of the Walnut Street Presbyterian Church in St. Louis, Missouri. Brookes may well have been one of the several pastors that met and were favorably disposed towards Darby during one of his missionary visits to St. Louis.[175] According to H.A. Ironside, Brookes and Darby were very well acquainted. **Brookes** unquestionably held Darby in high esteem, exclaiming that, "Darby was a man of decided ability, extensive learning, profound acquaintance with the Word of God."[176] Brookes had such a high regard for Darby, that he invited him to fill his pulpit on several occasions at the Walnut Street Presbyterian Church. **H.A. Ironside** has stated that, "Dr. Brookes knew and loved many of the them [i.e., the Plymouth Brethren]. His pulpit had often been open to them. J.N. Darby, Malachi Taylor, Paul J. Loizeaux and

---

[172] *The Roots of Fundamentalism* - Earnest R. Sandeen - The University of Chicago Press, 1970, p.72.

[173] *The Roots of Fundamentalism* - Earnest R. Sandeen - The University of Chicago Press, 1970, p.74.

[174] *The Blessed Hope* - George Eldon Ladd, Wm. B. Eerdmans Publishing Company, 1980, p.43.

[175] *The Roots of Fundamentalism* - Earnest R. Sandeen, The University of Chicago Press, 1970, pp.74-75.

[176] *The Truth*, 21, May 1895, *Plymouth Brethren*, James H. Brookes, p.249, as quoted in *The Hermeneutics of Dispensationalism* - Daniel Payton Fuller, Northern Baptist Theological Seminary, Doctoral Dissertation, 1957, p.80.

others had preached in his church at various times."[177] Not surprisingly, Brookes played a major role in popularizing Darby's Dispensationalism in America through his writing and his involvement in the American prophetic conference movement.

7b. The Circulation of Dispensational Books and Tracts.

A second important element that facilitated the spread and acceptance of Darby's prophetic teaching was the circulation of Brethren books and tracts. While John Darby was traveling throughout the cities of America, his Brethren associates, William Kelly, C.H. Mackintosh, and William Trotter were writing numerous pamphlets and books that advocated Darby's Dispensational interpretation of Scripture. These writings were highly effective in popularizing Darby's secret, any-moment rapture teaching.[178] The far-reaching effects of these early Brethren writings cannot be overstated. Consider their effect on D.L. Moody (1837-1899), who in turn affected millions more through his numerous evangelistic campaigns. **H.A. Ironside** has recorded that, "Mr. Moody ever confessed his indebtedness to the writings of the Brethren for much help in the understanding of the Word, but it was C.H. Mackintosh and Charles Stanley[179] who had the greatest influence. The writings of the former he always highly commended."[180] Moody himself has testified just how profoundly he was influenced by the writings of C.H. Mackintosh. **Moody** stated that the writings of Mackintosh were instrumental in persuading him to accept much of Darby's Dispensational teaching, declaring, "... I had my attention called to C.H.M.'s *Notes*, and was so much pleased and at the same time profited by the way they opened up Scripture truths, that I secured at once all the

---

[177] *A Historical Sketch of the Brethren Movement* - H.A. Ironside, Loizeaux Brothers, Inc., 1985, p.196.

[178] Josiah Teulon, who was the vice-principal of The Theological College at Chichester, England, and a contemporary of John Darby, commented on the spread of Brethrenism, stating that, "It has found a home in many continental States; it is well known in the colonies, and in America...Though it employs evangelistic agencies to make its tenants known, and gather up its converts, *the main instrument of its propagation has been the press rather than the pulpit*, and numbers, to whom the society itself is little more than a name, have unconsciously imbibed its principles from a perusal of *its periodicals, its pamphlets and its leaflets*...They have produced a large number of writers, by whose works the principles of Brethrenism have been disseminated far and wide." *The History and Teaching of the Plymouth Brethren* - J.S. Teulon, Society for Promoting Christian Knowledge, London, 1883, pp.5-6,19.

[179] Charles H. Mackintosh, aka C.H.M. (1820-1896) was a Brethren pastor, evangelist, writer and educator. He authored many tracts and books that promoted Darby's Dispensational teachings. Charles Stanley (1821-1888) was a Brethren evangelist and writer. He preached throughout England and authored numerous tracts under the initials "C.S."

[180] *A Historical Sketch of the Brethren Movement* - H.A. Ironside, Loizeaux Brothers, Inc., 1985, p.82.

writings of the same author...They have been to me a very key to the Scriptures."[181] Not surprisingly, by 1877, **D.L. Moody** was teaching the secret, any-moment coming of Jesus Christ, declaring, "...he [i.e., Christ] is to come unexpectedly and suddenly...at any moment he may come...Now I can't find any place in the Bible where it tells me to wait for signs of the coming of the millennium...but it tells me to look for the coming of the Lord; to watch for it; to be ready at midnight to meet him...The trump of God may be sounded, for anything we know, before I finish this sermon."[182]

7c. The American Prophetic Conference Movement.

A third and extremely important factor that contributed to the rapid spread of Darby's new Dispensational teaching in America was the American Bible Conference Movement. During the last decades of the 19th century and early years of the 20th century, leading conservative millenarians regularly met in various cities to study and discuss prophetic subjects. The first of these influential interdenominational conferences was held in 1868. However, the most important and influential Bible conferences were known as the Niagara Conferences. In 1883, millenarian leaders made the decision to regularly convene prophetic conferences at a beautiful and secluded resort at Niagara, on the shores of Lake Ontario. This location was utilized until 1897. The Niagara conferences were widely attended by millenarians from across America. James Hall Brookes, who was very active in the pre-Niagara conferences, became one of the primary organizers and president of the Niagara Conferences. The overwhelming majority of the Niagara leaders and speakers openly advocated and taught the key elements of Darby's Dispensational approach to Scripture - specifically, the secret, any-moment pretribulational rapture of the Church; the Church age parenthesis; and the dichotomy between Israel and the Church. Some of the more famous and influential ministers of the day that were regularly represented at the Niagara Conferences were,

---

[181] *The Roots of Fundamentalism* - Earnest R. Sandeen, The University of Chicago Press, 1970, p.173, as quoted from *Watchword and Truth*, No. 22, (1900), p.255.
[182] *Moody: His Words, Works and Workers* – Dwight Lyman Moody, edited by W.H. Daniels, Nelson & Phillips, 1877, pp.470,472.

Arthur Tappan Pierson,[183] Nathaniel West,[184] William G. Moorehead,[185] William J. Erdman,[186] Adoniram Judson Gordon,[187] Robert Cameron,[188] Samuel H. Kellogg,[189] Henry W. Frost,[190] William E. Blackstone[191] and Henry M. Parsons.[192]

In 1880, D.L. Moody, who had already adopted many of the major elements of Darby's Dispensationalism, launched his own series of very influential Bible conferences. These were known as the Northfield Conferences. These conferences were held at Moody's church at East Northfield, Massachusetts. The speakers were handpicked by Moody and were nearly all Dispensational millenarian leaders who were already well known in the Bible Conference Movement. The prestigious Northfield Conferences provided a highly effective forum that did much to legitimize and popularize Darby's secret, any-moment rapture teaching with the evangelical leaders of America. A.J. Gordon, a close friend and associate of Moody, oversaw these conferences from 1892 to 1894, while Moody was conducting revival campaigns in Great Britain. These conferences were so popular that they continued for several years after Moody's death. Interestingly, at one of the later conferences (circa 1895), Moody invited a then unknown pastor from Dallas, Texas to address the gathering. His name was Cyrus Ingerson Scofield.[193] Shortly thereafter, Moody installed C.I. Scofield as pastor of the Congregational Church at East Northfield and appointed him president of the Northfield Bible Training School

---

[183] **A.T .Pierson** (1837-1911) was a highly respected clergyman and author. During C.H. Spurgeon's last illness, Pierson filled the pulpit of the Metropolitan Tabernacle in London.

[184] **Nathaniel West** (1826-1906) was a recognized and respected Biblical scholar, Presbyterian pastor and professor at Danville Theological Seminary and a leader of the Niagara conferences.

[185] **William G. Moorehead** (1836-1914) was the president of the United Presbyterian Seminary at Xenia, Ohio and editor of the prophetic periodical *Truth*.

[186] **William J. Erdman** (1834-1923) was a highly respected and influential Presbyterian minister, and active in the Bible conference movement.

[187] **A.J. Gordon** (1836-1895) was the pastor of Clarendon Street Baptist Church in Boston, editor of the prophetic journal, *Watchword*, and a highly respected leader of the Niagara prophetic conferences.

[188] **Robert Cameron** (1839-1927) was a Baptist pastor at Brantford, Ontario, Canada and member of the Niagara Executive Committee. He edited the prophetic periodical *Watchword and Truth*.

[189] **Samuel H. Kellogg** (1836-1899) was a professor at the Presbyterian Seminary at Allegheny, PA.

[190] **Henry W. Frost** (1858- ?) was the homeland director of the Inland China Mission for 36 years, author and recording secretary for the Niagara Conferences.

[191] **William E. Blackstone** (1841-1935) was a lay worker within the Methodist Episcopal Church. He was very active in the Niagara Bible Conference Movement and his book, *Jesus Is Coming* did much to spread and popularize Darby's Dispensational teaching in America.

[192] **H.M. Parsons** (1828-1913) was a Presbyterian minister, having held pastorates in New York and Ontario. He was an early member and leader within the Niagara conference movement.

[193] **C.I. Scofield** (1843-1921) was converted at 37 years of age and was discipled by James H. Brookes.

(Moody's home church and Bible school).[194] Thus, Darby's secret rapture teaching continued to gain widespread acceptance and popularity within the American Bible Conference Movement, and by the last decade of the 19th century, it had unquestionably become the predominate view. However, not all of the conference participants accepted Darby's pretribulationalism. Some began to seriously question the Biblical legitimacy of this teaching, and by 1900, what had begun as an honest theological disagreement, escalated into an open and bitter controversy.

7d. The Bible Institute Movement.

A fourth, and vitally important element that contributed to the spread of Darby's Dispensational teaching in America was the Bible Institute Movement. Conservative premillenarians soon realized the need for conservative Bible training schools that would prepare and equip Christian workers, evangelists, missionaries and pastors. Unlike the liberal seminaries, the Bible institutes emphasized the teaching of the Bible as God's inspired and inerrant Word, endeavoring to impart to their students an appreciation and understanding of the harmony and unity of the Scriptures. And unlike the traditional seminaries, the Bible institutes accepted both men and women students. Their mission was to impart both Biblical knowledge and practical ministerial skills that would yield genuine benefits to the Church. Thus, these schools developed straightforward, no-nonsense programs designed to train Sunday school teachers, church secretaries, church musicians, Bible teachers, missionaries and pastors.[195]

These Bible institutes also played a major role in unifying the conservative evangelical movement in America because they shared and propagated a common theology, purpose and culture. And one of the major unifying doctrines that most of these schools held in common was J.N. Darby's premillennial Dispensationalism.[196] By 1900 there were approximately fourteen Bible schools in operation - by 1920 another twenty-six were added and by 1945, there were some sixty-eight more schools.[197] Over the years,

---

[194] *The Story of the Scofield Reference Bible* - Frank E. Gaebelein, Oxford University Press, 1959, p.8.
[195] *Training God's Army* - Virginia Lieson Brereton, Indiana University Press, 1990, pp.63,64,139.
[196] *Training God's Army* - Virginia Lieson Brereton, Indiana University Press, 1990, p.88.
[197] Some of the more notable Bible institutes are: Missionary Training Institute (Nyack College), 1882; Moody Bible Institute, 1886; Boston Missionary Training School (Gordon College), 1889; Training School for Christian Workers (Azusa College), 1899; Bible Institute of Los Angeles (BIOLA), 1908; Prairie Bible Institute, 1922; Multnomah School of the Bible, 1936. See *Training God's Army* - Virginia Lieson Brereton, Indiana University Press, 1990, pp.71-76.

these Bible institutes thoroughly trained thousands upon thousands of Christian workers, missionaries and pastors in the Dispensational method of Bible interpretation.

7e. Publishing.

The fifth important element that facilitated the spread and acceptance of Darby's Dispensationalism in America was the highly effective use of the print media. **Paul J. Loizeaux** (1841-1916), a French Huguenot, immigrated to America in 1860. In 1870, he was invited to attend a Brethren conference in Guelph, Ontario, Canada, where John Darby was speaking. After a private meeting with Darby, he immediately joined the Brethren movement. In 1876, Paul Loizeaux, and his brother **Timothy Ophir Loizeaux** (1843-1927), founded the Bible Truth Depot (later renamed Loizeaux Brothers). This publishing enterprise was, "Devoted to the Lord's Work and to the Spread of His Truth," effectively becoming the primary publishing house for Brethren books and tracts in America.[198]

Another highly significant and effective publishing endeavor was the publication in 1888, of C.I. Scofield's tract, *Rightly Dividing the Word of Truth*. This pamphlet systematically outlined the major principles for the Dispensational method of Scripture interpretation. In his brief introduction, **Scofield** stated that, "The purpose of this pamphlet is to indicate the more important divisions of the Word of Truth,"[199] which according to Scofield were essential to a correct understanding of the Bible. **Scofield** warned his readers that, "The Word of Truth, then, has right divisions, and it must be evident that, as one cannot be 'a workman that needeth not to be ashamed' without observing them, so any study of that Word which ignores those divisions must be in large measure profitless and confusing."[200] Scofield's pamphlet experienced a wide circulation and is still readily available today. It is important however to note that Scofield's famous pamphlet was essentially a restatement of what he learned during his three years of discipleship training under the tutelage of Dr. John Hall Brookes. Commenting on Scofield's training under Dr. Brookes, **Lewis Sperry Chafer** has observed that Brookes, "...was a firm believer in prophecy, an ardent premillenarian

---

[198] *A Historical Sketch of the Brethren Movement* - H.A. Ironside, Loizeaux Brothers, Inc., 1985, pp.73-74, and *The History of the Brethren* - Napoleon Noel, edited by William Knapp, 1936, pp.113,133.
[199] *Rightly Dividing the Word of Truth* - C.I. Scofield, Loizeaux Brothers Inc., 1896, p.3.
[200] *Rightly Dividing the Word of Truth* - C.I. Scofield, Loizeaux Brothers Inc., 1896, p.3.

who knew how to divide the Word of truth rightly.[201] At the feet of this choice servant of Christ, Scofield took his place. Here he learned what he could not have learned in any of the theological seminaries of that time. Being instructed by Dr. Brookes in Bible study, he soon mastered, with his fine analytical mind, the ABC's of the right division of the Word of God, which he later embodied in a small brochure, *Rightly Dividing the Word of Truth.*"[202] Then, in 1907, Scofield published, *The Scofield Correspondence Course*, which comprised seven volumes covering the entire Bible. This Bible study course was designed to thoroughly instruct laymen in the Dispensational system of Bible interpretation and was sponsored and administered by The Moody Bible Institute in Chicago. The complete course has remained in constant publication well into the late 1990s and is still readily available.

But without question, one of the most effective publications that contributed to the spread and acceptance of John Darby's Dispensationalism is *The Scofield Reference Bible*. The idea of publishing a Dispensational study Bible was first raised by C.I. Scofield in 1901, at the Gaebelein sponsored Sea Cliff Bible Conference on Long Island, New York. It is important to understand the strong influence that Brethrenism had on the production of Scofield's Bible. First, three prominent Brethren businessmen, Francis Fitch, Alwyn Ball and John T. Pirie, provided the necessary financial support.[203] Incidentally, Francis Fitch also published *The Scofield Correspondence Course*, and A.C. Gaebelein's periodical, *Our Hope*. Second, at Scofield's request, A.C. Gaebelein, who had adopted all of Darby's Dispensational teachings, played a major advisory role in determining the interpretation of many of the prophetic passages. In a letter to Gaebelein, **Scofield** deferred to Gaebelein's judgment, declaring, "I sit at your feet when it comes to prophecy, and congratulate in advance the future readers of the reference Bible on having in their hands a safe, clear, sane guide through what to most

---

[201] When Dispensationalists refer to the "divisions" of the Word or of "rightly dividing the Word," they are alluding to the process by which they determine which verses of the New Testament apply to the Church and which verses apply to a future Jewish remnant. This process is also referred to as interpreting the Bible "dispensationally." See footnotes 161 and 162.

[202] *Moody Monthly*, Nov. 1942, p.129, *The Story of the Scofield Reference Bible, Part II – A Brief Biographical Sketch* - Arno C. Gaebelein.

[203] See *The Hermeneutics of Dispensationalism* - Daniel Payton Fuller, Northern Baptist Theological Seminary, Doctoral Dissertation, 1957, p.115, and *Dispensationalism in America* - C. Norman Kraus, John Knox Press, 1958, p.113.

is a labyrinth." [204]

Scofield began working on his Reference Bible in 1902. By 1907, the project was completed and published by the Oxford University Press. It was revised in 1917 and renamed, *The Scofield Study Bible*. Scofield's primary objective was to systematically present the Dispensational interpretation of Scripture, making it readily accessible to the common Christian reader. In this endeavor he unquestionably succeeded. From its first appearance, *The Scofield Study Bible* found immediate and widespread acceptance among conservative evangelicals. Still popular today, it has sold millions of copies world-wide.

Another very important book that significantly contributed to the acceptance of Darby's Dispensational approach to Scripture was written by William Eugene Blackstone, a lay Christian evangelist. Blackstone's interest in Bible prophecy led him to write a book entitled, *Jesus Is Coming*. This book has been continuously in print since its first publication in 1878, and has experienced a worldwide circulation, having been translated into 40 different languages. Because the book presents Darby's Dispensational teachings in a very popular and readable format, it has played an important role in popularizing Darby's secret, pretribulational rapture teaching.

7f. The Emotional Appeal of The Pretribulational Rapture Doctrine.

A sixth element that contributed to the widespread acceptance and popularity of the Dispensational doctrine of a pretribulation rapture is its comforting promise of deliverance from persecution and suffering. The idea of being exempt from the future persecutions of the Antichrist and the associated sufferings of the Great Tribulation unquestionably offers a tremendous psychological and emotional appeal. Nobody wants to suffer, or see those whom they love suffer. People are therefore naturally inclined to accept a teaching that promises them deliverance from the harsh realities of the last days. The positive emotional appeal of being exempt from the final great persecution is

---

[204] *Moody Monthly*, Feb. 1943, p.344, *The Story of the Scofield Reference Bible, Part V – The Work Begun in 1902, Published in 1909* - A.C. Gaebelein. See also, *Dispensationalism in America* - C. Norman Kraus, John Knox Press, 1958, p.113.

fully recognized by Dispensationalists. For example, **John Walvoord** candidly observes that, "The issue of whether the church will go through the tribulation or be raptured before this time of unprecedented trouble is more than a theological argument…the argument between pretribulationists and post-tribulationists…involves an *emotional element*."[205] And it is this "emotional element" that Dispensationalists frequently appeal to in their advocacy of the pretribulation rapture. Consider the following examples:

C.H. Mackintosh, promises the Church complete exemption from the Tribulation when he explains that, "The plain fact is, the church will not be on earth during that solemn period. She will be with her Head and Lord, in the divine retirement of the Father's house… There blessed be God, they will be, while the seals are being opened, the trumpets sounded, and the vials poured out."[206]

William Trotter, while referring to the approaching Great Tribulation, assures Christians that, "Ere the coming crisis opens upon the world, the Church will have been received into heaven, at the descent of Christ into the air." **Trotter** goes on to exclaim, "We, my brethren, are…comforted…by the hope of being gathered to meet the Lord in the air; as that when the judgments come, we shall not be amid the scene on which they are poured, but in the heavens whence they issue."[207]

W.E. Blackstone, first warns Christians of the coming "…period of unequalled trial, sorrow and calamity, spiritual darkness and open wickedness. It is the night of the world." And then reassures them that, "…the true Church, which is not of the night, being watchful and prayerful, will be accounted worthy to escape it, by the Rapture, and to stand before the Son of Man…"[208]

C.I. Scofield, while explaining the course of the present world, describes the Tribulation at the end of this "present age" as, "…the period which culminates in the unprecedented horror of the Great Tribulation, which covers the last 3 1/2 years of the period, and into which the Church does not enter." **Scofield** then goes on to declare that,

---

[205] *The Blessed Hope and the Tribulation* - John F. Walvoord, Zondervan Publishing House, 1976, p.10.
[206] *Papers on the Lord's Coming* - C.H.M., Loizeaux Brothers, n.d., p.30.
[207] *Plain Papers* - W. Trotter, Loizeaux Brothers, n.d., pp.74,100-101.
[208] *Jesus is Coming* - W.E.B., Fleming H. Revell Company, 1932, pp.98-99.

"...the last three and one-half years of the age stand out as supreme among all the horrors of human history..."[209]

A.C. Gaebelein, in his commentary on the book of Revelation warns that, "Judgments, tribulation and wrath are swiftly coming upon this age. Out of all this our gracious Lord has delivered us," because as Gaebelein later promises in his notes on chapter four, "We are no longer on earth but are transported into heaven... the blessed hope of the Church, has suddenly come to pass. The departure of the true Church from the earth will be as sudden as its beginning (Acts ii:1-2)."[210]

H.A. Ironside, in a discussion about whether or not the Church will pass through the Tribulation declares, "...we look for Him [i.e., Jesus Christ] as the One who is coming to snatch us away from the wrath that is soon to fall upon this earth. This exactly accords with the promise of Revelation 3:10. And it is in this way that the Church will be kept from that hour of trial. Before the judgments fall the Lord Jesus will descend from heaven with a shout, the dead in Christ will be raised, and the living saints changed, and we will be snatched away, caught up to be with Him before the indignation is poured out upon this guilty scene." **Ironside** concludes his discussion by confidently affirming that, "...the Church, the Body of Christ, is not to look forward to a time when the wrath of God will be poured out upon this world, but is to live in daily expectation of the Lord's return to take us to be with Himself ere the time of grief begins." [211]

Dwight Pentecost, vividly describes the coming Tribulation when he explains that, "Many different words are used to describe it, but the Lord, speaking of the character of it, said that it would be 'great tribulation' - tribulation unprecedented, unmatched and unparalleled in its severity. Talk of the tribulation is enough to strike dread or terror into the heart of any man who has read Scripture concerning the nature of this seven-year period. Thank God for the hope given in Scripture that before this awful time breaks on

---

[209] *Will the Church Pass Through the Great Tribulation?* - C.I. Scofield, Philadelphia School of the Bible, Inc., 1917, pp.6,8.
[210] *The Revelation* - Arno C. Gaebelein, Loizeaux Brothers, 1961, pp.21,44.
[211] *Not Wrath, But Rapture* - H.A. Ironside, Loizeaux Brothers, n.d., pp.22,48.

the earth, believers will be translated out of this world, away from the experiences of the tribulation period, caught up into the Lord's presence."[212]

Tim LaHaye, appeals directly to his readers worst fears when he asks, "Are you able to look at your children playing in the sunlight and believe firmly in your heart that they will not have to endure the monstrous horrors of the Tribulation?" **LaHaye** contrasts "that comforting belief" of the rapture with "the horrors of the Great Tribulation...the most gruesome period the world has ever known;" and "the mind-boggling terror and turmoil of the Tribulation;" warning that "the Tribulation will be a horrifying, grisly period;" therefore, "if the church were to go through the Tribulation, she would not survive it."[213]

8. The American Controversy Over the Secret Rapture Teaching.

Reminiscent of the doctrinal dispute that erupted within the early Brethren movement, American premillennialists likewise soon became bitterly divided over the question of the time of the rapture. As a result of the growing controversy over the rapture question, many of the conference leaders and participants began to give careful consideration to the relationship between the Great Tribulation and the rapture of the Church. Upon closer examination, many who had originally accepted Darby's secret rapture teaching, rejected it as unbiblical. Referring to the almost universal acceptance of pretribulationalism within the early prophetic conference movement, **George Ladd** has observed that, "Later in the movement, when greater emphasis began to be laid upon the details, the teachers began to study the Word more carefully, and many of them came to realize that along with sound Biblical premillennialism, they had accepted a teaching which upon mature reflection and study they decided was not Biblical. They had the courage publicly to reverse themselves at this point without in any way giving up the essentials of a Biblical doctrine of the Lord's premillennial return."[214] The exact number of conference leaders and participants that changed their minds is not known. To be sure it was a minority. However, some of the more notable leaders within the conference movement who rejected Darby's Dispensational scheme were Robert

---

[212] *Will Man Survive?* - J. Dwight Pentecost, Zondervan Publishing House, 1980, pp.69-70.
[213] *No Fear of the Storm* - Tim LaHaye, Moody Press Books, 1992, pp.14,50,51,56.
[214] *The Blessed Hope* - George Eldon Ladd, Wm.B. Eerdmans Publishing Company, 1980, p.52.

Cameron, Nathaniel West, Henry Frost, William Erdman, Charles Erdman, A. J. Gordon and William G. Moorehead.

The simmering doctrinal dispute over Darby's secret rapture teaching soon came to a hard boil. The leadership of Niagara began to take up sides, and within several years, conference participants were polarized over the issue. Both pro and con articles were regularly appearing in the numerous prophetic journals. For example, in a series of 15 articles, published from 1893 to 1895 in *The Episcopal Recorder*, Nathaniel West strongly denounced the secret rapture teaching that was so prevalent at Niagara, referring to it as, "the any moment theory." In 1895, James H. Brookes, the Niagara conference president published a rebuttal to West in a series of articles written by George N.H. Peters in the periodical *The Truth*. Also, in 1895, the prophetic periodical *The Truth*, published an article written by Robert Cameron that refuted the pretribulational rapture teaching, contending that neither Jesus nor the Apostles taught a secret, imminent rapture of the Church.[215] Although attempts were made to reconcile the two opposing positions, none were successful. The last Niagara Conference was held at Asbury Park, New Jersey in 1900. Due to the growing bitterness and rancor over the secret rapture teaching, the 1901 Niagara Conference was cancelled. Premillennialists had effectively separated over the rapture question. A.C. Gaebelein immediately responded by announcing a new series of annual prophetic conferences to be held at Sea Cliff, on Long Island, New York, beginning in July of 1901. Gaebelein insured that the only prophetic view represented at Sea Cliff was Darby's imminent, secret rapture teaching. Arno C. Gaebelein and C.I. Scofield emerged from this controversy as the undisputed leaders of premillennial Dispensationalism in America.

Arno Gaebelein was a German immigrant who came to America in 1879. As a Methodist minister he initially labored among the Jews of New York City. To facilitate his missionary work among the Jews of New York City, Gaebelein published a periodical entitled *Our Hope*. However, as a direct result of the break between premillennialists over the secret rapture teaching, Gaebelein redefined the purpose of his magazine. Originally dedicated to furthering Jewish evangelism, the magazine's

---

[215] *The Truth*, XXI, March, 1895, *Discrediting the Second Advent*, pp.165-171, as referenced in *The Hermeneutics of Dispensationalism* - Daniel Payton Fuller, Northern Baptist Theological Seminary, Doctoral Dissertation, 1957, p.99.

newfound purpose was to actively promote Dispensationalism and the secret rapture teaching.

Both Gaebelein and Scofield proved to be able defenders and promoters of Darby's secret rapture doctrine. Like Scofield, Gaebelein, enthusiastically embraced the full scope of Darby's Dispensational teachings, declaring, "I had become acquainted with the work of those able and godly men who were used in the great spiritual movement of the Brethren in the early part of the nineteenth century, John Nelson Darby and others. I found in his writings, in the works of William Kelly, Mcintosh, F.W. Grant, Bellett and others the soul food I needed. I esteem these men next to the Apostles in their sound and spiritual teaching."[216] Not surprisingly, Gaebelein proved to be a tireless and tenacious defender of Darby's secret rapture doctrine.

---

[216] *Half a Century* - Arno C. Gaebelein, pp.84-85 as quoted in *The Hermeneutics of Dispensationalism* - Daniel Payton Fuller, Northern Baptist Theological Seminary, Doctoral Dissertation, 1957, p.106.

Chapter Three
The Dispensational Hermeneutic

Outline of Chapter Three:
1. The Use of Inference.
2. The Dispensationalizing of the New Testament.
2a. The Distinction Between Israel and the Church.
2b. The Division of the New Testament into Jewish and Christian Sections.
3. Summary.

Dispensationalists promote and defend the concept of a pretribulational rapture by employing two essential interpretative methods. First, they depend heavily upon the use of *inference*. And second, they interpret the New Testament Scriptures, *dispensationally*.

1. The Use of Inference.

Dispensationalists consistently and uniformly claim to employ a literal method of interpretation of the Scriptures. For example, **Lewis Sperry Chafer** maintains that, "The outstanding characteristic of the dispensationalist is the fact that he believes every statement of the Bible and gives to it the plain, natural meaning its words imply."[217] **John Walvoord** claims that, "Pretribulationalism is based on a literal interpretation of key Scriptures..."[218] **Charles Ryrie** maintains that, "Dispensationalists claim that their principle of hermeneutics is that of literal interpretation."[219] **Dwight Pentecost** stresses that, "Words must be interpreted, then, in the usual, natural, literal sense."[220] And **Gerald Stanton** affirms that the Scriptures are to be, "...understood in a normal, grammatical, literal fashion."[221]

For the most part, the Dispensationalist's claim of employing a literal method of interpretation is true. However, when it comes to the prophetic Scriptures,

---

[217] *Dispensationalism* - Lewis Sperry Chafer, Dallas Seminary Press, 1936, p.105.
[218] *The Rapture Question* - John F. Walvoord, Zondervan Publishing House, 1981, p.55.
[219] *Dispensationalism Today* - Charles Caldwell Ryrie, Moody Press, 1970, p.86.
[220] *Things To Come* - J. Dwight Pentecost, Zondervan Publishing House, 1964, p.36.
[221] *Kept From the Hour* - Gerald B. Stanton, Zondervan Publishing House, 1956, p.140.

Dispensationalists routinely abandon the use of their literal hermeneutic and resort to the use of *inference*[222] in order to support their doctrine of a secret, imminent, pretribulational rapture of the Church.

Dispensationalists indirectly admit the inferential nature of their pretribulation rapture teaching. For example, **Lewis Sperry Chafer**, while discussing his belief that the Church will be delivered from the suffering of the Tribulation via the rapture, confesses that, "The evidence of the Scriptures is gained from that which may be *deduced*."[223] [224] **E. Schuyler English** affirms that, "...Scripture upon Scripture *intimates* [225] that the Church will be permitted to go through no part whatever of the Tribulation..."[226] **Gerald Stanton** acknowledges, "Of course, the Bible does *not* come out in so many words and say, 'The rapture of the Church will be pretribulational.'"[227] He goes on to add, "Now it is rather obvious that one will search in vain if he looks for a crystallized statement such as, 'The rapture will precede the revelation by seven years.'" **Stanton** therefore reasons that, "The solution to all Bible problems do not lie on the immediate surface, but must be settled by *inference*..."[228] **Leon Wood** contends that, "Several passages in the New Testament *imply*[229] that the rapture of the church is near..."[230] And **Renald Showers** explains that he, "...believes that biblical *inferences* concerning the Rapture of the church favor the Pretribulation Rapture view."[231]

Because the Bible does *not* clearly state or describe a pretribulational Coming and rapture, Dispensationalists are forced to base their teaching solely on inferences and analogies. The operative question then becomes, "Are the *inferences* of

---

[222] *Inference* refers to the human reasoning process, whereby facts are analyzed and conclusions are drawn. If the reasoning process is sound and the facts are analyzed correctly, inferences can be valid. However, if the reasoning process is flawed or the facts misunderstood or misapplied, the inference can be false.

[223] *Deduce* means "To derive by reasoning...to infer by deduction." *Webster's Collegiate Dictionary*, Fifth Edition, G. & C. Merriam Co., 1941.

[224] *Systematic Theology* - Lewis Sperry Chafer, Kregel Publications, 1993, vol.4, p.367.

[225] *Intimate* means to, "Suggest obscurely or indirectly; hint." *Webster's Collegiate Dictionary*, Fifth Edition, G.& C. Merriam Co., 1941.

[226] *Re-Thinking the Rapture* - E. Schuyler English, Loizeaux Brothers, 1954, p.114.

[227] *Kept From the Hour* - Gerald B. Stanton, Zondervan Publishing House, 1956, p.43.

[228] *Kept From the Hour* - Gerald B. Stanton, Zondervan Publishing House, 1956, p.252.

[229] *Imply* means, "To express indirectly; to hint or hint at." *Webster's Collegiate Dictionary*, Fifth Edition, G.& C. Merriam Co., 1941.

[230] *The Bible and Future Events* - Leon J. Wood, The Zondervan Corporation, 1974, p.79.

[231] *Maranatha-Our Lord, Come!* - Renald E. Showers, The Friends of Israel Gospel Ministry, 1995, p.13.

Dispensationalism logical and valid, and do they harmonize with the overall testimony of Scripture?" I submit that they *are not* and *do not.* Rather, the *inferences* of Dispensationalists are highly subjective, speculative, arbitrary and contradictory to the plain statements of the Biblical text. Yet, Dispensationalists confidently herald their *inferences* as established Biblical facts. But inferential assumptions, suppositions and analogies are *not* facts. And sound doctrine must rest upon Biblical facts and not mere human speculation and conjecture.

The Dispensationalist's tendency to employ *inference* was recognized by critics at the outset of the Brethren movement. For example, **B.W. Newton**, while commenting on the arguments advanced by John Darby and his followers, observed that, "I might almost say that there are none [i.e., arguments in favor of the pretribulation rapture], which I have heard drawn immediately from Scripture. Nearly all rest upon *analogy*;[232] and is there anything more dangerous than *analogy*, unless we are watchfully guided in our use of it by the plain declarations of the word?"[233] Likewise, **Samuel P. Tregelles** observed that, "When proofs have been asked for the doctrine of the secret advent and the secret removal of the Church, certain supposed *analogies* have been sometimes presented instead, which were thought to bear upon the subject. But as *analogy* is a resemblance of relations, it is needful that the facts should be first known and demonstrated instead of their being merely supposed."[234]

The Dispensational doctrine of the secret, any moment rapture of the Church is *not* the result of a careful, deliberate and literal exegesis of the Biblical text as frequently claimed. Rather, it is based entirely upon the use of *inference* and *analogy*. Dispensationalists routinely disregard the plain statements and immediate context of the Scriptures in favor of what they *assume* the Scriptures are *implying*. The entire argument for the pretribulation rapture is based exclusively upon obscure, indirect suggestions and hints that are *inferred* from the New Testament text and *not* the plain, ordinary, literal statements of the Scriptures.

---

[232] *Analogy* means, "A form of *inference* in which it is reasoned that if two (or more) things agree with one another in one or more respects, they will (probably) agree in yet other respects." *Webster's Collegiate Dictionary*, Fifth Edition, G.& C. Merriam Co., 1941.

[233] *Five Letters* - Benjamin Wills Newton, London, 1877, *Fifth Letter*, p.80.

[234] *The Hope of Christ's Second Coming* - S.P. Tregelles, The Sovereign Grace Advent Testimony, n.d., p.40.

2. The Dispensationalizing of the New Testament.

Dispensationalists do *not* believe that all of the New Testament Scriptures are singularly Christian in their application. They maintain that large portions of the New Testament, especially within the Gospels, and the book of Revelation, apply specifically and primarily to the "Jews." The term *"dispensationalizing"* refers to the practice of determining which verses in the New Testament apply to the "Jews" and which verses apply to the "Church." This exercise of making *"dispensational distinctions"* within the New Testament is the foundation upon which modern Dispensationalism rests and is crucial to preserving, protecting and defending the pretribulational rapture doctrine. The proposition that large portions of the New Testament apply to a future unbelieving Jewish remnant and *not* to the Church was popularized by John Darby and his followers. **Lewis Sperry Chafer** has recognized and commented on the historical connection when he observed that, "...a worthy and scholarly research of the Bible with *dispensational distinctions* in view was made during the last century in England by J.N. Darby, Charles H. Mackintosh, William Kelly, F.W. Grant, and others who developed what is known as the Plymouth Brethren movement."[235]

Beginning with John Darby and his early followers, Dispensationalists have uniformly and consistently taught that the New Testament must be interpreted "dispensationally." This means that the New Testament interpreter must carefully distinguish between those sections of the New Testament that apply to "the Jews" and those sections that apply to "the Church." For example, while referring to the Olivet Discourse, **John Darby** declares, "I still believe that Matthew 24... is addressed to the disciples as Jews...and *I do not think it addressed to the church* as the church...The standing, therefore, of Peter and his companions on the Mount of Olives was clearly not our standing at all...they ought to have been addressed, if at all, as a *Jewish remnant*."[236] **William Trotter** maintains that there are, "...many passages in the Gospels which would *not strictly apply to the Church*, as such."[237] **A.C. Gaebelein** declares that, "...the Gospel of Matthew, as the *Jewish Gospel*...[is] *dispensational throughout*...

---

[235] *Dispensationalism* - Lewis Sperry Chafer, Dallas Theological Press, 1936, 1951, p.11.
[236] *The Collected Writings of J.N. Darby* - edited by William Kelly, Stow Hill and Tract Depot, Prophetic No.4, Vol.11, n.d., pp.3,14,15,17,18.
[237] *Plain Papers* - William Trotter, Loizeaux Brothers, n.d., p.373.

everything must be looked upon from the ***dispensational point of view.***"[238] **E. Schuyler English** insists that, "...Matthew's Gospel is ***dispensational*** in its teaching. In the study of the words of our Lord, in this Gospel, therefore we must be particularly ***careful to determine of what age*** He is speaking."[239] While referring to the Gospel of John, **Lewis Sperry Chafer** asserts that, "...it is essential to recognize, also, that, with the ***exception of chapters 13-17***, the words of Christ contained in that Gospel were ***spoken to Jews.***"[240] **Chafer** also cautions that, "There is a ***dangerous and entirely baseless sentiment*** abroad which assumes that every teaching of Christ must be binding during this age simply because Christ said it."[241] And **C. I. Scofield** maintains that, "With the exception of the few brief chapters of the Gospels which record the resurrection and ascension of our Lord, ***all Scripture up to the Acts...has the Jew primarily in view.***"[242] And again, **Scofield** asserts that "...the Gospels are transitional between law and grace...the ***Gospels are necessarily largely Jewish in coloring***, since Christ was to the Jews a minister of the circumcision."[243] In the study notes contained in his *Study Bible*, **Scofield** refers to the New Testament Epistles of Hebrews, James, First and Second Peter as, "The Jewish-Christian Epistles."[244] **Scofield** then asserts that, "They [i.e., The Jewish-Christian Epistles] are ***not*** to be taken as the ***summit and final word of revelation for this dispensation***. That word was given to the great apostle to the Gentiles.[245] Doctrinally, the Jewish-Christian writings group with the Gospels and the Acts 1-9."[246] In other words, according to **Scofield**, half of the New Testament must be interpreted "dispensationally," that is, applied primarily to the Jews and ***not*** to the Church.

Dispensationalists unanimously argue that the New Testament Scriptures ***cannot*** be correctly understood and applied unless they are interpreted "dispensationally." Again,

---

[238] *The Gospel of Matthew* - Arno C. Gaebelein, Loizeaux Brothers, 1910, 1982, p.7.
[239] *Studies in the Gospel According to Matthew* - E. Schuyler English, Zondervan Publishing House, 1938, p.169.
[240] *Systematic Theology* - Lewis Sperry Chafer, Kregel Publications, 1993, vol.4, p.57.
[241] *Systematic Theology* - Lewis Sperry Chafer, Kregel Publications, 1993, vol.4, p.224.
[242] *Scofield Bible Correspondence Course, Volume IV, The Epistles and the Revelation* – C.I. Scofield, Moody Bible Institute, 1960, p.634.
[243] *Scofield Bible Correspondence Course, Volume IV, The Epistles and the Revelation* - C.I. Scofield, Moody Bible Institute, 1960, p.656.
[244] *The Scofield Study Bible* - C.I. Scofield, Oxford University Press, 1945, p.1289.
[245] Scofield is obliquely referring to the Apostle Paul.
[246] *Scofield Bible Correspondence Course, Volume IV, The Epistles and the Revelation* - C.I. Scofield, Moody Bible Institute, 1960, p.874.

this means that the "Jewish" portions of the New Testament must be properly identified and carefully distinguished from the "Christian" portions. For example, **E. Schuyler English** claims that, "No one can understand the word of God in its fullness unless he has a thorough grounding in *dispensational truth*..."[247] And **A.C. Gaebelein** asserts that, "...the gospel of Matthew is preeminently the Jewish Gospel...Because it is the Jewish Gospel, it is *dispensational throughout*...a person, no matter how learned or devoted, who does not hold the clearly revealed *dispensational truths* concerning the Jews, the Gentiles and the church of God will fail to understand Matthew."[248] Dispensationalists are united in their insistence that unless the New Testament Scriptures are interpreted "dispensationally" they cannot be correctly understood. In other words, the interpreter must carefully distinguish between the so-called "Jewish" and "Christian" portions of the New Testament, if the Scriptures are to be correctly understood and applied.

But Dispensationalists go even further by asserting that anyone who denies the pretribulational rapture teaching, and the interpretative methods used to support it, are actually enemies of the truth. **John Nelson Darby**, was the first to set the caustic tone of this debate when he declared that, "The great object of the enemy in denying the rapture of the saints *before* the appearing of the Lord, and in the consequent rejection of a distinct Jewish remnant, with Jewish hopes and Jewish piety, is to deny and destroy the proper faith of the church of God, and to set the church itself aside...They are deceived by the enemy..."[249] **William Kelly**, charged that all who deny the any-moment, pretribulational rapture of the Church, "...are actuated by the self-same spirit of unbelief; that they are the antagonists, I am grieved to say, of the truth of God, as far as this grave subject is concerned."[250] And **Charles Mackintosh**, while emphasizing the distinction between the "coming" of Christ *before* the Tribulation and the "appearing" of Christ *after* the Tribulation, charged that, "The great object of the enemy is to drag down the church of God to an earthly level - to set Christians entirely astray as to their divinely appointed hope - to lead them to confound things which God has made to differ, to occupy them with earthly things - to cause them to so mix up the *coming* of Christ for His people with His *appearing* in judgment upon the world, that

---

[247] *Studies in the Gospel According to Matthew* - E. Schuyler English, Zondervan Publishing House, 1935,1938, p.182.
[248] *The Gospel of Matthew* - Arno C. Gaebelein, Loizeaux Brothers, 1910, 1982, p.5.
[249] *The Collected Writings of J.N. Darby* - Edited by William Kelly, Stow Hill Bible and Tract Depot, n.d, Prophetic No.4, Vol.11, p.129.
[250] *Lectures on the Second Coming* - William Kelly, Believers Bookshelf, 1970, p.186.

they may not be able to cultivate those bridal affections and heavenly aspirations which become them as members of the body of Christ."[251] **Arno C. Gaebelein,** in his comments on Matthew 24, obliquely makes reference to Robert Cameron and Nathaniel West. Both of these men were a part of the early Bible Conference Movement in America and initially embraced Darby's Dispensational teachings. However, after carefully examining the doctrine, they both publicly rejected it outright, declaring it to be completely unbiblical. **Gaebelein** caustically lashed out, declaring, "We know some who taught and believed the imminency of the coming of the Lord. All at once their voices were silent as to the blessed hope. Why? In some way they became ensnared in teachings, which put off the glorious event till after the great tribulation, the manifestation of the Antichrist, etc., and this unscriptural view silenced their testimony completely. It is sad to see this, and we fear, if the Lord tarries, some of these men (as it has been already the case) will act the part of the evil servant in a still more pronounced way."[252] And **C.I. Scofield,** while commenting on First Thessalonians 4, attributes the rejection of the pretribulation rapture teaching to Satanic subterfuge, when he declared, "Undoubtedly, Satan has a peculiar hatred of the doctrine of 1Thessalonians 4:14-18. He either breeds disbelief of the whole doctrine, or, as in the case of the Thessalonians, robs the blessed hope of all its joy and comfort by convincing saints that the horrors of the 'Day of the Lord' must precede the catching up of the church."[253]

The question naturally arises, "Upon what hermeneutical principles do Dispensationalists base their claim that the New Testament Scriptures *must* be interpreted "dispensationally?" The answer to this crucial question is twofold: **First**, Dispensationalists argue that Israel (Old Testament Jewish believers and or a future Jewish remnant) and the Church (New Testament believers who live in a parenthetical period between the close of the Old Testament and the beginning of the future Tribulation) represent two separate and distinct groups of redeemed believers, that must be carefully distinguished. **Second**, Dispensationalists claim that large portions of the New Testament Scriptures apply specifically to those Jews and *not* to the Church.

---

[251] *Papers on the Lord's Coming* - C.H.M., Loizeaux Brothers, n.d., pp.31-32.
[252] *The Gospel of Matthew* - Arno C. Gaebelein, Loizeaux Brothers, 1910, 1982, p.522.
[253] *Scofield Correspondence Course, Vol.IV, The Epistles and Revelation* - C..I. Scofield, Moody Bible Institute, 1960, 1975, p.660.

2a. The Distinction Between Israel and the Church.

Dispensationalists have uniformly taught that Israel (OT Jewish believers and or a future Jewish remnant) and the Church (New Testament believers) are two separate and distinct groups, with different purposes and programs. **John Darby** argued that, "...the church is not of the world. It, as such, sits in heavenly places in Christ, where prophecy reaches not. It never will be established on earth, as the Jews...With the Christian, it is to prepare him for heaven; with the Jews, on the contrary, it is to display God's righteousness on earth..."[254] Thus, Darby maintained that God is pursuing two distinctly different purposes - one "earthly" concerning Israel and another, "heavenly" concerning the Church. Significantly, all of Darby's followers have accepted and echoed his conviction that Old Testament believers and New Testament believers are eternally distinct and separate. For example, **William Trotter,** an early convert and active promoter of Darby's teachings, stressed the necessity for Christians to "...apprehend the difference between Israel's earthly and the Church's heavenly calling - the earthly hopes of Israel, and the heavenly hopes of the Church."[255] **Charles Mackintosh**, another of Darby's early followers, declared that, "...the church forms no part of the ways of God with Israel and the earth. The church does not belong to time, but to eternity. She is not earthly, but heavenly."[256] And **Lewis Sperry Chafer,** founder of Dallas Theological Seminary, taught that it was necessary to, "...distinguish the heavenly character of the Church in contrast to the earthly character of Israel."[257] **Chafer** went on to assert that, "Little true understanding of prophecy will be gained until it is recognized that the divine purpose for the earth is centered about Israel."[258] **C.I. Scofield**, author of the famous *Scofield Reference Bible*, maintained that, "...the elementary distinction between Israel and the church is that the former is of and for the earth, the latter of and for heaven..."[259] And **Arno C. Gaebelein**, an early leader and active promoter of Dispensationalism in America, succinctly declared that, "Israel's calling is earthly;

---

[254] *The Collected Writings of J.N. Darby* - Edited by William Kelly, Stow Hill Bible and Tract Depot, n.d., Prophetic No.4, Vol.11, pp.46-47.
[255] *Plain Papers* - William Trotter, Loizeaux Brothers, n.d., p.389.
[256] *Papers on the Lord's Coming* - C.H.M., Loizeaux Brothers, n.d., p.104.
[257] *Systematic Theology* - Lewis Sperry Chafer, Kregel Publications, 1993, vol.4, p.32.
[258] *Systematic Theology* - Lewis Sperry Chafer, Kregel Publications, 1993, vol.4, p.341.
[259] *The Scofield Bible Correspondence Course, Vol.1, Old Testament* - C.I. Scofield, Moody Bible Institute of Chicago, 1907, p.25.

theirs is an earthly kingdom, ours is altogether heavenly."[260] Thus, Dispensationalists are convinced that God's purpose for Israel is "earthly" and that His purpose for the Church is "heavenly." They assert that God has two different plans, and is pursuing two different programs, with two different groups of believers. For instance, **Lewis Sperry Chafer** explains that, "The dispensationalist believes that throughout the ages God is pursuing two distinct purposes: one related to the earth with earthy people and earthly objectives involved, which is Judaism; while the other is related to heaven with heavenly objectives involved, which is Christianity."[261]

Dispensationalists further maintain that because Israel is an "earthly" people, with an "earthly" calling and purpose, they do ***not*** enjoy the same spiritual standing before God as New Testament saints. Dispensationalists reason that because the Church is a "heavenly" people with a "heavenly" calling and purpose, their spiritual standing is much higher and nobler than that of the "earthly" Old Testament saints. To illustrate, **John Darby** asserted that, "Those who believe in the rapture of the church before the appearing of Christ hold that the ***church has a special and peculiar character and connection with Christ***..."[262] Although **William Trotter** recognized that, "...Christ has relations to Israel as well as to the Church," he also insisted that, "...it is beyond doubt that His relations to the latter [i.e., the Church] are ***unspeakably more tender and intimate*** than His relations to the former [i.e., Israel]..."[263] **A.C. Gaebelein** maintained that, "We as Christian believers are ***higher in our standing*** than the Old Testament saints."[264] And **Lewis Sperry Chafer** contended that, "...New Testament saints are advanced to a ***higher position of standing*** than Old Testament saints..."[265] As an example of Israel's inferior spiritual position, consider **Chafer's** contention that, "To Israel, God is known by His primary titles, but ***not*** as the Father of the individual Israelite."[266]

---

[260] *The Gospel of Matthew* - Arno C. Gaebelein, Loizeaux Brothers, 1910, 1982, p.110.

[261] *Dispensationalism* - Lewis Sperry Chafer, Dallas Seminary Press, 1936, 1951, p.107.

[262] *The Collected Writings of J.N. Darby* - Edited by William Kelly, Stow Hill Bible and Tract Depot, n.d., Prophetic No.4, Vol.11, p.119.

[263] *Plain Papers on Prophetic and Other Subjects* - William Trotter, Loizeaux Brothers, n.d., p.341.

[264] *The Gospel of Matthew* - Arno C. Gaebelein, Loizeaux Brothers, 1910, 1982, p.224.

[265] *Systematic Theology* - Lewis Sperry Chafer, Kregel Publications, 1993, vol.4, p.63.

[266] *Systematic Theology* - Lewis Sperry Chafer, Kregel Publications, 1993, vol.4, p.32. Chafer apparently failed to consider, the Jewish exclamation contained in Isaiah 63:16, which declares, "Thou, O LORD art our Father, our Redeemer from of old is Thy name." And again, in Isaiah 64:8, "But now, O LORD, Thou art our Father, we are the clay, and Thou our potter; and all of us are the work of Thy hand."

It is this contrived distinction between Old and New Testament believers that leads Dispensationalists to conclude that Old Testament saints are *not* a part of the Church. For example, **John Darby** emphatically declared that, "The church, or God's assembly, Christ's body, what He builds on earth, is solely what is His between Pentecost and His coming...I deny that saints before Christ's first coming, or after His second, are part of the church." **Darby** goes on to say that it is a "...gross and unscriptural error, that all the saved belong to the church."[267] **William Kelly,** the close friend and associate of Darby, warns that, "...the greatest mischief has been done to souls by mingling...the Church with...the Old Testament saints...the Church differs essential from the Old Testament saints."[268] **William E. Blackstone**, an early American convert to, and highly effective promoter of Dispensationalism, declared that, "...the church...is not to be confused with the coming kingdom, nor does it include the Old Testament saints..."[269] And **Lewis Sperry Chafer** emphatically declared, "Judaism is not the bud which has blossomed into Christianity."[270] **Chafer** further maintained that "...Judaism did not merge into Christianity...the Church is a new, heavenly purpose of God..." **Chafer** went on the say that the Church is *not*, "...an ever increasing company of redeemed people gathered alike from all ages of human history..."[271]

Thus, Dispensationalists reject the idea that the Church represents a continuation of a single redemptive plan. They are convinced that the Church is, in the words of **Chafer**, "a new, heavenly purpose of God." They therefore reason that since the Church is a new work of God, in a new dispensation, Old Testament saints cannot logically be a part of it. For instance, **Renald Showers,** maintains that, "There is a distinction between the saved Jews of the Church and the saved Jews of the Old Testament Israel...Old Testament Israel and the Church are not essentially the same."[272] **Charles Ryrie** justifies the Dispensational practice of excluding Old Testament saints from the Church by reasoning that the Church's "...existence is distinctive to this present dispensation, which makes the Church distinct from Israel..."[273]

---

[267] *The Collected Writings of J.N. Darby* - Edited by William Kelly, Stow Hill Bible and Tract Depot, n.d., Prophetic No.4, Vol.11, pp.345-346.

[268] *Lectures on the Second Coming* - William Kelly, Believers Bookshelf, 1970, pp.147,149.

[269] *Jesus is Coming* - William E. Blackstone, Kregel Publications, 1989, p.203.

[270] *Systematic Theology* - Lewis Sperry Chafer, Kregel Publications, 1993, vol.4, p.248.

[271] *Systematic Theology* - Lewis Sperry Chafer, Kregel Publications, 1993, vol.4, p.34.

[272] *Maranatha, Our Lord Come!* - Renald E. Showers, The Friends of Israel Gospel Ministry, Inc., 1995, p.230.

[273] *Dispensationalism Today* - Charles Caldwell Ryrie, Moody Press, 1970, p.154.

Dispensationalists uniformly maintain that the Church is a new work of God, compartmentalized within this present dispensation, and therefore cannot include Old Testament saints. But are Dispensationalists correct in their contention that God is pursuing two distinct and separate "purposes" - one earthly and the other heavenly? Do Old Testament saints and New Testament saints really comprise two separate and distinct groups of believers? And do the New Testament Scriptures actually support the contention that Old Testament saints do not possess the same spiritual standing and privileges as New Testament saints? The short answer to all of these questions is a resounding, "No." The erroneousness of these Dispensational teachings becomes immediately evident when they are examined in the light of the Biblical doctrine of salvation.

The New Testament knows nothing of multiple plans of salvation or different categories of believers. The New Testament is emphatic in its declaration that God has only one plan of salvation for mankind – faith in the person and work of the Lord Jesus Christ, God's only-begotten Son. While referring to Christ Jesus, the Apostle Peter declared, "And there is salvation in no one else; for there is no other name under heaven that has been given among men by which we must be saved" (Acts 4:12). Individuals are saved when they believe what God has said about Jesus Christ and put their faith and trust in Him. (1Jn.3:23; Jn.6:28-29).

When Old Testament saints believed what God said about the promised Messiah, He reckoned their faith to them as righteousness. This is made evident by the example of Abraham (see Ro.4:3; Gal.3:6-9 cp. Gn.15:6 [274]). Likewise, when New Testament saints believe what God says about His Son, their faith is also reckoned to them as righteousness (see Ro.4:22-25 cp. Phil.3:8-11). Thus, all who have been saved or will be saved are saved by faith in the Lord Jesus Christ (Eph.2:8-9; Gal.2:16). And the basis of this salvation is the substitutionary and sacrificial death of Jesus Christ on the Cross (1Pt.2:24). It is the sacrificial death of Christ that provides the legal grounds for God's forgiveness of our sins (Ro.3:21-26; 1Pt.3:18). If Old Testament saints are saved (and Dispensationalists agree that they are), then they are completely saved. The Bible

---

[274] While the level of redemptive detail revealed to Old Testament saints differed substantially from that revealed to New Testament saints, the salient question is: "Did Old Testament saints believe what God did reveal?" Those that did believe what God said were saved. Those that did not believe what God said were lost. While New Testament saints have a much fuller revelation of God's redemptive plan, the necessity of believing what God has said remains exactly the same.

knows nothing of a partial salvation - you either are, or you are not. And if you are saved, you experience the full benefit of the cross-work of Jesus Christ. And one of the many benefits of salvation is adoption,[275] which is why all believers are referred to as the "children of God" (Ro.8:14-16; 1Jn.3:1-2). We therefore, cannot accept the Dispensational proposition that Old Testament saints, who in faith looked forward to the fulfillment of the Messianic promises of God, and who have been saved by the cross-work of Christ, have no part in the Church of Christ, which is called "the household of God" (1Tim.3:15). The only difference between the two groups is that Old Testament believers looked *forward* to the fulfillment of God's promise of Messianic redemption (1Pt.1:10-11 cp. Is.53:1-12), while New Testament believers look *backward*, to the historical accomplishment of that redemption at the Cross of Calvary (1Cor.15:1-8).

The confusion of Dispensationalists on this point is illustrated by **Lewis Sperry Chafer**, who teaches that, "The Church is a new purpose of God...the fact that *Jews are now invited into fellowship in one Body with Gentiles* is no warrant for the belief that Old Testament saints are included in this new divine purpose."[276] Note carefully that Chafer asserts that the Church represents a new purpose of God that invites Jews "into fellowship ...with Gentiles." However, the problem is that the Scriptures do *not* say that *Jews are invited into fellowship with Gentiles*. On the contrary, the exact opposite is true! The Scriptures plainly declare that it was the *Gentiles who were invited into the Church by believing Jews!*

The New Testament reveals the logical continuation of God's redemptive plan for humanity. It is here that the redemptive hopes and promises of the Old Testament are realized.[277] And it is here that we clearly see God's intention to gather together both Jewish and Gentile believers into one body under the headship of Jesus Christ (Gal.3:8-9). It is important however, to understand the historical context of this issue. Initially the Church was entirely "Jewish." It was comprised of Jewish Apostles and disciples who followed and believed in the Jewish Messiah, who came in fulfillment of hundreds

---

[275] In addition to Adoption, the Cross-work of Christ provides Propitiation, Redemption, Justification, Reconciliation, Sanctification, Illumination and ultimately Glorification for every believer.
[276] *Systematic Theology* - Lewis Sperry Chafer, Kregel Publications, 1993, vol.4, p.77.
[277] It should be pointed out that the Old Testament is thoroughly Messianic in its character and purpose. See for example, Lk.24:27,44; Jn.5:39; 8:56 cp. Gal.3:8.

of Old Testament Jewish prophecies. This is the historical backdrop when, in Ephesians 2:11-21, the Apostle Paul ("a Hebrew of Hebrews," Phil.3:5) calls upon the Gentile believers at Ephesus to "remember" that they were once called "the Uncircumcision" (v.11) and were "separate from Christ, excluded from the commonwealth of Israel, and strangers to the covenants of promise, having no hope and without God in the world" (v.12). Paul clearly states that it was the Gentiles who were separated from God, alone and without hope in the world. "But now" Paul says, "in Christ Jesus you [i.e., Gentiles] who formerly were far off have been brought near by the blood of Christ" (v.13). Thus, it is Jesus Christ (the Jewish Messiah) who has brought the Gentiles into fellowship with God's chosen people (the Jews). It is Christ who has "broke down the barrier of the dividing wall," (v.14) which effectively separated Gentiles from believing Jews for millennia. It is Christ who now reconciles both Jews and Gentiles "...in one body to God through the cross..." (v.16). Paul declares that "you [Gentiles] are no longer strangers and aliens, but you [Gentiles] are fellow citizens with the saints and are of God's household"[278] (v.19). Paul is plainly teaching that through the Gospel, Gentile believers are now brought into fellowship with the original recipients of "the covenants of promise," who he identifies as "the commonwealth of Israel" (v.12) – a clear and unmistakable reference to God's Old Testament people.

This truth is further developed in Ephesians 3:1-6, where Paul speaks of the "mystery of Christ" which in former generations was hidden, declaring, "...that the Gentiles are fellow heirs and fellow members of the body[279] and fellow partakers of the promise in Christ Jesus through the gospel" (Eph.3:4-6). And with whom are the Gentiles "fellow heirs" and "fellow members" and "fellow partakers" of Christ with? In the context of Ephesians 2 and 3, they were the believing Jews who initially comprised that "body" (i.e., the early Church). Likewise, in Romans 11:11-24, Paul again refers to this same truth when he explains that it was the Gentiles (the wild olive branches), who were grafted into the rich root of the cultivated olive tree (Israel) - and *not* vice-a-versa. Thus, Gentile believers were brought into fellowship with Jewish believers through the Gospel. I should also remind my readers that Acts 15 records an important meeting of the "Jewish" Jerusalem Council, which debated and deliberated upon the question of requirements and conditions upon which believing Gentiles could be admitted into the

---

[278] The phrase "God's household" is a clear reference to the Church, which Paul describes as "the household of God" in 1Tim.3:15.
[279] The phrase "the body" clearly refers to the Church (see Eph.1:22-23; Col.1:18,24).

then exclusively "Jewish" Church! Dispensationalists have erred greatly by reversing this whole process, when they erroneously assert that it was the Gentiles who invited the Jews into the Church, when in fact the exact opposite is true!

Furthermore, Dispensationalists have no textual justification for segregating Old Testament believers from New Testament believers. Especially in light of the fact that the New Testament clearly describes the unity that exists between Old and New Testament saints. Carefully consider Roman 4:1-25. Paul clearly states that Abraham is the father of *all* who come to God by faith (v.16). In verses 11-12, Paul declares that Abraham is "…the father of all who believe without being circumcised [*i.e., Gentile believers*] …and the father of circumcision to those who not only are of the circumcision, but who also follow in the steps of the faith of our father Abraham… [*i.e., Jewish believers*]" (v.12). Are we really willing to accept the Dispensational proposition that Abraham, to whom God "…preached the gospel beforehand…" (Gal.3:8) and who is referred to as the father of *all* the faithful, has no part in the Church of Jesus Christ? Is it reasonable to accept the claim that Old Testament believers, who have followed Abraham's example of faith in God, are excluded from fellowship in the Church of their Savior? The defective reasoning of these Dispensational assertions is made evident by Paul when he rhetorically asks, "…is God *the* God of Jews only? Is He not *the* God of Gentiles also? Yes, of Gentiles also, since indeed God who will justify the circumcised [i.e., Jews] by faith and the uncircumcised [i.e., Gentiles] through faith is one" (Ro.3:29-30). Paul again underscores the unity of all believers when he declares that there is only "…*one* body and *one* Spirit, just as you were called in *one* hope of your calling; *one* Lord, *one* faith, *one* baptism, *one* God and Father of *all*…"(Eph.4:4-6, emphasis added).[280]

It is important to emphasize that Dispensationalists have no textual basis for segregating Old Testament saints from New Testament saints. We must ask, "Where is the Biblical text that declares that God is pursuing two different redemptive plans, with two different groups of believers, for two different purposes?" The short answer is, "Nowhere." It simply does *not* exist. The entire scheme is based upon subjective and imaginative speculation - not the clear, authoritative statements of Scripture.

---

[280] The unity of all believers is clearly established by the teachings of Christ. Carefully consider John 10:16 cp. Is.52.10; 56:8; John 11:52; 17:20-21 and Luke 13:28-30.

Dispensationalists segregate Old Testament saints from Church saints for one reason only: to promote and preserve the doctrine of the secret pretribulation rapture. It is this contrived division of the people of God into two distinct and separate groups (one "earthly" and the other "heavenly") that legitimizes their argument for a pretribulation rapture. For example, it was this artificially created dichotomy between Israel and the Church which permitted **John Darby** to rhetorically ask, "Now who are in this tribulation in the passages which speak of it in Scripture?" **Darby's** answer was, "...the Jews are in it - the church not...the tribulation regards the Jews...as regards the church who await Christ...they shall be kept out of it...it is for the Jews and not for the church."[281]

The problem that Dispensationalists are attempting to evade is that the New Testament clearly reveals that there will be believers on earth during the Tribulation period *after* the supposed pretribulation rapture of the Church. The question that immediately arises is, "If Christians are really raptured before the Tribulation begins, then who are these believers in the Tribulation?" Thus, in order to rescue the doctrine of the rapture from the obvious implications of this question, Dispensationalists simply declare these suffering saints to be "earthly" Jews and not "heavenly" Christians.[282]

2b. The Division of the New Testament into Jewish and Christian Sections.

Dispensationalists have always maintained that the Scriptures cannot be correctly understood, unless the "dispensational distinction" between Israel and the Church is recognized, accepted and applied. For example, **E. Schuyler English** stresses that, "No one can possibly have a clear perception of Scripture as a whole, or of Bible prophecy

---

[281] *The Collected Writings of J.N. Darby* - Edited by William Kelly, Stow Hill Bible and Tract Depot, n.d., Prophetic No.4, Vol.11, pp.164-165.

[282] Consider the comments of Charles R. Erdman (1866-1960), who participated in the early prophetic conference movement. While referring to Dispensationalists, Erdman observed that, "They take all the predictions of blessing, and apply them to the church, and heap upon poor Israel all the prophecies of woe. They teach that the church is to be 'caught away secretly' from this scene of sorrow and distress, and then, under the Man of Sin, Israel is to suffer unparalleled anguish. Therefore, as our Lord, in His great prophetic discourse of Matthew twenty-four and five, alludes to a Great Tribulation, these teachers hold that our Lord was giving messages intended only for the Jews and not the church. Similarly, great corresponding portions of all the Gospels are designated as 'Jewish'; and on the same principle, all of the Apocalypse, from chapter four to chapter nineteen, is said 'to belong to the Jews,' and to have no relation to the church." *The Return of Christ* - Charles R. Erdman, George Doran Company, 1922, p.74.

in particular, who does not discern the distinction between two of the things that differ, namely Israel and the Church...The differentiation between the calling of Israel and the Church...is equally manifest in predictive prophecy."[283] This "dispensational distinction" between Old Testament and New Testament saints is foundational to Dispensational doctrine. **John Walvoord**, underscores this fact when he succinctly states that, "The distinction of these *two programs* [i.e., Israel and the Church] is an *essential feature* of contemporary dispensationalism..."[284] And **Charles Ryrie**, also emphasizes the crucial nature of this distinction when he declares that, "...the clear distinction between Israel and the Church...is a *vital part* of dispensationalism."[285] **Ryrie** underscores the importance of this doctrine when he explains that, "The *distinction* between Israel and the Church leads to the belief that the Church will be taken from the earth before the beginning of the Tribulation."[286] And **John Walvoord**, emphasizes the importance of separating Old Testament and New Testament believers when he explains that, "A proper *distinction* between the church and Israel naturally leads to pretribulationalism..."[287] **Walvoord** goes on to say that, "...a proper understanding of the doctrine of the church as a body *distinct* from Israel and from saints in general...is...an *indispensable foundation* in the study of pretribulationism. It is safe to say that pretribulationism *depends on a particular definition of the church*..."[288]

The reason why the "dispensational distinction" between Israel and the Church is such an, "indispensable foundation in the study of pretribulationism" is because in the words of **Walvoord**; "pretribulationism *depends* on a particular definition of the church." In other words, if Old Testament Jewish believers and New Testament believers are all equally a part of the Church of Jesus Christ, then pretribulationalism *cannot* be true. **Walvoord** clearly recognizes this fact when he cautions, "If the term church includes saints of all ages, then it is self-evident that the church will go through the Tribulation, as all agree that there will be saints in this time of trouble."[289] It is "self-evident" because if the numerous New Testament passages that clearly place *believers* in the

---

[283] *Re-Thinking the Rapture* - E. Schuyler English, Loizeaux Brothers, 1954, pp.34,37.
[284] *The Rapture Question* - John F. Walvoord, Zondervan Publishing House, 1979, p.56.
[285] *Dispensationalism Today* - Moody Press, 1970, Charles Caldwell Ryrie, p.159.
[286] *Dispensationalism Today* - Moody Press, 1970, Charles Caldwell Ryrie, p.159.
[287] *The Rapture Question* - John F. Walvoord, Zondervan Publishing House, 1979, p.20.
[288] *The Rapture Question* – John F. Walvoord, Zondervan Publishing House, 1979, p.21.
[289] *The Rapture Question* - John F. Walvoord, Zondervan Publishing House, 1979, p.21.

Tribulation period do in fact apply to the Church, and not to an imaginary future Jewish remnant, then obviously the Church will go through the Tribulation. Therefore, Dispensationalists *must* insist that Old Testament and New Testament believers represent two different and distinct groups of believers in God's redemptive economy. This distinction is vital to the pretribulation rapture doctrine because it allows Dispensationalists to assert that *all* New Testament passages that refer to believers suffering in the Tribulation apply to a future Jewish remnant, and *not* to the Church.

To illustrate the importance of this "dispensational distinction" consider the Olivet Discourse of Matthew 24. This chapter contains one of the most detailed explanations of the events of the last days and the end of the age contained in the New Testament. Within this chapter, the Lord Jesus Christ reveals numerous prophetic events leading up to and encompassing the Great Tribulation. Without question, the Lord is speaking to *believers* in this discourse. This is made evident by the fact that He is speaking directly to His disciples - specifically, to Peter, James, John and Andrew (Mt.24:1 cp. Mk.13:3). Jesus warns His disciples that, "...they will deliver **you** to tribulation, and will kill **you**, and **you** will be hated by all nations on account of My name" (Mt.24:9, emphasis added). The crucial question is, "Who does the "**you**" represent? The traditional premillennial position is that the "**you**" of Matthew 24 refers to the disciples, who in turn represent the Church. However, the Dispensational position is that the disciples represent a future Jewish remnant that will be living during the Tribulation period. **John Darby** popularized this teaching. **Darby** writes; "For imbedded in the Sermon on the Mount are words of our Lord which *apply far more closely to Jews or the remnant than to the church*... Matthew 24 and 25...relates to the Jews and the remnant up to the last days."[290] Following Darby's lead, **William Kelly**, while also commenting on Matthew 24, insists that, "This future Jewish remnant is represented by the men that were then before the Lord, who therefore begins, you may have observed, with their place as Jewish disciples...What am I to *infer* from it all? That it is *not* a description of Christians, which the Lord is here pursuing, but of godly Jews, and at the end of the age especially."[291] Notice that Kelly is *inferring* that the Olivet Discourse "is not a description of Christians" but of "godly Jews." Likewise, **Charles Mackintosh** assumes that, "...this godly remnant [i.e., the future Jewish remnant] is represented by the

[290] *The Collected Writings of J.N. Darby* - Edited by William Kelly, Stow Hill Bible and Tract Depot, n.d, Prophetic No.4, Vol.11, p.179.
[291] *Lectures on the Second Coming* - William Kelly, Believers Bookshelf, 1970, pp.247-248.

handful of disciples which gathered round our Lord on the Mount of Olives. We feel persuaded that if this be not seen, the true scope, bearing, and application of this remarkable discourse must be lost."[292]

Clearly, there is nothing within the text or context of Matthew 24 to justify the Dispensational claim that the Lord's disciples represent a "future Jewish remnant." This notion is nothing more than unsubstantiated speculation motivated by desperate necessity. Dispensationalists have developed and embraced this highly questionable interpretation because they realize that the viability of the entire pretribulation rapture doctrine depends upon it. They understand that the Lord's disciples in Matthew 24 cannot be allowed to represent Christians. Thus, without any textual justification whatsoever, they simply decree that the Lord's disciples represent a "future Jewish remnant" and not the Church.

John Darby declared, "I still believe that Matthew 24, at least to verse 31, is addressed to the disciples as Jews, as believing Jews no doubt, but as Jews... I do *not* think it addressed to the church. *Nothing* indeed was addressed to the church by the Lord in Person, because the church did not yet exist to be addressed..."[293] **Darby** explains elsewhere that, "...in chapter 23... The multitude and the disciples are both put on distinct *Jewish ground*[294]...The Lord then proceeds in Matthew 24 to announce the judgment of Jerusalem, and the circumstances of His disciples in connection with the end of the age."[295] **Charles H. Mackintosh,** while discussing Matthew 24, declares, "We shall find nothing about the church of God, the body of Christ, here...We are entirely on *Jewish ground*, surrounded by Jewish circumstances and influences." **Mackintosh** then concludes that, "The persons addressed are not on proper *Christian ground*[296]. The entire scene is earthly and Jewish, not heavenly and Christian."[297] And **Arno C. Gaebelein** also asserts that the disciples who are addressed in Mathew 24

---

[292] *Papers on the Lord's Coming* - C.H.M., Loizeaux Brothers, n.d., p.68.
[293] *The Collected Writings of J.N. Darby* - Edited by William Kelly, Stow Hill Bible and Tract Depot, n.d, Prophetic No.4, Vol.11, p.3.
[294] The phrase "Jewish ground" was coined by John Darby and readily adopted by his followers. In typical Dispensational parlance it means, "This passage does *not* apply to the Church, but to a future Jewish remnant."
[295] *The Collected Writings of J.N. Darby* - Edited by William Kelly, Stow Hill Bible and Tract Depot, n.d, Prophetic No.4, Vol.11, p.146.
[296] The term "Christian Ground" is used by Dispensationalists to refer to Scripture that applies specifically to the Church.
[297] *Papers on the Lord's Coming* - C.H.M., Loizeaux Brothers, n.d., p.64, 72.

must be regarded as "Jewish" and not as "Christian." **Gaebelein** maintains that, "In reading over the first part of the discourse of our Lord we find that it relates to disciples, which of necessity must be Jewish...The reference to Daniel and the great tribulation, which never concerns the church, but Israel, shows us that we are not on *Christian ground*, but *Jewish ground*."[298] **E. Schuyler English**, in his comments on Matthew 24 explains that, "... pre-tribulationists identify verses four to thirty-one *not* as part of the Church Age, but as Jewish..."[299] **English** goes on to say that, "...the disciples knew nothing of the Church Age; they were living in a Jewish Age..." therefore, **English** concludes that, "...we believe that these prophecies have to do *entirely* with the Tribulation of Israel..."[300] And **Dwight Pentecost**, commenting on Matthew 24:4-26, declares that the prophetic elements of the Olivet Discourse strictly apply *only* to Israel and *not* the Church. **Pentecost** contends that, "Consistency of interpretation would seem to *eliminate any application* of this portion of Scripture to the church or the church age, inasmuch as the Lord is dealing with the prophetic program for Israel."[301] Likewise, **Gerald Stanton** explains that, "...dispensationalists hold that Matthew 24 speaks of Israel in the Tribulation and *not* of the Church, which they believe to be already raptured..."[302]

Thus, Dispensationalists have determined that the disciples addressed in Matthew 24 are representative of a future Jewish remnant and *not* the Church.[303] And this astonishing conclusion is based solely upon the dubious observation that it rests upon "Jewish ground!" Dispensationalists confidently conclude that Matthew 24 cannot be addressed to the Church because it is thoroughly "Jewish" in its subject matter and character. *But how does the fact that the Olivet Discourse is "Jewish" in character prove that the discourse does not apply to the Church?* After all, the entire Bible is "Jewish" in its subject matter and character. Jews wrote the Old and New Testaments.[304]

---

[298] *The Gospel of Matthew* - Arno C. Gaebelein, Loizeaux Brothers, 1982, pp.465,469.

[299] *Studies in the Gospel According to Matthew* - E. Schuyler English, Zondervan Publishing House, 1935,1938, p.171.

[300] *Studies in the Gospel According to Matthew* - E. Schuyler English, Zondervan Publishing House, 1935,1938, p.172.

[301] *Things To Come* - J. Dwight Pentecost, Zondervan Publishing House, 1964, p.278.

[302] *Kept From the Hour* - Gerald B. Stanton, Zondervan Publishing House, 1956, p.57.

[303] It should be noted at this point that Dispensationalists also maintain that the parallel passages of the Olivet Discourse contained in Mark 13 and Luke 21 are also on "Jewish ground." For example, referring to Luke 21, **Dwight Pentecost** declares, "...the primary reference in this chapter is to the nation of Israel, who is already in the tribulation period, and therefore this is *not* applicable to the church." *Things to Come* - J. Dwight Pentecost, Zondervan Publishing House, 1964, p.161.

[304] Luke, a Gentile physician and companion of the Apostle Paul is the only exception.

It is filled with "Jewish" images, Hebraisms, references and terms. The apostles were all Jewish. Jesus is the Jewish Messiah. And salvation itself is from the Jews (Jn.2:4:22)! It would be amazing indeed if the Bible lacked its Jewishness! If the Olivet Discourse does not apply to the Church because of its "Jewishness," then why does any other part of the New Testament apply to the Church? For example, why does the Last Supper recorded in Matthew 26, from whence the Church derives the ordinance of Communion, apply to the Church? This event was the Jewish Passover celebration. It was held in Jerusalem, the Jewish capital of the Jewish nation. They sang Jewish hymns. The Jewish Apostles participated in it and the Jewish Messiah officiated! The Dispensational argument that Matthew 24 cannot apply to the Church because it rests "entirely on Jewish ground" is contrived. The Jewishness of Matthew 24 does not prove that the words of the Lord Jesus apply to a future Jewish remnant. Nowhere do the Scriptures state or even imply that the Lord's disciples are representative of a future Jewish remnant. However, the Scriptures do clearly declare that the apostles are representative of the Church. In Ephesians 2:19-20, Paul says, "So then you [Gentiles] are no longer strangers and aliens, but you are fellow citizens with the saints, and are of God's household, having been built upon the **foundation of the apostles and prophets**..." (Emphasis added).

There is absolutely nothing in the text or the context of the Olivet Discourse of Matthew 24 that supports the Dispensational argument that the words of Jesus Christ, which are addressed directly to His disciples, refer to a future Jewish remnant and not to Christians. These "dispensational distinctions" are a pure fiction that rest upon the assumptions and inferences of men, in direct disregard for the straightforward intention of the Biblical text. These "dispensational distinctions" actually blunt the "plain, ordinary and literal" meaning of the prophetic Scriptures - Scriptures that if interpreted literally, would immediately contradict the pretribulation rapture scheme. Yet, in order to preserve the all-important doctrine of a secret, any moment, pretribulational rapture, Dispensationalists are prepared to declare that large portions of the New Testament rest upon "Jewish ground" and therefore have no direct application or relevance to Christians specifically, or to the Church generally.

Not surprisingly, *every* New Testament text that presents an exegetical problem for the pretribulation rapture teaching, is conveniently set aside by simply declaring it to be upon "Jewish ground" and therefore irrelevant to the Church.[305] It is here that Dispensationalists commit an error of enormous magnitude. By what principle of interpretation do Dispensationalists claim the insight and ability to divide the New Testament Scriptures into "Jewish" and "Christian" portions? For the answer to this all important question, carefully consider the words of **Lewis Sperry Chafer**, who, in his *Systematic Theology*, declares that the New Testament Scriptures present a;

"...*twofold character* of the work and teachings of Christ. He was both a minister to Israel to confirm the promises...and a minister to the Gentiles that they might glorify God for His mercy...these *two widely different revelations* are not separated in the Scriptures by a well-defined boundary of chapter and verse; they are *intermingled in the text* and are to be *identified*...by the *character of the message* and *circumstances* under which given."[306]

Thus, **Chafer** would have us believe that it is the task of the Bible interpreter to distinguish between the "twofold character of the work and teachings of Christ" which are "intermingled in the text," thereby separating the "Jewish" portions of Scripture from the "Church" portions. And this is to be accomplished on the arbitrary and subjective basis of the "character of the message and circumstances under which given." This is utter and complete rubbish. The entire premise is artificial, manufactured and contrived. There is absolutely no exegetical justification for the Dispensational claim that the so-called "twofold character of the work and teachings of Christ" must be distinguished so that the New Testament can be interpreted "dispensationally." Nonetheless, Dispensationalists uniformly accept Chaffer's interpretative approach. Consider **John Walvoord's** advice: "One of the important principles to be kept in view in the study of prophecy is *distinguishing* the prophecies that relate to *Israel and her program from* the prophecies that relate to the *church and her program*."[307] And again, while contending that the Lord's disciples represent Israel in the Olivet Discourse of

---

[305] "Whatever has been felt to be a difficulty has been set aside by saying that it is 'Jewish'; and that one word has been deemed to be quite enough to show that it has nothing to do with the Church. On this principle the application of very much of the New Testament has been avoided...An undefined term becomes an easy mode of explaining away distinct statements which cannot be reconciled to a theory; because in this manner no meaning whatever is assigned to the passages whose testimony has to be avoided. This has been the case with the word 'Jewish' in connection with the Scriptures which teach the manifest appearing of the Lord in glory. In this manner the three first Gospels have been called Jewish, whenever any portion of their teaching was felt as a difficulty. So, too, the Epistle to the Hebrews, and those of James and Peter."
The Hope of Christ's Second Coming – S.P. Tregelles, The Sovereign Grace Advent Testimony, n.d. (ca.1864), pp.37-38.
[306] *Systematic Theology* - Lewis Sperry Chafer, Kregel Publications, 1993, Vol.4, pp.171-172.
[307] *Major Bible Prophecies* - John F. Walvoord, Zondervan Publishing House, 1994, p.353.

Matthew 24, **Walvoord** explains that, "The question as to whom any particular passage is addressed cannot be settled by the fact that it was given to the disciples, because they represent in some sense ***both*** Israel and the church. The issue must be settled on the subject matter..."[308]

This dispensational principal of distinguishing between "Jewish" and "Christian" portions of the New Testament was popularized by John Darby and is euphemistically referred to by Dispensationalists as "rightly dividing the word of truth." Referring to this highly questionable practice, **Earnest Sandeen** explains that, "Since for Darby the ministry of Jesus was divided into two parts (his earthly appeal to the Jews as earthly Messiah and his later role as founder of the church), the exegesis of the Gospels ***required a careful separation of passages referring to Jewish or churchly promises and admonitions***. The ***task of the expositor*** of the Bible was, in a phrase that became the hallmark of dispensationalism, ***'rightly dividing the word of truth.'***"[309] However, the Dispensational practice of "rightly dividing the word" represents an entirely new and unheard of hermeneutic. The historic view of the Church has always been that the New Testament, from Matthew to Revelation, represents Christian Scripture - ***not*** an admixture of Jewish and Christian writings that must be subjectively and arbitrarily "divided" on the basis of their perceived Jewish character and circumstances!

Dispensationalists fully recognize that their secret, any moment pretribulational rapture teaching is based upon ***inferences*** and ***assumptions,*** which in turn are dependent upon ***dispensationalized*** New Testament passages. In an attempt to level the interpretive playing field, Dispensationalists make two allegations against post-tribulationalism. First they confidently assert that there is no New Testament text that places the Church in the Tribulation. For example, **Lewis Sperry Chafer** declares that, "...no Scripture ever relates the Church to the 7 years of tribulation[310]...the Church never enters or passes through the tribulation...no New Testament Scripture necessitates the placing of the Church in that period[311]...no Scripture intimates that the Church is in the tribulation, nor is the Church warned as though in danger of so great a trial."[312] And **John**

---

[308] *The Blessed Hope and the Tribulation* - John F. Walvoord, Zondervan Publishing House, 1976, p.86.
[309] *The Roots of Fundamentalism* - Ernest R. Sandeen, The University of Chicago Press, 1970, p.67.
[310] *Systematic Theology* - Lewis Sperry Chafer, Kregel Publications, reprinted 1993, Vol.4, p.340.
[311] *Systematic Theology* - Lewis Sperry Chafer, Kregel Publications, reprinted 1993, Vol.4, p.364.
[312] *Systematic Theology* - Lewis Sperry Chafer, Kregel Publications, reprinted 1993, Vol.4, p.367.

Walvoord likewise asserts that, "None of the New Testament passages on the Tribulation mention the church (Matt.13:30, 39-42, 48-50; 24:15-31; 1Thess.1:9-10, 5:4-9; 2 Thess.2:1-11; Rev.4-18)."[313] And secondly, Dispensationalists assert that since there is no Scripture that places the Church in the Tribulation, post-tribulationalism like pretribulationalism is necessarily based upon *inferences*. For instance, **John Walvoord** alleges that, "...both pretribulationism and posttribulationism...[are] an *induction* based on scriptural facts rather than an explicit statement of the Bible."[314] And **Renald Showers**, while discussing the time of the rapture declares, "...every person who studies the subject of the Rapture is forced to look for *inferences* of its time from different details presented in the Bible."[315] Dispensationalists thereby attempt to reduce the disagreement over the time of the rapture, to a determination over which side can produce the most convincing *inferences*.

However, the Dispensational claim that the time of the rapture is a matter of "induction" and that Bible students must therefore "look for inferences" is simply false. First of all, this assertion can be made only *after* the Dispensationalist has declared every passage in the New Testament that clearly depicts believers in the Tribulation as being on "*Jewish ground*" and therefore *not* applicable to the Church. Thus, only *after* all pertinent Scriptures have been thoroughly "dispensationalized" can the Dispensationalist assert that there is *no Scripture* that places the Church in the Tribulation. However, if the Scriptures are truly interpreted in their "literal, usual, natural, plain, ordinary and normal sense," they clearly and unmistakably declare that Christians will indeed pass through the coming Tribulation - for the Lord Himself plainly warned His disciples; "Then they will deliver *you* to *tribulation*, and will kill *you*, and *you* will be hated by all nations on account of My name" (Matt.24:9). Only when the "you" is forced to mean "them" can one escape from the plain and literal meaning of this and other similar texts.[316]

---

[313] *The Rapture Question* - John F. Walvoord, Zondervan Publishing House, 1979, p.271.

[314] *The Rapture Question* - John F. Walvoord, Zondervan Publishing House, 1979, p.181.

[315] *Maranatha - Our Lord Come!* - Renald Showers, The Friends of Israel Gospel Ministry, Inc. 1995, p.13.

[316] For example, the popular radio Bible teacher, **J. Vernon McGee**, while commenting on Matthew 24:9, states, "'Then they shall deliver you up to be afflicted' – who is the *you*? Obviously, He [Jesus] is not addressing the church but the nation of Israel. The affliction He is talking about is anti-Semitism on a worldwide scale." *Thru the Bible with J. Vernon McGee* – J. Vernon McGee, Thru the Bible Radio, Pasadena, CA, Vol. IV, Matthew – Romans, p.126.

Additionally, the Dispensational charge that "both pretribulationism and post-tribulationism" rely upon "induction...rather than an explicit statement of the Bible"[317] is an attempt to place both "pretribulationism" and "post-tribulationism" on an equal footing. The words, "pretribulation" and "post-tribulation" are *not* Bible words. Rather, they are theological terms that have been developed to describe two different views about the time of the rapture. The question therefore is, "Which view do the Scriptures describe?" Clearly, the belief that Jesus Christ will return *before* the Tribulation to rapture the Church is an *inference* because there is *no* Biblical text that describes a pretribulational Coming of Jesus Christ in the New Testament. However, the post-tribulational Coming of Christ is mentioned numerous times throughout the New Testament.[318] Therefore, there is absolutely no question that Jesus Christ is returning to this world *after* the Tribulation. Furthermore, there is no question that the rapture of the Church occurs at the time of Christ's Second Coming.[319] Thus, the certainty of a post-tribulational rapture which coincides with the post-tribulational Coming is a matter of logical deduction, and *not* speculative inference and assumption. Surely, if Christ were coming *before* the onset of the Great Tribulation there would be at least one clear statement in Scripture describing this event. Yet, the indisputable fact is there is *not* one verse in the entire New Testament that describes a pretribulational Coming of Jesus Christ for any reason whatsoever – not one! Thus, we must ask, "In the absence of any clear Scriptural reference to a pretribulational Coming of Christ, how can Dispensationalists possibly know that Jesus Christ is Coming to rapture the Church *before* the onset of the Great Tribulation?"

3. Summary.

There are two major premises upon which the pretribulation rapture teaching rests. **First**, Dispensationalists have abandoned a truly literal interpretation of the prophetic portions of the New Testament. Instead, they have based the doctrine of the pretribulation rapture entirely upon *inferences*, which are nothing more than *subjective*

---

[317] *The Rapture Question* - John F. Walvoord, Zondervan Publishing House, 1979, p.181.

[318] New Testament verses that clearly describe the post-tribulational Advent of Jesus Christ are; Mt.16:27; 24:27-31; 25:31; Mk.8:38; 13:24-27; Lk.9:26; 17:22-24, 26-30; 21:25-27; 2Thess.1:6-10; 2:1-8; 1Pt.4:13; Jude 14-15; Rv.1:7; 6:14-17; 11:15-19; 19:11-16.

[319] New Testament verses that clearly link the Second Coming (i.e., *parousia*) of Christ with the rapture are 1Thess.4:13-17; 2Thess.2:1-4 cp. Mt.24:27-31, wherein the Scriptures clearly teach that Christ's Second Coming (i.e., *parousia*) will occur *after* the Tribulation.

opinions of what they *assume* the Biblical text is *implying.* Their entire argument is based upon supposition, speculation, and conjecture, *not* sound exegetical principles of Biblical interpretation.

Second, in order to support the pretribulation rapture teaching, Dispensationalists are forced to argue that the New Testament Scriptures must be interpreted "dispensationally." This means that the supposed Jewish and Christian portions of the New Testament must be carefully identified and distinguished. This argument is based upon *two major assumptions*. Dispensationalists first-of-all *assume* that Israel (Old Testament believers and or a future Jewish remnant) and the Church (New Testament believers) represent two separate and distinct groups of believers. Each group has their own separate redemptive "program" - one earthly (the Jews) and the other heavenly (the Church). Next, Dispensationalists *assume* that the New Testament is a hodgepodge of "Jewish" and "Christian" Scriptures that must be carefully distinguished and separated so that they can be applied to the appropriate group (either Jews or Christians). This extraordinary approach enables Dispensationalists to promote a pretribulational rapture by applying *all* New Testament passages that speak of believers being present on earth during the future Tribulation period to a hypothetical future Jewish remnant instead of the Church.[320] And these astounding *assumptions* are confidently heralded as established Biblical facts!

---

[320] New Testament references that clearly describe "believers" being present on the earth during the Tribulation period are; Mt.24:1-51, (notice the word "you"), vv. 4, 6, 9, 15, 23, 25-26, 32-34, 42-44,47. Compare also Mk.13:5-37, and Lk.21:5-36. See also, Rv.7:14; 12:11,17; 13:7,10; 14:12-13; 16:6; 17:6; 18:4,24; 20:4.

Chapter Four
The Doctrine of Imminence

Outline of Chapter Four:
1. Imminence Defined.
2. The Rapture is a Signless Event.
3. Signs of a Signless Event.
4. The Importance of the Doctrine of Imminence.
5. The Doctrine of Imminence is Supported Entirely by Inference.

1. Imminence Defined.

Dispensationalists define "imminence" as the unexpected, unannounced, any moment coming of Jesus Christ to rapture the Church *before* the start of the Great Tribulation. **John Nelson Darby** popularized the claim that, "...Christ's coming may be expected at any time..."[321] Modern Dispensationalists have uniformly adopted Darby's teaching of "imminence." For example, **Leon Wood** affirms that, "Christ's coming for His Church will be sudden and unannounced. No advance warning will be given."[322] **John Walvoord** assures us that, "...the Lord could come at any moment..."[323] And **Renald Showers** stresses that, "...church saints are to be continuously alert or on the watch for Christ to come, because...He could come at any moment."[324] Thus, Dispensationalists teach that Christians should be watching for an "any moment" coming of Christ that will be sudden and without warning. Furthermore, Dispensationalists teach that this any moment coming of Christ is the very next prophetic event to be fulfilled on the prophetic calendar. For example, **E. Schuyler English** declares that, "The rapture or translation of the Church is the *next event* in predictive prophecy."[325] Likewise, **Louis Talbot** teaches that, "...the *very next event* will be the translation of the church!"[326]

---

[321] *The Collected Writings of J.N. Darby* - Edited by William Kelly, Stow Hill Bible and Tract Depot, n.d, Prophetic No.4, Vol.11, p.344.
[322] *The Bible and Future Events* - Leon J. Wood, Zondervan Publishing House, 1974, p.47.
[323] *The Blessed Hope and the Tribulation* - John F. Walvoord, Zondervan Publishing House, 1976, p.70.
[324] *Maranatha, Our Lord Come!* - Renald Showers, The Friends of Israel Gospel Ministry, Inc., 1995, p.103.
[325] *A Companion to the New Scofield Reference Bible* - E. Schuyler English, Oxford University Press, 1972, p.136
[326] *God's Plan for the Ages* - Louis T. Talbot, published by Louis T. Talbot, 1936, 1943, p.139.

2. The Rapture is a Signless Event.

Because the pretribulation rapture is believed to be the "very next event" in "predictive prophecy," and because that event could occur at "any moment," Dispensationalists maintain that there are no Biblical prophecies indicating when the rapture will take place. Thus, while referring to the pretribulational rapture of the Church, **John Darby** confidently asserts that, "There is no earthly event between it and heaven...the church is properly heavenly; in its calling and relationship with Christ, forming no part of the course of events of the earth, which makes its rapture so simple and clear...*there is no event, I repeat, between us and heaven.*"[327] Following Darby's lead, **William Kelly** teaches that, "The coming of the Lord, in its bearing upon the Christian, is our hope...Never, in any passage of the word of God, is a single incident put before it as necessary to be accomplished before the church can legitimately look for Him...*there are no defined periods or visible harbingers to intimate that He is coming to receive us*..."[328] **Charles H. Mackintosh**, while referring to the pretribulational rapture assures his readers that, "This hope may be realized this very night. There is *nothing* whatever to wait for - *no* events to transpire amongst the nations - *nothing* to occur in the history of Israel - *nothing* in God's government of the world - *nothing* in short, in any shape or form whatsoever..."[329] **William Blackstone** emphatically declares that the Church has, "...*no date* and *no sign* which might so definitely indicate the time of her Rapture..."[330] **Dwight Pentecost** reasons that, "Since the church is given the hope of an *imminent* return of Christ there can be *no signs* given to her as to when this event will take place."[331] And **John Walvoord** assures us that, "...the Lord could come at *any moment* and that there are *no necessary intervening events*."[332]

Thus, when Dispensationalists refer to the "imminent" return of Jesus Christ, they mean that Christ's Coming to rapture the Church will be a sudden, unannounced, any moment, pretribulational event without any prior prophetic warnings or signs to indicate when it will occur.

---

[327] *The Collected Writings of J.N. Darby* - Edited by William Kelly, Stow Hill Bible and Tract Depot, n.d, Prophetic No.4, Vol.11, p.156,157.
[328] *Lectures on the Second Coming* - William Kelly, Believers Bookshelf, 1970, pp.216, 223.
[329] *Papers on the Lord's Coming* - C.H.M., Loizeaux Brothers, n.d., p.23.
[330] *Jesus is Coming* - William E. Blackstone, Kregel Publications, 1989, p.211.
[331] *Things to Come* - J. Dwight Pentecost, Zondervan Publishing House, 1964, p.155.
[332] *The Blessed Hope and the Tribulation* - John F. Walvoord, Zondervan Publishing House, 1976, p.70.

3. Signs of a Signless Event.

However, it is both amazing and contradictory, that the very people, who maintain that the rapture can occur at *any moment* and that there are *no prophetic signs* to indicate when it will occur, are also the very same people who point to *prophetic signs* as *proof* that the "imminent" pretribulation rapture is near! For example, **William Blackstone** paradoxically dedicates an entire chapter to "Signs of Christ's Imminent Coming."[333] This is an obvious contradiction in terms. How can there be "signs" to indicate the proximity of a "signless" event? Nonetheless, **Blackstone** proceeds to list the fulfillment of numerous Biblical prophecies as proof that the "signless" pretribulation rapture is "imminent."[334] But not only do Dispensationalists point to prophetic signs to prove that the signless rapture is at hand, they use verses of Scripture which they have previously declared to be exclusively "Jewish" in their application and therefore *not* applicable to the "Church." Consider the comments of **E. Schuyler English**, in his commentary on the Gospel of Matthew, who points to the fulfillment of prophetic "signs" as indicators of the nearness of the "imminent" pretribulation rapture. **English** refers to Matthew 24:32-36 (i.e., the *Parable of the Fig Tree*), explaining that, "Israel has been barren, but one day it will put forth leaves; then know that the Lord's return is near...*Yes, this is Tribulation teaching*, but Christians, can we not see things today which point to a near accomplishment of these things...The summer is nigh - soon, sooner than we think, we may go to be with our Lord."[335] Likewise, **C. I. Scofield,** also refers to in Matthew 24:32-36, to emphasize the nearness of the imminent pretribulation rapture. **Scofield** teaches that, "According to the parable we are to watch the fig tree...Watch the fig tree! When you see the first buds you know that the time is at hand."[336] But one has to wonder exactly how a prophetic portion of Scripture, which Dispensationalists say applies specifically to the future Tribulation period can possibly be a "sign" of the imminent pretribulation rapture of the Church.[337]

---

[333] *Jesus is Coming* - William E. Blackstone, Kregel Publications, 1989, p.231.

[334] According to Blackstone, definitive "signs" pointing to the nearness of the rapture are, "The Prevalence of Travel and Knowledge, Perilous Times, Spiritualism, Apostasy, Worldwide Evangelism, Rich Men, Israel, & Zionism." *Jesus is Coming* - William E. Blackstone, Kregel Publications, 1989, pp.231-246.

[335] *Studies in the Gospel According to Matthew* - E. Schuyler English, Zondervan Publishing House, 1935,1938, pp.178-179.

[336] *Prophecy Made Plain* - C. I. Scofield, The Gospel Hour, 1967, p.126.

[337] Dispensationalists uniformly agree that the *Parable of the Fig Tree* refers to Israel during the Tribulation period. For example, A.C. Gaebelein teaches that this parable refers, "...to the end of the Jewish Age...But learn the parable from the figtree...The figtree is the picture of Israel...The figtree will bud again...This is the lesson here. Israel's blessing, new life,

Under the paragraph heading *Signs of the Times*, **Leon Wood** explains that while no one can know the exact date of Christ's Coming, "...the Christian may be alerted to the time in general." **Wood** goes on to say that "Many of the more general signs are set forth in Matthew 24:6-12: 'wars and rumors of wars,' 'famines, and pestilences, and earthquakes,' persecution of Christians, betrayal by friends, the appearance of false prophets, and abounding iniquity."[338] But again, the question begs: How can "signs" alert the Christian to the pretribulational coming of Christ if it is a "signless" event? The contradiction is apparent! Furthermore, how can dispensationalized portions of Scriptures that supposedly apply only to a future Jewish remnant during the Tribulation period indicate the nearness of a pretribulation rapture, which is supposed to have occurred years before these "signs" transpire? Obviously, if the rapture occurs *before* the prophetic signs, those signs cannot possibly indicate the approach of the rapture!

Nonetheless, Dispensationalists see no contradiction in pointing to "signs" as proof that a "signless" pretribulational rapture is near. For example, consider **Tim LaHaye's** attempt to justify this practice when he argues that, "...there are *no signs* associated with Christ's rapture of His church. All sign prophecies...relate to the Glorious Appearing. Pre-Tribulationists may be ridiculed by some for writing books about 'signs' of the coming of Christ even while insisting that no specific signs exist for the rapture. These critics overlook an important fact. The signs predicted for the end of this age...will cast long shadows before them and serve as general warnings to Christians...it is possible for diligent students of prophecy to anticipate the season of the rapture."[339] Thus, **LaHaye** asserts that all of the "sign prophecies" refer to the "Glorious Appearing" that occurs at the end of the Tribulation. He further maintains that there are "no specific signs" associated with the rapture. Yet, **LaHaye** paradoxically maintains that the signs that point to the post-tribulational "Glorious Appearing" will also "cast long shadows" which will yield "general warnings" that will indicate when the pretribulation rapture is near. Thus, according to **LaHaye**, the non-signs are actually signs. The inherent contradiction in **LaHaye's** argument is painfully obvious. However,

---

fruit and glory will quickly be realized in those last days. When in these last seven years, and especially the last 1,260 days, all these things come to pass…" Yet Gaebelein paradoxically goes on to say, "The other application, that *now* we behold Israel like a budding figtree, signs of new national life and in this a sign of the times is certainly not wrong. It tells us of the nearness of the end." *The Gospel of Matthew* – Arno C. Gaebelein, Loizeaux Brothers, 1982, pp.512-513.

[338] *The Bible and Future Events* - Leon J. Wood, Zondervan Publishing House, 1974, p.18.

[339] *No Fear of the Storm* - Tim LaHaye, Multnomah Press Books, 1992, p.67.

Dispensationalists routinely ignore these apparent inconsistencies in their unwavering defense of their essential doctrine of imminence because they recognize that the doctrine of imminence is essential to the viability of the pretribulation rapture theory. Without it, the entire argument for a pretribulational rapture immediately collapses.

4. The Importance of the Doctrine of Imminence.

In his defense of the Dispensational doctrine of imminence, **John Walvoord** declares that, "The *central feature* of pretribulationism, the doctrine of imminency, is however, a prominent feature of the doctrine of the early church."[340] And again, **Walvoord** observes that, "...the doctrine of imminency...is the *heart of pretribulationism*..."[341] Furthermore, **Walvoord** maintains that the, "...imminency of the Lord's return...is an *essential doctrine* of pretribulationism."[342] But exactly why is the Dispensational doctrine of the "imminency of the Lord's return" so crucial to the doctrine of the pretribulational rapture?

The doctrine of imminence is essential to pretribulationalism because *there is no text of Scripture that actually describes a pretribulational Coming of Jesus Christ.* The doctrine of imminence was developed out of necessity to legitimize the concept of a pretribulational Coming and rapture. Early on, Dispensationalists faced a major dilemma in their advocacy for the pretribulation rapture. Their principal problem was and remains the fact that there is not a single text of Scripture that describes a pretribulational Coming of Jesus Christ. Rather, every passage in the New Testament that indicates a timeframe for Christ's Second Coming, describes that Coming as a *post-*tribulational event.[343] We would reasonably expect that a doctrine of such monumental importance as the Coming of Christ to rapture His Church before the onset of the Great Tribulation would be described at least once in Scripture. However, such a description does not exist. The Scriptures are completely silent about a pretribulational Coming of Jesus Christ. Dispensationalists have therefore necessarily developed the doctrine of

---

[340] *The Rapture Question* – John F. Walvoord, Zondervan Publishing House, 1979, p.51.
  See **Appendix B** for a refutation of this frequent claim by Dispensationalists.
[341] *The Rapture Question* - John F. Walvoord, Zondervan Publishing House, 1979, p.53.
[342] *The Rapture Question* - John F. Walvoord, Zondervan Publishing House, 1979, p.270.
[343] New Testament verses that clearly describe the post-tribulational Advent of Jesus Christ are; Mt.16:27; 24:27-31; 25:31; Mk.8:38; 13:24-27; Lk.9:26; 17:22-24, 26-30; 21:25-27; 2Thess.1:6-10; 2:1-8; 1Pt.4:13; Jude 14-15; Rv.1:7; 6:14-17; 11:15-19; 19:11-16.

imminence to obliquely explain *why* the pretribulational Coming and rapture is *not* specifically mentioned in Scripture.

The doctrine of imminence *assumes* that since the Scriptures do *not* mention a pretribulational Coming of Christ, nor a pretribulational rapture, the aforementioned Coming and rapture must therefore be a secret, signless, pretribulational event that could occur at any moment!

Dispensationalists *assume* that *all* Biblical texts that refer to the rapture *automatically imply* that it will be *imminent* (i.e., a secret, signless, unannounced event that could occur at any moment). The primary rapture passages referred to by Dispensationalists are **John 14:1-3; 1Corinthians 15:50-53; 1Thessalonians 4:13-18; 5:1-6** and **2Thessalonians 2:1-3.** A careful and objective review of these texts will confirm that none of these texts actually describes an imminent pretribulational Coming of Jesus Christ. Dispensationalists simply *assume* that these texts depict an imminent Coming and rapture. Their assumption rests upon the observation that none of these passages describe any Tribulational events that precede the rapture. Because there are no specific Tribulational events described as preceding the rapture in these texts, Dispensationalists *assume* that the rapture must therefore occur *before* these unmentioned Tribulational events. Carefully consider **John Walvoord's** comment on First Thessalonians 4:13-18, when he asserts that, "...the rapture here, as elsewhere, is presented as an imminent event *without any prophetic events taking place first.*"[344] And again, while commenting on First Corinthians 15:50-53, **Walvoord** declares that, "There is *no* reference to any *preceding events* such as will *precede* the second coming. Rather the Rapture is an imminent event."[345] Thus, **Walvoord** *assumes* that the rapture is an imminent event because these texts do not describe any other preceding tribulational events. In other words, **Walvoord** *assumes* that because there are no other tribulational events described as occurring before the rapture in these particular passages, the rapture must therefore necessarily occur before these unmentioned events. But, these conclusions are nothing more than highly subjective *inferences* that are based upon what the Scriptures do *not* say and *not* upon what the Scriptures *do* say!

---

[344] *Major Bible Prophecies* - John F. Walvoord, Zondervan Publishing House, 1994, p.317.
[345] *Major Bible Prophecies* - John F. Walvoord, Zondervan Publishing House, 1994, p.325.

The subjective nature of the Dispensational doctrine of imminence is further underscored by **John Walvoord's** admission that, "The view that the Rapture is pretribulational - that is, more than seven years before the second coming of Christ - involves certain *prior assumptions*."[346] It is highly significant that **Walvoord** does not state that the pretribulation rapture doctrine is based upon clear declarations of Scripture, but rather on "*certain prior assumptions*." Furthermore, **Walvoord** concludes a detailed discussion of John 14:2-3, 1Thessalonians 4-5, 2Thessalonians 2, and 1Corinthians 15:51-58, by stating that, "In all these *major passages* on the Rapture, the *implication* is that the time of trouble follows the Rapture rather than precedes it..." **Walvoord** then goes on to say that, "These are the major passages on the doctrine of the Rapture...they uniformly *imply* that the Rapture is *imminent* with *no prophesied preceding events*."[347] Carefully consider the fact that **Walvoord** acknowledges that these verses do *not* clearly state that the rapture is either imminent or pretribulational. Rather, **Walvoord** candidly admits that these "major passages on the Rapture" only "*imply*" that the rapture is imminent and pretribulational - an implication that is both highly subjective and questionable at best.

Dispensationalists have invented the concept of an unannounced, signless, any moment coming of Christ (imminence) to advance a teaching (the pretribulation rapture) that the Scriptures are completely silent about. This is precisely why the early Dispensationalists referred to the pretribulation rapture as being "secret." Secret in the sense that the Scriptures make absolutely no mention of it - secret in the sense that it will suddenly come upon the Church without any advance indication or warning - secret in the sense that it will be invisible and unobserved by the unbelieving world.

5. The Doctrine of Imminence is Supported Entirely by the Use of Inference.

The Dispensational doctrine of *imminence* rests entirely upon assumptions of men, and *not* the clear, authoritative declarations of Scripture. Carefully consider the candid admission by **Renald Showers**, who declares that, "The concept of the *imminent*

---

[346] *Major Bible Prophecies* - John F. Walvoord, Zondervan Publishing House, 1994, p.330.
[347] *Major Bible Prophecies* - John F. Walvoord, Zondervan Publishing House, 1994, pp.325,351.

coming of Christ is a ***significant inference*** for the Pretribulation Rapture of the Church."[348]

This is a very revealing statement. What Showers is obliquely saying is that, "The ***concept*** [i.e., the idea] of the ***imminent*** [i.e., the secret, signless, unannounced, any moment] coming of Christ is a ***significant inference*** [i.e., a major assumption] *for* [i.e., that supports] the Pretribulation Rapture of the Church." In other words, it is the doctrine of imminence that makes the idea of the pretribulational rapture viable.

Showers further asserts that, "Many Bible scholars...have concluded that the New Testament teaches or ***implies*** the imminent coming of Christ in the following passages: 1 Corinthians 1:7; 4:5; 15:51-52; 16:22; Philippians 3:20; 4:5; 1Thessalonians 1:10; 2Thessalonians 3:10-12; Titus 2:13; James 5:8-9; 1 John 2:28; Revelation 3:11; 22:7,12,17,20."[349] However, a careful review of these passages cited by Showers will reveal no statement of imminence as defined by Dispensationalists. All of these passages clearly teach the "soon" or "near" Coming of Christ. However, Scriptural declarations of the near or soon appearing of Christ are ***not*** proof of a secret, signless, any moment, pretribulational rapture. Even **Showers** himself has acknowledged that, "...imminent is ***not*** equal to soon."[350] Likewise, the well-known Dispensational radio Bible teacher, **J. Vernon McGee,** while commenting on 1Thessalonians 4:13-18, has stated, "We now come to...one of the most important prophetic passages in the Scriptures. It teaches the ***imminent*** and ***impending*** coming of Christ for His church. That does ***not*** mean the ***immediate*** or ***soon*** coming of Christ."[351] Therefore, according to Dispensationalists themselves, the numerous passages which speak of Christ's near or soon Coming do ***not*** mean imminent. So, if soon, near, or immediate does not mean imminent, where exactly are the verses that describe the imminent (i.e., the secret, signless, unannounced, any moment) Coming of Jesus Christ to be found?

The inferential nature of the Dispensational doctrine of imminence is clearly illustrated by **Fredrick W. Grant**, who was an early Brethren Dispensational leader and

---

[348] *Maranatha, Our Lord Come!* - Renald Showers, The Friends of Israel Gospel Ministry, Inc., 1995, p.127.
[349] *Israel My Glory* - May/June 2007, *Why Study Biblical Prophecy?* - Renald Showers, p.34.
[350] The complete quotation is, "Thus, 'imminent' is not equal to 'soon.'" *Maranatha, Our Lord Come!* - Renald Showers, The Friends of Israel Gospel Ministry, Inc., 1995, p.127.
[351] *Thru the Bible with J. Vernon McGee* - J. Vernon McGee, Thru the Bible Radio, 1983, vol.V, p.393.

contemporary of John Darby. While commenting on the concept of the pretribulation rapture, **Grant** explains, "...no one would understand that between this gathering up of the saints to meet the Lord and His appearing in glory with them there should be an interval of months and years of earthly history. Nor can one be blamed, therefore, for being slow to assent to such a statement as this. Yet it is the truth; and one which can be perfectly established from Scripture, *although there is not a single text which states it.*"[352]

The well-known Bible teacher and pastor, **J. Oswald Smith** testifies that, "After years of study and prayer, I am absolutely convinced there will be no rapture before the tribulation...when I began to search the Scriptures for myself, whether these things were so, I discovered that *there is not a single verse in the Bible that upholds the pre-tribulation theory*; but that the uniform teaching of the Word of God is for a post-tribulation rapture."[353]

The entire Dispensational argument for an imminent pretribulational rapture of the Church is based entirely upon the *subjective assumptions and inferences* of men and *not* the clear, objective statements of Scripture. This fact is frequently made evident by Dispensational teachers themselves. For example, carefully consider the teaching of **Lehman Strauss**. While referring to John 14:1-3, **Strauss** asserts that, "When our Lord discussed with His disciples His coming for His own, He used the *language of imminency*...These verses *indicate* that there are *no intervening events* between Christ's going to the Father's house in heaven and His return to take His own from earth to heaven."[354]

Let's look at John 14:1-3. The text states;

"Let not your hearts be troubled; believe in God, believe also in Me. In My Father's house are many dwelling places; if it were not so, I would have told you; for I go to prepare a place for you. And if I go and prepare a place for you, I will come again and receive you to Myself; that where I am, there you may be also."

[352] *The Revelation of Christ to His Servants of the Things That Are, and Things That Shall Be* – F.W. Grant, Loizeaux Brothers, Bible Truth Depot, 63 Fourth Ave., New York, n.d., Part I, pp.22-23.

[353] *Tribulation Till Translation* - George L. Rose, Rose Publishing Company, 1943, p.246, quoting *God's Future Program* - Dr. J. Oswald Smith, pp.52-53.

[354] *God's Plan for the Future* - Lehman Strauss, Zondervan Publishing House, 1965, p.84.

Strauss contends that Jesus is using "the language of imminency." But in all honesty, how can these consoling words of Christ possibly be construed to mean that He will come unannounced, at any moment, before the onset of the Tribulation? Obviously they do not. First of all, there is no mention of the rapture or the Tribulation. Second, Christ does not give any indication whatsoever as to when He will come - only that He will. Further, **Strauss** himself seems only partially convinced by his own argument, when he concludes that "*the language of imminency*" only "*indicates* that there are no intervening events" prior to the rapture.

Consider **Leon Wood's** assertion that New Testament verses, which urge Christians to watch for the Second Coming of Christ, refer specifically to the imminent coming of Christ. **Wood** declares that, "Pre-tribulationists believe *these urgings require the second coming to be imminent.*"[355] **Wood** goes on to say that, "...the 'watching' passages *require an imminency* for the coming, for they clearly *imply* that there will be no warning signal for last-minute preparation."[356] Then, while discussing "evidences" for the pretribulation rapture, **Wood** refers specifically to Matthew 24:42-44, maintaining that, "...Jesus there *urges* the disciples to watch diligently for His coming...one may safely take it as an *implied* reference to the rapture."[357] Let's look carefully at the text in question. Matthew 24:42-44 states;

 "Therefore be on the alert, for you do not know which day your Lord is coming. But be sure of this, that if the head of the house had known at what time of the night the thief was coming, he would have been on the alert and would not have allowed his house to be broken into. For this reason, you be ready too; for the Son of Man is coming at an hour when you do not think *He will.*"

There are three important points that the reader should carefully consider.

First, there is the question of the validity of **Wood's** assertion that the "urgings" to "watch for" the coming of Christ, "require the second coming to be imminent." But, exactly why should these "urgings" to be alert and watchful for the Lord's return require imminency? **Wood** does not leave us wondering as to the answer to this question. He tells us that these urgings to be watchful for the Lord's return, "*imply* that there will be

[355] *Is the Rapture Next?* - Leon J. Wood, Zondervan Publishing House, 1956, p.29.
[356] *Is the Rapture Next?* - Leon J. Wood, Zondervan Publishing House, 1956, p.118.
[357] *The Bible and Future Events* - Leon J. Wood, Zondervan Publishing House, 1974, p.91.

no warning" and therefore we "may safely take it as an *implied* reference to the rapture." Note carefully that **Wood** does not demonstrate from the Biblical text that "urgings" to be alert and watchful for the return of Christ demand imminency (i.e., a secret, unannounced, any moment Coming of Christ). On the contrary, by his own words, he admits that these urgings to be watchful are "an *implied reference* to the rapture." The word "implied" denotes that which is inferentially and indirectly referred to, as opposed to that which is clearly and specifically stated.

Second, the "urgings" which **Wood** refers to in Matthew 24:42-44, occur toward the end of the Olivet Discourse (see also the parallel passages in Mark 13:33-37; Luke 21:34-36) and are plainly in the context of the Great Tribulation. It is significant that these "urgings" to watch for the Lord's return immediately follow the delineation of numerous prophetic events that will find fulfillment prior to and during the Tribulation period. Jesus clearly links His "urgings" to be alert and watchful for His return to the fulfillment of specific Tribulational events. For example, in Matthew 24, Jesus warns His followers that, many false Christs will arise (v.5), and that "nation shall rise against nation and kingdom against kingdom," and that "there will be famines and earthquakes" (v.7). The Lord goes on to say that, "there will be a great tribulation" unparalleled in the history of the world (v.21-22); that "false Christs and false prophets" will arise and will "show great signs and wonders, so as to mislead, if possible, even the elect" (v.24); that the "sun will be darkened, and the moon will not give its light, and the stars will fall from the sky and the powers of the heavens will be shaken" (v.29). Immediately after revealing these specific signs that will precede His glorious Coming, Jesus instructs His followers in Matthew 24:32-33;

"Now learn the parable from the fig tree: when its branch has already become tender, and puts forth its leaves, you know that summer is near; even so you too, when you see all these things, recognize that He is near, right at the door."

Thus, just as the budding of the fig tree announces the soon arrival of summer, the fulfillment of these prophetic events described by Christ, will announce that His Coming is near. In other words, it is the fulfillment of these specific prophetic events that will make it evident to those who are alert and watching, that the return of the Lord "is near, right at the door."

Third, the Dispensational doctrine of imminence is exactly backwards. Dispensationalists maintain that Christ's coming will be "sudden, unannounced and unexpected" for believers. But a careful consideration of the Biblical text reveals that the exact opposite is true. Believers who heed Christ's admonition to be alert and watchful will see the fulfillment of these prophetic signs and fully understand that the coming of Christ is near. However, mere professors and outright unbelievers will not recognize the significance of these prophetic events. Thus, the coming of Christ will come upon them suddenly, unexpectedly and without warning!

Look carefully at Matthew 24:48-51. Here the Lord makes it clear that it is *not* the believer who will be surprised by His coming, but the unbeliever! While describing the behavioral characteristics of the "evil slave," Christ declares that,

"...the Master of that slave will come on a day when he does **not expect** him and at an hour which he does **not know**" (v.50. Emphasis added.)

Consider Matthew 24:37-39, that clearly states that just as it was in the days of Noah, it is the unbeliever, *not* the believer who will be surprised by Christ's Second Coming. Here, in the immediate context of the *Parable of the Fig Tree*, Jesus declares;

"For the coming of the Son of Man will be just like the days of Noah. For as in those days which were before the flood they were eating and drinking, they were marrying and giving in marriage, until the day that Noah entered the ark, and they **did not understand** until the flood came and took them all away; so shall the coming of the Son of Man be." (Emphasis added).

Thus clearly, Jesus Christ will come suddenly and unexpectedly upon the unbelieving world, who because of their unbelief will fail to understand the significance of the prophetic signs revealed in Scripture. However, for those who believe and are alert and watching, these prophetic signs will clearly announce the soon coming of Christ and the approach of the end of the age. This fact is underscored in Luke 21:28. Immediately after describing the prophetic events that will precede His glorious Second Coming, Jesus told His disciples;

"But when these things begin to take place, straighten up and lift up your heads, because your redemption is drawing near."

The whole point of the Olivet Discourse of Matthew 24 (as well as the parallel accounts in Luke 21 and Mark 13) is to make the followers of Christ aware of the prophetic signs that will precede His glorious Second Coming. While the believer cannot know the exact day nor hour of Christ's return (Mt.24:36 cp. Mk.13:32-37) he can most certainly know that Christ's coming is near when he sees the unfolding of these prophetic events described by the Lord. Thus, the entire context of the Olivet Discourse resoundingly refutes the Dispensational teaching of a secret, signless, unannounced, unexpected, any moment coming of Jesus Christ for believers![358]

There is one more important point that needs to be addressed with respect to the doctrine of imminence. Dispensationalists frequently speak of this doctrine as an established Biblical fact. For example, consider **John Walvoord's** assertion that, "The Rapture, as described in Scripture, is an imminent event and therefore will precede the Tribulation."[359] **Walvoord** further maintains that, "The *fact* that the rapture is presented as an *imminent event* is a major argument for distinguishing the rapture from the second coming of Christ to the earth."[360] Thus, **Walvoord** maintains that one of the primary reasons for separating the rapture from the post-tribulational Coming of Christ is the *"fact"* that the rapture is presented as *"an imminent event."* But as we have seen, the Dispensational doctrine of a secret, signless, unannounced, any moment coming of Christ is *not* an established Biblical "fact" as **Walvoord** alleges. That Jesus Christ is coming again *after* the Tribulation is an established Biblical fact that is based upon the clear, straightforward declarations of Scripture. However, the Dispensational assertion that Jesus Christ is also coming secretly and unannounced *before* the Tribulation is based upon nothing more than speculation and conjecture. ***There is not one Biblical text that states Jesus Christ is coming <u>before</u> the Tribulation - nor is there one Biblical text that <u>describes</u> a pretribulational rapture of the Church!*** The entire notion rests upon nothing more than subjective assumptions and inferences. Again, the pretribulation rapture theory is *not* supported by what the Scriptures are plainly saying, but by what Dispensationalists *imagine* the Scriptures are *implying*! Sound doctrine must be built upon the clear, authoritative statements of Scripture and not unsupported assumptions and highly imaginative speculations! Thus, the unsubstantiated

---

[358] Likewise, compare the testimony of Paul in 1Thessalonians 5:1-6, where he tells the Thessalonian believers, "...But you brethren are not in darkness, that the day should overtake you as a thief...so then let us not sleep as others do, but let us be alert and sober." (Emphasis added).

[359] *Major Bible Prophecies* - John F. Walvoord, Zondervan Publishing House, 1994, p.337.

[360] *The Blessed Hope and the Tribulation* - John F. Walvoord, Zondervan Publishing House, 1976, p.163.

Dispensational doctrine of "imminence" provides no legitimate reason for separating the rapture of the Church from the post-tribulational Coming of the Lord Jesus Christ.

Chapter Five
The Theological Contradictions
Created by the
Pretribulation Rapture Teaching

Outline of Chapter Five:
I. The Practice of Doubling Key Bible Doctrines.
II. Two Second Comings of Jesus Christ.
III. Two Gospels.
IV. Two First Resurrections.
V. Two Days of the Lord.

Chapter Five, Part I
The Practice of Doubling Key Bible Doctrines.

The *pretribulation rapture doctrine* is the be-all and end-all of Dispensational theology. The entire theological system revolves around it and is designed to support it. Dispensationalism has one singular objective – protect and defend the concept of the pretribulation rapture doctrine at all costs and by any means! The Dispensational system necessarily relies heavily upon the use of analogy, inference, and assumption. This approach has resulted in an extremely complex and convoluted interpretative system. Very few Christians fully understand the interpretative process that Dispensational scholars use to advance their argument for the pretribulation rapture. While many evangelical Christians readily accept the premise of a pretribulational rapture, most do not fully understand the interpretative principles that Dispensational scholars use to advance this doctrine.

For the sake of illustration, the interpretative methods that support the pretribulation rapture doctrine can be viewed as a great cathedral where every individual component of the structure – its foundation, walls and pillars are all designed to uphold the ornate crowning dome. Likewise, the pretribulational rapture doctrine – the capstone of Dispensationalism, is supported by an elaborate interpretive system that is specifically designed to protect and advance the concept of the pretribulational rapture of the

Church. Just like a great cathedral, Dispensationalism has its foundation, walls and pillars that are explicitly designed to support the all-important crowning dome of the pretribulation rapture (see chart on page 99)!

In their support of the pretribulation rapture doctrine, Dispensationalists employ *two essential interpretative principles - inference* and *dispensationalizing* the New Testament Scriptures. They also make one *critical assumption* - imminence. In Chapter 3, it was explained that the use of *inference* allows Dispensationalists to *assume* whatever facts are necessary to defend the doctrine of the pretribulation rapture. While the practice of *dispensationalizing* the New Testament Scriptures permits Dispensationalists to apply all New Testament passages that contradict the premise of a pretribulation rapture to a future Jewish remnant instead of the Church. And in Chapter Four, it was demonstrated that the *assumption of imminence* permits Dispensationalists to promote the rapture as a secret, signless, any moment event in spite of the fact that there is not one New Testament text that actually mentions or describes a pretribulational Coming of Jesus Christ.

In addition to these three highly questionable interpretative methods (i.e., inference, dispensationalizing and imminence) Dispensationalists have found it necessary to *double* numerous Bible doctrines. For example, in their defense of the pretribulation rapture doctrine, Dispensationalists have created different categories of redeemed people by *dividing* the people of God into *two* distinct and separate groups - one "Jewish" and the other "Christian." They have *divided* the New Testament Scriptures into *two* different portions - one that applies only to "Israel" and the "Jews" and the other which applies solely to the "Church" and "Christians." They maintain that there are *two New Covenants* - one for the Church and one for a future Jewish remnant. They assert that there are *two elections* - one for Israel and one for the Church. They maintain that God is pursuing *two different programs and purposes* - one earthly (for Israel) and one heavenly (for the Church). They contend that there are *two different kingdoms* - the kingdom of heaven (which is earthly) and the kingdom of God (which is universal). They claim that the phrase, "the kingdom of heaven" has *two meanings* - it can refer to either the earthly theocratic kingdom or apostate Christendom. And they insist that Jesus revealed *"two distinct lines of truth"* - one as Israel's Messiah and the other as the

Savior of the world.[361] Dispensationalists further maintain that the three principal New Testament words used to describe the Second Advent of Jesus Christ have a *double meaning* and therefore refer to *both* a pretribulational and post-tribulational Coming, Appearing and Revelation.[362]

The use of this *doubling methodology* is the principal method by which Dispensationalists resolve textual problems created by the pretribulation rapture doctrine. It is important to understand that Dispensationalists are able to advance the concept of a pretribulational rapture of the Church only *after* they have *doubled* numerous Bible doctrines that would otherwise flatly contradict their claim. It is this *doubling methodology* that provides the primary means of support for the Dispensational teaching that Jesus Christ will return before the onset of the Tribulation. Without the use of this *doubling methodology* it would be impossible for Dispensationalists to defend the concept of a pretribulational Coming and rapture. However, the unintended consequence of *doubling* key Biblical doctrines has created an extremely intricate and complex theological system that confuses and confounds the revealed order of end-time events. Even Dispensationalists recognize the overly complex and elaborate nature of their theological system. For example, while discussing the differences of opinions that exist between fellow Dispensationalists regarding end-time terminology, **John Walvoord** observes that, "Only the premillennialist *[note, that Walvoord uses the term "premillennialist" here as if it were synonymous with "dispensationalist"]* is in the position of attempting to establish a *complicated sequence of events* in which too often both the theologue and the theologian become *lost in the detail.*"[363]

This strange interpretative approach to the Scriptures has also created some very serious theological inconsistencies and contradictions. Four of the more glaring incongruities are the Dispensational claims of "*two*" Second Comings of Jesus Christ, "*two*" different and distinct Gospels, "*two*" first resurrections of the righteous, and "*two*" Days of the Lord. However, the concept of "two" Second Comings, "two" Gospels, "two" first

---

[361] See Chafer's *Systematic Theology*, vol.4, pp. 31; 49; 82-86; 98-99; 223-224; 320; and E. Schuyler English - *Matthew*, p.91.

[362] These words are *parousia* (Coming), *epiphaneia* (Appearing) and *apokalupsis* (Revelation) and are discussed in Chapter Five, Part II.

[363] *New Testament Words for the Lord's Coming* - John F. Walvoord, *Bibliotheca Sacra*, 101:284, July 1944.

resurrections of the righteous and "two" Days of the Lord are *not* objectively taught in the Scriptures. Dispensationalists have necessarily developed these teachings via their *doubling methodology* to support, promote and defend their notion of a secret, signless, any moment pretribulational rapture of the Church. Without *doubling* these four key Bible doctrines the concept of a pretribulation rapture would be entirely indefensible.

Before engaging in a detailed analysis of these four essential Dispensational doctrines, consider the following brief introductory overview.

First, Dispensationalists maintain that there are *two Second Comings* of Jesus Christ - the first is secret, signless and unannounced, *before* the Tribulation, and the second is visible, public and glorious, *after* the Tribulation.

Second, Dispensationalists claim that there are *two distinct and different Gospels* revealed in the New Testament - one for the Church (i.e., the Gospel of Grace), which was preached by Paul in the Epistles, and one for the Jews (i.e., the Gospel of the Kingdom), which was originally preached by John the Baptist, Jesus and the Apostles, and will yet again be preached by a future Jewish remnant during the Tribulation period.

Third, Dispensationalists assert that there are *two first resurrections* of the saints. The first occurs *before* the Tribulation at the time of the secret rapture when all Church saints will be raised. The second occurs some seven years later, *after* the Tribulation when the Old Testament saints and the Tribulation saints will be raised.

Fourth, Dispensationalists maintain that there are *two Days of the Lord* - one *broad* (encompassing the entire Tribulation period and Millennium) and the other *narrow* (confined to one day at the very end of the Tribulation period when Christ returns in judgment).

The
Pretribulation Rapture
Doctrine

"Two" People of God [5]

"Two" Gospels [6]

"Two" Second Comings [7]

"Two" First Resurrections [8]

"Two" Days of the LORD [9]

The Indispensable Pillars of Support [4]

The Vital Methodology [3]
Doubling Key Bible Doctrines

The Critical Assumption [2]
Imminence

The Two Essential Interpretative Principles [1]
Inference and the Dispensationalizing of the NT Scriptures

Chart Notes

Note 1: Inference: The use of *inference* allows Dispensationalists to *assume* what they cannot prove. Inference provides the principal means by which Dispensationalists promote the concept of the pretribulation rapture. The argument for the pretribulational rapture is based solely upon speculation, assumption and analogy - not the plain, ordinary, literal statements of Scripture. **Dispensationalizing of the NT Scriptures:** Dispensationalists maintain that large portions of the New Testament apply solely to a future Jewish remnant and not to the Church. It is the job of the Bible interpreter to "rightly divide" the Word by determining which sections of the New Testament apply to Israel and which sections apply to the Church.

Note 2: There is no verse in the New Testament that describes a pretribulational Coming or rapture. Dispensationalists have therefore invented the doctrine of *imminence* which states that the Coming of Christ to rapture the Church will be a secret, signless, unannounced, any moment event without any prophetic indication as to when it will occur.

Note 3: The concept of a pretribulational rapture is not legitimately derived from the Biblical text. Rather, it is forced upon the text through the use of *inference*, *dispensationalizing* and the assumption of *imminence*. This has caused numerous textual contradictions. In an attempt to resolve these contradictions Dispensationalists have *doubled* numerous Bible doctrines.

Note 4: The *doubling* of key Bible doctrines is the only means by which Dispensationalists have been able to preserve the concept of the pretribulation rapture. It is this *doubling methodology* that provides the ultimate support for the pretribulation rapture theory. Remove any one of these five pillars of support, and the possibility of a pretribulational rapture immediately disappears.

Note 5: Dispensationalists divide the people of God into *two* separate groups. Israel, comprised of both Old Testament saints and a fictitious future Jewish remnant, and Christians or Church saints, comprised of individuals saved between Pentecost and the start of the Tribulation.

Note 6: Dispensationalists maintain that there are *two* distinct and different Gospels - the **Gospel of the Kingdom** preached by John the Baptist, Jesus and the disciples, and the **Gospel of Grace** preached by Paul and Christian ministers.

Note 7: Dispensationalists teach that there are *two* Second Comings of Jesus Christ. The "first" Second Coming occurs **before** the Tribulation. The "second" Second Coming occurs **after** the Tribulation.

Note 8: Dispensationalists assert that there are *two* first resurrections. The "first" first resurrection occurs at the "first" Second Coming **before** the Tribulation. The "second" first resurrection occurs at the "second" Second Coming **after** the Tribulation.

Note 9: Dispensationalists contend that there are *two* Days of the Lord. The **Broad Day of the LORD** covers an extended period of time that begins with the rapture of the Church at the "first" Second Coming (before the Tribulation) and includes the Millennium. The **Narrow Day of the LORD** covers a very limited period of time that begins with the "second" Second Coming at the very end of the Tribulation and ends shortly thereafter.

Chapter Five, Part II
"Two" Second Comings of Jesus Christ

Outline of Chapter Five, Part II:
1. Terminology of the Second Coming.
2. Contrasting Details.
3. Dividing the Second Coming.
4. The Promise of a Pretribulation Rapture.
5. The Hope of the Church.
6. Dispensational Proof for the Pretribulation Rapture.
   6a. First Thessalonians 4:13-18.
   6b. The Connection Between Matthew 24 and 1&2 Thessalonians.

1. Terminology of the Second Coming.

Any discussion about the Second Coming of the Lord Jesus Christ ultimately revolves around the meaning of three New Testament words. *Parousia*, which refers to the Coming of Christ and thus His physical presence.[364] *Epiphaneia*, which refers to the manifestation or appearance of Christ.[365] *Apokalupsis*, which refers to the revealing or revelation of Christ.[366] Generally speaking, post-tribulational premillennialism maintains that these three New Testament words - *parousia* (Coming), *epiphaneia* (Appearing), and *apokalupsis* (Revelation), describe the one and only Second Coming of Jesus Christ *after* the Tribulation.

However, early Dispensationalists taught that the word *parousia* referred specifically to the secret, pretribulational **Coming** of Christ to rapture the Church *before* the beginning of the Tribulation, whereas the words *epiphaneia* and *apokalupsis* referred to the post-tribulational **Appearing** of Christ to judge the world and establish His millennial kingdom *after* the Tribulation. John Darby originated this teaching. For example,

---

[364] "παρουσία [*parousia*]…being present, presence…a coming, arrival, advent…" *A Manual Greek Lexicon of the New Testament* – G. Abbott-Smith, Charles Scribner's Sons, 1953, p.347.
[365] "ἐπιφανεία [*epiphaneia*]… a manifestation, appearance…" *A Manual Greek Lexicon of the New Testament* – G. Abbott-Smith, Charles Scribner's Sons, 1953, p.176.
[366] "ἀποκάλυψις [*apokalupsis*]…an uncovering, laying bare…Metaph., a revealing, revelation: a disclosure of divine truth, or a manifestation from God…" *A Manual Greek Lexicon of the New Testament* – G. Abbott-Smith, Charles Scribner's Sons, 1953, p.50.

Darby declared that, "…our hope of Christ's **Coming** [*parousia*] for us is not properly His **Appearing** [*epiphaneia*]…His **Coming** [*parousia*]…is the rapture of the saints…at their rapture He has not **Appeared** [*epiphaneia*] yet…at His **Appearing** [*epiphaneia*] He will execute judgment against the ungodly"[367] Early Dispensationalists unanimously embraced Darby's teaching that the word *parousia* applied specifically to the rapture of the saints **before** the Tribulation, whereas, the word *epiphaneia* referred to the judgment of the world **after** the Tribulation.

However, later Dispensationalists ultimately realized that Darby's restriction of the word *parousia* to a pretribulational Coming was indefensible, since the word is clearly used to refer to the *post*-tribulational Coming of Christ (see Mt.24:27; 2Thess.2:8). Thus, to save the doctrine of the pretribulation rapture, Dispensationalists found it necessary to modify Darby's original definitions. Dallas Seminary spearheaded the effort. While retaining Darby's major premise of "two" Comings - one *for* and one *with* the saints - they simply modified Darby's original definitions, declaring that the words *parousia*, *epiphaneia* and *apokalupsis* were used interchangeably in the New Testament to describe *both* the secret, pretribulational Coming as well as the visible, glorious post-tribulational Coming. For example, **Lewis Sperry Chafer**, founder of Dallas Seminary, taught that, "*Parousia* is a Greek word for the 'coming' of someone or 'being present by reason of coming.' It is not restricted to either form of Christ's appearing, but is used *both* of His return *for* and *with* His saints."[368] Likewise, **John Walvoord**, who succeeded **Chafer** as president of Dallas Seminary, affirmed that these three Greek words - *parousia*, *epiphaneia*, and *apokalupsis*, "…are not in themselves technical words…"[369] **Walvoord** further maintained that "…all three terms are used in a *general* and *not a technical sense* and they are descriptive of *both* the *rapture and the glorious return* of Christ to the earth…"[370] Modern Dispensationalist have uniformly followed Chafer and Walvoord in maintaining that all three of these words are used interchangeably in the New Testament to describe *both* the pretribulation rapture and the glorious return of Christ after the Tribulation.

---

[367] *The Collected Writings of J.N. Darby* – Edited by William Kelly, Prophetic No.4, Vol.11, Stow Hill Bible and Tract Depot, n.d., pp.115,154,155.
[368] *Systematic Theology* - Lewis Sperry Chafer, Kregel Publications, 1993, Vol.7, p.248.
[369] *The Blessed Hope And The Tribulation* - John F. Walvoord, Zondervan Publishing House, 1976, p.49.
[370] *New Testament Words for the Lord's Coming* – John F. Walvoord, *Bibliotheca Sacra*, 101:284-89, July, 1944, p.284.

Let us carefully consider the Dispensational claim that these three words have a *dual meaning*. With respect to the word *parousia* (Coming) **Walvoord** asserts, "That it is used frequently of the rapture of the church is clear in the following references (1Cor.15:23; 1Thess.2:19; 4:15; 5:23; 2Thess.2:1(?): James 5:7-8; 2Pet.3:4(?); 1John 2:28). While it is not always evident in the context and room must be left for difference of opinion, some references are specific."[371] Despite **Walvoord's** claim of specific references to a pretribulational Coming of Christ, a careful and impartial reading of these texts cited by Walvoord will reveal no indication whatsoever of a pretribulational *parousia* of Christ. In fact, none of these texts give any indication as to whether the coming of Christ is pre or post-tribulational. Rather, they are all *time neutral*. However, conversely, Matthew 24:27-31 and 2Thessalonians 2:8 clearly and unmistakably describe the *parousia* of Jesus Christ as a post-tribulational event!

With respect to the word *epiphaneia* (Appearing), **Walvoord** maintains that, "...two instances are found where it refers to the rapture of the church...it would seem sound exegesis to classify 1Timothy 6:14 and 2Timothy 4:8 as referring to the rapture."[372] Once again, a careful reading of these two passages reveals no indication or statement of a secret, imminent pretribulational Appearing of Christ. Interestingly, **Walvoord** also observes that, "...two instances *seem* to refer to the second coming of Christ... In 2Timothy 4:1 and Titus 2:13, however, there *seems* to be reference to His second coming."[373] It is amazing that Walvoord sees a secret, pretribulational rapture in 1Timothy 6:14 and 2Timothy 4:8 where there is none, and yet only *seems* to recognize the visible, glorious, post-tribulational Appearing that is clearly described in 2Timothy 4:1 which states, "...the Lord Jesus Christ, who shall judge the quick and the dead at His **appearing** and His kingdom" (KJV), and Titus 2:13 which speaks of "...the **appearing of the glory** of our great God and Savior, Christ Jesus."[374]

---

[371] *New Testament Words for the Lord's Coming* - John Walvoord, *Bibliotheca Sacra*, 101:284-89, July, 1944, p.285.
[372] *New Testament Words for the Lord's Coming* - John Walvoord, *Bibliotheca Sacra*, 101:284-89, July, 1944, p.288.
[373] *New Testament Words for the Lord's Coming* - John Walvoord, *Bibliotheca Sacra*, 101:284-89, July, 1944, p.288. Note that Walvoord uses the term "Second Coming" to refer to Christ's post-tribulational Coming. For example, **Walvoord** explains that, "...the term *rapture* or *translation* is used for the coming of Christ for His church, while the term *second coming* is uniformly used as a reference to His coming to the earth to establish His millennial kingdom, an event that all consider posttribulational." *The Rapture Question* - John F. Walvoord, Zondervan Publishing House, 1979, p.269.
[374] This is clearly a post-tribulation reference due to the fact that the judgment of the world occurs when Jesus appears in "glory." See Mt.16:27; 24:30;.25:31.

Walvoord further claims that the word *apokalupsis* (Revelation) is used to describe the pretribulational Revelation of Christ. He maintains that the word *apokalupsis*, "...is clearly used in reference to the coming of Christ in the air for His church (1Cor.1:7; Col.3:4; 1Pet.1:7,13) ... His revelation to the church will precede His revelation to the world as a whole."[375] Again, all of these verses describe various aspects of the Revelation of Christ. However, a careful reading of these texts will again confirm the fact that they are *time neutral* and do *not* describe a pretribulational Revelation of Jesus Christ. However, Luke 17:29-30; 2Thessalonians 1:7 and 1Peter 4:13 clearly and unmistakably describe the visible, glorious, post-tribulational Revelation of Jesus Christ.

There is one more important point that needs to be made with respect to **Walvoord's** argument that the words *parousia, epiphaneia* and *apokalupsis* are general terms, and as such are used in Scripture to refer to both a pretribulational and post-tribulational Coming of Christ. While commenting on the supposed dual nature of the word *apokalupsis*, **Walvoord** states that;

"The world in the flesh has never seen Christ in His glory. The church will 'see Him as He is' (1John 3:2) at the time of their gathering up from the earth at the rapture. *The world will see Him in His glory when He returns in power* with His saints and angels to rule over the earth."[376]

Walvoord, like all Dispensationalists, accepts the concept of a *secret*, pretribulational rapture. Note carefully that **Walvoord** clearly states that Christ will be revealed to the Church at the time of the rapture. However, the world will *not* see Christ until He returns in glory *after* the Tribulation to rule over the world. It is important to understand that the viability of the pretribulation rapture teaching is entirely dependent upon the premise of a "secret rapture." Dispensationalists teach that Jesus Christ is coming to rapture the Church seven years before He comes to judge the world and establish His Millennial reign upon the earth. *However, the New Testament Scriptures do **not** describe two visible Comings of Jesus Christ at the end of this age. The only visible appearing described in Scripture is clearly and undeniably post-tribulational.* Thus, if there is a pretribulational rapture, it necessarily must be "unseen" or "secret." But, many modern Dispensationalists are uncomfortable with the necessity of a "secret rapture"

---

[375] *New Testament Words for the Lord's Coming* - John Walvoord, *Bibliotheca Sacra*, 101:284-89, July, 1944, p.287.
[376] *New Testament Words for the Lord's Coming* - John F. Walvoord, *Bibliotheca Sacra*, 101:284-89, July, 1944, p.287.

and attempt to either ignore it altogether or claim that it is not an important issue. The problem for Dispensationalists is that if the pretribulational rapture is "visible" then they are at once placed in the untenable position of teaching that the unsaved world will be eye-witnesses to the pretribulational Coming of Christ, the resurrection of the righteous dead and the "catching up" of the saints in the air to be with Christ. There are no other options - either the pretribulational Coming of Christ is "secret" and unobserved by the world, or "visible" and observed by the unbelieving world. Early Dispensationalists chose the first option - secrecy. Modern Dispensationalists for the most part, attempt to conveniently ignore the issue, while at the same time obliquely accepting the premise of secrecy as demonstrated by Walvoord's statement above.

However, the very words used in Scripture that describe the Coming of Christ and the rapture of the Church clearly convey the idea of "visibility" and not "secrecy." For example, the word *parousia* refers to the personal presence of Christ by virtue of His Coming. If someone is "present" they are "visible." *Epiphaneia* refers to the brilliant manifestation of the glory of Christ when He appears. When someone "appears" they are "visible." *Apokalupsis* refers to the unveiling, or revelation of the glorious person of Christ. When someone is "revealed," they are made "visible." Therefore, the Divine glory, majesty and radiant splendor of the risen, glorified Christ will be *Revealed* when He *Appears* at His *Coming*. Thus, the very words used by Scripture to describe the Second Advent of Jesus Christ testify against the concept of an unobserved and secret Coming. The claim made by Dispensationalists that these three words are used interchangeably in Scripture to describe "two" different Comings of Christ - one secret and the other visible is flatly contradicted by the literal meaning of the words themselves!

Furthermore, Dispensationalists have also failed to provide any legitimate linguistic or exegetical basis to justify their contention that the words *parousia, epiphaneia* and *apokalupsis* have a *double meaning*. An examination of the Biblical texts in which these words appear positively refutes the Dispensational claim that these words are used interchangeably to describe two different Comings of Christ. The indisputable fact is that there is not one New Testament text where these words are used to describe a

pretribulational Coming, Appearing or Revelation of Jesus Christ – not one! [377]
Therefore, we must ask, "In the absence of any Biblical description of a pretribulational
Coming, Appearing or Revelation, how can Dispensationalists possibly know that Jesus
Christ is returning before the Tribulation?"

The only reason that Dispensationalists argue that the words *parousia, epiphaneia* and
apokalupsis have a **double meaning** is because the viability of the pretribulation rapture
doctrine depends upon it! These three words have been illegitimately redefined by
Dispensationalists for the singular purpose of advancing the concept of the
pretribulation rapture. Mark it carefully, the entire Dispensational argument for a
pretribulation rapture hinges upon the redefinition of these three key words. Therefore,
John Walvoord carefully instructs his fellow Dispensationalists on the proper meaning
and use of the words *parousia, epiphaneia* and *apokalupsis* by insisting that, "...these
are **general** rather than **specific** terms and that all three of them are used of the coming
of Christ at the translation [i.e., the rapture] and may also refer to His coming at the
Second Advent."[378] However, the literal meaning of these words coupled with their
linguistic use in Scripture resoundingly refutes Walvoord's contention.

2. Contrasting Details.

Dispensationalists maintain that the words *parousia, epiphaneia* and *apokalupsis* are
used in a "general" and not a "specific or technical" manner and therefore **cannot** be
used to distinguish or differentiate between the pretribulational rapture and the post-
tribulational Coming of Christ.[379] For example, **Charles Feinberg**, while referring
specifically to the words *parousia, epiphaneia* and *apokalupsis* states that,

---

[377] The reader is encouraged to closely examine the usage of these words with respect to the Second Advent of Jesus
Christ. *Parousia* (Coming) occurs in Mt.24:3,27,37,39; 1Cor.15:23; 1Th.2:19, 3:13, 4:15, 5:23; 2Th.2:1,8; Jas.5:7,8;
2Pt.3:4; 1Jn.2:28. *Epiphaneia* (Appearing) occurs in 2Th.2:8; 1Tim.6:14; 2Tim.4:1,8; Tit.2:13. *Apokalupsis* (Revelation)
occurs in 1Cor.1:7; 2Th.1:7; 1Pt.1:7,13, 4:13; and *Apokalupto* (Revealed) Lk.17:30.
[378] *The Rapture Question* – John F. Walvoord, Zondervan Publishing House, 1979, p.172.
[379] In point of fact, the words *parousia, epiphaneia* and *apokalupsis* are technical words that refer specifically to the post-
tribulational Coming of Christ at the end of this age. Consider the comments of Charles R. Erdman. While commenting on
the "literal, visible, bodily return of Christ," Erdman states that, "...the terms used to describe the return of our Lord are
definite and distinct. For instance, the word 'coming,' ...is the Greek word, '*parousia*,' and invariably means, in relation to
Christ, his future, glorious, visible appearing. From the earliest centuries this appearing, therefore, has been designated by
Christian writers as 'the second coming of Christ' to distinguish it from the 'first coming,' which took place in the
incarnation and earthly career of our Lord. Therefore, whenever in the New Testament we read of the '**coming** (*parousia*)

"We conclude, then, that from a study of the Greek words themselves the distinction between the coming of Christ *for* His saints and *with* His saints is *not* to be gleaned."[380]

This is both an amazing and a revealing statement. It apparently has never occurred to Dispensationalists that the reason why these words do *not* denote a "distinction between the coming of Christ *for* His saints and *with* His saints" is because there is no distinction to be made. The fact that these three words are never used in Scripture to describe a pretribulational Coming of Christ should give every Dispensationalist serious pause. Furthermore, if we cannot determine the dual nature of Christ's return based on the words used to describe that return, then exactly how are we to make a distinction between the pretribulational rapture and the post-tribulational Second Coming?

Feinberg explains that, "The differentiation between the Rapture and the Revelation is made clear by a *comparative study* of the Scriptures on the coming of the Lord Jesus Christ."[381]

Thus, because the words used to describe Christ's Second Coming do *not* convey the *dual nature* of that Coming, we are told that we must derive that distinction by "a comparative study of the Scriptures." What Feinberg means is that the specific details and circumstances described in the various passages dealing with the Second Coming must be subjectively evaluated so that a determination can be made as to which Coming the passage is referring to. **John Walvoord** explains this process of "*comparative study*" when he stresses that,

"...most pretribulationists distinguish the rapture from the coming of Christ to set up His kingdom because the two events are presented with such *contrasting details* in the New Testament[382]...no two events could be more dissimilar than the rapture of the church and the second coming of Christ to set up His kingdom...They involve the same person, Jesus Christ, but the *details* attributed to the two events in Scripture are entirely different."[383]

---

of Christ,' we can be absolutely certain that the reference is to his glorious return. Much the same might be said of the word **'appearing,'** once used of the first advent (2Tim.1:10), but elsewhere of the glorious return from heaven (1Tim.6:14; 2Tim.4:1,8; Titus 2:13; 2Thess.2:8), or of the word **'revelation,'** when employed in relation to Christ (2Thess.1:7 etc.), or the phrases 'The day of the Lord,' 'That day,' or 'The day of Jesus Christ'... all of them point to the return of our Lord." *The Return of Christ* - Charles R. Erdman, George H. Doran Company, 1922, pp.31-32.

[380] *Premillennialism or Amillennialism?* - Charles L. Feinberg, Zondervan Publishing House, 1936, p.207.
[381] *Premillennialism or Amillennialism?* - Charles L. Feinberg, Zondervan Publishing House, 1936, p.207.
[382] *The Blessed Hope And The Tribulation* - John F. Walvoord, Zondervan Publishing House, 1976, p.64.
[383] *The Blessed Hope and the Tribulation* - John F. Walvoord, Zondervan Publishing House, 1976, p.156.

Thus, it is the "*comparative study*" of the "*contrasting details*" described in the text, which Dispensationalists use to determine which Coming of Christ is in view. For instance, as described above, **Walvoord** claims that 1Timothy 6:14 and 2Timothy 4:8 both refer to a pretribulational appearing of Christ to rapture the Church. **Walvoord** reasons that, "Both references connect the coming of Christ with specific fulfillment of His purpose for the church and are therefore used in relation to the rapture."[384] Let's look at these two passages;

1Tim.6:14 - "that you keep the commandment without stain or reproach until the **appearing** [*epiphaneia*] of our Lord Jesus Christ." (Emphasis added).

2Tim.4:8 – "in the future there is laid up for me the crown of righteousness, which the Lord, the righteous Judge, will award to me on that day; and not only to me, but to all who have loved His **appearing** [*epiphaneia*]. (Emphasis added).

Both of these passages clearly refer to the *Appearing* of Jesus Christ. However, neither of these passages specifically mentions a pretribulational rapture or pretribulational appearing of Christ. Yet, based solely upon the perceived "*contrasting details*," **Walvoord** confidently asserts that both of these passages refer to a pretribulational rapture because they "connect the coming of Christ with specific fulfillment of His purpose for the church." But exactly how does the fulfillment of Christ's purpose for the Church establish the fact of a secret pretribulational *Appearing* and rapture? In point of fact it does not. The entire argument is designed to create a pretribulational *Appearing* where none objectively exists.

Dispensationalists further assert that if a Biblical text refers to the Coming of Christ but fails to mention other tribulational events, it necessarily describes a pretribulational Coming. For example, **Walvoord** argues that if, within a text, there are "…no fundamental changes in the world situation…" or "…no indication of worldwide judgment..." or "…no indication that a millennial reign of Christ immediately follows" or "…no judgment upon the nation of Israel…" or "...no judgment of the nations..."[385] then the passage describes a pretribulational Coming of Christ to rapture the Church.

---

[384] *New Testament Words for the Lord's Coming* - John F. Walvoord, *Bibliotheca Sacra*, 101:284-89, July, 1944, p.288.
[385] *The Blessed Hope and the Tribulation* - John F. Walvoord, Zondervan Publishing House, 1976, pp.154-155.

These are the types of **"contrasting details"** that Dispensationalists say "prove" that the "rapture passages" teach a pretribulational Coming of Christ.[386]

However, just because the so-called "rapture passages"[387] do not mention other tribulational events, does **not** prove that the rapture is pretribulational. This is an argument from silence, and is therefore no argument at all. The fact is that no one Scripture contains all revealed truth on any given subject. It is only when all the pertinent passages on a given subject are brought together that the whole counsel of God can be discerned. For example, when Paul told the Philippian jailer to, "Believe in the Lord Jesus and you shall be saved, you and your household" (Acts 16:31), there is no mention of "the Gospel," which is "the power of God for salvation" (Ro.1:16) or of confessing "Jesus as Lord" or of believing that "God raised Him from the dead" (Ro.10:9; 1Cor.15:3-5) or of "repentance" (Acts 2:38; 26:20). Obviously Acts 16:31 is abbreviated and does not contain everything that the Bible has to say about salvation. Thus, in exactly the same way, just because the so-called "rapture passages" do not refer to other end-time events in no way justifies the conclusion that they are pretribulational. This line of reasoning is nothing more than subjective speculation. It is an attempt to determine what the Scriptures mean by what they **don't** say! On the contrary, sound Biblical exegesis determines what the Scriptures mean by what they **do** say!

It is highly significant that these "contrasting details" within the "rapture passages" represent the "most important" arguments that Dispensationalists can offer in support of the pretribulation rapture! Consider the statement of **John Walvoord,** who acknowledges that;

"Probably the ***most important reason*** for pretribulationism is the evident ***contrast between the details*** revealed concerning the rapture and the description given of the second coming of Christ to establish

---

[386] Walvoord presents what could fairly be described as a "contextual argument" which accurately represents modern Dispensational thinking. Consider the following example: "The term *parousia* is used of Christ's Second Coming as a whole, and of individual events (e.g., the Rapture); *only context* can determine which is being discussed." *AMG's Annotated Strong's Dictionaries* - James Strong, edited by Warren Baker and Spiros Zodhiates, AMG Publishers, 2009, p.848.

[387] The primary "rapture passages" referred to by Dispensationalists are Jn.14:1-3; 1Cor.15:50-53; 1Thess.4:13-18; 1Thess.5:1-6; 2Thess.2:1-3.

His kingdom...these *contrasts* describe these two events as different in purpose, character, and result."[388]

Mark it well, according to **Walvoord**, "the most important reason for pretribulationism" is *not* that the Scriptures plainly and specifically describe a pretribulational Coming of Christ - but the subjective observation that there is a "contrast between the details" or stated another way; that there are no other Tribulational events described in these rapture passages. But, the fact that specific Tribulational events are not mentioned in every passage that refers to the Coming of Christ is neither peculiar nor surprising. The obvious intended purpose of the "rapture passages" is to inform, encourage and comfort Christians by revealing God's ultimate deliverance of His people, and not to delineate the entire sequence of end-time events, which are clearly revealed elsewhere. For instance, in 1Thessalonians 4:13-18, Paul closes his discussion of the rapture with the encouraging admonition, "Therefore comfort one another with these words" (v.18). And again, in 1Corinthians 15:51-57, Paul closes his discussion of the rapture by triumphantly declaring, "O death, where is your victory? O death, where is your sting? ...but thanks be to God who gives us the victory through our Lord Jesus Christ" (v.57). Again, Paul's intent is not to provide a detailed chronology of end-time events, but rather to encourage believers by declaring God's ultimate victory over evil and the final deliverance of His people!

3. Dividing the Second Coming.

As previously mentioned, Dispensationalists divide the "Second Coming" of Jesus Christ into "two" distinct and separate Comings - one before the Tribulation to rapture the Church and one some seven years later to judge the world. They commonly refer to these "two comings" as different *"stages," "phases"* or *"movements."* Often these *"stages," "phases"* or *"movements"* are referred to as Christ's coming *"for"* His saints (before the Tribulation) as opposed to Christ's coming *"with"* His saints (after the Tribulation).

John Darby popularized this distinction between the "*Coming*" of Christ to rapture the Church *before* the Tribulation and the "*Appearing*" of Christ to judge the world *after*

---

[388] *The Blessed Hope and the Tribulation* - John F. Walvoord, Zondervan Publishing House, 1976, p.161.

the Tribulation. **Darby** declared that, "Those who believe in the rapture of the church before the appearing of Christ hold that the church has a special and peculiar character and connection with Christ..."[389] **Darby** taught that, "...this coming to receive us to Himself is not His appearing...our hope of Christ's coming for us is not properly His appearing...His coming...is the rapture of the saints, preceding their and Christ's appearing...So that at the rapture He has not appeared yet...At the appearing comes the judgment of this world...He will take us up to be with Himself at His coming...The coming of Christ has a *double* aspect. As regards...the world...Scripture speaks of His appearing...As regards the body of Christ, it speaks of His coming, and our taking up to Himself."[390]

Thus, **Darby** divided the Second Coming into two separate and distinct events. He maintained that the *Coming* (i.e., the *parousia*) of Christ referred to the secret rapture of the Church *before* the Tribulation, whereas the *Appearing* (i.e., the *epiphaneia;* as well as the *apokalupsis* or the Revelation) of Christ referred to the visible Coming of Christ to judge the world *after* the Tribulation.[391] Darby's followers uniformly adopted this teaching. For example, **William Trotter,** while referring to the pretribulational rapture, declares that, "This is the *first stage* in His return to earth."[392] **William Blackstone** likewise divided the Second Coming into "two" separate events, declaring that, "At the Rapture, Christ comes in the air *for* His saints. At the Revelation, He comes to the earth *with* them... So we have no date for the Rapture, only that it will precede the Revelation. That is, Christ will come *for* His church before He comes *with* His church, the period of the Tribulation lying between the *two*." [393] **E. Schuyler English** explains that, "There are *two phases* to the Lord's return described in the Word of God: (1) The rapture. The Lord's coming *before* the Tribulation *for* His own... (2) The Lord's return in glory. His return *after* the Tribulation *with* His own to reign upon the earth..."[394] **Lehman Strauss** teaches that, "...the Seventieth week of Daniel, occurs

---

[389] *The Collected Writings of J.N. Darby* - Edited by William Kelly, Stow Hill Bible and Tract Depot, n.d., p.119.
[390] *The Collected Writings of J.N. Darby* - Edited by William Kelly, Stow Hill Bible and Tract Depot, n.d., pp.153, 154, 155, 260, 279.
[391] As previously pointed out, later Dispensationalists, associated with Dallas Seminary modified Darby's original definition of the words *parousia, epiphaneia* and *apokalupsis*, asserting that all three terms were used interchangeably in Scripture to refer to *both* the pretribulational rapture and the post-tribulational Second Coming. See Chapter Five, Part II, No.1, *Terminology of the Second Coming.*
[392] *Plain Papers on Prophetic and Other Subjects* - William Trotter, Loizeaux Brothers, n.d., p.44.
[393] *Jesus Is Coming* - William E. Blackstone, Kregel Publications, 1989, pp.77-78, 210.
[394] *Studies in the Gospel According to Matthew* - E. Schuyler English, Zondervan Publishing House, 1938, p.224.

between the *two phases* of Christ's coming, between the Rapture when he comes *for* His saints (John 14:3; 1Thessalonians 4:16,17), and the Revelation when He comes to earth *with* his saints (1Thessalonians 3:13; Jude 14)."[395] And **Nigel Turner**[396] maintains that, "There is no alternative but to understand that the *parousia* of Christ takes place in *two distinct phases*, each separated from the other by an interval of time." **Turner** further stresses that the first phase of the *parousia*, "...will be a *preliminary phase* and seems to be quite *secret*."[397]

However, some Dispensationalists refer to the concept of Christ's Coming "for His saints" and His Coming "with His saints" for what it truly is - "two" different Comings. For example, **Leon Wood** explains that, "Christ's coming at the rapture must be distinguished from His coming at what is commonly called His revelation. The later appearance will not occur until after the tribulation period...There is some value here, however, in listing some basic distinctions between the *two comings*. First, the revelation does not occur until after the tribulation, rather than before as does the rapture...This means that the *two appearances* are separated by no less than seven years...He comes in the revelation *with* His saints, rather than *for* them, as at the rapture."[398] Likewise, **Henry Thiessen** maintains that Christ, "...will come into the air and...he will come to the earth...These *two comings* must be distinguished."[399] **John Walvoord** teaches that, "Though both the Rapture and the Second Coming are described as comings...the *two comings* are *entirely different*...The *two events* have *nothing in common* except that both are referred to as a 'coming.'"[400] And **Renald Showers** straightforwardly explains that, "...the Rapture and the coming of Christ with His angels will be *two separate events*."[401]

However, not all Dispensationalists are as candid and direct as **Wood, Thiessen, Walvoord** and **Showers**. Some Dispensationalists, while strictly adhering to the

---

[395] *God's Plan for the Future* – Leman Strauss, Zondervan Publishing House, 1965, p.163.
[396] Nigel Turner is a recognized Bible scholar and translator. He is known for his work on J.H. Moulton's *Grammar of New Testament Greek, Interpreter's Dictionary of the Bible*, Hasting's *Dictionary of the Bible*, Manson's *Companion to the Bible* and numerous scholarly articles.
[397] *Christian Words* - Nigel Turner, Thomas Nelson Publishers, 1981, p.405.
[398] *The Bible and Future Events* - Leon J. Wood, Zondervan Publishing House, 1974, p.42.
[399] *Lectures in Systematic Theology* – Henry C. Thiessen, revised by Vernon D. Doerksen, William B. Eerdmans Publishing House, 1986, p.347.
[400] *Major Bible Prophecies* - John F. Walvoord, Zondervan Publishing House, 1994, pp.337, 313.
[401] *Maranatha - Our Lord Come!* - Renald Showers, The Friends of Israel Gospel Ministry, Inc., 1995, p.176.

doctrine of "two Comings," argue that Dispensationalism teaches that there is only "one" Coming of Christ that has different "phases." For example, in defense of the pretribulation rapture doctrine, **Tim LaHaye** asserts that, "I see no contradiction in viewing the Second Coming as a *single event in two phases*...I realize some will accuse me of teaching *two comings* of Christ, but that is untrue…" However, **LaHaye** immediately goes on to say, "…one *cannot combine into a single event* the *two comings* of Christ: *once* for His church and *secondly* to the world with great power and glory."[402] **LaHaye** effectively demonstrates the impossibility of denying the obvious and at the same time making sense. No matter how hard one tries, two Comings cannot be sensibly described as one Coming. Language simply will not permit it. Likewise, **Gerald Stanton** attempts to argue that, "...the rapture and the revelation, together with the intervening events, are merely *different phases* of the *one second coming* of Christ. Pretribulationists do *not* believe that there are two second comings... but that there is *one coming incorporating two separate movements*..."[403] However, **Stanton's** attempt to disguise the Dispensational doctrine of two Comings of Christ as *"two separate movements"* is nothing more than verbal sleight-of-hand.

Dispensationalists clearly teach *two* separate and distinct Comings of Christ, at *two* different times, for *two* entirely different purposes. Dispensationalists teach that Christ is coming from heaven to rapture Christians and then take them back to heaven. Dispensationalists then teach that some seven years later, Christ is coming again from heaven a second time to judge the world and establish His Millennial Kingdom. No amount of verbal gymnastics can transform *two* different appearings, which have *two* different purposes, which occur at *two* different times, and involve *two* different groups of people, into one and the same appearing. The attempt to do so represents a serious disregard for the literal meaning of words - "two" is *not* "one" - despite all the creative attempts by Dispensationalists to disguise this obvious fact by substituting words such as, *"stages," "phases"* or *"movements."*

4. The Promise of a Pretribulation Rapture.

Dispensationalists confidently promise Christians that an imminent pretribulational

---

[402] *No Fear of the Storm* - Tim LaHaye, Multnomah Press Books, 1992, p.32.
[403] *Kept From the Hour* - Gerald B. Stanton, Zondervan Publishing House, 1956, p.19.

rapture of the Church will occur before the onset of the Great Tribulation. **John Darby** is commonly credited as being the first to assure Christians that, "The church...will be caught up to heaven out of the evil."[404] **Darby's** immediate followers were instrumental in helping to popularize this claim. **William Trotter** guaranteed believers that, "We, my brethren, are...comforted...by the hope of being gathered to meet the Lord in the air; so that when the judgments come, we shall not be amid the scene on which they are poured, but in the heavens whence they issue."[405] Modern Dispensationalists have continued to reassure the Church of an imminent pretribulational rapture. For example, **Leon Wood** promises that, "The first occurrence in the sequence of last-day events is the rapture of the church."[406] And **Charles Ryrie** reassures Christians that, "...the church will be raptured before the tribulation begins."[407]

Dispensationalists advocate for a pretribulational rapture because they are convinced that there is no Scripture that specifically places the Church in the Tribulation. For example, **John Walvoord** confidently assures his readers that, "...a careful and literal exegesis of the Scriptures reveals no evidence whatever that the Church will go through the Tribulation."[408] And again, **Walvoord** stresses that, "...there is no mention of the Church in any passage describing the future Tribulation..."[409] Likewise, **Leon Wood** affirms that, "There is a lack of any definite Scripture passage which indicates that the Church will endure the Tribulation."[410] And **Lehman Strauss** emphatically states that, "In none of the Tribulation passages do we find any reference to the Church."[411]

However, it is important to understand that these statements are based solely upon *one colossal assumption*. Dispensationalists *assume*, without any textual justification whatsoever, that the numerous New Testament passages that clearly place "the saints," "the elect" and "the disciples" in the midst of the Great Tribulation refer to a hypothetical future Jewish remnant and *not* to Christians. The problem for

---

[404] *The Collected Writings of J.N. Darby* - Edited by William Kelly, Stow Hill Bible and Tract Depot, n.d., p.116..
[405] *Plain Papers on Prophetic and Other Subjects* - William Trotter, Loizeaux Brothers, n.d., p.100.
[406] *The Bible and Future Events* - Leon J. Wood, Zondervan Publishing House, 1974, p.29.
[407] *Dispensationalism Today* - Charles Caldwell Ryrie, Moody Press, 1965, p.56.
[408] *The Rapture Question* – John F. Walvoord, The Zondervan Publishing House, 1979, p.59.
[409] *The Rapture Question* - John F. Walvoord, The Zondervan Publishing House, 1979, p.65.
[410] *Is the Rapture Next?* - Leon J. Wood, Zondervan Publishing House, 1956, p.21.
[411] *God's Plan for the Future* - Lehman Strauss, Zondervan Publishing House, 1965, p.163.

Dispensationalists is that there is no mention of a "future Jewish remnant" in the New Testament or any indication that these believers are anything other than Christians.

For example, in Matthew 24, Jesus addresses His end-time teaching directly to His disciples. Likewise, the parallel passages in Mark 13 and Luke 21 are also directed to the Lord's disciples. In Revelation, chapters 5-18, believers are referred to as those, "...who keep the commandments of God and hold to the testimony of Jesus." (12:17); "...the saints..." (13:7); "...the saints who keep the commandments of God and their faith in Jesus." (14:12); "...those who are with Him are the called and chosen and faithful." (17:14). There is absolutely no exegetical or textual reason to justify the Dispensational *assumption* that these references to the followers of Jesus Christ apply to a "future Jewish remnant" instead of "Christians." It is only *after* the Scriptures have been thoroughly and completely "dispensationalized"[412] that Dispensationalist can insist that, "In none of the Tribulation passages do we find any reference to the Church." In this manner the Dispensationalist conveniently and effectively sets aside every New Testament passage that refers to Christians suffering persecution and death during the Great Tribulation. Dispensationalists simply allege that these believers are part of a future Jewish remnant and therefore not members of the Church. But we must ask, "Where exactly in the New Testament do we find the doctrine of a future unbelieving Jewish remnant that will be converted to Christ during the Tribulation?" The simple answer is, "Nowhere!" The concept exists only in the imaginations of Dispensationalists who have invented it for the singular purpose of rescuing the doctrine of the pretribulation rapture from the plain testimony of Scripture. The entire concept is an absurd fabrication that has no foundation in Biblical fact. The claim is simply preposterous!

5. The Hope of the Church.

The pretribulation rapture teaching is the defining doctrine of Dispensationalism – it is the mainspring that drives and determines how all Biblical texts are interpreted. **John Darby** set the tone when he declared that, "The *rapture of the church*...is the *fulfillment of the highest blessings of sovereign grace* - Christ's coming to take us to

---

[412] As previously stated, to interpret the Scriptures "dispensationally" is to separate the Jewish portions of the New Testament Scriptures from the Christian portions. See Chapter 3 - The Dispensational Hermeneutic, 2. Dispensationalizing the New Testament.

Himself, that where He is, there we may be also."[413] Dispensationalists have unanimously echoed Darby's sentiments. **William Trotter** taught that, "...the descent of Jesus into the air to raise His sleeping saints, and transform those that are alive, translating both into His own presence in glory, is the *one, true, scriptural hope* of the Church...[414] This is the *Church's, even the Christian's hope*."[415] **Charles Mackintosh** declared that, "...the rapture, or the catching up of the saints...is the distinct and *only proper hope of the church*..."[416] **Macintosh** goes on to say that, "...the rapture of the saints...[is] the *brightest hope of the church* of God, and of the individual believer."[417] **Lewis Sperry Chafer** maintained that, "...the *Christian's hope* is the prospect of the *imminent coming of Christ* to take away His Church from the earth...The imminent return of Christ to receive His Church is held before every believer as a 'blessed hope.'"[418]

Dispensationalists constantly refer to Titus 2:13 in support of the imminent, pretribulational appearing of Christ to rapture His Church. Dispensationalists uniformly equate "the blessed hope" mentioned in Titus 2:13 with the pretribulational rapture of the Church. For example, while discussing the rapture, **Lehman Strauss** promises that, "This event is the Christian's 'blessed hope' (Titus 2:13)."[419] And **John Walvoord** assures Christians that, "The blessed hope is the rapture of the church before the great tribulation."[420] Really? Look carefully at the text, which declares;

"For the grace of God has appeared, bringing salvation to all men, instructing us to deny ungodliness and worldly desires and to live sensibly, righteously and godly in the present age, looking for the blessed hope and the appearing of the glory of our great God and Savior, Christ Jesus." Titus 2:11-13.

Paul here encourages Christians to be "looking for the blessed hope and the *appearing* of the glory of our great God and Savior, Christ Jesus." (Emphasis added). The word

---

413 *The Collected Writings of J.N. Darby* - Edited by William Kelly, Stow Hill Bible and Tract Depot, n.d., p.186.
414 *Plain Papers on Prophetic and Other Subjects* - William Trotter, Loizeaux Brothers, n.d., p.432.
415 *Plain Papers on Prophetic and Other Subjects* - William Trotter, Loizeaux Brothers, n.d., p.23.
416 *Plain Papers on the Lord's Coming* - C.H.M., Loizeaux Brothers, n.d., p.28.
417 *Plain Papers on the Lord's Coming* - C.H.M., Loizeaux Brothers, n.d., p.34.
418 *Systematic Theology* - Lewis Sperry Chafer, Kregel Publications, 1993, Vol.4, pp.23, 367.
419 *God's Plan for the Future* - Lehman Strauss, Zondervan Publishing House, 1965, p.79.
420 *The Blessed Hope and the Tribulation* - John F. Walvoord, Zondervan Publishing House, 1976, p.163.

"appearing" is *epiphaneia*. It refers to a glorious appearance or manifestation[421] hence, a shining forth[422] or brilliant display of brightness and glory.[423] In the ancient Greek world, the word was used to describe the appearance of the gods to mortal men[424] as well as the formal arrival of royalty.[425] Thus, for the Greeks it came to mean a glorious, visible manifestation or appearance. In the New Testament, *epiphaneia* refers to the bright and glorious appearing of the Lord Jesus Christ.[426] Thus, Paul's use of the word *epiphaneia* is not a reference to a secret, unobserved coming of the Lord, but to the visible appearance and manifestation of His Divine glory! This statement is confirmed by the fact that the word *epiphaneia* is unquestionably used to describe the glorious, visible, post-tribulational appearing of Christ. Paul tells us plainly in 2Thessalonians 2:8 that Jesus Christ will destroy the antichrist, "...by the appearance [*epiphaneia*] of His coming [*parousia*]..." Or as the King James Version translates the passage, "...by the **brightness** of His coming..." Thus, it is the glorious appearance of Jesus Christ, at His Second Coming, after the Tribulation that brings about the destruction of the Antichrist. Therefore, Paul's reference to, "the blessed hope and the **appearing** of the glory of our great God and Savior, Christ Jesus," clearly and unmistakably refers to the

---

[421] *The Analytical Greek Lexicon Revised* - Harold K. Moulton, Zondervan Publishing House, 1978 edition reprinted 1982, p.163, "ἐπιφανεία,...glorious display, 2Thes.2:8." Likewise, "*The Greek-English Lexicon to the New Testament* - William Greenfield, Zondervan Publishing House, 1981, p.73, "ἐπιφανεία, ...glorious display, 2Thes.2:8."

[422] *The Thessalonian Epistles* - D. Edmond Hiebert, Moody Press, 1971, p.316. Hiebert, a recognized Dispensational scholar states, "The noun *manifestation*...basically means 'a shining forth' (our English word Epiphany)." The English word Epiphany denotes, "A manifestation, esp. of divinity." See *Webster's Collegiate Dictionary*, Fifth Edition, 1941. See also *An Expository Dictionary of New Testament Words* - W.E. Vine, Thomas Nelson Publishers, third printing, n.d., p.58, "EPIPHANEIA (ἐπιφανεία)... (c) the shinning forth of the glory of the Lord Jesus 'as the lightning cometh forth from the east, and is seen even unto the west,' Mt.24:27..."

[423] Both the Geneva Bible (1599) and the King James Bible (1611) translate the word *epiphaneia* (ἐπιφανεία) in 2Thess. 2:8 as, "brightness." See also, "*A Commentary on the Old and New Testaments* - Robert Jamieson, A.R. Fausset and David Brown, Hendrickson Publishers, Inc., Vol.3, p.476, "[ἐπιφανεία] appearing ("brightness") refers to the coming itself."

[424] *Thayer's Greek-English Lexicon of the New Testament* - Joseph H. Thayer, Hendrickson Publishers, 2005, p.245, "Often used by the Greeks of a glorious manifestation of the gods, and esp. of their advent to help;" See also, *An Expository Dictionary of New Testament Words* - W.E. Vine, Thomas Nelson Publishers, third printing, n.d., p.57, "2. EPIPHANEIA (ἐπιφανεία), Eng., epiphany, lit. 'a shining forth,' was used of the appearance of a god to men..."

[425] *The International Standard Bible Encyclopedia* - James Orr, General Editor, Hendrickson Publishers, 2002, vol. III. p.2251. "Like the word Parousia, this term [i.e., *epiphaneia*] in Hellenistic Greek is employed to denote the ceremonial arrival of rulers." Compare also, *Christian Words* - Nigel Turner, Thomas Nelson Publishers, 1982, p.408, "The ascension of the 'divine' emperor Claudius was described as an *epiphaneia*."

[426] "ἐπιφανεία... In the New Testament it is not inappropriate to find the word used...to describe that bright Coming in which He [i.e., Jesus Christ] triumphantly confronts the Man of Sin (2Th.2:8)." *Christian Words* - Nigel Turner, Thomas Nelson Publishers, 1982, p.408

visible, glorious manifestation of Jesus Christ and *not* to a secret pretribulational rapture.

The contention by Dispensationalists that the *epiphaneia* of Christ refers to an unobserved appearance is a contradiction in terms. There is no such thing as an "appearance" that is "invisible"! Some Dispensationalists attempt to counter the serious implications presented by the literal meaning of *epiphaneia* by asserting that Paul is actually referring to both the pretribulational rapture and the glorious Second Coming in Titus 2:13. For example, while commenting on Titus 2:13, **John Walvoord**, declares that;

"The Titus passage apparently contrasts the *two expectations* of the Christ: the 'blessed hope' of Christ's return for them, and the 'glorious appearing of the great God and our Saviour Jesus Christ,' which will change the 'present world' of Titus 2:12 to millennial conditions. Here again the proof is not absolute, and there is room for divergent opinion."[427]

Thus, **Walvoord** cautiously contends that the phrase, "... looking for the blessed hope" refers to the pretribulational rapture, while the very next phrase, "...and the appearing of the glory of our great God and Savior, Christ Jesus" refers to the post-tribulational Second Coming.[428] However, **Walvoord's** contention that Titus 2:13 presents "two expectations," is grammatically untenable. Paul is unmistakably referring to one appearing *not* two. This fact is made evident by the grammatical construction of the sentence. Simply put, the use of a single definite article with two nouns in the same case, connected by the word "and," designates that both of the nouns refer to the same thing.[429]

---

[427] *New Testament Words for the Lord's Coming* - John F. Walvoord, Bibliotheca Sacra, 101:284-289, July 1944, p.288.

[428] This is a common Dispensational assertion. For example, Tim LaHaye, teaches that, "...Titus 2:13, which refers in a single verse to the Rapture as the 'blessed hope,' and the coming to earth as the 'glorious appearing.'" *No Fear of the Storm* – Tim LaHaye, Multnomah Press, 1992, p.73.

[429] "We have Granville Sharp's rule here, which says that when there are two nouns in the same case connected by *kai* (and), the first noun having the article, the second noun not having the article, the second noun refers to the same thing as the first noun does and is a further description of it. Thus, that blessed hope is the appearing of our Lord. The translation should read, 'that blessed hope, even the appearing of the glory of our great God and Saviour, Jesus Christ." *Word Studies in the Greek New Testament* - Kenneth S. Wuest, Wm.B. Eerdmans Publishing Company, 1999, *The Pastoral Epistles in the Greek New Testament - The Exegesis of Titus* vol.2, p.195. Note also that Wuest is a respected Dispensational scholar.

Thus, grammatically "the blessed hope and appearing"[430] are one and the same event - the blessed hope *is* the visible, glorious appearing of Jesus Christ.

Further, the Dispensational claim that the secret, pretribulational rapture is "the only legitimate hope of the Church" is an unwarranted imposition upon the text. Titus 2:13 does *not* say that the rapture (neither *pre* nor *post*) is the hope of the Church. On the contrary, the only legitimate hope for the Christian is the person and work of the Lord Jesus Christ - "who is our hope" (1Tim.1:1). Thus, we are to look for the glorious, personal appearance of Jesus Christ - our great God and Savior. Our hope is Christ, not the rapture!

6. Dispensational Proof for the Pretribulation Rapture.

6a. First Thessalonians 4:13-18

When asked to provide textual proof for the pretribulation rapture theory, Dispensationalists invariably point to First Thessalonians 4:13-18. It is this text, according to Dispensationalists, which provides the **principal textual support** for the doctrine of a pretribulational rapture of the Church.

John Walvoord explains that, "Probably the *main reason* for many pretribulationalist' holding to a rapture before the Tribulation is the exhortation of 1Thessalonians 4:18."[431] And again, **Walvoord** makes it clear that, "Probably more pretribulationists *base their conclusion* for a pretribulational rapture on 1Thessalonians 4 than any other single passage of Scripture."[432] **Gerald Stanton** observes that, "It is recognized by most Bible students that 1Thessalonians 4:13-18 is the *primary passage* of the Word of God on the subject of the rapture of the Church." **Stanton** goes on to declare that,"...1Thessalonians 4 is the *cardinal passage* on the rapture of the saints..."[433] **Leon Wood** asserts that, "One of the *fullest treatments* of the rapture is found in First Thessalonians 4:13-18."[434] **Lehman Strauss** maintains that, "The *outstanding prophetic passage* in the New

---

[430] Literally, "τὴν μακαρίαν ἐλπίδα καὶ ἐπιφάνειαν " - "the blessed hope and appearing"
[431] *The Rapture Question* - John F. Walvoord, Zondervan Publishing House, 1979, p.209.
[432] *The Blessed Hope And The Tribulation* - John F. Walvoord, Zondervan Publishing House, 1976, p.94.
[433] *Kept From The Hour* - Gerald B. Stanton, Zondervan Publishing House, 1956, pp.83,90.
[434] *The Bible and Future Events* - Leon J. Wood, Zondervan Publishing House, 1974, p.42.

Testament which describes in some detail the nature of the Rapture is 1Thessalonians 4:13-18..."[435] **E. Schuyler English** explains that, "The *classic text* that pertains to the translation of the Church is...1Thessalonians 4:15-17, for therein *more detail* is given about the united up-calling...than anywhere else in the Scriptures."[436] And **Renald Showers** claims that, "First Thessalonians 4:13-18 is the *most extensive* New Testament passage dealing with the Rapture of the Church."[437]

Thus, Dispensationalists uniformly point to First Thessalonians 4:13-18 as the single most important New Testament text in support of the pretribulational rapture. Dispensationalists refer to this text as "the primary passage of the Word of God on the subject of the rapture" - "the cardinal passage on the rapture of the saints" - "the outstanding prophetic passage in the New Testament which describes...the rapture" - "the classic text that pertains to the translation." Dispensationalists further assert that in First Thessalonians 4:13-18, "more detail is given about the united up-calling...than anywhere else in the Scriptures." Because this passage is considered by Dispensationalists to be "the most extensive New Testament passage dealing with the Rapture," they maintain that, "more pretribulationists base their conclusion for a pretribulational rapture on 1Thessalonians 4 than any other single passage of Scripture." Surely then, this text must clearly and unquestionably reveal a pretribulational Coming of Jesus Christ. Look carefully at First Thessalonians 4:13-18.

"(v.13) But we do not want you to be uninformed, brethren, about those who are asleep, that you may not grieve, as do the rest who have no hope. (v.14) For if we believe that Jesus died and rose again, even so God will bring with Him those who have fallen asleep in Jesus. (v.15) For this we say to you by the word of the Lord, that we who are alive, and remain until the **coming** [i.e., *parousia*] of the Lord, shall not precede those who have fallen asleep. (v.16) For the Lord Himself will descend from heaven with the voice of the archangel, and the trumpet of God; and the dead in Christ shall rise first. (v.17) Then we who are alive and remain shall be caught up together with them in the clouds to meet the Lord in the air, and thus we shall always be with the Lord. (v.18) Therefore comfort one another with these words." (Emphasis added).

According to Dispensationalists, First Thessalonians 4:13-18, reveals two crucial things about the Coming of Jesus Christ. First, it is claimed that this text declares that Jesus

---

[435] *God's Plan for the Future* - Lehman Strauss, Zondervan Publishing House, 1965, p.85.
[436] *Re-Thinking the Rapture* - E. Schuyler English, Loizeaux Brothers, 1954, p.41.
[437] *Maranatha - Our Lord Come!* - Renald Showers, The Friends of Israel Gospel Ministry, Inc., 1995, p.198.

Christ will come *before* the beginning of the Tribulation, and second, that that Coming will be *imminent*. For example, **John Walvoord** assures us that, "...in 1 Thessalonians 4:13-18...The church is promised *the comfort of translation*, and this *seems* to be regarded in 1 Thessalonians as an *imminent event*."[438] However, a careful and thoughtful reading of this text will find no description whatsoever of an imminent (i.e., secret, unannounced, any moment)[439] pretribulational Coming of Jesus Christ. This passage simply and straightforwardly declares that at the **Coming** (i.e., the *parousia*, v.15) of Jesus Christ, the righteous dead shall "rise first" and then the living saints will be "caught up" together with them, to meet the Lord in the air. Thus, the entire argument over whether the rapture is pretribulational or post-tribulational hinges upon the meaning of the word *parousia* (Coming) - because, according to this text, it is at the *parousia* of Jesus Christ that the resurrection and rapture of the saints will occur.

The word *parousia* is used fifteen times in the New Testament to describe the Second Coming of Jesus Christ.[440] The lexical definition of *parousia* denotes, "presence, a coming, arrival, advent,"[441] "the presence of one coming, hence the coming, arrival, advent."[442] It is important to note that the definition of words is determined primarily by their linguistic usage. Thus, a careful examination of *how* the word *parousia* is used with respect to the Second Coming of Christ is crucial. A careful examination reveals some very important details about the nature of Christ's Coming and the effect that His "coming, arrival, advent and presence" will have upon both believers and unbelievers alike.

Matthew 24:3 - The *parousia* of Christ is associated with the *end of the present age*.

The disciples asked Jesus, "...what will be the sign of Your **coming** *[parousia]* and the end of the age?" (Emphasis added).

---

[438] *The Rapture Question* – John F. Walvoord, Zondervan Publishing House, 1979, p.35.
[439] As previously pointed out, Dispensationalists define the word "imminent" as the secret, unannounced, any moment Coming of Jesus Christ to rapture the Church. See Chapter Four, *The Doctrine of Imminence* for a thorough discussion of the topic.
[440] See Mt.24:3,27,37,39; 1Cor.15:23; 1Thess.2:19; 3:13; 4:15; 5:23; 2Thess.2:1,8; Jas.5:7,8; 2Pt.3:4; 1Jn.2:28.
[441] *The Analytical Greek Lexicon Revised* - Harold K. Moulton, Zondervan Publishing House, 1982, p.307.
[442] *Thayer's Greek-English Lexicon of the New Testament* - Joseph H. Thayer, Hendrickson Publishers, 2005, p.490.

Matthew 24:27 - The *parousia* of Christ will be an observable event, as *bright* as the *lightning flashing* across the sky.

"For just as the lightning comes from the east and flashes even to the west, so shall the **coming** *[parousia]* of the Son of Man be." (Emphasis added).

Matthew 24:37-39 - The *parousia* of Christ will be *completely unexpected* by the unbelieving world.

"For the **coming** *[parousia]* of the Son of Man will be just like the days of Noah. For as in those days which were before the flood they were eating and drinking, they were marrying and giving in marriage, until the day that Noah entered the ark, and they did not understand until the flood came and took them all away; so shall the **coming** *[parousia]* of the Son of Man be." (Emphasis added).

1Corinthians 15:22-23 - Paul links the *resurrection of believers* to the *parousia* of Christ.

"For as in Adam all die, so also in Christ all shall be made alive. But each in his own order: Christ the first fruits, after that those who are Christ's at His **coming** *[parousia]*." (Emphasis added).

1Thessalonians 2:19 - Paul declares that the *spatial separation of believers* will cease at the *parousia*, when at last, believers will be united together in the presence of Christ.

"For we wanted to come to you - I, Paul, more than once - and yet Satan thwarted us. For who is our hope or joy or crown of exultation? Is it not even you, in the presence of our Lord Jesus at His **coming** *[parousia]*?" (Emphasis added).

1Thessalonians 3:13 - Paul reveals that *all the saints* will accompany Christ at His *parousia*.

"so that He may establish your hearts unblameable in holiness before our God and Father at the **coming** *[parousia]* of our Lord Jesus with **all** His saints." (Emphasis added).

1Thessalonians 4:13-15 - Paul declares that *both* the resurrection of the righteous and the catching up of the living saints will occur at the *parousia* of Christ.

"(v.13) But we do not want you to be uninformed, brethren, about those who are asleep, that you may not grieve, as do the rest who have no hope. (v.14) For if we believe that Jesus died and rose again, even so God will bring with Him those who have fallen asleep in Jesus. (v.15) For this we say to you by the word of the Lord, that we who are alive, and remain until the **coming *[parousia]*** of the Lord, shall not precede those who have fallen asleep. (v.16) For the Lord Himself will descend from heaven with the voice of the archangel, and the trumpet of God; and the **dead in Christ shall rise first**. (v.17) **Then we who are alive and remain shall be caught up together with them in the clouds to meet the Lord in the air**, and thus we shall always be with the Lord. (v.18) Therefore comfort one another with these words." (Emphasis added).

1Thessalonians 5:23 - Paul reveals that the believer will be *entirely sanctified* and *without blame* at the *parousia* of Christ.

"Now may the God of peace Himself **sanctify you entirely**; and may your spirit and soul and body be preserved complete, **without blame** at the **coming *[parousia]*** of our Lord Jesus Christ." (Emphasis added).

2Thessalonians 2:1-2 - Paul connects the *parousia* of Christ with both the *rapture* and the *Day of the Lord*.

"Now we request you, brethren, with regard to the **coming *[parousia]*** of our Lord Jesus Christ, and **our gathering together to Him**,[443] that you may not be quickly shaken from your composure or be disturbed either by a spirit or a message or a letter as if from us, to the effect that the **day of the Lord** has come." (Emphasis added).

2Thessalonians 2:8 - Paul declares that the man of lawlessness (i.e., the Antichrist) will be destroyed at the *parousia* of Christ.

"And then that lawless one will be revealed whom the **Lord will slay with the breath of His mouth and bring to an end** by the appearance of His **coming *[parousia]***;" (Emphasis added).

James 5:7-8 - Although the coming of Christ is near, and is to be expected soon, James instructs believers to *wait patiently* for the *parousia* of Christ.

"**Be patient**, therefore, brethren, until the **coming *[parousia]*** of the Lord. Behold the farmer waits for the precious produce of the soil, being patient about it, until it gets the early and late rains. You too **be patient**; strengthen your hearts, for the **coming *[parousia]*** of the Lord is at hand." (Emphasis added).

---

[443] Dispensationalists uniformly agree that the phrase "our gathering together to Him" refers to the rapture of the Church.

2Peter 3:3-4 - Peter reveals that in the "last days" the doctrine of the *parousia* of Christ will be rejected and scoffed at by unbelievers.

"Know this first of all, that in the **last days mockers will come with their mocking**, following after their own lusts, and saying, 'Where is the promise of His **coming *[parousia]*?** For ever since the fathers fell asleep, all continues just as it was from the beginning of creation.'" (Emphasis added).

1John 2:28 - John tells us that the anticipation of the *parousia* should motivate all believers to be faithful and obedient to Christ.

"And now, little children, abide in Him, so that when **He appears**, we may have confidence and not shrink away from Him in shame at His **coming *[parousia]*.**" (Emphasis added).

Thus, we can readily see from the combined testimony of Scripture, that the *parousia* of Jesus Christ will occur at the end of this age - that it will be completely unexpected and mocked at by unbelievers - while believers are encouraged to live godly lives, pleasing to God as they wait patiently for His Coming - which will be a personal, brilliant manifestation of radiant glory, visible to all - when the righteous dead will be raised and the living saints raptured as the Lord comes to destroy the Antichrist and establish His millennial kingdom reign upon the earth.

Not surprisingly, Dispensationalists intentionally ignore these Biblical statements that shape and define the nature and character of the *parousia*. They argue that the word is *not a technical term.* Rather, they claim that the word *parousia* is a "general" term that simply refers to the "presence" of Christ and therefore describes *both* a pretribulational and post-tribulational "presence" or Coming. For example, while referring to the word *parousia,* **John Walvoord** explains that, "A brief survey of its usage in the New Testament includes its reference to the 'coming of Stephanas and Fortunatus and Achaicus,' Paul's friends (1Cor.16:17), to the coming of Titus (2Cor.7:6,7), to the coming of Paul himself (Phil.1:26), to the coming of the lawless one (2Thess.2:9)...All must concede that these instances are *general* and *not technical*."[444]

On the basis of the supposed non-technical nature of the word *parousia,* Dispensationalists argue that only by evaluating the "contrasting details" of a text, can it

---

[444] *New Testament Words for the Lord's Coming* - John Walvoord, *Bibliotheca Sacra*, 101:284-89, July, 1944, p.285.

be determined whether the word *parousia* refers to a pretribulational or post-tribulational Coming of Christ.[445] For example, **Walvoord** maintains that First Thessalonians 4:13-18 refers to a pretribulational Coming of Christ on the basis that the text does not mention the fulfillment of any other prophetic events. **Walvoord** contends that, "Most important is the fact that this event, as described, is presented as an *imminent* event with *no preceding order of events* that had to be enacted."[446] In other words, according to Walvoord, if a "rapture passage"[447] does *not* mention other end-time events taking place prior to Christ's Coming it is automatically *assumed* to be describing a secret, unannounced, any moment, pretribulational Coming. Mark it carefully, none of the so-called "rapture passages" actually describes a pretribulational Coming of Jesus Christ – Dispensationalists simply *assume* that these passages are referring to a pretribulational Coming and rapture because these texts do not mention any other *"preceding order of events" (i.e., other Tribulational events)* occurring before the described Coming of Christ.

John Walvoord's contention that the word *parousia* is used in Scripture to describe the coming and presence of individuals other than Christ is true. However, this does not mean that the word lacks special significance when used of the Coming of Christ. Consider the word "lord" (*kurios*). It is used in the New Testament to refer to earthly masters or overlords (Acts 16:16),[448] political rulers (Acts 25:26),[449] idols (1Cor.8:5)[450] and as a general title of respect (1Pt.3:6).[451] However, when the word "lord" (*kurios*) is used to describe the person of Jesus Christ, it assumes a far greater significance and meaning. The word denotes Christ's identification and equality with the Father, and thus His divine character, privileges, prerogatives, and supreme authority. In exactly the same way, the Coming (*parousia*) of the Lord Jesus Christ has far greater significance and meaning than the coming of Paul or Titus or Stephanas and Fortunatus and

---

[445] See Chapter Five, Part II, No. 2, *Contrasting Details*, for a discussion of the technical nature of the word *parousia* in relation to Jesus Christ.

[446] *The Rapture Question* - The Zondervan Publishing House, 1979, John Walvoord, p.202.

[447] The principal "rapture passages" referred to by Dispensationalists are Jn.14:1-3; 1Cor.15:50-53; 1Thess.4:13-18; 1Thess.5:1-6; 2Thess.2:1-3.

[448] Acts 16:16 - Referring to the slave girl having the spirit of divination (lit. the spirit of Python), it is said that she "...was bringing her masters [*kurios*] much profit by fortunetellng."

[449] Acts 25:26 - Festus confesses that he has, "...nothing definite to write to my lord [*kurios*]" regarding the Apostle Paul.

[450] 1Cor.8:5-6 "For even if there are so-called gods whether in heaven or on earth, as indeed there are many gods and many lords [*kurios*], yet for us there is but one God..."

[451] 1Pt.3:6 "Thus Sarah obeyed Abraham, calling him lord [*kurios*]..."

Achaicus! Thus, when used of the Coming of the Lord Jesus Christ, the word *parousia* takes on a very specific and technical meaning.[452]

Consider the insights and observations of **Adolf Deissmann,**[453] with respect to the meaning of the word *parousia*. **Deissmann** explains that, "We may now say that the best interpretation of the Primitive Christian hope of the *parusia* is the old Advent text, 'Behold, thy King cometh unto thee' (Zech.ix.9; Matt.xxi.5). From the Ptolemaic period down into the 2nd century A.D. we are able to trace the word in the East as a *technical expression* for the arrival or the visit of the king or the emperor."[454] The word *parousia* was commonly used to describe the official and formal arrival of a king or emperor.[455] Such arrivals were characterized by great fanfare, pomp and ceremony.[456] As the emperor arrived in a city, his large entourage of advisors, aides, military guards and musicians accompanied him to the cheers of the residents who lined the streets to observe the procession. It was a public spectacle characterized by great feasts and games. Coins were struck to commemorate the arrival, statues were erected and special taxes were levied to pay the expenses.[457] **Deissmann** further observes, "How graphically it must have appealed to the Christians of Thessalonica, with their living conception of the *parusiae* of the rulers of this world, when they read in saint Paul's second letter[458] of the Satanic '*parusia*' of Antichrist, who was to be destroyed by 'the manifestation of the *parusia*' of the Lord Jesus!"[459]

---

[452] A.T. Robertson observes that, "The word *parousia* was the *technical word* for the arrival or visit of the king or emperor and can be traced from the Ptolemaic period into the second century A.D." *Word Pictures in the New Testament*, Broadman Press, 1931, vol. IV, p.191.

[453] Adolf Deissmann (1866-1937) was a respected German Lutheran linguist and theologian. Additionally, he was a recognized authority on the Greek Papyri and their linguistic relationship to the New Testament.

[454] *Light From the Ancient East* - Adolf Deissmann, Hendrickson Publishers, 1995, p.368.

[455] "A coming, arrival, advent; in late writers as a *technical term* for the visit of a king; hence in NT, specifically of the Advent or Parousia of Christ." *A Manual Greek Lexicon of the New Testament* - G. Abbott-Smith, Charles Scribner's Sons, 1953, p.347.

[456] "...the NT uses *Parousia* for the glorious coming of the Lord Jesus at the end of time, his Second Coming. This return of Christ must somehow be filled out with the pomp and magnificence that characterized royal and imperial visits." *Theological Lexicon of the New Testament* – Ceslas Spicq, Edited by James D. Ernest, Hendrickson Publishers, 2012, vol.3, παι–ψευ, pp.54-55.

[457] See the *Theological Lexicon of the New Testament* – Ceslas Spicq, Edited by James D. Ernest, Hendrickson Publishers, 2012, vol.3, παι–ψευ, p.55.

[458] Deissmann is referring to 2Thessalonians 2:8-9.

[459] *Light From the Ancient East* - Adolf Deissmann, Hendrickson Publishers, 1995, p.371.

Thus, in Matthew 24:3, when the disciples asked Jesus, "...what will be *the sign of your coming [parousia]* and the end of the age?" (emphasis added), They were asking, "What will be the sign of your glorious and public manifestation as King?" Jesus answers their question in verses 27-30, when He declares,

"For just as the lightning comes from the east, and flashes even to the west, so shall the **coming** *[parousia]* of the Son of Man be. Wherever the corpse is, there the vultures will gather. But **immediately** <u>after</u> **the tribulation** of those days the sun will be darkened, and the moon will not give its light, and the stars will fall from the sky, and the powers of the heavens will be shaken, and then the sign of the Son of Man will appear in the sky, and then all the tribes of the earth will mourn, and they will see the Son of Man coming on the clouds of the sky with power and great glory." (Emphasis added).

Consequently, in answer to the disciple's question about the time of His *parousia*, Jesus declares that it would occur *after* the Tribulation. Furthermore, Jesus describes His *parousia* as a visible, personal, spectacular and glorious event! The Apostle Paul underscores this fact in Second Thessalonians 2:8, where he declares that the "...lawless one will be revealed whom the Lord will slay with the breath of His mouth and bring to an end by the **appearance** *[epiphaneia]* of His **coming** *[parousia]*." (Emphasis added). Paul is clearly describing a visible, post-tribulational Coming of Jesus Christ, which will abruptly end the malevolent reign of the Antichrist. Therefore, contrary to the unfounded claims of Dispensationalists, the word *parousia* does *not* refer to a secret, unobserved, Coming of Christ *before* the Tribulation, but to the visible, public, personal, glorious appearance of Jesus Christ *after* the Tribulation, as the victorious King of kings and Lord of lords!

Yet, Dispensationalists insist that the Scriptures are vague and inconclusive as to the time of the rapture. For example, **John Walvoord** claims that, "There is not a single Scripture in either the Old or New Testament that relates the translation of the church to a post-tribulational coming of Christ."[460] Referring to the time of the rapture, **Renald Showers** insists that, "The Scriptures do not give a specific statement concerning the *time* of this event."[461] And **E. Schuyler English,** while referring specifically to 1Thessalonians 4:13-18, states that, "While this is the most detailed description of the

[460] *The Rapture Question* - John F. Walvoord, Zondervan Publishing House, 1979, p.171.
[461] *Maranatha Our Lord Come!* - Renald E. Showers, The Friends of Israel Gospel Ministry, Inc., p.13.

saint's translation that is written in the Scriptures, nothing is said here, as all will agree, as to *when* this will happen in relation to the Tribulation."[462] However, the Scriptures are not as ambiguous as the Dispensationalists claim. The fact is the Scriptures do reveal *when* the rapture takes place in relation to the Tribulation. 1Thessalonians 4:13-18 plainly tells us that the rapture occurs at the *parousia* of Jesus Christ. And both Jesus and the Apostle Paul clearly state that the *parousia* occurs *after* the Tribulation (see Mt.24:27-31 & 2Thess.2:1-8). Obviously, if the *rapture* occurs at the *parousia*, and the *parousia* occurs *after* the tribulation, then the rapture must also occur *after* the Tribulation.

Again, Paul tells us plainly in 2 Thessalonians 1:5-10, that the persecution and suffering of Christians will cease *when* Jesus Christ is *revealed* from heaven. The Thessalonian Christians were subjected to severe persecution for their faith in Christ (see 1Thess.1:6; 2Thess.1:6-7). Paul himself was forced to leave Thessalonica because of this persecution (Acts 17:1-10). In 2Thessalonians, Paul writes to encourage the Thessalonians, promising them relief from suffering *when* the Lord Jesus Christ is revealed. Look closely at 2Thessalonians 1:5-10,[463] which declares;

"This is a plain indication of God's righteous judgment so that you may be considered worthy of the kingdom of God, for which indeed you are suffering. For after all, it is only just for God to repay with affliction those who afflict you, and to give relief to you who are afflicted and to us as well **when [*en*]** the Lord Jesus shall be **revealed [*apokalupsis*]** from heaven with His mighty angels in flaming fire, dealing out retribution to those who do not know God and to those who do not obey the gospel of our Lord Jesus. And these will pay the penalty of eternal destruction, away from the presence of the Lord and the glory of His power, when He comes to be glorified in His saints on that day, and to be marveled at among all who have believed - for our testimony to you was believed."(Emphasis added).

---

[462] *Re-Thinking the Rapture* - E. Schuyler English, Loizeaux Brothers, 1954, p.58. This is a remarkable statement by English. He asserts that this is the most detailed passage regarding the rapture in all of Scripture, and then says that it does *not* indicate whether the rapture will be pre or post-tribulational. If this "most detailed description of the saint's translation" does *not* state that the rapture is pretribulational, then exactly where in Scripture do Dispensationalists find such a statement?

[463] Compare 1Peter 4:12-13 which declares, "Beloved, do not be surprised at the fiery ordeal among you, which comes upon you for your testing, as though some strange thing were happening to you; but to the degree that you share the sufferings of Christ, keep on rejoicing; so that at the **revelation [*apokalupsis*] of His glory,** you may rejoice with exultation." (Emphasis added).

Carefully note that Paul tells the Thessalonian Christians that they would experience relief from their persecutions and sufferings, "*when [en]* the Lord Jesus shall be *revealed [apokalupsis]* from heaven with His mighty angels in flaming fire, dealing out retribution to those who do not know God and to those who do not obey the gospel of our Lord Jesus." Paul clearly and unmistakably describes a *post*-tribulational *Revelation* of Jesus Christ that will result in deliverance for His followers and judgment for His enemies as He comes with His angels in "flaming fire." Significantly, Paul does *not* tell the Thessalonian believers that their sufferings would cease unexpectedly at any moment, at a secret, imminent, pretribulational rapture. On the contrary, Paul plainly and unmistakably fixes the cessation of Christian suffering at the *post*-tribulational *Revelation* of Jesus Christ!

Not surprisingly, Dispensationalists attempt to avoid the crushing force of Paul's statement by first generalizing it, and then summarily dismissing it. For example, **John Walvoord** declares that, "The Thessalonians are being told that God in His *own time* will destroy their persecutors...the passage does *not contribute to the debate over the Tribulation*."[464] Paul is certainly *not* saying that God will destroy the Thessalonian "persecutors" in His "own time," as if the deliverance of suffering Christians was a vague and undefined future event. On the contrary, Paul precisely and specifically declares that God will destroy their persecutors "...*when* the Lord Jesus shall be *revealed [apokalupsis]* from heaven with His mighty angels in flaming fire..." **Walvoord** then attempts to dismiss the entire argument by declaring that, "...the passage does not contribute to the debate over the Tribulation." It more than contributes to the debate over the Tribulation - it settles it for those who are truly willing to accept the "plain, literal and normal" meaning of Scripture! Paul clearly and unmistakably links the deliverance of suffering Christians with the post-tribulational Revelation of Jesus Christ. This fact is clear, indisputable and inescapable!

However, **E. Schuyler English** also attempts to minimize the significance of Paul's declaration that Christians will be delivered from persecution "...*when* the Lord Jesus shall be *revealed [apokalupsis]* from heaven..." by calling into question the accuracy of the translation. **English** declares that, "...the Greek of verse 7 does not state, '*when* the Lord Jesus shall be revealed, etc.' but '*in* the revelation of the Lord Jesus' (*en tee*

---

[464] *The Blessed Hope and the Tribulation* - John F. Walvoord, Zondervan Publishing House, 1976, pp.123-124.

apokalupsei)..."[465] **English** is correct when he states that the preposition *en* can be translated "*in*." For example, the *Wycliff Bible* (1380) translates verse 7, "and to you that been troubled: rest with us, *in* the showing of the Lord Jesus from heaven..."[466] (Emphasis added). However, translating the preposition *en* as *in* does not alter or change the plain meaning of the text - deliverance from persecution will be experienced "in" the Revelation of Christ. However, it must also be noted that there is absolutely no problem with the Biblical translation of the preposition *en* as "when."[467] For example, the *Tyndale New Testament* (1526 and 1534) translates verse 7, "and to you which are troubled rest with us, *when* the Lord Jesus shall show himself from heaven..." (Emphasis added). The *Geneva Bible* (1557 and 1559) translates verse 7, "And to you which are troubled, rest with us *when* the Lord Jesus shall show himself from heaven..." (Emphasis added). The *King James Bible* (1611) translates verse 7, "And to you who are troubled, rest with us, *when* the Lord Jesus shall be revealed from heaven..." (Emphasis added).[468] The salient point is that whether the preposition *en* is translated "*in* the revelation of Jesus Christ"; or "*when* Jesus Christ is revealed," the plain meaning of the text is not altered - believers will at last be delivered from their persecutions and sufferings *in* that Revelation, and *when* that Revelation occurs. In either case, the fact remains that the deliverance of believers coincides with the ***post-***tribulational ***Revelation*** of Jesus Christ!

After calling into question the accuracy of the translation, **English** then suggests that Paul's intention is to simply convey a ***general idea*** of deliverance and ***not*** to indicate any ***specific time*** of deliverance. **English** contends that, "...it is not so much the ***moment*** that these things will occur that is at issue here, but...When the ungodly are

---

[465] *Re-Thinking The Rapture* – E. Schuyler English, Loizeaux Brothers, 1954, p.65.

[466] See also *The English Hexapla*, 1841edition published by Samuel Bagster and Sons, London, reprinted by Still Water Revival Books, n.d.

[467] Commenting on 2Thessalonians 1:7, the renowned Greek scholar, **A.T. Robertson** observes that, "They shared suffering with Paul (verse 5) and so they will share the *rest. At the revelation of the Lord Jesus* (*en tei apokalupsei tou Kuriou Iesou*). Here the *Parousia* (1Thess.2:19; 3:13; 5:23) is pictured as a Revelation (Un-veiling, *apo-kalupsis*) of the Messiah...At this Unveiling of the Messiah there will come the *recompense* (verse 6) to the persecutors and the *rest* from the persecutions." *Word Pictures in the New Testament* - Archibald Thomas Robertson, Broadman Press, 1931, vol. IV, p.43.

[468] For the *Wycliff Bible* (1380), *Tyndale New Testament* (1534), *Geneva Bible* (1557), and *King James Bible* (1611) see *The English Hexapla*, 1841edition published by Samuel Bagster and Sons, London, reprinted by Still Water Revival Books, n.d. For the *Tyndale New Testament* (1526) see *The New Testament*, translated by William Tyndale, reprinted by The British Library, 2000, W.R. Cooper, Editor. For the *Geneva Bible* (1599) see *The Geneva Bible 1599*, reprinted by L.L. Brown Publishing, 2003.

suffering under the righteous judgment of God, His own people will be enjoying eternal rest."[469] This statement is utter nonsense. Paul clearly links the believer's deliverance from suffering to the post-tribulational Revelation of Jesus Christ. The *"moment"* of the believer's deliverance from persecution is precisely what Paul is describing. It is *when* Jesus Christ is revealed from heaven with His mighty angels in flaming fire that the Christian's persecution and suffering will cease - *not* seven years before that event! [470]

6b. The Connection Between Matthew 24 and 1&2 Thessalonians.

Dispensationalists teach that the doctrine of the rapture of the Church is a *new revelation*, unknown to the Church until the Apostle Paul revealed it. For example, while commenting on 1Thessalonians 4, **Gerald Stanton** declares that, "The rapture of chapter four is a *new mystery-revelation*..."[471] **E. Schuyler English** asserts that, "...the translation of the Church was not revealed by our Lord but that it was left for the Apostle Paul to declare this mystery as a *new revelation* (1Cor.15:51,52; 1Thess.4:13-18)."[472] And **John Walvoord**, while commenting on 1Thessalonians 4:13-18, stresses that, "There is no reasonable connection between this passage and the Olivet Discourse. The rapture of living saints is a *new revelation* not connected with the second coming of Christ in previous revelations..."[473] And again, **Walvoord** asserts that, "The Rapture is a *new doctrine*, distinct from the Second Coming."[474]

---

[469] *Re-Thinking the Rapture* - E. Schuyler English, Loizeaux Brothers, 1954, p.65. Note that Schuyler closely follows Darby here. While commenting on 2Thess.1:8-9, Darby asserted, "The moment of their entering into this rest is not at all the subject here, but the contrast between their actual condition and that which it would be if Jesus were [to] come...In His day they should be at rest, and the wicked in distress..." *Synopsis of the Books of the Bible* - J.N. Darby, Loizeaux Brothers, Vol.V, p.130.

[470] Referring specifically to 2Thessalonians 1:7, Charles Erdman observes that, "The time of this deliverance is to be 'at the revelation of the Lord Jesus from heaven with the angels of his power in flaming fire.' The rest comes when Christ comes...Paul mentions no interval between the time of deliverance and the time of retribution. No period of years elapses. The 'rest' and the 'destruction' follow in quick succession." *The Epistles of Paul to the Thessalonians* – Charles R. Erdman, Westminster Press, 1935, pp.80-81.

[471] *Kept From the Hour* - Gerald B. Stanton, Zondervan Publishing House, 1956, p.90.

[472] *Re-Thinking the Rapture* - E. Schuyler English, Loizeaux Brothers, p.49.

[473] *The Blessed Hope and the Tribulation* - John F. Walvoord, Zondervan Publishing House, 1976, p.106.

[474] *The Rapture Question* - John F. Walvoord Zondervan Publishing House, 1979, p.204.

Thus, the Dispensational proposition that the pretribulation rapture teaching is a "new doctrine" is predicated upon the assertion that there is "no reasonable connection" between the prophetic teachings of Jesus Christ in the Olivet Discourse (i.e., Mt.24; Mk.13; Lk.21) and the prophetic teachings of the Apostle Paul in the Thessalonian Epistles. Dispensationalists insist that the *gathering of the elect* in Matthew 24:30-31[475] does *not* refer to the rapture of the Church. For example, **John Walvoord** stresses that, "...the translation of living saints, which is the main characteristic of the rapture, is found nowhere in Matthew."[476] **Lehman Strauss** teaches that, "There are some verses in Matthew 24 which resemble the Rapture, however, those statements uttered by our Lord in the Olivet Discourse depict post-Rapture scenes."[477] **Gerald Stanton** maintains that, "...the Matthew passage contains a heavy Jewish cast and...its details are in contrast to, rather than in harmony with, the passage in 1Thessalonians 4."[478] And **E. Schuyler English** explains that, "In Matthew the Lord is speaking of a visible return to the earth. In Thessalonians the Word tells us of a meeting with the saints in the air..."[479]

It is important to understand that in order to protect and preserve the viability of the pretribulation rapture doctrine, it is absolutely essential that Dispensationalists deny any unity between Matthew 24 and the Thessalonian Epistles. The viability of the pretribulational rapture doctrine depends upon a complete disassociation from the teachings of the Lord in Matthew 24. The reason is that Matthew 24 clearly and undeniably describes a post-tribulational Coming of the Lord and a post-tribulational gathering of the saints. Any linkage therefore, between Matthew and the Thessalonian Epistles would immediately refute the Dispensational assertion of a pretribulational Coming and rapture. However, despite Dispensational claims to the contrary, there is a remarkably strong correlation and unity between the prophetic teachings of Jesus Christ in the Olivet Discourse and those of the Apostle Paul in the Thessalonian Epistles.

Consider the following parallels contained in the following chart:

---

[475] Matthew 24:30-31 states, "...and they will see the Son of Man coming on the clouds of the sky with power and great glory. And He will send forth His angels with a great trumpet and they will **gather together His elect** from the four winds, from one end of the sky to the other." (Emphasis added).

[476] *The Blessed Hope and the Tribulation* - John F. Walvoord, Zondervan Publishing House, 1976, p.90.

[477] *God's Plan for the Future* - Lehman Strauss, Zondervan Publishing House, 1965, p.87.

[478] *Kept From the Hour* - Gerald B. Stanton, Zondervan Publishing House, 1956, p.57.

[479] *Studies in the Gospel According to Matthew* - E .Schuyler English, Zondervan Publishing House, 1938, p.177.

Matthew 24	1&2 Thessalonians
vv.10 "...many will *fall away*..."	2Th.2:3 "...*the apostasy*..."
v.15 "...the abomination of desolation... standing in *the holy place*..."	2Th.2:4 "...he takes his seat in the *temple of God*, displaying himself as being God."
v.24 "...false Christs and false prophets will arise and show *great signs and wonders*..."	2Th.2:9 "...the one whose coming is in accord with the activity of Satan, with all *power* and *signs and false wonders*."
v.27 "...so shall the *parousia* of the Son of Man be."	1Th.4:15 "the *parousia* of the Lord..." 2Th.2:1 "...the *parousia* of our Lord Jesus Christ..."
v.27 "For just as the *lightning* comes from the east and *flashes* even to the west..." v.30 "...and *they will see* the Son of Man coming... with *power and great glory*."	2Th.1:7 "...the Lord Jesus shall be *revealed from heaven* with His mighty angels in *flaming fire*."
v.31 "He will send forth His *angels* with a *great trumpet*..."	1Th.4:16 "...the voice of the *archangel* and the *trumpet* of God."
v.30-31 "...and they will see the Son of Man coming on the *clouds of the sky*... and they will *gather together* His elect from the four winds, from one end of *the sky* to the other."	1Th.4:17 "...we who are alive and remain shall be *caught up* together with them in the *clouds* to meet the Lord in *the air*..."[480]
v.31 "...and they will *gather together* His elect..."	2Th.2:1 "...our *gathering together* to Him."

Significantly, the prophetic teachings of the Lord Jesus in Matthew 24 and the Apostle Paul in the Thessalonian Epistles both refer to the future apostasy from the truth - the desecration of the Temple - great signs and wonders performed by false prophets & teachers - a visible, glorious Coming (*parousia*) that is associated with the sky, clouds,

---

[480] Compare Mt.24:30-31 & 1Thess.4:17 with **Rev.1:7**, "Behold, He **comes with the clouds**, and every eye will see Him, even those who pierced Him; and **all** the tribes of the earth will mourn over Him. Even so, Amen." (Emphasis added.) Clearly a post-tribulational description of the Coming of Jesus Christ.

angels, trumpets, and a gathering together of the elect. It should be obvious, even to the most casual reader, that the eschatologies of Matthew 24 and 1&2 Thessalonians are parallel. Or put another way, the eschatology of Paul harmonizes perfectly with the teachings of Christ as revealed in Matthew 24. As previously mentioned, this should not be surprising, since the Apostle Paul has testified that he received his teaching by direct revelation from the Lord Jesus Christ (Gal.1:11-12). We can therefore conclude that Paul's eschatology is wholly dependent upon the Lord's teachings and therefore does not represent a "new" end-time doctrine at all, but rather an amplification of established doctrine long understood and accepted by the early Church.

It is also highly significant that Jesus refers to believers as His "elect" three times within the Olivet Discourse.[481] The word "elect" (*eklektos*) simply means to be "chosen" or "selected."[482] It is frequently used in the New Testament to refer to those individuals who have been selected or chosen by God for salvation. For example, in Romans 8:33, Paul rhetorically asks, "Who will bring a charge against God's **elect** (*eklektos*)? God is the one who justifies; who is the one who condemns?" In Colossians 3:12, Paul refers to the Colossian Christians as "...those who have been **chosen** (*eklektos*) of God, holy and beloved..." In Second Timothy 2:10, Paul declares that he endures all things, "...for the sake of those who are **chosen** (*eklektos*)..." In Titus 1:1, Paul announces that he is an Apostle of Jesus Christ "...for the faith of those **chosen** (*eklektos*) of God..." The Apostle Peter addresses his first epistle to those "...who are **chosen** (*eklektos*), according to the foreknowledge of God the Father, by the sanctifying work of the Spirit, that you may obey Jesus Christ and be sprinkled with His blood..." (1Pt.1:1-2).

Throughout the New Testament, the word *eklektos* is unquestionably used to describe Christians. However, in Matthew 24, Dispensationalists argue that the word *eklektos*

---

[481] **Mt.24:22** "And unless those days had been cut short, no life would have been saved; but for the sake of the **elect** those days shall be cut short." **Mt.24:24** "For false Christs and false prophets will arise and show great signs and wonders, so as to mislead, if possible, even the **elect**." **Mt.24:31** "And He will send forth His angels with a great trumpet and they will gather together His **elect** from the four winds, from one end of the sky to the other." (Emphasis added).

[482] "ἐκλεκτός [*eklektos*]...chosen out, selected; in N.T. chosen as a recipient of special privilege, elect..." *The Analytical Greek Lexicon Revised* – Harold K. Moulton, Zondervan Publishing House, 1978, p.125. "ἐκλεκτός [*eklektos*]...choice, select...chosen..." *A Manual Greek Lexicon of the New Testament* – G. Abbott-Smith, Charles Scribner's Sons, 1953, p.139. "ἐκλεκτός [*eklektos*]...picked out, chosen...chosen by God...to obtain salvation through Christ...hence Christians are called...the chosen or elect of God..." *A Greek-English Lexicon of the New Testament* – Joseph Henry Thayer, T.&T. Clark, Edinburgh, 1953, p.197.

refers to Israel and *not* to Christians. For example, while referring to Matthew 24, **Arno Gaebelein** states that, "...the word *elect* refers to the literal Israel." **Gaebelein** goes on to say that, "...the '*elect*,' [is] a term which in this chapter as well as throughout the Gospels always means His earthly people; in the Epistles the word 'elect' always means the church."[483] **E. Schuyler English** follows Gaebelein almost verbatim, teaching that, "...in the Gospels the '*elect*', means Israel, the chosen people; in the Epistles the '*elect*' means the Church, the body of believers..."[484] **C.I. Scofield** refers specifically to Matthew 24:22, declaring that God will shorten the time of the Tribulation, "...because there will be in the world those whom He calls the '*elect*,' Israel beloved for the fathers sake."[485] And **Lewis Sperry Chafer** maintains that, "...throughout the entire Olivet Discourse, the '*elect*' is Israel."[486]

Thus, Dispensationalists argue that the word "elect" (*eklektos*) is used in the New Testament to describe *two* separate and distinct redeemed bodies - the Church and Israel. For example, **John Walvoord** argues that, "...saints in the church and saints who are Israelites...can *both be elect* and *not* the same company"[487] It is important to understand that this is an unsubstantiated assumption that is based solely upon two inferences. First, Dispensationalists *assume* that there are two separate groups of redeemed people - Israel (Old Testament believers and a future Jewish remnant) and the Church (New Testament believers exclusively). Second, they *assume* that large portions of the New Testament narratives apply specifically to the Jews and *not* to the Church.[488] However, there is absolutely no textual or exegetical reason to justify these highly speculative and subjective inferences. If however, the Gospels are accepted as Christian Scriptures that apply specifically to the Church, then the elect of the Gospels and the elect of the Epistles logically refer to the same body of redeemed individuals.

Dispensationalists further argue that there will be *two* separate and distinct "gatherings" of these "elect." For example, **Dwight Pentecost,** while referring to Matthew 24:31

---

[483] *The Gospel of Matthew* - Arno C. Gaebelein, Loizeaux Brothers, 1982, pp.473,504.
[484] *Studies in the Gospel According to Matthew* - E. Schuyler English, Zondervan Publishing House, 1938, pp.177-178.
[485] *Prophecy Made Plain* - C.I. Scofield, The Gospel Hour, Inc., 1967, p.132.
[486] *Systematic Theology* - Lewis Sperry Chafer, Kregel Publications, 1993, vol.4, p.319
[487] *The Rapture Question* - John F. Walvoord, Zondervan Publishing House, 1979, p.60.
[488] See Chapter Three, *The Dispensational Hermeneutic*, Part 2, *The Dispensationalizing of the New Testament*, for a discussion of the Dispensational practices of dividing the New Testament Scriptures into "Jewish" and "Christian" sections.

states that, "Verse 31 *suggests* that the event to follow the second advent will be the regathering of Israel...the 'elect' of verse 31 must have reference to the saints of that program with which God is then dealing, that is, Israel."[489] And **Renald Showers** claims that, "...there is good reason for concluding that the gathering of the elect in Matthew 24:31 refers, *not* to the Rapture, but to the gathering of the believing *remnant* of Israel alive in the earth at Jesus' coming after the Great Tribulation."[490] **Showers** goes on to say that, "...in 2 Thessalonians 2:1 Paul was referring to the coming of Christ that will involve the Rapture of the church..."[491]

Thus, Dispensationalists teach that there will be *two* distinct gatherings of *two* separate groups, at *two* different times - one before the Tribulation (i.e., the Church) and one after the Tribulation (i.e., a Jewish remnant). However, the Scriptures do not support this theory. It is highly significant that both the Lord Jesus Christ and the Apostle Paul refer to a future "gathering" of believers in the immediate context of the *parousia*. In Matthew 24, Jesus declared that at "...the **coming** [*parousia*] of the Son of Man...immediately **after** the tribulation... He will send forth His angels with a great trumpet and they will **gather together** [*episunago - ἐπισυνάγω*] His elect..." (vv.27,29,31, emphasis added). In 2Thessalonians 2:1, Paul writes that, "...with regard to the **coming** [*parousia*] of our Lord Jesus Christ, and our **gathering together** [*episunagoge - ἐπισυναγωγή*] to Him..." (Emphasis added). It is conspicuous that both the Lord Jesus and the Apostle Paul employ different forms of the same word, which mean to "gather together." Jesus uses the verbal form, *episunago* (**ἐπισυνάγω); while** Paul uses the noun form *episunagoge* (**ἐπισυναγωγή**)[492] to refer to the *gathering together* of believers at the *parousia*. Since there is only one *parousia*, it logically follows that there is only one *gathering together* of believers. It therefore, becomes readily apparent from the context of these passages and the terminology employed that both the Lord Jesus Christ and the Apostle Paul are describing the gathering of the Church at the *parousia* - an event that both Jesus and Paul place *after* the Tribulation (see Mt.24:27-31, and 2Thess.2:1,8).

---

[489] *Things to Come* - J. Dwight Pentecost, Zondervan Publishing House, 1964, p.280.
[490] *Maranatha Our Lord Come!* - Renald E. Showers, The Friends of Israel Gospel Ministry, Inc., p.182.
[491] *Maranatha Our Lord Come!* - Renald E. Showers, The Friends of Israel Gospel Ministry, Inc., p.226.
[492] The noun *episunagoge* refers to the future prospect of being "gathered together" to Christ, while the verb *episunago* refers to the act of being "gathered together" unto the Lord. See *Expository Dictionary of Bible Words* - Stephen D. Renn, Editor, Hendrickson Publishers, 2005, p.427, and *The Analytical Greek Lexicon Revised* - Harold K. Moulton, Zondervan Publishing House, 1982, p.161.

If the Scriptures really teach that Jesus Christ is Coming *before* the Tribulation to rapture His Church, as Dispensationalists insist - then surely there should be at least one Scripture that clearly describes this pretribulational Coming. ***Yet, the indisputable fact is that there is not one verse in the New Testament that describes a pretribulational Coming, Appearing or Revelation of Jesus Christ - not one!*** It is an incontrovertible fact that the New Testament Scriptures consistently and uniformly describe the ***Second Coming*** of Jesus Christ as a *post*-tribulational event. Carefully consider the following textual evidence:

Matthew 16:27, describes the glorious coming of Christ, with the angels of heaven to render recompense to all men for their actions. This is clearly a post-tribulational description of Divine judgment and reward.

"For the Son of Man is going to come in the **glory** of His Father with **His angels**; and will then **recompense every man** according to his deeds." Emphasis added. Compare the parallel passages in Mark 8:38 and Luke 9:26.

Matthew 24:27, portrays the visible, post-tribulational Coming of Christ at the end of this age.

"For just as the **lightning** comes from the east, and **flashes** even to the west, so shall the **coming** [*parousia*] of the Son of Man be." Emphasis added.

Matthew 25:31, depicts the glorious coming of Jesus Christ with all the angels of heaven to establish His earthly reign and to judge the nations. Clearly a description of post-tribulational events synonymous with those described in Matthew 16:27.

"But when the Son of Man comes in His **glory**, and **all the angels** with Him, then He will sit on His glorious throne. And all the nations will be gathered before Him..." Emphasis added.

Mark 13:24-26, describes the post-tribulational Coming of Christ, which will be accompanied by cataclysmic celestial events.

"But in those days, **after the tribulation** the **sun will be darkened**, and the **moon will not give its light**, and the **stars will be falling from heaven**, and the **powers of the heavens will be shaken**. And then they will see the Son of Man coming in the clouds with great power and glory." Emphasis added. Compare parallel passages in Matthew 24:29-30 and Luke 21:25-26.

Luke 17:23-24, explains that the Second Coming of Jesus Christ will be visible, *not* secret. It will be as bright, obvious and observable as the lightning flashing across the sky - clearly and unmistakably a post-tribulational description of Christ's glorious Coming.

"And they will say to you, 'Look there!' 'Look here!' Do not go away, and do not run after them. For just as the **lightning**, when it **flashes** out of one part of the sky, **shines** to the other part of the sky, so will the Son of Man be in His day." Emphasis added. Compare the parallel passage in Matthew 24:26-27.

Luke 17:26-30, declares that the judgment of the Flood and the destruction of Sodom and Gomorrah prefigure the Divine judgments that will fall upon this present world at the *Revelation* of Jesus Christ - clearly, a post-tribulational description of God's judgment upon the ungodly.

"... in the **days of Noah**...the **flood** came and destroyed them all. It was the same as happened in the **days of Lot**...it rained **fire and brimstone from heaven** and destroyed them all. It will be **just the same** on the day that the Son of Man is **revealed**." (Emphasis added).

Luke 21:25-27, plainly reveals that the Second Coming of Christ will be visible, powerful and glorious - and that it will occur *after* the cataclysmic astronomical events of the Tribulation.

"And there will be **signs in the sun and moon and stars**, and upon the earth dismay among nations, in perplexity at the roaring of the sea and the waves, men fainting from fear and the expectation of the things which are coming upon the world; for the **powers of the heavens will be shaken**. And then they will see the Son of Man coming in a cloud with power and great glory." Emphasis added. Compare the parallel passage in Matthew 24:29-30.

Second Thessalonians 1:6-10, graphically describes the visible, post-tribulational Coming of Jesus Christ with His angels to deliver His people and to judge the unbelieving world.

"For after all it is *only* just for God to repay with affliction those who afflict you, and to *give* relief to you who are afflicted and to us as well when the **Lord Jesus shall be revealed from heaven** with His **mighty angels in flaming fire**, dealing out retribution to those who do not know God and to those who do not obey the gospel of our Lord Jesus. And these will pay the **penalty of eternal destruction**, away from the presence of the Lord and from the glory of His power, when He comes to be glorified in His saints on that day, and to be marveled at among all who have believed - for our testimony to you was believed." Emphasis added.

Second Thessalonians 2:8, depicts the post-tribulational destruction of the Antichrist at the Coming of Christ.

"And then that **lawless one** will be revealed whom the Lord will **slay with the breath of His mouth** and bring to an end by the appearance of His **coming [*parousia*]**." Emphasis added.

Jude 14-15, describes the post-tribulational Coming of Christ in judgment upon the ungodly.

"About these also Enoch, in the seventh generation from Adam, prophesied, saying 'Behold, the Lord came with many thousands of His holy ones, to **execute judgment upon all**, and to **convict all the ungodly** of all their ungodly deeds which they have done in an ungodly way, and of all the harsh things which ungodly sinners have spoken against Him." Emphasis added.

Revelation 1:7, explains that the Second Coming of Jesus Christ will be a visible event, witnessed by all, causing great emotional distress among all the inhabitants of the earth – clearly a description of the visible post-tribulational Coming of Christ at the end of the age.

"Behold, He comes with the clouds, and **every eye will see Him**, even those who pierced Him; and all the tribes of the earth will mourn over Him. Even so, Amen." Emphasis added.

Revelation 11:15-19, announces that at the sounding of the seventh trumpet, (i.e., the last trumpet cp. 1Cor.15:52) the reign of Jesus Christ will be established over the kingdoms of the world, His servants rewarded, and His enemies destroyed. This passage clearly refers to post-tribulational events.

"And the seventh angel sounded; and there arose loud voices in heaven, saying, 'The kingdom of the world has become the kingdom of our Lord, and of His Christ; and He will reign forever and ever.' ...And the nations were enraged, and Thy wrath came, and the time came for the dead to be judged, and the time to give their reward to Thy bond-servants the prophets and the saints and to those who fear Thy name, the small and the great, and to destroy those who destroy the earth."

Revelation 19:11-16, graphically describes the visible and glorious Coming of the Lord Jesus Christ *after* the Tribulation; the terrible judgment of the nations which will then ensue; and the establishment of His millennial rule over those nations. This passage is clearly parallel to the events of the seventh trumpet depicted in Revelation 11:15-19.

"And I saw heaven opened; and behold, a white horse, and He who sat upon it is called Faithful and True; and in righteousness He judges and wages war...And He is clothed with a rob dipped in blood; and His name is called the Word of God...And from His mouth comes a sharp sword, so that with it He may smite the nations; and He will rule them with a rod of iron; and He treads the wine press of the fierce wrath of God, the Almighty."

The Scriptures clearly testify to the fact that there is only *one* Second Coming of Jesus Christ – and that Coming will be *post*-tribulational. The textual evidence is indisputable. Yet, without one clear statement from Scripture, Dispensationalists maintain that the Lord will also come secretly, before the Tribulation for the sole purpose of rapturing His Church. In support of this proposition, Dispensationalists have constructed a complicated and convoluted interpretative system that relies upon human speculation, assumption, analogy and inference instead of clear statements from Scripture. Mark it carefully and consider it thoughtfully: there is not one verse in the entire New Testament that describes a pretribulational Coming of Jesus Christ – not one! Nor is there one verse in the entire New Testament that describes a secret, unannounced, any moment pretribulational rapture of the Church - not one! This simple fact should give every proponent of the pretribulation rapture theory pause for serious reflection.

Chapter Five, Part III
"Two" Gospels

1. Different Gospels

Dispensationalists teach that the New Testament reveals *two* different Gospels. They maintain that the phrases "the Gospel of the Kingdom" and "the Gospel of the grace of God" refer to two distinctly different Gospel messages. In support of this claim, Dispensationalists point to the fact that in the Gospel of Matthew, we are told that Jesus went about preaching "the gospel of the kingdom," whereas the Apostle Paul preached "the gospel of the grace of God."[493] Dispensationalists therefore conclude that there are "two" different Gospels with "two" fundamentally different messages - the "gospel of the kingdom" which heralds the establishment of an earthly theocratic kingdom for national Israel and "the gospel of God's grace" which reveals God's saving grace and offers personal salvation to sinners.

---

[493] The Biblical texts alluded to are: **Mt.4:23,** "And Jesus was going about in all Galilee, teaching in their synagogues, and proclaiming the *gospel of the kingdom*..." (Emphasis added; see also Mt.9:35; Lk.16:16). **Mt.24:14,** "And this *gospel of the kingdom* shall be preached in the whole world for a witness to all the nations, and then the end shall come." **Acts 20:24,** "But I do not consider my life of any account as dear to myself, in order that I may finish my course, and the ministry which I received from the Lord Jesus, to testify solemnly of the *gospel of the grace of God*." (Emphasis added).

John Darby was the first to assert that there were multiple Gospels. For example, while commenting on Matthew 24:14, **Darby** explains that, "It is 'this gospel of the kingdom' which is here spoken of; it is *not* the proclamation of the union of the Church with Christ, *nor* redemption in its fullness, as preached and taught by the apostles after the ascension, but the kingdom which was to be established on the earth, as John the Baptist, and the Lord Himself, had proclaimed."[494] **William Kelly** succinctly states that, "The gospel of God's grace is *not* the same as the gospel of the kingdom."[495] **Charles Mackintosh** instructs his followers that, "The church must not be confounded with the kingdom; nor yet the gospel of the grace of God with the gospel of the kingdom. *The two are perfectly distinct;* and if we confound them, we shall understand neither the one nor the other."[496] In his Bible correspondence course, **C.I. Scofield** teaches that, "The gospel of the kingdom (Matt.4:23; 24:14) is to be *distinguished* from the gospel of the grace of God (Acts 20:24)."[497] **A.C. Gaebelein** explains that, "There is a *difference* between the Gospel of the Kingdom and the Gospel of Grace."[498] **Renald Showers** explicitly states that, "...Jesus gave *two distinct gospels* to His disciples to preach." According to **Showers**, "...the content of the *first gospel* was, 'The kingdom of heaven is at hand'... Paul defined the *second gospel* in 1Corinthians 15:1-5... An examination of these *gospels* indicates that *their contents were quite distinct*."[499] And **John Walvoord** cautions Christians that, "The gospel of the kingdom should *not be confused* with the gospel of Salvation..."[500]

Does the New Testament really reveal "two" distinctly different Gospels with two fundamentally different messages? Is the "gospel of the kingdom" (Mt.4:23) really different than the "gospel of God's grace" (Acts 20:24)? Despite Dispensational claims to the contrary, there are *not* "two" Gospels. There is only *one* Gospel revealed in the New Testament. This fact is made evident when the Scriptures are actually interpreted "literally."

---

[494] *Synopsis of the Books of the Bible* - J.N. Darby, Loizeaux Brothers, 1950, *Matthew-John*, Vol.III, p.172.
[495] *Lectures on the Gospel of Matthew* - William Kelly, Loizeaux Brothers, 1943, p.440.
[496] *Papers on the Lord's Coming* - C.H.M., Loizeaux Brothers, n.d., p.71.
[497] *Scofield Correspondence Course, Vol.V, Twenty-Six Great Words of Scripture* - C.I. Scofield, Moody Bible Institute, 1960, p.1284.
[498] *The Gospel of Matthew* - Arno C. Gaebelein, Loizeaux Brothers, 1961, p.488.
[499] *There Really is a Difference* - Renald E. Showers, The Friends of Israel Gospel Ministry, Inc., 2002, p.3.
[500] *Major Bible Prophecies* - John F. Walvoord, Zondervan Publishing House, 1994, p.300.

We are told in Matthew 4, that after John the Baptist had been arrested (see v.12), "Jesus was going about in all Galilee, teaching in their synagogues, and proclaiming *the gospel of the kingdom*..." (Mt.4:23, emphasis added). However, the parallel passage in the Gospel of Mark declares, "And after John had been taken into custody, Jesus came into Galilee, preaching *the gospel of God*, and saying, "The time is fulfilled, and the kingdom of God is at hand; repent and believe in *the gospel*." (Mk.1:14-15, emphasis added). Clearly, the phrases "*the gospel of the kingdom*," "*the gospel of God*" and "*the gospel*" are equivalent terms.[501] These three different phrases are used interchangeably to describe the message preached by Christ in Galilee. Are we to seriously believe that Christ preached three different messages throughout Galilee? Certainly not. The phrases "*the gospel of the kingdom*" and the "*the gospel of God*" simply describe different characteristics or aspects of "*the Gospel*." The equivalency of these phrases is further confirmed by parallel passages in Matthew 24 and Mark 13. In Matthew 24:14, Jesus declared: "And this *gospel of the kingdom* shall be preached in the whole world for a witness to all the nations, and then the end shall come." However, in the parallel passage in Mark 13:10, we are told: "And *the gospel* must first be preached to all the nations." The phrases, "*this gospel of the kingdom*" and "*the gospel*" refer to the same message that is to be preached to all the nations and are therefore clearly equivalent.

Consider first of all, the phrase, "gospel of the kingdom." The word "gospel" (*euanggelion - εὐαγγέλιον*) literally means "glad tidings" or "good news." The word "kingdom" (*basileia - βασιλεία*) refers to the sovereign power, authority and dominion of a king.[502] Thus, the phrase "*the gospel of the kingdom*" refers to the good news of God's sovereign administration and rule over the earth as its King. The phrase "*the gospel of God*"[503] expresses the idea that the glad tidings or good news of the

---

[501] Likewise, consider Luke 9:2 & 9:6. In v.2, we are told that Jesus sent out the Twelve to "...proclaim the **kingdom of God**, and to perform healing." Verse 6, states that they departed and "...began going about among the villages, preaching **the gospel**, and healing everywhere." Clearly, the proclamation of the kingdom of God is synonymous with the preaching of the Gospel.

[502] "βασιλεία...sovereignty, royal power, dominion..." *A Manual Greek Lexicon of the New Testament* - G. Abbott-Smith, Charles Scribner's Sons, 1953, p.77. "βασιλεία...royal power, kingship, dominion, rule...a kingdom, i.e., the territory subject to the rule of a king..." *Thayer's Greek-English Lexicon of the New Testament* - Joseph H. Thayer, T & T Clark, 1953, p.96. "βασιλεία...a kingdom, realm, the region or country governed by a king; kingly power, authority, dominion, reign; royal dignity, the title and honour of a king." *The Analytical Greek Lexicon Revised* - Harold K. Moulton, Zondervan Publishing House, 1982, p.67.

[503] See also Rom.15:16; 2Cor.11:7; 1Thess.2:2; 2:8-9 for the phrase "the gospel of God."

Gospel is Divine in its origin - its source is directly from God and not from man. This is precisely Paul's point when he testified to the Galatians that, "...*the gospel* which was preached by me is not according to man. For I neither received it from man, nor was I taught it, but I received it through a revelation of Jesus Christ" (Gal.1:11-12). Paul testifies that he received "*the gospel*" by direct revelation from God. Moreover, in Acts 20:24 Paul declares that it was his life's ambition "...to testify solemnly of *the gospel of the grace of God*." However, in the very next verse Paul declares that, "...I went about *preaching the kingdom*..." (v.25). Are we to believe that Paul was preaching two different and distinct Gospels at the same time? Certainly not. Clearly, Paul's "*preaching the kingdom*" is synonymous with his divine call to "*testify solemnly of the gospel of the grace of God*."

Likewise in Acts 28, we are told that while Paul was under arrest in Rome, he was "...solemnly testifying about *the kingdom of God*, and trying to persuade them [i.e., the Jewish leaders] *concerning Jesus*..." (v.23, emphasis added). We are also told that Paul was "...welcoming all who came to him, *preaching the kingdom of God*, and teaching concerning *the Lord Jesus Christ*..." (v.30-31, emphasis added). Again, are we to seriously entertain the proposition that the Apostle Paul was preaching two different and distinct Gospels to these people - one pertaining to an earthly theocratic kingdom for the Jews and the other pertaining to salvation by grace for Jews and Gentiles? The context of these passages makes it readily apparent that all of these phrases are used interchangeably, the one modifying the other. For example, it is evident that Paul's preaching about "*the kingdom*" and "*the kingdom of God*" pertained specifically to "*the Lord Jesus Christ*." Proof that Paul's message was one of grace and salvation is made evident when Paul rebuked the Jewish leaders who refused to believe his proclamation of the "good news" about Jesus Christ, declaring that, "...*this salvation of God* has been sent to the Gentiles; they will also listen" (v.28) - in other words, the very same message that was rejected by these Jews, was then delivered to, and accepted by the Gentiles. Contextually, the phrase, "*this salvation of God*" concisely synthesizes what Paul had previously been "...explaining to them [i.e., the Jews] by solemnly testifying to them about the kingdom of God, and trying to persuade them concerning Jesus..." (v.23). Paul was clearly preaching the message of salvation through Jesus Christ.

144

Carefully consider the testimony of Acts 8. Here we are told that Phillip went to Samaria, "...and began *proclaiming Christ* to them" (v.5), with the result that many, "...believed Phillip *preaching the good news about the kingdom of God* [504]..." (v.12, emphasis added). We are then told that when the Apostles in Jerusalem heard that the Samaritans "...had received *the word of God*" (v.14, emphasis added), Peter and John traveled from Jerusalem to Samaria, where they prayed for these new believers. Then, after Peter and John, "...had solemnly testified and spoken *the word of the Lord*, they started back to Jerusalem, and were preaching *the gospel* to many villages of the Samaritans" (v.25, emphasis added). Phillip was then directed by an angel to engage an Ethiopian eunuch, who was reading Isaiah 53 while traveling on the road from Jerusalem to Gaza. Phillip approached the Ethiopian and "...beginning from this Scripture he *preached Jesus* to him" (v.35, emphasis added). Thereafter, Phillip miraculously found himself at Azotes where he "...kept preaching *the gospel* to all the cities..." (v.40). Now then, are we to believe that Phillip, Peter and John were all preaching different Gospels? Clearly, the terms *"proclaiming Christ," "preaching the good news about the kingdom of God," "the word of God," "the word of the Lord"* and *"the gospel,"* are all equivalent terms and are used interchangeably to refer to the one true Gospel message.

The New Testament frequently uses terms that emphasize different characteristics or aspects of the Gospel message. For example:

In **Acts 20:24,** we have the phrase, *"the gospel of the grace of God."* This phrase reveals that the message of God's grace towards sinners is an essential element of the Gospel message.

In **Romans 1:9,** we have the phrase, *"...the gospel of His Son..."* This phrase indicates that the one true Gospel pertains specifically to God's only begotten Son - Jesus Christ. In other words, the Gospel reveals good news about the person, nature and work of the Lord Jesus Christ on behalf of sinners.[505]

---

[504] Literally, "...they believed Phillip *preaching the gospel (εὐαγγελιζομένῳ)*, the things about the kingdom of God..." Acts 8:12.

[505] The equivalent phrase "the gospel of Christ" occurs in Ro.15:19; 1Cor.9:12; 2Cor.2:12; 9:13; 10:14; Gal.1:7; Phil.1:27; 1Thess.3:2.

In **2 Corinthians 4:4,** we have the phrase, *"...the light of the gospel of the glory of Christ, who is the image of God."* This phrase reveals that the Gospel discloses the Divine splendor, grandeur, magnificence and majesty of the Lord Jesus Christ.

In **Ephesians 6:15,** we have the phrase, *"...the gospel of peace."* This phrase reveals that the Gospel presents terms of peace - it announces the "good news" that God has provided a way for fallen, lost, ruined sinners to be reconciled to God through the Lord Jesus Christ.

In **1Timothy 1:11,** Paul refers to "...the *glorious gospel* of the blessed God..." This phrase refers to the fact that the Gospel reveals a body of Divine redemptive truth that is immensely splendid, marvelous and wonderful beyond description - it is glorious!

In **Revelation 14:6,** we see an angel "...having an *everlasting gospel* to preach to those who live on the earth..." The Gospel is eternal - Jesus Himself declared that, "Heaven and earth will pass away, but My words will not pass away" (Mk.13:31).

Thus, the phrases, *"the gospel of the grace of God," "the gospel of His Son," "the light of the gospel of the glory of Christ," "the gospel of peace," "the glorious gospel"* and the *"everlasting gospel"* do not describe different Gospels. Rather, these phrases describe different aspects or characteristics of the one true Gospel. In exactly the same way, the phrases *"the gospel of the kingdom"* and *"the gospel of the grace of God"* describe different characteristics or aspects of the one true Gospel and *not* two distinct and different Gospel messages!

2. The Gospel of the Kingdom Explained

According to Dispensationalists, the "gospel of the kingdom" is the message that God sent Jesus Christ, the King, to establish an earthly, theocratic, political kingdom for Israel. Once again, **John Darby** was the first to assert that, "In chapter 10, Christ sends out the twelve.[506] They were...to go to the lost sheep of the house of Israel, and *declare the kingdom of heaven at hand*; to inquire who was worthy, i.e., seek the righteous remnant, *not* poor sinners... Here we find the Lord establishing a ministry exclusively to

---

[506] Darby is referring to Matthew, chapter 10.

Israel...*to gather out a remnant and prepare a people for the kingdom which was at hand*. Such is the direct teaching of the Lord."[507] Following **Darby's** lead, **William Blackstone** declares that, "The gospel of the kingdom is the good news, or glad tidings of the kingdom come."[508] **A.C. Gaebelein** rhetorically asks, "What then is the Gospel of the Kingdom?" He then answers, "...the Gospel of the Kingdom is the good news that the promised kingdom of the Old Testament was about to be established with the manifestation of the King."[509] And **C.I. Scofield** explains that, "...the Gospel of the kingdom...is the good news that God purposes to set up on earth...a kingdom, political, spiritual, Israelitish, universal..."[510]

Dispensationalists insist that the Gospels of Matthew, Mark, Luke and John are directed principally to the Jews and pertain to the establishment of an earthly theocratic kingdom for Israel. For example, **C.I. Scofield** stresses that, "The mission of Jesus was, *primarily* to the Jews..."[511] And according to Dispensationalists, the most important aspect of Christ's ministry to "the Jews" was His offer of an earthly theocratic kingdom to the Jewish nation. In his *Systematic Theology*, **Lewis Sperry Chafer** maintains that, "...the earthly ministry of Christ [was] addressed to Israel *exclusively* and concerning their kingdom as at hand. The evidence is complete respecting the fact that Israel's kingdom was offered to that nation by Christ at His first advent."[512] **Chafer** goes on to explain that, "...the New Testament opens with the appearance of the King and the offer to Israel of her long predicted kingdom...."[513] Thus, Dispensationalists claim that the primary purpose of Christ's earthly ministry was to establish an earthly kingdom for Israel.

But are Dispensationalists correct when they insist that the New Testament teaches that Jesus came to offer an earthly theocratic kingdom to the nation of Israel? Was this really the emphasis of the earthly ministry of Christ? Thus, the operative question becomes, "What was the primary purpose of the Incarnation of the Son of God?" Was it

---

[507] *The Collected Writings of J.N. Darby* - Edited by William Kelly, Stow Hill Bible and Tract Depot, n.d., Prophetic No.4, Vol.11, pp.145.
[508] *Jesus is Coming* - William E. Blackstone, Kregel, Publications, 1989, p.133.
[509] *The Gospel of Matthew* - Arno C. Gaebelein, Loizeaux Brothers, 1961, p.488.
[510] *The Scofield Study Bible* - C.I. Scofield, Oxford University Press, 1909, 1917, 1939, 1945, p.1343.
[511] *The Scofield Study Bible* - C.I. Scofield, Oxford University Press, 1909, 1917, 1939, 1945, p.989.
[512] *Systematic Theology* - Lewis Sperry Chafer, Kregel Publications, 1993, Vol.4, p.266.
[513] *Systematic Theology* - Lewis Sperry Chafer, Kregel Publications, 1993, Vol.4, p.385.

to establish an earthly political kingdom for the Jews, or was it to accomplish God's eternal plan of redemption for a fallen humanity? Fortunately, God has not left us to wonder and speculate as to the purpose of Christ's earthly ministry. The Scriptures are crystal clear on this point. They plainly state *why* Jesus Christ became flesh and dwelt among us. Prior to the birth of Christ, the angel declared to Joseph that Mary would, "...bear a Son; and you shall call His name Jesus, for it is He who will save His people from their sins" (Mt.1:21). Significantly, the English name "Jesus" is derived from the Greek *Iesous*, which is equivalent to the Hebrew, *Yeshuah* (Joshua) which literally means "God is salvation."[514] Not surprisingly, Jesus Himself, clearly and repeatedly testified that the purpose of His preaching was *redemptive* and *not political*. For example, Jesus declared that, "...I did not come to call the righteous, but sinners" (Mt. 9:13 cp. Mk.2:17). In Luke 5:32, Jesus stated, "I have not come to call the righteous but sinners to repentance." Again, in Matthew 18:11, Jesus explained, "For the Son of man has come to save that which was lost." (cp. Lk.19:11). And in response to James and John's offer to call fire down from heaven upon a Samaritan village (Lk.9:52-54) Jesus, in verse 56, declared, "...for the Son of Man did not come to destroy men's lives but to save them." In Matthew 20:28, Jesus declared, "The Son of Man did not come to be served, but to give His life a ransom for many." (cp. Mk.10:45). Thus, Jesus Himself clearly defined the purpose of His earthly ministry as redemptive and *not* political. Underscoring this indisputable fact, the Apostle Paul states that, "It is a trustworthy statement, deserving full acceptance, that Christ Jesus came into the world to save sinners..." (1Tim.1:15). Likewise, the Apostle John declares that, "You know that He [Jesus] appeared in order to take away sins…" (1John 3:5).

Yet, Dispensationalists insist that Jesus' primary mission was to offer an earthly, political kingdom to the Jews in spite of the fact that there is *not a single New Testament verse that makes this claim.* In fact, the Scriptures refute the entire proposition out-right. In the Gospel of John we have the record of the miraculous feeding of the five thousand by Jesus while He was ministering in Galilee (see Jn.6:1-14). The people were so impressed by this miracle that they intended to declare Jesus their King. However, we are told that, "Jesus, therefore perceiving that they were intending to come and take Him by force, to make Him king, withdrew again to the

---

[514] *Expository Dictionary of Bible Words* – Stephen D. Renn, Hendrickson Publishers, 2005, p.533. The idea conveyed in the name "Jesus" is that salvation is provided by God.

mountain by Himself alone" (Jn.6:15). Clearly, Jesus had no intention of establishing Himself as King over an earthy theocratic kingdom in Israel at His first Advent. His immediate and deliberate withdrawal from the multitude that would have recognized Him as their King effectively demonstrates this fact.

Beginning with **John Darby**, Dispensationalists have also insisted that the "gospel of the kingdom" makes no provision for individual salvation. While commenting on Matthew 24:14, **Darby**, contends that, "...this *gospel of the kingdom* which is here spoken of; it is *not* the proclamation of the union of the Church with Christ, *nor redemption in its fullness*, as preached and taught by the apostles after the ascension, but the kingdom which was to be established on the earth..."[515] Likewise, **Lewis Sperry Chafer** stresses that, "The first ministry of Christ was, then, to Israel as her King. In this He appeared, *not as a personal Savior*, but as her long-expected Messiah..."[516] **Chafer** further insists that, "The gospel of the kingdom...is the announcement of the presence of the long-expected Messiah and His predicted blessings for Israel...The *kingdom gospel*, since it concerns Israel's national hope, was properly restricted to them...this gospel call was *not for the salvation even of Israel, but was for revival and restoration.*"[517] And **Clarence Larkin** maintains that "The Gospel of the Kingdom...is the Good News that God purposes to set up a Kingdom on this earth...This Gospel is to be preached again after the Church is taken out. It will be the fulfillment of Matt.24:14...This has *no reference* to the Gospel that is now being preached to the nations [i.e., the Gospel of Salvation] but the *Gospel of the Kingdom is not for salvation* but for a witness, that is, it is the announcement that the time has come to set up the kingdom."[518]

Thus, according to Dispensationalists, the hope of Israel is not individual salvation, but national restoration and political revival. This view is emphasized by **Louis Talbot**, who declares that, "The gospel of grace points to a Saviour and a Bridegroom; it offers to the bride citizenship in heaven and joint-heirship with Him. The gospel of the kingdom will offer *citizenship in His millennial kingdom*, a literal, earthly

---

[515] *Synopsis of the Books of the Bible* - J.N. Darby, Loizeaux Brothers, 1950, *Matthew-John*, vol.3, p.172.
[516] *Systematic Theology* - Lewis Sperry Chafer, Kregel Publications, 1993, Vol.4, p.174.
[517] *Dispensationalism* - Dallas Seminary Press, Lewis Sperry Chafer, 1936, 1951, pp.83-84.
[518] *The Book of Revelation* - Clarence Larkin, Rev. Clarence Larkin Estate, 1919, p.133.

kingdom."[519] Therefore, according to **Talbot**, it is "the gospel of grace" that offers salvation and a heavenly citizenship, whereas, "the gospel of the kingdom" offers a temporal, earthly citizenship in the Millennial Kingdom. This same premise is latent in **Charles Ryrie's** description of the kingdom gospel, when he declares that, "...dispensationalists insist that the kingdom Jesus preached was the Davidic kingdom...It was the Davidic kingdom which Jesus offered and *not* the general rule of God over the earth or *His spiritual reign in individual lives*."[520] Likewise, **Dwight Pentecost** draws a sharp distinction between the temporal and spiritual aspects of the two gospels when he announces that, "The gospel of the kingdom was the good news that the promised King was soon to appear on the scene to offer the promised kingdom...the gospel of the kingdom was *not primarily soteriological* but eschatological in concept."[521] What Pentecost is saying, is that the Gospel of the Kingdom does not pertain to Israel's salvation but to her kingdom hopes. Lest there should be any doubt about what **Pentecost** meant, he immediately goes on to say that, "The gospel of the kingdom *did not offer a way of salvation,* but rather offered the hope of the fulfillment of Israel's eschatological promises, which contained within them the fulfillment of their soteriological hopes..."[522] **Pentecost** does not explain how "the fulfillment of Israel's eschatological promises" would fulfill their "soteriological hopes," especially in light of his emphatic claim that the "gospel of the kingdom did *not* offer a way of salvation." Likewise, **John Walvoord** also draws a sharp distinction between the redemptive characteristics of the Gospel of Grace and the political and social reformation of the Gospel of the Kingdom, when he asserts that, "The gospel of the kingdom should *not* be confused with the gospel of salvation, which relates to the first coming of Christ, his death on the cross, and his provision of salvation and eternal life...The gospel of the kingdom, however, is God's answer to the wickedness of our modern civilization. It is the bright hope that when Jesus comes the wickedness will be judged and righteousness will characterize the world."[523] Thus, Dispensationalists teach that the "gospel of the kingdom" announces a non-redemptive message that is primarily concerned with the Divine subjugation of the earth, and the establishment of an earthly

---

[519] *God's Plan for the Ages* - Louis C. Talbot, published by Louis C. Talbot, 1943, p.161.

[520] *Dispensationalism Today* - Charles Caldwell Ryrie, Moody Press, 1970, pp.172-173.

[521] *Things to Come* - J. Dwight Pentecost, Zondervan Publishing House, 1964, p.272. In systematic theology, *soteriology* refers to the doctrine of salvation and *eschatology* refers to the doctrine of last things.

[522] *Things to Come* - J. Dwight Pentecost, Zondervan Publishing House, 1964, p.272.

[523] *Major Bible Prophecies* - John F. Walvoord, Zondervan Publishing House, 1991, p.300.

theocratic kingdom that will result in political and social reform, wherein Jesus Christ is seen primarily as a King and *not* as a Savior.

Dispensationalists maintain that there are "two" different Gospels, with "two" different messages, with "two" different purposes, intended for "two" different groups of people. However, at the same time they paradoxically attempt to minimize and obscure these differences by blending elements of the Gospel of Grace with the Gospel of the Kingdom. For example, **Charles Ryrie**, who asserts that the "gospel of the kingdom" does *not* pertain to God's, "spiritual reign in individual lives" also claims that "Even if one makes a distinction between the gospel of the grace of God and the gospel of the kingdom, this does not mean that the gospel of the kingdom will not *include the message of the cross*. It will *add* the aspect of good news which announces the coming kingdom *along with the message of the cross*."[524] Likewise, **Dwight Pentecost** who declared that the "gospel of the kingdom did *not* offer a way of salvation" elsewhere maintains that, "The fact of the *good news of the kingdom* does not eliminate the *good news of salvation* from its message."[525] **Pentecost** further claims that, "...this gospel of the kingdom *entails the preaching of the death of Christ and the blood of Christ as the way of salvation*."[526] Thus, Dispensationalists have created a hybridized Gospel that blends the redemptive elements of the Gospel of Grace with the political aspirations of the Gospel of the Kingdom. The Gospel of the Kingdom therefore becomes a fictitious admixture of salvation and political restoration and reform.

Clearly, Dispensationalists do a serious disservice to the Christian community when they teach that there are two Gospels. They commit an even more egregious error when they insist that the redemptive elements of the Gospel of Grace are incorporated into the Gospel of the Kingdom. But, Dispensationalists cannot have it both ways. They cannot at the same time reasonably maintain that the "gospel of the kingdom" and the "gospel of grace" are both different and the same. This proposition represents an obvious contradiction in terms. If they are different, then they are not the same. And if they are the same, they are not different. But they cannot be both different and the same! The simple fact of the matter is that the New Testament does not so much as even hint at the existence of multiple Gospels. Rather, the Scriptures reveal only one true Gospel, and

---

[524] *Dispensationalism Today* - Charles Caldwell Ryrie, Moody Press, 1970, p.56.
[525] *Things to Come* - J. Dwight Pentecost, Zondervan Publishing House, 1964, p.273.
[526] *Things to Come* - J. Dwight Pentecost, Zondervan Publishing House, 1964, p.419.

issues a sobering warning against all who would dare preach "another gospel" (Gal.1:6-9)! The Dispensational doctrine of multiple Gospels would seem to come perilously close to incurring Paul's frightening Anathema (Gal.1:8,9).

Some Dispensationalists fully recognize the seriousness of this issue. They therefore attempt to evade the ominous implications created by their doctrine of *two* Gospels by asserting that there is actually only one Gospel that emphasizes different aspects at different times, or assumes different forms as new revelations are added. For example, **J. Vernon McGee** maintains that the differences between the Gospel of the Kingdom and the Gospel of Grace are only differences of "emphasis," when he explains that, "...during the Tribulation Period the gospel of the kingdom will again be preached. It is not for our day, because we are to preach the gospel of the grace of God. Is the gospel of the kingdom another gospel? No, my friend, it is not. It is the same gospel with a *different emphasis*."[527] **William Kelly** explains that, "...the term 'gospel'...is used in scripture with much more latitude than men are now accustomed to...we have *different messages, different glad tidings*, according to the various subjects or hopes that God was presenting at *different times*."[528] This concept of *"different messages"* and *"different glad tidings"* at "different times" is more fully described by **H.A. Ironside.** While commenting on Revelation 14:6,[529] **Ironside** teaches that the, "...everlasting gospel is *not* to be distinguished from the gospel that has been proclaimed throughout the centuries...it is *identical with the gospel as proclaimed from the beginning.* It is the good news, of all the ages, that God is sovereign, and man's happiness consists in recognizing His authority...To this blessed fact is *added*, in the present dispensation, the *full truth of the gospel of the grace of God*. The Gospel of the kingdom is but *another aspect* of this *same news* from heaven...There can be *only one gospel*...But that *one gospel* has *different phases*." And according to **Ironside**, "...the gospel of the kingdom...[is] the very *last phase* of that gospel..."[530] In other words, according to **Ironside**, the "one gospel" is the result of ongoing revelations which began in ages past - it is therefore an amalgamation or combination of various "phases," each building

---

[527] *Thru the Bible with J. Vernon McGee* – J. Vernon McGee, Thru the Bible Radio, vol. IV, Matthew-Romans, p.127.
[528] *Lectures on Revelation* - William Kelly, A.S. Rouse, 1897, p.325.
[529] Rev.14:6 - "And I saw another angel flying in midheaven, having an eternal gospel to preach to those who live on the earth, and to every nation and tribe and tongue and people."
[530] *Lectures on the Book of Revelation* - H.A. Ironside, Loizeaux Brothers, 1971, pp.257-258.

upon the other, yet paradoxically, we are also told that it remains "...identical with the gospel as proclaimed from the beginning."

This concept of different "phases" in the development of the "one gospel" is the underlying premise of **C.I. Scofield's** assertion that, "*Four forms* of *the Gospel* are to be *distinguished*." **Scofield** defines these "four forms" as, "(1) The Gospel of the kingdom...this is the good news that God purposes to set up on the earth...a kingdom, political, spiritual, Israelitish, universal...(2) The Gospel of the grace of God...This is the good news that Jesus Christ, the rejected King, has died on the cross for the sins of the world...This *form of the gospel* is described in many ways...(3) The everlasting Gospel...This is to be preached to the earth dwellers at the very end of the great tribulation...*It is neither the Gospel of the kingdom, nor of grace*...its burden is judgment *not salvation*...(4) That which Paul calls 'my Gospel' (Ro.2:16). This is *the Gospel of the grace of God* in its *fullest development*...It is the distinctive truth of Ephesians and Colossians..."[531]

Scofield's admonition that these "Four forms of the Gospel are to be distinguished"[532] naturally leads to the conclusion that they must be essentially different. The word "distinguish" refers to the separation of things based upon the criteria of recognizable and identifiable differences. Thus, we can only distinguish between those things that are different. If things are the same, there is no difference, and therefore no way to distinguish. It is therefore, a contradiction in terms to argue that the "one" Gospel can be distinguished from itself. If there is only "one" Gospel, then there is nothing to compare it to, or to distinguish it from. If however, the Gospel of Grace can be distinguished from the Gospel of the Kingdom, then the two must have differences and therefore cannot logically be the same. Thus, the insistence by some Dispensationalists that there is "only one Gospel" that exists in different "forms" or "phases" is nothing more than euphemistic double talk, designed to maintain the appearance of orthodoxy. Dispensationalists cannot have it both ways. They cannot on the one hand legitimately insist that there are different and distinct Gospels, and then on the other hand, maintain that there is really only one true Gospel. The entire proposition is ludicrous.

---

[531] *The Scofield Study Bible* - C.I. Scofield, Oxford University Press, 1909, 1917, 1939, 1945, p.1343. Also see Clarence Larkin who follows Scofield almost verbatim in his commentary, *The Book of Revelation*, pp.133-134.
[532] *The Scofield Study Bible* - C.I. Scofield, Oxford University Press, 1909, 1917, 1939, 1945, p.1343.

The simple truth is that there is only one true Gospel revealed in the New Testament. And that one Gospel reveals both the redemptive mission and the kingly reign of Jesus Christ. In fulfillment of numerous Old Testament prophecies, Christ came the first time, humbly (Mt.21:4-5; Zech.9:9), as the Suffering Servant of Jehovah (Is.53; Ps.22). His singular purpose was to accomplish the Father's redemptive plan (Heb.10:7; Jn.4:34) which required His substitutionary death for man's sins on the Cross (Mt.16:21; Jn.12:27). Thus, by His perfect life and sacrificial death, with His Divine glory veiled and the exercise of His Divine prerogatives voluntarily curtailed (Phil.2:6-8), the Lord Jesus Christ accomplished the Father's eternal plan of redemption by providing salvation for a fallen, sin-ruined humanity.[533] This was the primary purpose of the First Advent of Jesus Christ. However, Christ will also come a second time, at the end of this age, to judge the world in righteousness and to establish God's sovereign rule and authority over this earth during the Millennium. At present, the world remains under the influence of Satan (1Jn.5:19; Jn.14:30), in open rebellion against God and in defiance of God's authority. But, ultimately the sovereign rule and rightful reign of God will be visibly extended over this entire earth. It is at the glorious Second Coming of Jesus Christ at the end of this age, when Christ appears in the glory of the Father with all the angels of heaven, (Mt.25:31) that every knee will bow and every tongue confess that Jesus Christ is Lord to the glory of the Father (Phil.2:9-11). It is then that the knowledge of the true and the living God will cover the earth as the waters cover the sea (Is.11:9). Thus, the one true Gospel, as revealed in the New Testament, presents Jesus Christ both as the Savior of the world and the King of kings and Lord of lords. Christ is simultaneously our Prophet (revealing God's will to us), our Priest (making sacrifice for our sins and interceding for us), and our King (ruling and directing our lives through the indwelling Holy Spirit).

The entire Dispensational premise of "two" Gospels is based upon an artificial distinction that is made between the phrases, "the kingdom of heaven" and the "kingdom of God." Dispensationalists assert that the proclamation of John the Baptist and Jesus Christ to, "Repent, for the kingdom of heaven is at hand" (see Mt.3:2; 4:17) was the announcement of God's intention to establish an earthly political kingdom for the Jews. Thus, according to Dispensationalists, "the gospel of the kingdom" was the

---

[533] I am **not** hinting at universal salvation here. While Christ's death was certainly **sufficient** to save all mankind, it is **efficient** only for the elect, who were chosen by God before the foundation of the world (see Eph.1:4; 2Thess.2:13; Rv.17:8).

proclamation that "the kingdom of heaven" (i.e., the earthly Davidic Kingdom) was about to be established on earth. For example, while referring specifically to Matthew 4:17, **Arno Gaebelein** states that, "He [i.e., Jesus] announces that the Kingdom has drawn nigh in that He, the King, is standing in their midst to establish that Kingdom."[534] **C.I. Scofield** teaches that "The kingdom of heaven...means the earthly, Davidic, Messianic kingdom of the Lord Jesus Christ."[535] And **Lewis Sperry Chafer** asserts that, "A distinction should be made between the kingdom of God and the kingdom of heaven.[536] **Chafer** further explains that, "The phrase, the *kingdom of heaven*...refers to the rule of God in the earth...it is to be distinguished from the *kingdom of God*, which is the rule of God throughout the bounds of the universe."[537]

However, this Dispensational distinction between "the kingdom of heaven" and the "kingdom of God" is contrived and will not stand-up to close scrutiny. For example, in Matthew 19, after the rich young ruler refused to heed Christ's advice to sell his possessions and follow Him, Christ declared to His disciples, "Truly I say to you, it is hard for a rich man to enter *the kingdom of heaven*. And again I say to you, it is easier for a camel to go through the eye of a needle, than for a rich man to enter *the kingdom of God*" (Mt.19:23-24, emphasis added). The two phrases, "the kingdom of heaven" and "the kingdom of God" are clearly used interchangeably and are synonymous. Both phrases refer to the same thing - entering the realm of God's sovereign rule and authority - a rule and authority that currently affects one individual believer at a time, but will ultimately be extended to encompass the entire inhabited earth when Jesus Christ returns in glory.

There is a simple explanation as to why the Gospel of Matthew frequently employs the phrase, "the kingdom of heaven" instead of the more direct phrase, "the kingdom of God." Matthew's Gospel was written to demonstrate to the Jews that Jesus Christ was indeed the promised Messiah. The Jews commonly refrained from using the name of God for fear of using His holy name in vain. They would therefore commonly substitute other expressions and phrases. For example, after Jesus' Triumphal Entry into

---

[534] *The Gospel of Matthew* - Arno C. Gaebelein, Loizeaux Brothers, 1982, p.100.
[535] *Scofield Bible Correspondence Course, Vol.V, Twenty-Six Great Words* - C.I. Scofield, Moody Bible Institute, 1960, p.1280.
[536] *Systematic Theology* - Lewis Sperry Chafer, Kregel Publications, 1993, vol.7, p.224.
[537] *Systematic Theology* - Lewis Sperry Chafer, Kregel Publications, 1993, vol.4, p.173.

Jerusalem, the Jewish leaders challenged His authority when they asked, "By what authority are You doing these things, and who gave You this authority?" (Mt.21:23). Jesus responded by asking, "The baptism of John was from what source, from *heaven* or from men?" (Mt.21:25, emphasis added). Jesus was clearly contrasting the authority of men, with the authority of God, yet He substituted the word "heaven" in place of the word "God." Again, when Jesus was on trial, the high priest inquired, "Are You the Christ, the Son of *the Blessed One*?" (Mk.14:61, emphasis added). The phrase, "the Blessed One" stands in place of the word "God." The high priest was asking, "Are You the Son of God?"[538] When the *Prodigal Son* confessed, "Father, I have sinned against *heaven* and in your sight: I am no longer worthy to be called your son." (Lk.15:21). The plain meaning is "I have sinned against *God* and in your sight..." Thus, the phrase, "the kingdom of heaven" was a common Hebrew idiom used in place of the more direct phrase "the kingdom of God."

The problem is that Dispensationalists unnecessarily delimit the kingdom of God to a future earthly Millennium. They fail to accept the fact that the kingdom of God is both a *present spiritual reality* (Lk.17:20-21 cp. Mt.12:28; Lk.11:20) as well as a *future earthly certainty* (Rv.11:15 cp. Rv.19:11-15). The kingdom of God is now advancing one person at a time. Through the preaching of the Gospel people believe and enter the kingdom of God. They are delivered from the domain of darkness and transferred into the kingdom of God's beloved Son (Col.1:13; Gal.1:4). They are set free from the bondage of sin (Jn.8:31-34; Ro.6:12-14) and experience the transforming power of the risen Christ in their daily lives. They have become new creatures (2 Cor.5:17), with a new heart (Ez.36:26) and a new mind (1Cor.2:16), partaking of a new covenant (Lk.22:20), while expectantly looking forward to a new heaven and new earth in which righteousness will dwell (2Pt.3:13; Rv.21:1,5 cp. Is.65:17; 66:22) – gladly and willingly submitting to the kingly rule and authority of the Lord Jesus Christ in their individual lives (Jn.14:15; 2Cor.5:9; 1Jn.5:3).

In light of the plain teaching of Scripture, we are forced to ask, "Why do Dispensationalists persist in arguing that there are "two" distinctly different Gospels?" The answer is that **the doctrine of two Gospels is absolutely necessary to support the**

---

[538] Compare the parallel passage in Lk.22:70, "And they all said, 'Are you the Son of God, then?' And He said to them, 'Yes, I am.'"

concept of a pretribulation rapture. Dispensationalists fully realize that if they concede that "the Gospel of the Kingdom" and "the Gospel of God's Grace" are indeed synonymous, the all-important doctrine of imminence (i.e., the secret, unannounced, any moment pretribulational Coming of Christ to rapture the Church) would immediately be destroyed. As previously pointed out, the Dispensational doctrine of "imminence" maintains that there are *no* prophetic events that must be fulfilled before the rapture can occur. In other words, the rapture can occur at any moment without any prophetic indication or warning. **Renald Showers** explains the importance of this concept when he states, "...Christ could come at any moment...If something else must happen *before* Christ's coming can take place, then Christ's coming is *not imminent*. The *necessity of something else taking place first destroys the concept of the imminent coming of Christ.*"[539] What **Showers** is saying is that if there is any predicted prophetic event that must transpire *before* Christ can come to rapture the Church, then the rapture cannot be a secret, unexpected, any moment, pretribulational event.[540]

The root of the dilemma for Dispensationalists hinges upon Matthew 24:14, wherein Jesus declares;

"And this **gospel of the kingdom** shall be preached in the whole world for a witness to all the nations, and **then the end shall come**." (Emphasis added).

This text plainly states that "the end" will come *after* the "gospel of the kingdom" has been preached to "all the nations." The word "end" denotes the completion or conclusion of something. In the context of Matthew 24, the phrase, "the end," refers to the completion or conclusion of this present age (v.3), when there shall be a great tribulation (v.20) which will culminate in the glorious appearing of Christ (vv.27-30), to deliver the righteous (v.31) and to execute judgment upon the unbelieving (vv.29-30 cp. 2Thess.1:6-10).

However, to protect the doctrine of a pretribulational rapture, Dispensationalists teach that there are "two Gospels" and therefore "two ends."

---

[539] *Maranatha - Our Lord, Come!* - Renald Showers, The Friends of Israel Gospel Ministry, Inc., 1995, p.149.
[540] See Chapter 4, *The Doctrine of Imminence*, Part 4, *The Importance of the Doctrine of Imminence*, and Part 5, *The Doctrine of Imminence is Supported Entirely by Inference*, for a thorough discussion of the critical nature of the doctrine of imminence and how it relates to the pretribulation rapture theory.

First, Dispensationalists maintain that this present age (commonly referred to as the Church Age) "ends" at the time of the secret, pretribulation rapture. For example, **Lehman Strauss** asserts that, "The Church Age will *end* at the Rapture, when Jesus comes in the air to catch away the redeemed."[541] Likewise, **Charles Ryrie** contends that, "...the Tribulation with its many judgments is from the Dispensational viewpoint *the end* of the economy of grace."[542]

Second, Dispensationalists teach that the "Gospel of the Kingdom" will be preached as a witness to all the nations during the Tribulation period by 144,000 Jewish evangelists before "the end" referred to in Matthew 24:14 occurs. For example, while referring specifically to Mathew 24:14, **Arno Gaebelein** explains that, "This verse relates exclusively to *the end* of the age, that is the Jewish age[543]...it is at *the end* of the age that the glad tidings of the Kingdom are to be heralded through the earth[544]...And who will be the preachers of this last witness...before the King appears in judgment?[545] ...The 144,000...constitute the remnant of God's earthly people, the preachers of the Kingdom Gospel during the great tribulation."[546]

To summarize for the sake of clarity, Dispensationalists maintain that;

[1] The "age of grace" and the preaching of the "Gospel of Grace" will **cease** when Christ comes secretly to rapture the Church **before** the start of the Tribulation.

[2] The Tribulation will immediately commence after the rapture of the Church. Sometime thereafter, 144,000 Jewish evangelists will begin preaching the "Gospel of the Kingdom" (Mt.24:14) to all the nations. Their preaching will **cease** at the **end** of the Tribulation period when Christ comes in judgment.

[3] Dispensationalists thereby protect the all-important doctrine of imminence, and with it the pretribulation rapture doctrine, by insisting that the "Gospel of the Kingdom"

---

[541] *The End of This Present World* - Lehman Strauss, Zondervan Publishing House, 1967, p.99.
[542] *Dispensationalism Today* - Charles Caldwell Ryrie, Moody Press, 1970, p.56.
[543] *The Gospel of Matthew* – Arno C. Gaebelein, Loizeaux Brothers Inc., 1961, p.486.
[544] *The Gospel of Matthew* – Arno C. Gaebelein, Loizeaux Brothers Inc., 1961, p.487
[545] *The Gospel of Matthew* – Arno C. Gaebelein, Loizeaux Brothers Inc., 1961, p.490
[546] *The Gospel of Matthew* – Arno C. Gaebelein, Loizeaux Brothers Inc., 1961, p.493.

referred to in Matthew 24:14 is different than the "Gospel of Grace" as found in the Epistles.

If however, there is in fact only *one* Gospel, then this means that there is a major prophetic event that *must* transpire *before* "the end" (including the rapture) can occur – that is, the one, true Gospel must be preached to all the nations. The rapture therefore, could *not* be an imminent event because it could *not* have occurred at any moment during the past 2,000 years, for the simple reason that the Gospel has *not* yet been preached to all the nations![547] Therefore, in order to rescue the doctrine of imminence and with it the secret pretribulation rapture, Dispensationalists have declared that there are actually *two different Gospels* - "the Gospel of the Kingdom" as revealed in the four Gospel narratives and the "Gospel of God's Grace" as revealed in the Epistles. This spurious claim permits Dispensationalists to argue that it is only the "Gospel of the Kingdom" which must be preached to all the nations before "the end" can come and *not* the "Gospel of Grace." But are there really two distinct and different Gospels? Is there really one Gospel for the "Church Age" and a different Gospel for the "Tribulation period?" The answer is a resounding "No!" There is no textual justification to validate the Dispensational claim of two different and distinct Gospels.[548]

While each of the four Gospel narratives were written with a different emphasis, they all uniformly reveal the redemptive ministry of Jesus Christ. For example, the Gospel of Mark portrays Christ as the Servant of Jehovah, who has come to accomplish the

---

[547] Early critics of the secret pretribulation rapture theory frequently pointed to Matthew 24:14 as decisive proof that the rapture could *not* possibly take place until the Gospel was proclaimed to all the nations. For example, "If Christ's servants be *secretly* caught up (as some think) *before* the judgments upon the earth, how shall the Gospel be preached up to the end? (Matt.xxiv.14.)" *A Commentary on the Old and New Testaments* – Robert Jamieson (1827-1880) - A.R.Fausset (1821-1910) David Brown (1803-1897), Hendrickson Publishers, reprinted 1997, vol.3, col.2, p.466. Also, "Now the questions put to the Lord Jesus by the disciples, and His reply to them, had to do with His coming in glory. They say, 'What shall be the sign of Thy coming, and of the end of the world?' (Matt.24:13)…In His answer, He first tells His disciples of *many and varied intervening events*…commotions amongst the nations – persecutions…and the *preaching of the Gospel* should be carried out as a witness amongst *all nations*…" *The Hope of Christ's Second Coming* – S.P. Tregelles, The Sovereign Grace Advent Testimony, n.d., (ca.1864), p.14.

[548] Matthew 24:15 and Mark 13:10 are parallel passages that refer to the same Gospel message. Mark 13:10 literally states, "And to all the nations must first be proclaimed *the gospel*." (καὶ εἰς πάντα τὰ ἔθνη δεῖ πρῶτον κηρυχθῆναι τὸ εὐαγγέλιον). Matthew 24:14 literally states, "And there will be proclaimed this *the gospel* of the kingdom in all the earth for a testimony to all the nations…" (καὶ κηρυχθήσεται τοῦτο τὸ εὐαγγέλιον τῆς βασιλείας ἐν ὅλῃ τῇ οἰκουμένῃ εἰς μαρτύριον πᾶσιν τοῖς ἔθνεσιν). (All emphasis added). There is no legitimate justification for distinguishing between the "the Gospel" (τὸ εὐαγγέλιον) mentioned in Matthew and Mark and "the Gospel" (τὸ εὐαγγέλιον) mentioned in Romans! See Romans 1:9,16; 2:16; 10:16; 11:28; 15:16,19,29; 16:25!!!

redemptive work of God. The Gospel of Luke portrays Christ as the Messianic Son of Man – the perfect Man and Savior, appealing to all of Adam's descendants irrespective of racial, ethnic or cultural differences. The Gospel of John was written to emphasize the supremacy and deity of Jesus Christ, God's only begotten Son and Savior. Matthew's Gospel was written to the Jews. His primary purpose was to demonstrate to the Jews that Jesus Christ was the greater Son of David (Mt.1:1), God's promised Messianic King (Mt.2:2,6; 27:11) and Israel's Savior (Mt.1:21), in fulfillment of numerous Old Testament prophecies.[549] It is therefore **not** surprising that the word "kingdom" appears frequently in Matthew's Gospel account. As previously pointed out, the word "kingdom"[550] denotes sovereign power, authority, dominion and rule.[551] Matthew's use of the word "kingdom" in association with the word "gospel" does **not** designate a different Gospel message as Dispensationalists claim. Rather, the "good news" of the "kingdom" is that the sovereign reign of God is now made manifest in individual lives - the kingdom of God has come upon us – it is now in our midst (Lk.17:20-21 cp. Mt.12:28) and is not far from each one of us (Acts 17:27). The "good news" that is to be proclaimed to all of the nations is that God has overlooked the times of ignorance (Acts 17:30-31) and is now freely justifying (Ro.3:23-28) and reconciling sinners to Himself (Ro.5:10-11). Like brands[552] plucked from the fire (Jude 23 & Zech.3:2), all who believe the Gospel and come to God through faith in Jesus Christ immediately receive forgiveness from their sins (Acts 10:43; Col.1:14) and become citizens of God's eternal kingdom (Phil:3:20). Indwelt (Ro.8:9-11; 1Cor.6:19), transformed (2Cor.5:17) and led by the Holy Spirit (Gal.5:16,25), they become willing servants of Christ (2Cor.5:9), looking forward to the day when the kingdom of this world will at last become the kingdom of our God and Savior (Rev.11:15; 12:10).

---

[549] "Matthew's gospel is saturated with the OT. Over fifty clear quotations…lifted bodily from the OT…Most of the quotations come through the LXX, the ancient Greek translation of the OT…" *The Zondervan Pictorial Encyclopedia of the Bible* – Merril C. Tenney, General Editor, The Zondervan Corporation, 1975, 1976, Vol.4 (M-P), *Matthew, Gospel of*, No.7, pp.132-133.

[550] The word "kingdom" is **basileia** (βασιλεία).

[551] "βασιλεία…sovereignty, royal power, dominion…" *A Manual Greek Lexicon of the New Testament* - G. Abbott-Smith, Charles Scribner's Sons, 1953, p.77. "βασιλεία…royal power, kingship, dominion, rule…a kingdom, i.e., the territory subject to the rule of a king…"*A Greek-English Lexicon of the New Testament* - Joseph H. Thayer, 1953, T & T Clark, p.96. "βασιλεία…a kingdom, realm, the region or country governed by a king; kingly power, authority, dominion, reign; royal dignity, the title and honour of a king." *The Analytical Greek Lexicon Revised* - Harold K. Moulton, Zondervan Publishing House, 1982, p.67.

[552] "A stick or piece of wood partly burned, whether burning or not." *Webster's Collegiate Dictionary*, G. & C. Merriam Company., Springfield, Mass., 1941.

Matthew 24:14 does *not* describe a different Gospel message. It simply indicates that once the proclamation of the Gospel is complete, this present evil age will be brought to an abrupt end by the visible reign of Jesus Christ upon this earth. Verse 14, is essentially saying;

"And this *good news* [gospel] of the *sovereign rule and reign of God* [kingdom] will be *proclaimed* [preached] in the whole world for a *testimony* [witness] to all the nations, and then *the cessation of this present rebellious world order* [the end] shall come."

We must ask, "Does the Scripture really support the Dispensational proposition that Jesus and His disciples preached a *different Gospel* than the Apostle Paul?" A careful consideration of related Biblical texts reveals that the Dispensational claim of different Gospels is both unjustified and untenable. For example, the Gospel of Matthew tells us plainly that Jesus went about Galilee, "…proclaiming the gospel of the kingdom…" (Mt.4:23 cp. Mt.9:35). However, this is the same message that Phillip the evangelist and the Apostle Paul preached. Consider the following texts:

- Acts 8:12, states that the Samaritans "…believed Phillip *preaching the good news about the kingdom of God* and the name of Jesus Christ…" [553]

- Acts 19:8, tells us that while in Ephesus, the Apostle Paul was "…reasoning and persuading *them* about *the kingdom of God*." (Emphasis added).

- Acts 20:25, records the testimony of Paul to the Ephesian elders, wherein the Apostle declared, "…I went about *preaching the kingdom*…" (Emphasis added).

- Acts 28:31, relates that during Paul's Roman imprisonment, he was "welcoming all who came to him, *preaching the kingdom of God*…" (Emphasis added).

Clearly, Jesus, Paul and Phillip all proclaimed "the kingdom of God." Are we to believe that Phillip and Paul were preaching the "good news" of the restoration of a Davidic

---

[553] Literally, "…Phillip, *proclaiming the gospel* about the kingdom of God and the name of Jesus Christ…" (…Φιλίππῳ εὐαγγελιζομένῳ τὰ περὶ τῆς βασιλείας τοῦ θεοῦ καὶ τοῦ ὀνόματος τοῦ Ἰησοῦ Χριστοῦ…) (Emphasis added).

theocratic kingdom to the Samaritans and the Gentiles? Are we to believe that this was the message that "turned the world upside down?" (Acts 17:6 KJV). Or is it far more reasonable to conclude that Jesus, Paul and Phillip were all proclaiming the "good news of the righteous rule and reign of God" in the lives of redeemed individuals now, and over the entire world in the future? The simple truth of the matter is that there is only one body of truth that has once and for all been delivered unto the saints, (see Jude 1:3 cp. Gal.1:6-9; 2Cor.11:4) – this Divinely revealed body of truth is *the Gospel*, which is "...the power of God for **salvation** to everyone who believes, to the Jew first and also to the Greek." (Ro.1:16, *Emphasis added*). This is the message that is to be proclaimed to "...all creation" (Mk.16:15), beginning in "...Jerusalem, and in all Judea and Samaria, and even to the remotest part of the earth." (Acts1:8). If any doubt remains about the message preached by Jesus, Hebrews 2:3 should definitively settle the issue. Here we are asked,

"...how shall we escape if we neglect so great a **salvation**? After it was at the first spoken through the Lord...(Heb.2:3).

Without question, Jesus preached a message of salvation – *not* the restoration of an earthly, political Davidic kingdom for Israel.[554]

3. The Gospel of Grace is Found Only in the Epistles.

Dispensationalists assert that the good news of individual salvation, as revealed by the "Gospel of Grace," is to be found *only* in the Epistles and *not* the Gospels. **John Darby** was the first to teach that, "...the church, [is] the special fruit of sovereign grace...Paul...alone in the epistles speaks at all of the church or even names it...no apostle speaks of the church...but Paul."[555] **C.I Scofield** instructs Christians: "Do not expect to find in the Gospels the doctrine of the Church. In the Gospels the Church is a subject of prediction merely...The great body of Christ's teaching has to do with the kingdom, *not* the Church..."[556] **Scofield** concludes that, "The doctrines of grace are to

---

[554] Consider the gracious words of Jesus Christ Himself: Mt.11:28-30; Mt. 20:28; Mk.10:45; Lk.9:55-56; Lk.19:9-10; Jn.3:16-17 cp. Jn.6:29; 1Jn.3:23; Jn.5:24.

[555] *The Collected Writings of J.N. Darby* - Edited by William Kelly, Stow Hill Bible and Tract Depot, n.d., Prophetic No.4, Vol.11, pp.333,335.

[556] *Scofield Bible Correspondence Course, Volume III, The Gospels and Acts* - C.I. Scofield, Moody Bible Institute, 1966, p.480.

be sought in the Epistles, *not* the Gospels..."[557] **Arno C. Gaebelein** insists that, "It is through Paul...that the Gospel of Grace as well as the mystery hid in former ages is made known. In the Epistles given through Paul we read, therefore, all concerning the Gospel of Grace, the church and the ministry, which is for this age, an age in which our Lord Jesus Christ is *not* King, but Lord in Glory."[558] **Gaebelein** goes on to say that, "Through Paul the full revelation of the assembly,[559] the one body, is given[560]...***all the truth concerning the church*** was revealed through Paul, the Apostle to the Gentiles."[561] **Lehman Strauss** contends that it is only, "In the New Testament epistles, where Church truth is to be found..."[562] whereas, **Gerald Stanton** concedes that, "Christ revealed a *few things* concerning the future Church, but the main body of Church truth is found in the epistles, *not* the gospels."[563] However, Dispensationalists fail to appreciate the harmony and symmetry that exists between the Gospels and the Epistles. They create an unnecessary tension between the teachings of Christ and the teachings of Paul when they assert that the Synoptic Gospels are primarily concerned with a Jewish remnant and the restoration of an earthly theocratic kingdom, whereas "Church truth" (i.e., the revelation of God's grace, mercy, forgiveness and salvation) is to be found exclusively in the Epistles of Paul.[564]

Contrary to Dispensational claims, the Gospels and the Epistles do *not* contain conflicting messages. Rather, the Gospels and the Epistles complement each other beautifully. For example, while the Epistles make numerous references to the person of Jesus Christ, it is the Gospel narratives that establish the Messianic credentials of Christ. The Gospels validate Christ's Messianic claims by recording the fulfillment of numerous Old Testament prophecies and by documenting the numerous authenticating miracles performed by Him. The Gospels provide the historical foundation upon which the Epistles build and develop Christological and Soteriological doctrine. For example, the Gospels record the historical fact of the death and resurrection of Jesus Christ.

---

[557] *The Scofield Study Bible* - C.I. Scofield, Oxford University Press, 1909, 1917, 1939, 1945, p.989.
[558] *The Gospel of Matthew* - Arno C. Gaebelein, Loizeaux Brothers, 1961, pp.205-206.
[559] Gaebelein's use of the term "assembly" in place of "Church" is borrowed from John Darby who commonly used this term to describe the Church.
[560] *The Gospel of Matthew* - Arno C. Gaebelein, Loizeaux Brothers, 1961, p.348.
[561] *The Gospel of Matthew* - Arno C. Gaebelein, Loizeaux Brothers, 1961, p.320.
[562] *God's Plan for the Future* - Lehman Strauss, Zondervan Publishing House, 1965, p.51.
[563] *Kept From the Hour* - Gerald B. Stanton, Zondervan Publishing House, 1956, p.60.
[564] If this Dispensational teaching were taken to its logical conclusion, the non-Pauline New Testament Epistles of 1&2 Peter; James; Hebrews; 1-2-3 John, Jude and Revelation would also contain no "Church truth" whatsoever!

However, it is within the Epistles that the theological significance is fully developed and explained.[565] Again, in John 3:3 Jesus told Nicodemas that, "...unless one is born again, he cannot see the kingdom of God." What Jesus meant by being "born again" is *not* fully explained in the Gospels. Rather, it is the Epistles that reveal the radical spiritual transformation and subsequent life-style changes that result from the new birth.[566]

4. The Synoptic Gospels Reveal Kingdom Truth.

Dispensationalists are convinced that the Synoptic Gospels are primarily concerned with Christ's "kingdom offer" to Israel. They therefore maintain that the preponderance of the Lord's teachings, contained within these Gospels, are "kingdom teachings." Dispensationalists insist that these "kingdom teachings" pertain specifically to the Jews and their earthly theocratic kingdom and *not* to the Church. **Lewis Sperry Chafer** explains that, "Large portions of the Synoptic Gospels..." describe "...the **requirements** that are to be **imposed** upon those who enter that kingdom... The essential elements of a *grace administration*...are *not* found in the kingdom administration."[567] What **Chafer** means is that the teachings of Jesus Christ contained within the Synoptic Gospels specifies the legal requirements necessary for entrance into the earthly theocratic kingdom. For example, **Chafer** maintains that, "In the Law of the kingdom, the Mosaic Law is carried forward and intensified...the law is intensified in the kingdom teachings...no element of the law of Moses has been subtracted. Rather, to the Mosaic revelation are added the *kingdom teachings* of Christ..."[568] Thus, according to **Chafer** the "kingdom teachings" of Christ amplify and intensify the Law of Moses. **Chafer** claims that, "The *kingdom teachings*, like the Law of Moses, are *based* on a *covenant of works*."[569] **Chafer** therefore concludes that, "The teachings of the kingdom are *purely legal*..."[570] and therefore, according to **Chafer,** "...the kingdom injunctions...hold over its subjects the danger of *hell fire*."[571] The "legal" character and nature of the

---

[565] See for example Ro.3:24-26; Ro.8:1-4; 1Cor.15:1-26; Eph.1:7-8; 1Pt.2:24; 3:18.
[566] See for example, Ro.8:14-16; 2Cor.5:17; Gal.5:22-24; Eph.2:8-10; Phil.2:1-4; Col.1:21-22; 1Pt.1:22-23; 2Pt.1:5-10; 1Jn.2:4-6; Rv.12:11.
[567] *Dispensationalism* - Lewis Sperry Chafer, Dallas Seminary Press, 1936, 1951, p.50.
[568] *Systematic Theology* - Lewis Sperry Chafer, Kregel Publications, 1993, vol.4, p.213.
[569] *Systematic Theology* - Lewis Sperry Chafer, Kregel Publications, 1993, vol.4, p.215.
[570] *Systematic Theology* - Lewis Sperry Chafer, Kregel Publications, 1993, vol.4, p.225.
[571] *Systematic Theology* - Lewis Sperry Chafer, Kregel Publications, 1993, vol.4, p.184.

Gospels is also taught by **C.I. Scofield** who asserts that, "The mission of Jesus was primarily to the Jews...Expect therefore, a strong *legal* and Jewish colouring up to the cross...The Gospels do *not* unfold the doctrine of the Church."[572]

Thus, Dispensationalists "dispensationalize" the teachings of Christ, insisting that the Gospels contain "kingdom truth" that is "purely legal" in its intent and purpose. They assert that the words of Jesus were spoken to "Jews" who were "living under the Law," and conclude that His teachings must therefore apply exclusively to Israel and *not* the Church. The unfavorable effect of this interpretative approach to the Gospels is most graphically illustrated by the Dispensational interpretation of the *Sermon on the Mount*, the *Beatitudes* and *The Lord's Prayer*.

4a. The Sermon on the Mount.

Dispensationalists consider the Lord's teachings contained within the *Sermon on the Mount* to be an essential part of the "Gospel of the Kingdom." According to Dispensationalists, Matthew, chapters 5 through 7, depict "kingdom truth" that defines and regulates human behavior within the bounds of the future theocratic kingdom. Once again, **John Darby** was the first to teach that the gracious words of Christ contained within the *Sermon on the Mount* apply specifically to the Jews and their earthly kingdom and *not* to the Church or individual Christians. **Darby** declared: "For embedded in the sermon on the Mount are words of our Lord which apply far more closely to Jews or the remnant than to the church."[573] Darby further maintained that the *Sermon on the Mount* was fundamentally legal in its application and purpose. He asserted that the Sermon applied specifically to the establishment of an earthly Jewish theocratic kingdom and *not* to the radical spiritual transformation that results when individuals are born again. For example, **Darby** claimed that, "In the sermon on the mount the *remnant* are *morally distinguished;* the qualities of those who should have a part in the kingdom, are clearly and fully stated...all this is *divine government*, *__not__ divine salvation*.[574] And again, **Darby** declared that, "...*the kingdom* is announced in

---

[572] *The Scofield Study Bible* - C.I. Scofield, Oxford University Press, 1945 pp. 989-990.
[573] *The Collected Writings of J.N. Darby* - Edited by William Kelly, Stow Hill Bible and Tract Depot, n.d., Prophetic No.4, Vol.11, p.179.
[574] *The Collected Writings of J.N. Darby* - Edited by William Kelly, Stow Hill Bible and Tract Depot, n.d., Prophetic No.4, Vol.11, pp.145-146.

the sermon on the Mount...***Redemption is not spoken of in it***; but the character and nature of the kingdom, and who could enter."[575] Thus, according to Darby, the *Sermon on the Mount* is essentially a legalistic discourse that describes the attitudes and behavioral qualities that must be possessed in order to gain entrance into the earthly theocratic kingdom. Furthermore, entrance into the kingdom is solely dependent upon human effort and works, ***not*** faith in Jesus Christ.

Dispensationalists have unanimously accepted and disseminated **Darby's** legalistic interpretation of the *Sermon on the Mount*. For example, while referring to the "kingdom teachings" of Christ contained in the *Sermon*, **Lewis Sperry Chafer** declares that, "...it will be found that the teachings of the kingdom presented in Matthew 5-7 are almost wholly in ***disagreement with the teachings of grace***."[576] **Chafer** also claims that, "...the Sermon on the Mount, which is evidently ***the manifesto*** of the King...declares the essential character of the conditions of entrance into the kingdom. This kingdom rule of life is ***purely legal***...In the kingdom teachings...the commands of Moses are advanced into requirements vastly more impossible with respect to detail, and this does not relieve, but rather intensifies, its character as ***strictly legal***...Christ does not disown the principle of the law in the unfoldings of kingdom requirements...He is rather presenting a ***new degree and standard of law*** which is adapted to the conditions which shall obtain in the kingdom..."[577] **Chafer** therefore deduces that, "The ***terms of admission into the kingdom*** as set forth in Matthew 5:1-7:27 are, in reality, ***the Mosaic requirements intensified*** by Christ's own interpretation of them."[578]

The extreme legalistic nature of this Dispensational teaching is underscored by **C.I. Scofield** who teaches that, "Matthew is distinctively The Gospel of the Kingdom, but you are reminded that the two other synoptic Gospels (Mark and Luke) contain a great deal of ***kingdom truth***, rather than distinctively Church truth...The Sermon on the Mount is not the constitution of the Church, but of the kingdom; it is ***not grace but law***."[579] In his *Reference Bible*, **Scofield** asserts that, "The Sermon on the Mount is ***law,***

[575] *Synopsis of the Books of the Bible* - J.N. Darby, Loizeaux Brothers, 1950, *Matthew-John*, vol.3, p.59.
[576] *Systematic Theology* - Lewis Sperry Chafer, Kregel Publications, 1993, vol.4, p.214.
[577] *Systematic Theology* - Lewis Sperry Chafer, Kregel Publications, 1993, vol.4, p.177.
[578] *Dispensationalism* - Lewis Sperry Chafer, Dallas Seminary Press, 1936, 1951, pp.95-96.
[579] *Scofield Correspondence Course, Vol.V, Twenty-Six Great Words of Scripture* - C.I. Scofield, Moody Bible Institute, 1960, p.1268.

not grace...Having announced the kingdom of heaven as 'at hand,' the King, in Mt.5-7, declares the *principles of the kingdom*. The Sermon on the Mount...gives *the divine constitution* for the righteous government of the earth...the Sermon on the Mount is *pure law*...in its primary application gives neither the privilege nor the duty of the Church. These are found in the Epistles."[580]

Likewise, **Arno C. Gaebelein** declares that, "The so-called sermon on the mount is a proclamation concerning the Kingdom, *the magna charta [sic] of the Kingdom of heavens*..."[581] **E. Schuyler English** confidently asserts that, "The Sermon on the Mount is *the manifesto of the constitution of the kingdom* of the heavens, which is to come upon the earth in the millennial reign of the Lord Jesus...Had the Holy Spirit meant the application to be for the Church, He would have brought the discourse to our attention after the Lord first mentioned the Church, in Matthew sixteen. *Church doctrine is revealed in the Epistles*. The Christian has a heavenly calling; the *Sermon on the Mount* is to a great extent *earthly in its application*."[582] In other words, according to *English*, the Sermon on the Mount is a legal document designed to govern the earthly theocratic kingdom. It has no application to the Church, because the Church has "a heavenly calling." **English** further asserts that, "The Sermon on the Mount...was spoken directly to the disciples of our Lord (Mt.5:1,2)...Now we must remember that the *disciples were Jewish believers*, that they were living under Law, *not* under Grace...And we must also bear in mind that the King was still presenting the Kingdom."[583] Likewise, **Charles Feinberg** explains that, "Every king must have *laws* for the regulation of conduct in his kingdom...Now He promulgates *laws* for the carrying on of that kingdom. There is *no message of salvation* in this Sermon...The Sermon on the Mount is *legal in its character*; it is the *law of Moses raised to its highest power*."[584] And **Charles Ryrie** also maintains that, "The dispensationalist... views the primary fulfillment of the Sermon and the full following of its *laws* as applicable to the Messianic kingdom... Dispensationalists often point out the *absence from the Sermon of Church truth*."[585]

---

[580] *The Scofield Study Bible* - C.I. Scofield, Oxford University Press, 1909, 1917, 1939, 1945, pp. 989,999-1000.
[581] *The Gospel of Matthew* - Arno C. Gaebelein, Loizeaux Brothers, 1961, p.106.
[582] *Studies in the Gospel According to Matthew* - E. Schuyler English, Zondervan Publishing House, 1938, p.46.
[583] *Studies in the Gospel According to Matthew* - E. Schuyler English, Zondervan Publishing House, 1938, p.51.
[584] *Premillennialism or Amillennialism?* - Charles Feinberg, Zondervan Publishing House, 1936, p.90.
[585] *Dispensationalism Today* - Charles Caldwell Ryrie, Moody Press, 1970, pp.107-108.

4b. The Beatitudes and The Lord's Prayer.

With respect to *The Beatitudes* (Mt.5:1-12) contained within the *Sermon on the Mount*, (Mt.5:1-7:29), **Lewis Sperry Chafer** teaches that, "This ***kingdom message*** opens with the record of the ninefold blessing which is promised and provided for the ***faithful child of the kingdom***. The blessings are ***won through merit***."[586] Likewise, with respect to *The Lord's Prayer* (Mt.6:9-13), **Chafer** contends that, "What is commonly called 'The Lord's Prayer'...is directly concerned with the issues of the ***coming kingdom***...The ***legal character of this great kingdom-prayer*** should not be overlooked..."[587] **A.C. Gaebelein** adamantly declares that, "...the use of this model for prayer, as the Lord's prayer given to the Church, to be used by the Church, ***is wrong***, ***decidedly unchristian***, nor can it be proven from the New Testament that it is intended for the Church...This perfect model of prayer was given by our Lord to His disciples to be used by them individually and previously to the gift of the Holy Spirit. It was then all on ***Jewish ground***; they were Jewish believers and as such they received this model prayer and used it in the transition state."[588] **E. Schuyler English** emphasizes both the Jewishness and legal nature of *The Lord's Prayer* when he explains that, "...we must remember that this was a prayer, in the ***Age of Law***, for the disciples, at a time when the ***Kingdom of the heavens*** was at hand. It is ***not*** a prayer for this age."[589] And again, **English** emphasizes that, "The Lord's Prayer...is a ***Kingdom prayer***..."[590] And **Charles Ryrie** asserts that, "Dispensationalists believe that the Golden Rule and the Lord's Prayer are excellent guides. But they also believe that the full, nonfudging, unadjusted fulfillment of the Sermon relates to the ***kingdom of Messiah***."[591]

Thus, according to accepted Dispensational teaching, the *Sermon on the Mount* is the new constitution of the kingdom - the manifesto of the King, wherein Jesus Christ introduces a new standard of Law that expresses the legal basis for entrance into, and the governing of, His earthly theocratic kingdom. The *Sermon* is said to intensify the Mosaic legal requirements, elevating the Law of Moses to its highest conceivable

---

[586] *Systematic Theology* - Lewis Sperry Chafer, Kregel Publications, 1993, vol.4, p.216.
[587] *Systematic Theology* - Lewis Sperry Chafer, Kregel Publications, 1993, vol.4, p.221.
[588] *The Gospel of Matthew* - Arno C. Gaebelein, Loizeaux Brothers, 1961, p.140.
[589] *Studies in the Gospel According to Matthew* - E. Schuyler English, Zondervan Publishing House, 1938, p.53.
[590] *Studies in the Gospel According to Matthew* - E. Schuyler English, Zondervan Publishing House, 1938, p.131.
[591] *Dispensationalism Today* - Charles Caldwell Ryrie, Moody Press, 1970, p.108.

power. *The Beatitudes* are deemed to be "blessings won through merit" and *The Lord's Prayer* is declared to be "decidedly unchristian" because it rests upon "Jewish ground." Furthermore, Dispensationalists uniformly insist that the *Sermon* lacks "Church truth" because of its "strictly legal" character and purpose. At this point we must pause and ask, "Where exactly in the Scripture do we find the factual basis for these shocking Dispensational claims?" Where is the verse that reveals that Jesus was presenting a new legal "constitution" or "manifesto" to govern an earthly theocratic kingdom? And, precisely where does Jesus offer this kingdom to Israel? The short answer is, "Nowhere!" Mark it carefully; there is absolutely nothing in either the text or the context of the *Sermon on the Mount* to justify any of the outlandish claims advanced by Dispensationalists! The entire scheme is designed for the singular purpose of lending credibility to the Dispensationalist's claim that the "Gospel of the Kingdom" proclaims an entirely different message than the "Gospel of God's Grace" - a distinction that is absolutely essential to the viability of the pretribulation rapture teaching. However, the entire proposition is a ridiculous fiction that rests upon nothing more than unbridled speculation and imagination. Contrary to Dispensationalist's claims, the whole character and demeanor of the *Sermon on the Mount* conveys Divine mercy and grace, not Law "elevated to its highest degree!" The *Sermon on the Mount* does not reveal a new intensified legal standard of personal righteousness attained by human effort, but a practical righteousness of life that is the direct result of the indwelling and transforming power of the Holy Spirit - a transforming power received by grace, through faith in the Lord Jesus Christ!

5. The Preaching of the Gospel of the Kingdom Ceased When Israel Rejected Their King.

Dispensationalists uniformly teach that the Jews flatly rejected Jesus as their theocratic King, along with His offer to establish an earthly theocratic kingdom. They therefore maintain that the kingdom has been "postponed" until the Second Advent at the end of this age. **William Blackstone** explains that "...the Jews rejected this kingdom and killed their King, Jesus Christ...therefore the kingdom did not immediately appear... He would have set up the kingdom (Mt.23:37-39) but they rejected and crucified Him."[592] **Blackstone** goes on to say that, "...their King was then visibly present, and ready to

---

[592] *Jesus is Coming* - William E. Blackstone, Kregel, Publications, 1989, pp.86,89.

usher in the universal manifestation of the kingdom...[but] they rejected and crucified their King and so the kingdom waits until they will accept Him..."[593] While commenting on Matthew, chapters 8 through 12, **Arno C. Gaebelein** explains that, "These five chapters, from the eighth to the twelfth, contain therefore the full manifestation of Jehovah-Jesus among His people and the rejection of the King...The King and the Kingdom is rejected, the Kingdom postponed...they did not and would not recognize Him. They remained cold and indifferent...[thus] *the Kingdom of the Heavens*..is to be postponed till the Son of Man comes again...The *preaching of the Kingdom* with its gracious blessings *stopped...with the twelfth chapter."*[594]

We might pause and ask exactly where in the 8th to 12th chapter of Matthew do we find the account of Israel's rejection of a theocratic kingdom? **Gaebelein**, who was a leader of early Dispensationalism and fairly represents mainstream Dispensational thinking, informs us that Israel's rejection of the King and Kingdom is recorded in Matthew 12:46-50. Look carefully at verses 46-50. Here we are told that someone in the crowd interrupts Jesus' public teaching to inform Him that, "Your mother and Your brothers are standing outside seeking to speak to you." (Mt.12:47). Jesus mildly rebukes His family for intruding into His public ministry by declaring, "For whoever does the will of My Father who is in heaven, he is My brother and sister and mother." (Mt.12:50). Commenting on this rebuff, **Gaebelein** maintains that, "At the close of the twelfth chapter the Lord by His *symbolical action* in refusing to see His mother and brethren, declared His relationship with His own to whom He had come, and who received Him not, broken..." [595] **Gaebelein** further declares that Matthew 13:1-2 further describes Israel's national rejection of Christ. The text declares that,

"On that day Jesus went out of the house, and was sitting by the sea. And great multitudes gathered to Him, so that He got into a boat and sat down, and the whole multitude was standing on the beach" (Mt.13:1-2).

Commenting on these verses, **Gaebelein** explains that, "Leaving the house means He *severed His relation with His people* as we saw at the close of the twelfth chapter...*the*

[593] *Jesus is Coming* - William E. Blackstone, Kregel, Publications, 1989, pp.124-125.
[594] *The Gospel of Matthew* - Arno C. Gaebelein, Loizeaux Brothers, 1982, pp.165,167, 233-234, 440. Gaebelein defines the "Kingdom of the Heavens" as "The Kingdom to be established in the earth, as predicted by the Old Testament prophets." (p.224).
[595] *The Gospel of Matthew* - Arno C. Gaebelein, Loizeaux Brothers, 1982, p.471.

sea typifying nations, shows His testimony to be given now, the mysteries to be revealed have a wider sphere; they are relative to the nations."[596] This interpretation by Gaebelein could hardly qualify as "literal" Bible interpretation. However, this statement does acutely demonstrate the extreme lengths to which Dispensationalists will resort in their determined effort to promote and support the pretribulation rapture doctrine.

Dispensationalists further teach that even after the Jews rejected and crucified their King, they were given a second chance to accept the legal terms of the earthly theocratic kingdom. For example, **Arno C. Gaebelein** teaches that within, "The opening chapters of the Book of Acts...we find the record of the second call to Israel...The preaching of the Kingdom is resumed for a brief period... No Gentile heard this message, nor was it meant for a Gentile; it was exclusively addressed to Jerusalem...It was to the Jews that Peter preached on the day of Pentecost. It is the *Gospel of the Kingdom* when Peter declared unto them...'Repent ye, therefore, and be converted, that your sins may be blotted out...' (Acts iii:19-20). This was the good news of the Kingdom."[597] **Gaebelein** goes on to say that, "Soon the nation rejected the last offer in the stoning of Stephen... With that event the preaching of the *Gospel of the Kingdom* ceased. *Another Gospel* was preached. The Lord gave it to the great Apostle...And Paul calls this Gospel, 'my Gospel.' It is the *Gospel of God's free grace* to all who believe..."[598] Closely following Gaebelein, **E. Schuyler English** teaches that, "The invitation to Israel as a nation is recorded in Acts 3:12-26. It was *not* the *Gospel of Grace* that Peter preached upon this occasion...This was not a message to the Gentiles; it was *Jewish exclusively*...God the Father was ready for the Son to return to reign; so the *Gospel of the Kingdom* was again preached: 'Repent ye.'"[599]

If what the Dispensationalists claim is true, we must wonder why Jesus didn't immediately return and establish the theocratic kingdom that was supposedly being offered to them? After all, there is no indication that the Jews rejected Peter's call to repentance (Acts 2:38). On the contrary, the text tells us plainly that, "...when they heard this, [i.e., the testimony about the ministry, death and resurrection of Jesus, who they had rejected, vv.22-36] they were pierced to the heart...So then, those who had

---

[596] *The Gospel of Matthew* - Arno C. Gaebelein, Loizeaux Brothers, 1982, p.260.
[597] *The Gospel of Matthew* - Arno C. Gaebelein, Loizeaux Brothers, 1982, pp.441,488.
[598] *The Gospel of Matthew* - Arno C. Gaebelein, Loizeaux Brothers, 1982, p.489.
[599] *Studies in the Gospel According to Matthew* - E. Schuyler English, Zondervan Publishing House, 1938, p.159.

received his word were baptized; and there were added that day about three thousand souls" (vv.37; 41). And to what were these three thousand souls added that day? Did they enter an earthy theocratic kingdom? No, they were added to the Church!

Peter's second sermon was preached at the temple (Acts 3:11-26) after he had healed a lame man at the temple gate called Beautiful (v.2-10). Once again, Peter called upon the Jews to repent of their rejection of Jesus Christ (v.14, 19-21) and once again, we are told that "...many of those who had heard the message believed; and the number of men came to be about five thousand" (Acts 4:4). But again, we must ask where did Peter specifically offer the Jews an earthly theocratic kingdom as the Dispensationalists assert? And where is the record that the Jews rejected that offer? The entire scheme is nothing more than a bizarre imaginary tale! There is not one word in the text of Acts 2:14-41 or Acts 3:1-26 that even hints at a kingdom offer to Israel or their rejection of that offer! Peter was not offering an earthly theocratic kingdom to the Jews - he was preaching *the Gospel* and calling upon each individual Jew who heard him, to repent and believe that Jesus Christ was indeed, "...the Prince of Life whom God raised from the dead..." (Acts 3:15)!

6. The Gospel of the Kingdom Will Be Preached Again by a Future Jewish Remnant.

Dispensationalists teach that the preaching of the "Gospel of Grace" will cease at the time of the pretribulation rapture. They further maintain that during the Tribulation period a Jewish remnant will go forth and preach the "Gospel of the Kingdom" to all the Gentile nations. This "Kingdom Gospel" will announce that the King is soon returning to establish His earthly theocratic kingdom - a kingdom that will be governed by a rigorous legal code of conduct referred to as the "kingdom teachings" of Christ. These "kingdom teachings" are said to amplify and intensify the Law of Moses, whereby Divine approval and acceptance is based solely upon personal righteousness and merit. It is therefore not surprising that Dispensationalists also teach that this future Jewish remnant will be zealous adherents of the Old Testament Law. For example, while commenting on the presumed Jewish nature and character of the Olivet Discourse in Matthew 24, **William Kelly** asserts that, "The foregoing indications point clearly and exclusively to *Jewish disciples* who will be found in Judea in the latter day, *cleaving to the law and to the testimony, keeping the commandments of God*...[and] ***not in the***

172

full privileges of Christians now."[600] Likewise, **A.C. Gaebelein** declares that, "We believe that the remnant will most likely consist of such Hebrews who are at this time still holding to the Messianic hope of a coming deliverer, *who hold fast the law and the testimony*, who firmly believe in the prophecies of their own Scriptures."[601] **Dwight Pentecost** maintains that this remnant will be "*saved to a special Jewish relationship.*"[602] And **John Walvoord** asserts that, "The godly remnant of the Tribulation are pictured as Israelites, *not members of the church...*"[603]

Thus, according to Dispensationalists, this future Jewish remnant will be comprised of non-Christian Israelites who do not possess "the full privileges of Christians now" but are saved to a "special Jewish relationship," while "cleaving unto the law," and "keeping the commandments of God." This remnant will proclaim the glad tidings of the coming theocratic kingdom to the Gentile nations. **Arno C. Gaebelein** explains that, "...there is a time coming when a Jewish remnant will again go forth to preach *the Gospel of the Kingdom*. This will be during the great tribulation[604]...this faithful Jewish remnant will go throughout the world proclaiming the *coming of the kingdom* and calling to repentance."[605] **E. Schuyler English** teaches that, "...the remnant of Israel shall take up the uncompleted proclamation, and once more shall they preach, *'The Kingdom of the heavens is at hand.*'"[606] Likewise, **Lehman Strauss** maintains that, "After the Rapture of the Church, Jewish evangelists will once more preach the *gospel of the kingdom...*"[607] And **Louis Talbot** declares that, "All Gentile nations will have the opportunity to receive or to reject the message...some nations will receive it...Other nations will reject the *message of the coming King and His kingdom...*"[608] The sole message of this "faithful Jewish remnant" will be that the King is coming to establish His earthly kingdom. As previously explained, this is the announcement of a political, theocratic kingdom that establishes, "...a new degree and standard of law..."[609] These "Jewish evangelists" are *not* proclaiming the necessity of individual saving faith in the

---

[600] *Lectures on the Second Coming* - William Kelly, Believers Bookshelf, 1970, p.248.
[601] *The Gospel of Matthew* - Arno C. Gaebelein, Loizeaux Brothers, 1982, p.491.
[602] *Things to Come* - J. Dwight Pentecost, Zondervan Publishing House, 1964, p.214.
[603] *The Rapture Question* - John F. Walvoord, Zondervan Publishing House, 1979, p.272.
[604] *The Gospel of Matthew* - Arno C. Gaebelein, Loizeaux Brothers, 1982, p.203.
[605] *The Gospel of Matthew* - Arno C. Gaebelein, Loizeaux Brothers, 1982, p.484.
[606] *Studies in the Gospel According to Matthew* - E. Schuyler English, Zondervan Publishing House, 1938, p.77.
[607] *The End of This Present World* - Zondervan Publishing House, 1967, p.99.
[608] *God's Plan for the Ages* - Louis C. Talbot, published by Louis C. Talbot, 1943, p.183.
[609] *Systematic Theology* - Lewis Sperry Chafer, Kregel Publications, 1993, vol.4, p.177.

person and work of the Lord Jesus Christ for the forgiveness of sins. Their message is not one of grace, but in the words of **Lewis Sperry Chafer**, these Jewish evangelists are proclaiming, "...terms of admission into the kingdom as set forth in Matthew 5:1-7:27..."[610]

Dispensationalists uniformly teach that the Gospel of Grace will *not* be preached during this period. **A. C. Gaebelein** emphasizes this important point when he explains; "Now during the time that the Kingdom was preached to be at hand [*i.e., during the earthly ministry of Christ*] the Gospel of Grace was *not* heard, and during the time the Gospel of Grace is preached [*i.e., during the present Church Age*] the Gospel of the Kingdom is *not* preached...As soon then as the church leaves this earthly scene...*the Gospel of the Kingdom will be sounded forth once more to all the nations*."[611] While commenting on the Tribulation period, **Charles Ryrie** affirms that, "...the gospel to be preached during that period is the *gospel of the kingdom* (Matt.24:14)."[612] And **Dwight Pentecost** likewise stresses that, "The tribulation will witness the preaching of the *gospel of the kingdom*. Matthew 24 makes this very clear."[613]

6a. The 144,000.

Dispensationalists refer to the future Jewish remnant who will proclaim the Gospel of the Kingdom, as the 144,000. **A.C. Gaebelein** makes it clear that, "...the 144,000 of whom we read in Rev. vii... is the Jewish remnant...they will preach the Gospel of the kingdom..."[614] **E. Schuyler English** teaches that, "The Gospel of the Kingdom will again be preached, when the 144,000 Jewish people shall proclaim the message of the coming King."[615] **Charles Feinberg** succinctly states that, "...the 144,000 sealed ones...proclaim the gospel of the kingdom..."[616] **Louis Talbot** asserts that, "During the 70th week of Daniel His missionaries will be 144,000 Jews...and they will go throughout the nations preaching 'the gospel of the kingdom'...they will proclaim the

---

[610] *Dispensationalism* - Lewis Sperry Chafer, Dallas Seminary Press, 1936, 1951, pp.95-96.
[611] *The Gospel of Matthew* - Arno C. Gaebelein, Loizeaux Brothers, 1982, p.490.
[612] *Dispensationalism Today* - Charles Caldwell Ryrie, Moody Press, 1970, p.55.
[613] *Things to Come* - J. Dwight Pentecost, Zondervan Publishing House, 1964, p.271.
[614] *The Gospel of Matthew* - Arno C. Gaebelein, Loizeaux Brothers, 1982, p.470.
[615] *Studies in the Gospel According to Matthew* - E. Schuyler English, Zondervan Publishing House, 1938, p.174.
[616] *Premillennialism or Amillennialism?* - Charles Feinberg, Zondervan Publishing House, 1936, p.130.

same message which John the Baptist, the Lord Jesus, and His disciples heralded."[617] And **Dwight Pentecost** explains that, "It is believed that the 144,000 of Revelation 7 and 14 constitute a special part of the remnant of Israel, set apart by a sovereign act of God, to be special witnesses during the tribulation period."[618]

But what evidence is there that the 144,000 mentioned in Revelation 7:4-8 and 14:1-5 are Jewish evangelists commissioned to preach the Gospel of the Kingdom to the Gentile nations? Look very carefully at these two texts. They certainly do not state that the 144,000 are evangelists, nor is there any indication that the 144,000 preach a kingdom Gospel to the Gentile nations. The entire proposition is a highly imaginative and questionable assumption. **E. Schuyler English** attempts to justify this crucial Dispensational supposition by insisting that, "It is *not amiss*...for us to *infer* that the 144,000 will be the publishers or evangelists of the Gospel of the kingdom to the whole world..."[619] Not amiss to infer? Really? Carefully consider the fact that there is absolutely nothing in these two texts to substantiate this Dispensational inference. These texts do not state or even imply that the 144,000 are "evangelists" commissioned to preach a "kingdom Gospel" to the Gentile nations. Once again, the entire teaching exists within the imaginations of the Dispensationalists and *not* the plain, ordinary, literal statements of the Scriptures. It is important to emphasize that this entire scenario is *not* the result of a careful and deliberate exegesis of the Biblical text. Rather, it is the product of highly *subjective assumptions* that are illegitimately imposed upon the text – assumptions that are necessary to defend and support the concept of a pretribulation rapture.

The book of Revelation presents a serious dilemma for Dispensationalists and their pretribulation rapture theory. This dilemma is created by the fact that the Book of Revelation frequently refers to *believers* being present upon the earth throughout the entire Tribulation period. If the Church is in fact removed from the earth before the beginning of the Tribulation as Dispensationalists maintain, then they must explain who these *believers* are. Dispensationalists attempt to answer this central question by asserting that the *believers* mentioned in the book of Revelation are individuals who are converted *after* the rapture when they accept the "Gospel of the Kingdom" that is

---

[617] *God's Plan for the Ages* - Louis C. Talbot, published by Louis C. Talbot, 1943, pp.160-161.
[618] *Things to Come* - J. Dwight Pentecost, Zondervan Publishing House, 1964, p.297.
[619] *Re-Thinking the Rapture* - E. Schuyler English, Loizeaux Brothers, 1954, p.102.

preached by the 144,000 Jewish evangelists. For example, **Arno C. Gaebelein** explains that, "When the Church is taken from the earth a *believing Jewish remnant* will give the witness and preach the Gospel of the Kingdom once more."[620] **Gaebelein** goes on to rhetorically ask, "And who will be the preachers of this last witness, the missionaries who reach all nations with this final message before the King appears in judgment? They are a *believing Israelitish remnant*."[621] Likewise, **Lehman Strauss** maintains that, "...the good news of the gospel of the kingdom..." will be proclaimed by "...the 144,000 *redeemed children of Israel*..." whom he refers to as "...those 144,000 Jewish missionaries..."[622] And **Gerald Stanton** asserts that, "...a *remnant from among Israel* shall be *redeemed* and become God's primary witnessing body during the Tribulation. The Church, her witness complete, will be already with the Lord."[623]

But this explanation raises another equally important question for Dispensationalists. Dispensationalists realize that immediately after the pretribulation rapture there will be no believers left on earth. For example, **John Walvoord** states that, "...at the time of the translation of the church *all* true believers are translated from earth to heaven...the nation Israel enters the Tribulation in an *unsaved condition*..."[624] Likewise, **Renald Showers** explains that, "...the Rapture will involve the *removal of believers* from the earth, but the *unbelievers will be left* on the earth to enter the next period of history."[625] Now then, if the Church is removed before the beginning of the Tribulation and the Gospel of Grace is no longer being preached, then exactly how do the 144,000 Jewish evangelists become "believers?" **Leon Wood** attempts to answer this crucial question by speculating that, "...the number of Jews who will turn in faith to Christ during the seven-year period will be quite large. Probably the first Jews to turn will do so as a result of *reading Bibles and religious books*...These in turn will witness to others, and finally the 144,000, or more, will be converted."[626] **Lehman Strauss** ignores the problem and simply asserts that, "This sealed remnant of Jews, not having had the gospel explained to them before, will *turn to Christ* after the rapture of the Church."[627]

[620] *The Gospel of Matthew* - Arno C. Gaebelein, Loizeaux Brothers, 1982, p.143.
[621] *The Gospel of Matthew* - Arno C. Gaebelein, Loizeaux Brothers, 1982, p.490.
[622] *The Book of the Revelation* - Lehman Strauss, Loizeaux Brothers, 1977, pp.175-176.
[623] *Kept From the Hour* - Gerald B. Stanton, Zondervan Publishing House, 1956, p.259.
[624] *The Rapture Question* - John F. Walvoord, Zondervan Publishing House, 1979, p.63.
[625] *Maranatha Our Lord Come!* - Renald Showers, The Friends of Israel Gospel Ministry, Inc., 1995, p.177.
[626] *The Bible and Future Events* - Leon J. Wood, Zondervan Publishing House, 1974, p.133.
[627] *The Book of the Revelation* - Lehman Strauss, Loizeaux Brothers, 1977, p.172.

Dwight Pentecost maintains that, "...after the rapture...Israel is still in **unbelief**...the nation, **unsaved** at the beginning of the tribulation, receives a **multitude of witnesses of various kinds** so that the individuals are experiencing salvation through the period..."[628] **Pentecost** speculates further, proposing that, "God uses **many different means** to bring all Israel to salvation during the seventieth week. The **Word of God is available and may be used**, so that those Jews who are hungering and thirsting **may search that Word** for a knowledge of Christ."[629]

Thus, Dispensationalists theorize that 144,000 unbelieving Jews will be saved through various unspecified means, which may include religious books and possibly even the "the Word of God." However, it is clear that the Gospel of Grace is **not** the means of their salvation. This fact is made clear by **John Darby**. While commenting on Romans 11:25, **Darby** flatly denies that the future salvation of Israel has any connection to the Gospel of Grace. **Darby** emphatically declared: "And so all Israel shall be saved...This is **not by the gospel as now preached**, for he [i.e., Paul] adds, 'As concerning the gospel they are enemies for your sake,' ...**our gospel is not the means**: they are as a nation enemies as respects that...Thus it is certain that God maintains His purpose as to them as a people, and it is **not by the gospel as now preached** they will be called in."[630]

So then, if the 144,000 are not "called in" by the Gospel of Grace as "now preached," then exactly how are they to be saved? Dispensationalists do not leave us wondering. **A. C. Gaebelein** explains that, "As soon then as the church leaves this earthly scene...the **Gospel of the Kingdom** will be sounded forth once more to all the nations."[631] While referring specifically to Matthew 24:14,[632] **Gaebelein** further explains that, "This verse relates exclusively to the end of the age, that is the Jewish age...it is at the end of the age that the **glad tidings of the Kingdom are to be heralded through the earth**...the preaching which the Lord speaks is a future witness to all the nations..."[633] Thus, according to **Gaebelein** it is the proclamation of the **"glad tidings of**

---

[628] *Things to Come* - J. Dwight Pentecost, Zondervan Publishing House, 1964, p.295.

[629] *Things to Come* - J. Dwight Pentecost, Zondervan Publishing House, 1964, p.295.

[630] *The Collected Writings of J.N. Darby* - Edited by William Kelly, Stow Hill Bible and Tract Depot, n.d., Prophetic No.4, Vol.11, p.267.

[631] *The Gospel of Matthew* - Arno C. Gaebelein, Loizeaux Brothers, 1982, p.490.

[632] Mt.24:14 - "And this gospel of the kingdom shall be preached in the whole world for a witness to all the nations, and then the end shall come."

[633] *The Gospel of Matthew* - Arno C. Gaebelein, Loizeaux Brothers, 1982, p.488.

the kingdom," that the future Jewish remnant will embrace and proclaim. As previously mentioned, Dispensationalists teach that the Gospel of the Kingdom is the "good news" that the King is about to establish His earthly theocratic kingdom and enact His kingdom constitution, which amplifies and intensifies the legal requirements of the Mosaic Law. These are the "glad tidings" that Dispensationalists assert the future Jewish remnant is going to accept and proclaim to all the nations of the earth.

But this is *not* a saving message! The problem for Dispensationalists is that the Scriptures plainly declare that salvation is exclusively the result of personal faith in the person and work of the Lord Jesus Christ [634] as revealed in the Gospel and *not* the imagined "glad tidings" of a forthcoming legalistic theocratic kingdom. Referring specifically to "Jesus Christ the Nazarene," Peter emphatically declares that "…there is salvation in no one else; for there is no other name under heaven that has been given among men, by which we must be saved."[635] Again, Jesus Himself declares that, "I am the way, and the truth, and the life; no one comes to the Father but through Me." (Jn.14:6). It could not be any clearer. There is no other saving message. God has decreed that the Gospel alone can deliver fallen people from their sins and restore them to fellowship with a holy and righteous God![636] Dispensational teachers do a serious disservice to the lost world by teaching that there is "another gospel" that can save lost souls!

6b. A Different Salvation.

Since Dispensationalists teach that those saved during the Tribulation will be converted through the preaching of a different Gospel, it is therefore not surprising that they also maintain that those converted during the Tribulation will experience a different quality of salvation than those within the Church. For example, **William Trotter** teaches that, "Unlike the Church, the remnant does *not possess the knowledge of salvation as an existing enjoyment*...those who compose the remnant are represented in prophecy as using language...*incompatible with any present assurance of salvation*."[637] **Trotter** then goes on to explain the difference between the Church and the remnant, asserting

---

[634] Ro.1:16; 10:9-13; Acts 16:30-31.
[635] Acts 4:10-12.
[636] 1Thess.3:13; 2Thess.2:13-14; Jas.1:18; 1Pt.1:23.
[637] *Plain Papers on Prophetic and Other Subjects* - William Trotter, Loizeaux Brothers, n.d., p.395.

that, "The Church stands in Christ; and has the knowledge of accomplished redemption: *the remnant do not*. The Church suffers for Christ's sake...*the remnant suffer for their own sins and those of the nation,* and *groan under the sense of God's wrath*."[638] While referring to the Jewish remnant, **William Kelly** asserts that, "They are redeemed of course. They are in bliss...but it is of a *lower character* than that of the heavenly saints...every one of these saints comes out of the great tribulation...They are blessed; they are washed in the blood of the Lamb; but they have *no distinctive properties of the church*...On one side is a body of blest Jews, on the other is this crowd of blest Gentiles. But there is *a special place for Christians...* [639] **Kelly** goes on to conclude that, "...although the sins of Israel will be as truly forgiven as ours... yet there will *not be the same communion, character, or measure* in the power of the Spirit formed by the knowledge of Christ."[640] And **Lewis Sperry Chafer** laments the fact that many Bible teachers "...carry the same realities which belong to the saved of this age over into the kingdom age and to the Jews and Gentiles alike...the *Church alone is accorded the heavenly position and glory*."[641]

It is a peculiar concept of salvation that differentiates between the spiritual standing and blessings of the saved of this age and the saved of the future Tribulation period. Not surprisingly, this difference in spiritual position and standing is the logical result of insisting that there are two different Gospels with two different messages. Obviously, if there is a different Gospel, then its intended purpose and effect would also necessarily be different - otherwise, it would not really be different. But where are we told in the New Testament that the "glad tidings" that the King is returning to establish His earthly theocratic kingdom is a saving message? Where are we told that God has determined to save sinners based upon their acceptance of a "kingdom message?" Dispensationalists are correct when they assert that Jesus Christ is returning to establish His Millennial Kingdom upon this earth. However, the acceptance of this Biblical fact is *not* a means of salvation.

The announcement of the future millennial reign of Christ is *not* a saving message! The simple fact of the matter is that God has determined to save fallen sinners solely by the

---

[638] *Plain Papers on Prophetic and Other Subjects* - William Trotter, Loizeaux Brothers, n.d., p.521.
[639] *Lectures on the Second Coming* - William Kelly, Believers Bookshelf, 1970, p.279.
[640] *Lectures on the Second Coming* - William Kelly, Believers Bookshelf, 1970, p.323.
[641] *Systematic Theology* - Lewis Sperry Chafer, Kregel Publications, 1993, vol.4, p.328.

preaching of the Good News of the sacrificial and substitutionary death of Jesus Christ upon the Cross of Calvary for our sins, and His glorious resurrection on the third day for our justification (Ro.4:25). There is no other redemptive message revealed in the New Testament – Jesus Christ died for our sins and we appropriate the eternal benefits of His substitutionary death by grace through faith in Jesus Christ. This redemptive message is referred to as "*the* Gospel," which is the good news of the sacrificial death, burial and resurrection of Jesus Christ for our sins (1Cor.15:1-8), coupled with the Divine admonition to repent and place our trust in Jesus Christ (Ro.10:9-10,17).

The term "salvation"[642] literally means "deliverance." Man needs to be delivered from sin because sin has completely ruined man and rendered him unfit for the purpose for which he was originally created - communion and fellowship with God. Thus, through Divine intervention, fallen, sinful men have been "saved," or "delivered" from the controlling power of sin and the Divine punishment that sin justly warrants. It is important to understand that the term "salvation" is an all-encompassing term that includes *all* of the benefits of the redemptive work of Christ. For example, someone who is "saved" is, *Regenerated* (born again, made spiritually alive); *Justified* (judicially declared righteous by God upon the grounds of Christ's righteousness which is imputed to the believer by faith); *Reconciled* (brought back into right relationship with God); *Redeemed* (delivered from the bondage and slavery of sin, and set free to serve and worship God in spirit and truth); *Adopted* (made a part of God's own household, which is the Church, the Body of Christ); *Sanctified* (the work of the Holy Spirit by which the believer's thoughts, desires and actions are brought into conformity with God's holy standards) and ultimately will be *Glorified* (the completion of the sanctification process when the believer is perfectly conformed to the moral image of Jesus Christ in body, soul and spirit). And this "deliverance" or "salvation" is found *only* in the person of Jesus Christ and rests *completely* upon the sacrificial and substitutionary death of Jesus Christ for our sins (Ro.5:8-9; 1Cor.15:3-8; 2Cor.5:21; Gal.1:3-4; 1Pt.2:24; 3:18; Heb. 9:11-14).

Thus, when viewed from the human perspective, salvation occurs when the historical proclamation of the Gospel is heard, understood and believed. All of the benefits of the

---

[642] "σωτηρία [soteria]...deliverance, preservation, salvation, safety...In NT esp. of Messianic and spiritual salvation." *A Manual Greek Lexicon of the New Testament* – G. Abbott-Smith, Charles Scribner's Sons, 1953, p.437.

redemptive work of Jesus Christ are then immediately applied to the believer and he immediately passes out of death into life - he is at once delivered from the domain of darkness and transferred into the kingdom of Christ (Col.1:13; Gal.1:4). It is the message of the Cross (i.e., the Gospel, which is the good news of the sacrificial death, burial and resurrection of Jesus Christ on behalf of sinners, 1Cor.15:1-5) which God has determined to use to effect the regeneration and transformation of fallen men - look carefully at Acts 15:7-9; Ro.1:16; 10:17; 1Cor.1:18; Eph.1:13; 1Thess.2:13; 2Thess.2:13-14; Jas.1:18; 1Pt.1:23. There is no other redemptive message! Dispensationalists commit a monumental error of enormous proportion when they teach that the acceptance of the "glad tidings" of a coming "theocratic kingdom" results in "salvation." They commit an even more egregious error when they attempt to disguise their doctrine of "two Gospels" by blending elements of the Gospel of Grace with their fictitious Gospel of the Kingdom; thereby creating a hybridized gospel that is really no Gospel at all.

Although Dispensationalists concede that their "future Jewish remnant" will truly be saved, they view their salvation as essentially inferior to the present experience of Christians. For example, Dispensationalists insist that those saved during the Tribulation period, through the preaching of their "kingdom Gospel" will not experience the benefit of the indwelling presence and enabling power of the Holy Spirit. They reach this conclusion via a complicated reasoning process that begins with the assumption that both the Holy Spirit and the Church will be removed from the earth *before* the beginning of the Tribulation. Once again, it was **John Darby** who popularized the view that the Holy Spirit would leave the earth at the time of the pretribulational rapture of the Church. While commenting on Second Thessalonians 2:6, **Darby** claimed that, "...when *the assembly* (the assembly, that is, as composed of the true members of Christ) *is gone*, and *consequently the Holy Ghost* as the Comforter *is no longer dwelling here below*, then the apostasy takes place..."[643] **William Blackstone**, follows Darby by connecting the supposed removal of the Holy Spirit with the rapture of the Church. **Blackstone** claims that, "When He, the restraining one, is taken out of the way (or out of the midst), at the rapture of the church...the lawless one will be revealed (2Thessalonians 2:7,8)."[644] Likewise, **Gerald Stanton** teaches that,

---

[643] *Synopsis of the Books of the Bible* - J.N. Darby, Loizeaux Brothers, 1950, vol.5, p.137.
[644] *Jesus is Coming* - William E. Blackstone, Kregel Publications, 1989, p.108.

"He who now restrains...is undoubtedly the Holy Spirit...When the spirit is removed, then the Church must also be snatched away...The removal of the Spirit takes place before the Wicked One shall be revealed, and this removal sets the time for the rapture of the Church."[645] **Edmond Hiebert** explains that, "The indwelling Spirit will be 'out of the midst' of this present scene when the returning Christ calls His church to Himself. When the Church is taken away to be with her Lord, then will He be also 'out of the midst;'...Since the removal of the Restrainer takes place before the manifestation of the lawless one, this identification *implies* a pretribulational rapture."[646] Implies a pretribulation rapture? Really? Look carefully at Second Thessalonians 2:6-7.

"And you know what restrains him [i.e., the antichrist] now, so that in his time he may be revealed. For the mystery of lawlessness is already at work; **only he who now restrains will do so until he is taken out of the way.**" (Emphasis added).

The problem for Dispensationalists is that this text does *not* say what the Dispensationalists claim it says. Dispensationalists *assume* that the phrase "he who now restrains" refers to the Holy Spirit. They further *assume* that the statement, "taken out of the way" refers to the removal of the Spirit from earth to heaven. Dispensationalists then circuitously reason that the Church, because it is indwelled by the Holy Spirit, must also be removed along with the Holy Spirit. Based upon this tenuous chain of assumptions, Dispensationalists conclude that this text describes the pretribulational rapture of the Church! However, a literal reading of this text does not support this Dispensational scenario. Even if, for the sake of argument, it is conceded that the phrase, "...he who now restrains *will do so* until he is taken out of the way" refers to the Holy Spirit, it does not substantiate the Dispensational contention that "taken out of the way" means that the Holy Spirit leaves the earth, or that the rapture then occurs. Mark it carefully, Dispensationalists are *assuming* that this text refers to the Holy Spirit; they are *assuming* that the phrase "he is taken out of the way" refers to the Spirit's removal from earth to heaven; and they are *assuming* that this all coincides with a pretribulation rapture of the Church. The entire proposition is an enormous *inference* that is supported by nothing more than unbridled speculation.

[645] *Kept From the Hour* - Gerald B. Stanton. Zondervan Publishing House, 1956, pp.106-107.
[646] *The Thessalonian Epistles* - D. Edmond Hiebert, Moody Press, 1982, p.313.

Carefully consider the torturous reasoning employed by **Lewis Sperry Chafer** who says, "...the Restrainer must be one with the Godhead...and since the Holy Spirit is the active Executer of the Godhead in the world during this age, it is reasonable to conclude that He it is who restrains...When His work of gathering out the Church is completed...He, the Spirit, the Restrainer, will be removed from the world...It is clearly asserted that the believer can never be separated from the Holy Spirit...therefore, when the Spirit, the Restrainer, is 'taken out of the way,' the Church will of necessity be removed with Him."[647] **Chafer's** entire argument is nothing more than assumptions heaped upon assumptions.

Dispensationalists further assume that after the rapture and the removal of the Spirit to heaven, His ministry will revert back to what it was during the Old Testament dispensation. For example, **A.C. Gaebelein** teaches that, "The Holy Spirit...will no longer be present on the earth as He is now; but He will still be working...in the same way as He did in the *Old Testament...*"[648] Likewise, **Charles Feinberg** says that, "The ministry of the Spirit after the Church age in the Tribulation Period will *approximate that of the Spirit in Old Testament times.*"[649] **Gerald Stanton** also affirms that, "When He, as restrainer, is removed, there will be a *reversal of Pentecost*, which will mean that the *Spirit will minister from heaven as during the Old Testament economy.*" [650]

Dispensationalists further assert that the Holy Spirit will *not* indwell those who are saved during the Tribulation period. For example, **Gerald Stanton** declares that, "He [i.e., the Holy Spirit] will be present but *not resident*; operating, but *no longer indwelling*. He will save souls but no longer baptize them into the body of Christ, for the Church will be complete and in heaven."[651] **Edmond Hiebert** maintains that, "...at Pentecost He [i.e., the Holy Spirit] assumed a special relationship to the church as its indweller...After the completion of His work in the church, He will *resume the relation to mankind that He had before Pentecost.*"[652] And **John Walvoord** assures us that, "While the Spirit will work in the tribulation period, *He will follow the pattern of the*

[647] *Systematic Theology* - Lewis Sperry Chafer, Kregel Publications, 1993, vol.4, p.372.
[648] *The Gospel of Matthew* - Arno C. Gaebelein, Loizeaux Brothers, 1982, pp.490-491.
[649] *Premillennialism or Amillennialism?* - Charles Feinberg, Zondervan Publishing House, 1936, p.219.
[650] *Kept From the Hour* - Gerald B. Stanton, Zondervan Publishing House, 1956, pp.105-106.
[651] *Kept From the Hour* - Gerald B. Stanton, Zondervan Publishing House, 1956, pp.105-106.
[652] *The Thessalonian Epistles* - D. Edmond Hiebert, Moody Press, 1982, p.314.

period before Pentecost rather than this present age of grace...the work...continues, but in a different way."[653] More pointedly, **Walvoord** explains that, "Pretribulationists hold that at the rapture we have a *reversal of what occurs on the day of Pentecost*...That the Spirit indwells all believers in the tribulation is *nowhere taught*."[654]

However, this "reversal of Pentecost" entails much more than a cessation of the Spirit's indwelling ministry. Dispensationalists further maintain that after the pretribulation Rapture of the Church, the distinction between Jews and Gentiles, which characterized the Old Testament economy, will once again be reinstated. Or put another way, the "dividing wall" that separated Jews and Gentiles and was removed by the death of Christ,[655] will once again be erected. For example, while referring to the future remnant, **William Kelly** asserts that, "By and by...God will have a people out of the Jews; He will have a people out of the Gentiles also; but...*they will not be mingled together*."[656] **William Trotter** says that, "The Jewish remnant, unlike the Church, *will recognize the distinction between Jew and Gentile*...when the Church has been caught up, and the Jewish nation and Jewish remnant are again in question before God, it is evident that the *distinction between Jew and Gentile is again in force*."[657] **Leon Wood** maintains that, "In the church age today, Jews who turn to Christ are made one with Gentiles in the unified body of Christ. Jews of the tribulation period, however, who turn to Christ, will do so as *members of the Jewish nation, quite as in Old Testament time*."[658] And **John Walvoord** states that, "After the translation of the church...believers in that tribulation period *retain their national characteristics* as saved *Gentiles* or saved *Jews*. Never are *tribulation saints* given the special and peculiar promises given to the church in the present age."[659] **Walvoord** further explains that, "...the redeemed people in the tribulation are described as *saved* Israelites and *saved* Gentiles, *not* as the Church."[660]

But where in Scripture are we informed that the effects of Pentecost are going to be "reversed" and that the ethnic distinctions between redeemed Jews and Gentiles are

---

[653] *The Rapture Question* - John F. Walvoord, Zondervan Publishing House, 1979, p.81.
[654] *The Blessed Hope and the Tribulation* - John F. Walvoord, Zondervan Publishing House, 1976, pp.127-128.
[655] See Eph.2:11-15.
[656] *Lectures on the Second Coming* -William Kelly, Believers Bookshelf, 1970, p.279.
[657] *Plain Papers on Prophetic and Other Subjects* - William Trotter, Loizeaux Brothers, n.d., p.394.
[658] *The Bible and Future Events* - Leon J. Wood, Zondervan Publishing House, 1974, p.155.
[659] *The Rapture Question* - John F. Walvoord, Zondervan Publishing House, 1981, p.65.
[660] *The Blessed Hope and the Tribulation* - John F. Walvoord, Zondervan Publishing House, 1976, p.67.

going to once again be "reinstated?" The fact is that there is nothing in the New Testament that substantiates these Dispensational claims. Rather, the testimony of the Scripture clearly and resoundingly refutes these claims. The Apostle Paul tells us plainly that there is "*one* body, *one* Spirit...*one* hope...*one* Lord, *one* faith, *one* baptism, *one* God and Father of *all*..." (Eph.4:4-5, emphasis added). The operative word here is "one." There are *not* different redeemed groups of believers - there is but "one." *All* believers, Jew and Gentile, are made *one* by faith in Jesus Christ (Gal.3:28; Col.3:11 cp. Jn.10:16; 11:52; 17:20-21).

Furthermore, the Dispensational claim that the Holy Spirit is going to "*resume the relation to mankind that He had before Pentecost*" and that He "*will follow the pattern of the period before Pentecost*" is refuted by the plain testimony of Scripture. The Epistle to the Hebrews refutes the Dispensational claim that God is going to reinstate certain elements of the Old Testament economy during the Tribulation period. This fact becomes obvious when it is realized that the conditions of the New Covenant have permanently replaced the conditions of the Old Covenant. God is no longer dealing with mankind on the basis of the Old Covenant because it has been rendered obsolete by the establishment of a new and better Covenant. Hebrews tells us that, "When He [God] said 'A new *covenant*,' He has made the first obsolete. But whatever is becoming obsolete and growing old is ready to disappear" (Heb.8:13). The Old Covenant was made obsolete when, "He [Christ] said, 'Behold, I have come to do Thy will.' He takes away the first in order to establish the second." (Heb.10:9). Thus, it is the new covenant (Jer.31:31-34) established by the blood of Jesus Christ (Lk.22:20) that permanently replaces the Old Covenant. Proof that the Old Covenant has become obsolete and has truly passed away is deduced from the fact that since the destruction of the Jewish Temple in 70 A.D., it is impossible for either Jew or Gentile to obey the terms and conditions of the Old Covenant. God is now approachable *only* on the basis of the conditions of the New Covenant. It is only by faith in the Lord Jesus Christ, that "...we have confidence to enter the holy place by the blood of Jesus, by a new and living way which He inaugurated for us through the veil, that is His flesh..." (Heb.10:19-20). This is precisely what Jesus meant when He said, "I am the way, and the truth, and the life, no one comes to the Father, but through Me." (Jn.14:6). The Dispensational claim that God is going to set aside the conditions of the New Covenant and then reinstate conditions of the obsolete Old Covenant is *not* the result of a careful, literal, exegesis of the Scriptures. Rather, it is part of a highly imaginative, complicated and convoluted

185

attempt by Dispensationalists to explain why believers are still present on earth after the pretribulation rapture has supposedly occurred. The entire proposition is simply preposterous and overtly contrary to the plain statements of Scripture.

7. Vast Multitudes Will Be Saved During the Tribulation

The book of Revelation clearly reveals that believers will be present on earth during the Tribulation period. Dispensationalists fully realize that they must explain who these believers are and why they are still on earth *after* the pretribulation rapture has supposedly occurred. Dispensationalists attempt to satisfy this demand by contending that immediately after the pretribulational rapture of the Church, an "unbelieving Jewish remnant" will be converted. This "Jewish remnant" will then go forth into all the nations and preach the "Gospel of the Kingdom." As a result, Dispensationalists declare that vast multitudes of both Jews and Gentiles will be saved. These new converts are the believers that Dispensationalists say are on earth during the Tribulation period. For example, **A.C. Gaebelein** declares that, "...the nations of Africa, China, India, the isles of the sea will hear and *accept the Gospel of the Kingdom* and gladly receive these messengers whom the Lord calls 'these my brethren' (Matthew xxv:31, etc.)."[661] **E. Schuyler English** maintains that, "...*many from among the Gentiles*, seeing the glory of God in His people Israel, *will also turn to the Lord*."[662] **Charles Feinberg** explains that, "...the 144,000...proclaim the gospel of the kingdom...The result of their testimony is seen in the *great multitude of Gentiles saved*...many Gentiles are saved out of the Great Tribulation as a result of the *preaching of the gospel of the kingdom* as a witness to all nations...salvation...will be brought about through the application of the Word by the Spirit to the hearts of individuals who have heard the message of God's witnesses."[663] **Gerald Stanton** succinctly states that, "*Multitudes are saved* during the Tribulation."[664] And **Dwight Pentecost** confidently asserts that, "...there will be a *multitude of believers* among the Gentiles who will believe and await His return."[665]

---

[661] *The Gospel of Matthew* - Arno C. Gaebelein, Loizeaux Brothers, 1982, p.494.

[662] *Re-Thinking the Rapture* - E. Schuyler English, Loizeaux Brothers, 1954, p.102.

[663] *Premillennialism or Amillennialism?* - Charles Feinberg, Zondervan Publishing House, 1936, pp.130,135,219.

[664] *Kept From the Hour* - Gerald B. Stanton, Zondervan Publishing House, 1956, p.270.

[665] *Things to Come* - J. Dwight Pentecost, Zondervan Publishing House, 1964, p.214.

And again, **Pentecost** insists that, "This witness is seen to be effective in that *multitudes of Jews are converted* during the tribulation period..."[666]

The problem for Dispensationalists is that the Scriptures clearly describe the Great Tribulation as a time of spiritual apostasy *not* unprecedented revival. For example, in the Olivet Discourse, Jesus warned His disciples that during the Tribulation, "... *many will fall away* and deliver up one another and hate one another" (Mt.24:10, emphasis added). Likewise, the Apostle Paul warns the Thessalonian Christians to, "Let no one in any way deceive you, for it [i.e., the Day of the Lord] will not come unless the *apostasy* comes first and the lawless one is revealed, the son of destruction..." (2Thess.2:1, emphasis added). The word "apostasy" refers to a rejection of sound doctrine and thus a falling away or departure from the truth. Paul further warns the Thessalonians that God will send a "deluding influence" upon the ungodly during the Tribulation period "so that they might believe what is false." (2Thess.2:10-12). Likewise, Paul cautions that, "...the Spirit explicitly says that in the *later times* some will *fall away from the faith,* paying attention to deceitful spirits and doctrines of demons..." (1Tim.4:1, emphasis added). Thus, the Scriptures clearly teach that the last days will be characterized by spiritual apostasy, *not* spiritual revival. The book of Revelation repeatedly emphasizes this fact. We are frequently told that during the Tribulation period, unregenerate men will blaspheme God and refuse to repent. Carefully consider the following texts:

Rv.9:20-21 "And the *rest of mankind,* who were not killed by these plagues, did *not repent* of the works of their hands...they did *not repent* of their murders nor of their sorceries nor of their immorality nor of their thefts." (Emphasis added).

Rv.16:8-9 "And the fourth angel poured out his bowl upon the sun; and it was given to it to scorch men with fire. And men were scorched with fierce heat; and they *blasphemed the name of God* who has the power over these plagues; and they did *not repent,* so as to give Him glory." (Emphasis added).

Rv.16:10-11 "And the fifth angel poured out his bowl upon the throne of the beast; and his kingdom became darkened; and they gnawed their tongues because of pain, and they *blasphemed the God of heaven* because of their pains and sores; and they did *not repent* of their deeds." (Emphasis added).

---

[666] *Things to Come* - J. Dwight Pentecost, Zondervan Publishing House, 1964, pp.237-238.

Rv.16:21 "And huge hailstones, about one hundred pounds each, came down from heaven upon men; and men **blasphemed God** because of the plague of the hail, because its plague was extremely severe." (Emphasis added).

Dispensationalists assert that the Tribulation period will be a time of unprecedented revival, with vast multitudes of Jews and Gentiles turning to the Lord. If this were truly the case, we would expect to find at least one text of Scripture that describes this unprecedented revival. ***Yet there is not a single verse that describes anyone being saved during the Tribulation period - not one!*** In fact, the exact opposite is true - we are repeatedly told that the last days will be a time characterized by *false teaching* and *apostasy* when men will *refuse* to believe!

Dispensationalists base their claim that multitudes of Jews and Gentiles will be saved during the Tribulation on assumptions that they draw from the text of Revelation 7:9-17. This text describes a great multitude of believers who are seen standing before the Lord, having come out of the Great Tribulation. Dispensationalists insist that this great multitude represents those who have been saved during the Tribulation as a direct result of the preaching of the Gospel of the Kingdom by the 144,000 Jewish evangelists (Rv.7:1-8). For example, **C.I. Scofield** teaches that, "The great tribulation will be, however, a *period of salvation*. An election out of Israel is seen sealed by God (Rev.7:4-8), and, with ***an innumerable multitude of Gentiles*** (Rev.7:9) are said to have 'come out of the great tribulation' (Rev.7:14)."[667] **H.A. Ironside** proposes that, "This great multitude...is the ***great ingathering of the coming dispensation***...During the dark days of the great tribulation they will heed the testimony which will be carried to the ends of the earth by ***Jewish missionaries***..."[668] **Leon Wood** emphasizes that, "...there will be those who will still turn to the Lord in repentance and faith. In fact, they are to be a *large number*. It seems probable that the ***preaching of the 144,000 Jews*** (Rev.7:14-17) who at this time become ***missionaries of the truth***, will have considerable effect toward bringing this about."[669] And **Charles Ryrie** affirms that, "The Tribulation period...will also be a ***time of much salvation***. ***Many Jews and multitudes of Gentiles*** will come to know the Lord (Rev.7)."[670]

---

[667] *The Scofield Study Bible* - C.I. Scofield, Oxford University Press, 1945 p.1337.
[668] *Lectures on the Book of Revelation* - H.A. Ironside, Loizeaux Brothers, 1971, pp.128-129.
[669] *Is the Rapture Next?* - Leon J. Wood, Zondervan Publishing House, 1956, p.22.
[670] *Dispensationalism Today* - Charles Caldwell Ryrie, Moody Press, 1970, p.56.

But look carefully at Revelation 7:4-17. The text makes no mention of Jewish missionaries or evangelists who preach a Kingdom Gospel to the Gentile nations. We are simply told that 144,000 are "sealed from every tribe of the sons of Israel." Furthermore, the "great multitude, which no one could count, from every nation and all tribes and peoples and tongues" are seen standing before the "the Lamb" suddenly and all at once, not incrementally over time. The language does not convey the idea of a progressive accumulation of the redeemed but a sudden and complete worldwide gathering. Furthermore, the text gives no indication that this multitude was saved by the preaching of a Kingdom Gospel or even that this multitude was saved during the Tribulation.

The highly imaginative and speculative nature of this entire Dispensational scheme is vividly illustrated by **Arno C. Gaebelein**, who explains that, "The Gospel preached is the Gospel of the Kingdom and the preachers are this faithful remnant of God's earthly people. *Nothing of this is said in chapter vii*, though the result, the gathered multitude coming out of the great tribulation is seen there."[671] Mark it carefully, **Gaebelein** admits that the text of Revelation 7, says *"nothing"* about the preaching of the Gospel of the Kingdom, or a faithful remnant of preachers, or multitudes of converts. According to **Gaebelein**, the mere fact that there is a "gathered multitude coming out of the great tribulation" substantiates the entire Dispensational scenario. Likewise, **Leon Wood** teaches that, "The existence of this group [i.e., the multitude of believers] is established especially by Revelation 7:9-17...The *implication* is that these people have died as martyrs during the tribulation..."[672] The implication? What implication? Note carefully, that the text states that this "great multitude" that have "come out of the great tribulation...have washed their robes and made them white *in the blood of the Lamb*" (v.14). This language does *not* describe individual martyrs who have shed their own blood, but believers whose sins have been "washed" away (i.e., cleansed) by the blood of Jesus Christ. What we have here is a clear description of those who have been saved by Christ and *not* those who have died for their testimony of Christ. In contrast carefully compare the straightforward language used to describe the martyrdom of

[671]*The Revelation* - Arno C. Gaebelein, Loizeaux Brothers, 1961, p.87.
[672] *The Bible and Future Events* - Leon J. Wood, Zondervan Publishing House, 1974, p.70.

believers in Revelation 6:9; 12:11; and 20:4.[673]

Furthermore, it should be pointed out that there are other, plausible, conservative, premillennial interpretations of these verses. For example, some see the sealing of the 144,000 of verses 1-8 as the fulfillment of Romans 11:26, wherein Paul declares, "...and thus, all Israel will be saved." Others see the 144,000 as symbolically representative of the entire company of God's redeemed (Old and New Testament saints; 12 tribes x 12 apostles = 144). While some see the sudden appearance of the "great multitude, which no one could count, from every nation and all tribes and peoples and tongues...**clothed in white robes**" (vv.9-17, emphasis added), as the rapture of the Church at the end of the Tribulation - compare Rv.19:7-8, "...his bride has made herself ready. And it was given to her to clothe herself in **fine linen, bright and clean**..." (Emphasis added). Still others maintain that these are Christian martyrs who perish during the persecutions of Antichrist during the Tribulation. Obviously, these are difficult verses to explain. The varied range of conservative interpretations underscores this fact.

However, the *singular purpose* of the Dispensational interpretation is to explain *why* there are still believers "coming out of the Tribulation" *after* the pretribulation rapture has supposedly occurred. In order to preserve the concept of the pretribulation rapture, Dispensationalists must reasonably explain *why* these believers were still present on the earth during the Tribulation. However, they attempt to meet this demand by offering only highly subjective assumptions instead of clear statements of Biblical fact. The entire Dispensational proposition is based upon a tenuous chain of highly speculative ideas that are supported by nothing more than unrestrained imagination. The undeniable fact remains that Dispensationalists cannot produce a single verse of Scripture that clearly affirms even one of their essential propositions. There is not one Biblical text that supports their contention that during the Tribulation period, God will send forth 144,000 Jewish evangelists, to preach a legalistic Kingdom Gospel to the Gentile nations, which will result in vast multitudes being saved. The entire body of Scripture is

---

[673] "And when He broke the fifth seal, I saw underneath the alter the souls of those who had been **slain** because of the word of God, and because of the testimony which they had maintained;" Rv.6:9 (Emphasis added). "And they overcame him because of the blood of the Lamb and because of the word of their testimony, and they did not love their life even to **death**." Rv.12:11 (Emphasis added). "...And I saw the souls of those who had been **beheaded** because of the testimony of Jesus and because of the word of God..." Rv.20:4 (Emphasis added).

completely silent regarding these Dispensational assertions. Yet Dispensationalists confidently teach these imaginative presuppositions as established Biblical facts!

8. The Tribulation Saints of Revelation.

The Book of Revelation repeatedly refers to *believers* being present on earth during the Tribulation period. For example,

Rv.7:9,14 "...a great multitude, which no one could count, from every nation and all tribes and peoples and tongues, standing before the throne and before the lamb, clothed in white robes...These are the ones who come out of the great tribulation..."

Rv.12:11 "And they overcame him [i.e., Satan, v.9] because of the blood of the Lamb and because of the word of their testimony, and they did not love their life even to death."

Rv.12:17 "And the dragon was enraged with the woman, and went off to make war with the rest of her offspring, who keep the commandments of God and hold to the testimony of Jesus."

Rv.13:7 "And it was given to him [i.e., the beast] to make war with the saints and to overcome them..."

Rv.13:10 "Here is the perseverance and the faith of the saints."

Rv.14:12-13 "Here is the perseverance of the saints who keep the commandments of God and their faith in Jesus...Blessed are the dead who die in the Lord from now on..."

Rv.16:6 "...they poured out the blood of saints and prophets..."

Rv.17:6 "And I saw the woman drunk with the blood of the saints, and with the blood of the witnesses of Jesus..."

Rv.18:4;24 "And I heard another voice from heaven, saying, 'Come out of her [i.e., Babylon the Great, v.2], my people, that you may not participate in her sins and that you may not receive of her plagues...Rejoice over her [i.e., her destruction], O heavens, and you saints... in her was found the blood of prophets and of saints and of all who have been slain on the earth."

Rv.19:2 "...HE [i.e., God] HAS AVENGED THE BLOOD OF HIS BOND-SERVANTS ON HER [i.e., Babylon the Great]."

Rv.20:4 "…the souls of those who had been beheaded because of the testimony of Jesus and because of the word of God…"

Who are these believers on earth during the Tribulation? Are they members of the Church or are they part of a Jewish and Gentile remnant saved after the pretribulation rapture of the Church? Apart from any clear evidence to the contrary, these believers would naturally be considered members of the Church. After all, they are referred to as "the witnesses of Jesus" - who have "washed their robes and made them white in the blood of the Lamb" - "who keep the commandments of God and hold to the testimony of Jesus" - "the saints" and "saints who keep the commandments of God and their faith in Jesus."

However, Dispensationalists insist that all of these references to believers on earth during the Tribulation period refer to non-Christian saints who are saved through the preaching of the Gospel of the Kingdom by a future Jewish remnant. For example, **John Walvoord** fairly represents the Dispensational position when he insists that, "…the church…***must not*** be confused with those described as saints…in the tribulation period."[674] This Dispensational distinction articulated by Walvoord is crucial to the pretribulation rapture theory. In order to preserve the feasibility of the pretribulation rapture, Dispensationalists must contend that the "saints" depicted in the book of Revelation are *not* a part of the Church. **Walvoord** emphasizes the critical nature of this fact when he explains that, "If these believers in the Tribulation are properly described as members of the church, it leads invariably to the conclusion that the church will go through the Tribulation."[675] **Walvoord** further explains that, "Scripture clearly indicates that there will be saints in the great Tribulation period. If *all saints* are in *the church*, then *the church would necessarily go through the Tribulation*…"[676]

Therefore, in order to preserve the pretribulation rapture doctrine, Dispensationalists must insist that the saints described in the book of Revelation are non-Church saints. They support their position with two lines of argumentation. First, Dispensationalists contend that the word "Church" (*ekklesia*) is limited in Scripture to Christian saints exclusively (i.e., to those saved between Pentecost and the pretribulation rapture).

---

[674] *The Rapture Question* - John F. Walvoord, Zondervan Publishing House, 1981, p.37.
[675] *The Rapture Question* - John F. Walvoord, Zondervan Publishing House, 1981, pp.19-20.
[676] *The Rapture Question* - John F. Walvoord, Zondervan Publishing House, 1981, p.161.

Second, Dispensationalists argue that the Church is not present on earth during the Tribulation because the word "Church" (*ekklesia*) is not specifically mentioned between chapters 5 through 18 of Revelation.

To protect and preserve the pretribulation rapture doctrine, Dispensationalists first-of-all restrict the word "Church" to believers of this present dispensation. For example, **John Walvoord** explains that, "Many pretribulationists...believe that, *the word church...is limited in Scripture to saints of the present dispensation.*"[677] In other words, **Walvoord** is asserting that the word "Church" refers exclusively to believers living between Pentecost and the pretribulation rapture. But this claim is demonstrably false. This is made evident by Stephen's testimony before the Jewish Council as recorded in Acts 7:1-60. In verse 38, while referring to Moses' ministry to Old Testament Israel, Stephen declared that, "This is the one who was in the *congregation* in the wilderness together with the angel who was speaking to him on Mount Sinai, and *who was* with our fathers; and he received living oracles to pass on to you." (Emphasis added). Note that the word "*congregation*" is *ekklesia* (Church). Stephen thus describes the Israelites as "...the *church* in the wilderness..." Furthermore, the Septuagint[678] commonly uses the word *ekklesia* (Church) to describe God's Old Testament people.[679] The word "Church" (*ekklesia*) is a compound word that is derived from the preposition *ek*, "out of" and the verb *kaleo*, "to call."[680] It refers to those who have been "called out"

---

[677] *The Rapture Question* - John F. Walvoord, Zondervan Publishing House, 1981, p.161.

[678] The *Septuagint*, designated by the Roman Numerals LXX, is a Greek translation of the Hebrew Old Testament. This translation was performed in Alexandria, Egypt during the 2nd century B.C. Dr. William Smith has observed that the "...writings of the Apostles and Evangelists...are full of citations and references, and imbued with the phraseology of the Septuagint." *Smith's Dictionary of the Bible* – William Smith, edited by H.B. Hackett, 1870 edition reprinted by Baker Book House, 1971, Vol. IV, p.2918. "It [i.e., the Septuagint] was the Bible of most writers of the NT. Not only are the majority of their express citations from Scripture borrowed from it, but their writings contain numerous reminiscences of its language." *The International Standard Bible Encyclopedia* – James Orr, General Editor, Wm.B.Eerdmans Publishing Co., 1939, 1956, Hendrickson Publishers, 2002, vol. IV, p.2722. The New Testament writers quoted from the *Septuagint* frequently. For example, there are some 58 citations within the four Gospels; Acts contains 23 more citations; Paul's letters contain another 78; and Hebrews has 28 citations. The *Septuagint* was the Bible for those Jews living in the Diaspora and served as the accepted Old Testament translation of the early Church. See *The Septuagint in the New Testament* by E.M. Blaiklock in *The Zondervan Pictorial Encyclopedia of the Bible* - General Editor, Merrill C. Tenney, Zondervan Publishing House, 1976, Vol. Five (Q-Z), pp.346-347.

[679] The word *ekklesia*, (church) is frequently used in the Septuagint to refer to the "assembly" or "congregation" of Israel. Consider the following examples in Dt.23:2; 31:30; Josh.8:35; Jud.21:8; 1Chron.29:1; Ps.22:22; 40:9.

[680] "The word *ekklesia* is derived from the two words *ek*, 'out' and *kaleo*, 'to call.'" *Dictionary of Theological Terms* – Alan Cairns, Ambassador Emerald International, 2002, p.88. "ἐκκλησία [*ekklesia*]...called out or forth..."*A Greek-English Lexicon of the New Testament* – Joseph Henry Thayer, T & T Clark, Edinburgh, 1953, p.195.

of the world and into fellowship with God. There is therefore a corresponding unity between both Old and New Testament believers - they have both been called out of the world and into God's assembly, congregation or Church.

Second, Dispensationalists argue that the believers mentioned throughout the book of Revelation are *not* part of the Church. For example, **H.A. Ironside** maintains that, "From the close of chapter 3, *we never see the church on earth* again through all the rest of this solemn book. We read of saints, but they are distinct altogether from the church of the present dispensation."[681] **Gerald Stanton** explains that, "Wicked men, godless nations, suffering Israel - these may be found in Revelation 6-18; but one *looks in vain for the Church of Christ*, which is His body, until he reaches the nineteenth chapter."[682] **Renald Showers** asserts that, "...there are *no references to the church* on the earth in chapters 4 through 18..."[683] **Showers** further observes that, "...the saints, who according to Revelation will be on the earth during the Tribulation, and the great multitude of Revelation 7 are *not the church*...the fact that Revelation has *no references to the church* on earth during the Tribulation strongly *infers* that the church will not be on earth during any part of the Tribulation...This then is a strong *inference* in favor of the Pretribulation Rapture view."[684] And **John Walvoord**, while referring to Revelation chapters 4 through 18 insists that, "...in this extended portion of Scripture *not one mention of the church*, the body of Christ, is found... *not one reference is found to the church*, *either by name itself* or by *any other title peculiar to believers* of this present age."[685]

Dispensationalists are correct when they state that the word "Church" does not occur in chapters 4 through 18 of Revelation. However, does this fact really mean that the Church is no longer present upon the earth, and that those believers referred to are non-Church saints? Not at all. Consider the fact that the Epistles of 1John, 2John, 1Peter, 2Peter, and Jude do *not* use the word "Church" either. Are we to conclude that these New Testament Epistles also refer to non-Church saints? Of course not! Then why would the absence of the word "Church" in chapters 4 through 18 of Revelation

[681] *Lectures on the Book of Revelation* - H.A. Ironside, Loizeaux Brothers, 1971, p.79.
[682] *Kept From the Hour* - Gerald B. Stanton, Zondervan Publishing House, 1956, p.36.
[683] *Maranatha Our Lord Come!* - Renald Showers, The Friends of Israel Gospel Ministry, Inc.,1995, p.245.
[684] *Maranatha Our Lord Come!* - Renald Showers, The Friends of Israel Gospel Ministry, Inc., 1995,p.251.
[685] *The Rapture Question* - John F. Walvoord, Zondervan Publishing House, 1981, p.46.

necessarily indicate that the Church has been raptured and that the believers referred to are non-Church saints? Especially in light of the fact that the entire book of Revelation is specifically addressed "to the seven churches of Asia." The book begins with the declaration, "John, to the *seven churches* of Asia..." (Rv.1:4). John is then commanded to, "Write in a book what you see, and send it to the *seven churches*..." (Rv.1:11). In Revelation 1:19, the Lord Jesus amplifies His command to "write" when He instructs John to, "Write therefore the *things which you have seen*, and the *things which are*, and the *things which shall take place after these things*." (Emphasis added). The third phrase, "the things which shall take place after these things" is a clear reference to the future Tribulational events described in chapters 6 through 19 - events, which are specifically addressed to the Churches!

Furthermore, the book of Revelation concludes with a clear statement that underscores the fact that these prophecies were written specifically for the Church and not for a fictitious future Jewish remnant. The Lord Himself declares, "I, Jesus, have sent My angel to testify to you these things **for the churches.**" (Rv.22:16, emphasis added). What things? Obviously, the things depicted throughout the book that John was commanded to write down and send "**to the seven churches of Asia.**" (Emphasis added). Do the inspired teachings delivered to "...the Church of God which is at Corinth..." (1Cor.1:2), "...to the church of the Thessalonians..." (2Thess.1:1) and "to the churches of Galatia" (Gal.1:2) authoritatively apply to the modern Church today? Of course they do. Then logically, the instructions delivered to the "seven churches of Asia" would also apply to the Church today. There is absolutely no textual evidence to the contrary.

One more point needs to be addressed. **John Walvoord's** assertion that "...not one reference is found to the church, either by *name itself* or by *any other title peculiar to believers of this present age*"[686] is demonstrably false. Throughout the book of Revelation, believers are repeatedly referred to as "saints."[687] The word saints is *hagios* (ἅγιος). It refers to those who have been redemptively set apart by God. The word is commonly applied to New Testament believers. For example, in the book of Acts,

---

[686] *The Rapture Question* - John F. Walvoord, Zondervan Publishing House, 1981, p.46.
[687] See Revelation 5:8; 8:3,4; 11:18; 13:7,10; 14:12; 18:20,24; 19:8; 20:9.

believers are referred to as "saints."[688] Romans is addressed "to all who are beloved of God in Rome, called *as* **saints**..." (Ro.1:7). First Corinthians is addressed to, "...the church of God which is at Corinth...**saints** by calling..." (1Cor.1:2 cp. 2Cor.1:1). Paul's letter to the Ephesians is addressed "...to the **saints** who are at Ephesus..." (Eph.1:1). Likewise, Philippians is addressed "...to all the **saints** in Christ Jesus who are at Philippi..."(Phil.1:1) and Colossians is addressed "to the **saints** and faithful brethren in Christ who are at Colossae..." (Col.1:2). Contrary to **Walvoord's** assertion, the term "saints" as found in the book of Revelation, is a "title peculiar to believers of this present age." The term "saints" is commonly used to refer to believers throughout the entire New Testament. Therefore, the Dispensational assertion that there is a fundamental difference between the "saints" of Revelation and the "saints" of the Epistles is totally unfounded. There is absolutely no textual reason to distinguish between the "saints" of the Epistles and the "saints" of Revelation. However, in the interest of protecting and preserving the concept of a pretribulation rapture of the Church, Dispensationalists are forced to make a sharp distinction between the believers described within chapters 6 through 18 of the book of Revelation and those of the Church. Thus, the "saints" mentioned in the book of Revelation are necessarily viewed as a completely new classification of believers who are said to be part of a future Jewish and Gentile remnant that will be saved after the pretribulational rapture of the Church. This "new" group of believers is carefully distinguished from "Church saints" and commonly referred to as "Tribulation saints" by Dispensationalists.

John Darby popularized the proposition that, "The book of Revelation *does not apply to the church* in its present state save in principle. *The saints* spoken of in it are...an entirely *new class of persons*..."[689] **Darby** further explains that, "*No general prophecy of the church itself is found in the course of the Apocalypse*...The reason is evident to one who knows what the church is. It is not of the world. It, as such, sits in heavenly places in Christ, where prophecy does not reach. It never will be established on earth as the Jews."[690] While commenting on chapters 6 through 18 of Revelation, **A.C. Gaebelein** declares that, "We are led back to *Jewish ground*. Events in connection with

---

[688] See Acts 9:13,32,41; 26:10.

[689] *The Collected Writings of J.N. Darby* - Edited by William Kelly, Stow Hill Bible and Tract Depot, n.d., Prophetic No.4, Vol.11, p.28.

[690] *The Collected Writings of J.N. Darby* - edited by William Kelly, Stow Hill Bible and Tract Depot, n.d., Prophetic No.4, Vol.11, p.46.

the Jewish people and Jerusalem are before us."[691] And again, while commenting on the martyrs seen under the alter in heaven in Revelation 6:9-11, **Gaebelein** rhetorically asks, "Who are these? *Not saints of the Church*…They are such of the *remnant of Jews* who began to give their witness after the church departed..."[692] **H.A. Ironside** teaches that, "...after the present dispensation has come to an end and the church has been removed to heaven...a *new company of saints* will be formed upon the earth, *altogether different* from the present heavenly company."[693] While referring to Revelation 13:7, **Lehman Strauss** states that, "The beast makes war with *the saints*. Now the *'saints'* here are *not* the believers of this present dispensation which make up the Church...The *saints* mentioned in our verse are the *saved during the tribulation* (Revelation 7)."[694] **E. Schuyler English** insists that, "Those who are termed *God's servants, or prophets, or saints* in The Revelation...are *not* the Church but God's *earthly people* of that era..."[695] And **Leon Wood** maintains that, "...*another religious group* will exist during the tribulation period. It will be comprised of persons commonly called *tribulation saints*..." [696]

Dispensationalists have thus concocted this astonishing hypothesis to support their contention that the Church will be raptured before the beginning of the Tribulation period. They maintain that 144,000 Jewish evangelists will be saved soon after the pretribulation rapture of the Church. This Jewish remnant will then begin preaching a legalistic Gospel of the Kingdom to the Gentile nations of the world. Their proclamation of the soon coming King and Kingdom will result in mass conversions, such as the world has never seen. These new believers are referred to as, "Tribulation Saints" and are described as a "new class" of believers who are denied the spiritual position and privileges of the Church because God will deal with them on the basis of Law rather than Grace. These are the amazing assertions that Dispensationalists must make in order to justify the concept of a pretribulational rapture of the Church! Yet, not one of these astounding claims is legitimately derived from a literal interpretation of the Scriptures. Rather, they are all forcefully read into the Biblical text. They are based

---

[691] *The Revelation* - Arno C. Gaebelein, Loizeaux Brothers, 1961, p.18.
[692] *The Gospel of Matthew* - Arno C. Gaebelein, Loizeaux Brothers, 1961, pp.483-484.
[693] *Lectures on the Book of Revelation*- H.A. Ironside, Loizeaux Brothers, 1971, p.111.
[694] *The Book of Revelation* - Lehman Strauss, Loizeaux Brothers, 1977, p.253.
[695] *Re-Thinking the Rapture* - E. Schuyler English, Loizeaux Brothers, 1954, p.112.
[696] *The Bible and Future Events* - Leon J. Wood, Zondervan Publishing House, 1974, p.70.

upon nothing more than **presumptions** and **assumptions** - *not* Biblical statements of fact. This is the inherent weakness of the pretribulation rapture doctrine. Dispensationalists must rely solely and completely upon **highly imaginative speculations** and **inferences** to support their contention of a pretribulation rapture! They must rely upon what they **imagine** the Scriptures are **implying,** and not what the Scriptures are literally stating! They must argue their case without one clear statement from Scripture to substantiate even one of their fantastic claims.

9. Proof of the Pretribulation Rapture in the Book of Revelation.

Dispensationalists offer two specific arguments from the book of Revelation to support their claim that rapture of the Church will be pretribulational.

9a. Dispensational Argument One: An Open Door in Heaven.

"After these things I looked, and behold, a door *standing* open in heaven, and the first voice which I had heard, like *the sound* of a trumpet speaking with me, said, 'Come up here, and I will show you what must take place after these things.'" (Rv.4:1).

Dispensationalists frequently point to Revelation 4, as proof for the pretribulation rapture. For example, **John Darby** emphatically declares that, "Chapter 4 shews the church in heaven."[697] In his notes on the Revelation, **Darby**, in his characteristically complicated and convoluted style, concludes his discussion of the Seven Churches (Rv.2-3), by explaining that,

"John's ministry in connection with the Lord's coming…" makes "…*no mention of the rapture*, yet the saints belonging to the assembly are always seen above after the seven assemblies are addressed…And it is to be remarked, that there is *no mention here of the fact of the Lord's coming* in reference to the assembly... the fact of His coming for His own, or the *assembly's rapture at any time, is not stated*…Even in chapter 12 , which remarkably confirms what I say, *the rapture is only seen as identified with the catching up of the Man-child, Christ Himself*…the saints belonging to the

---

[697] *The Collected Writings of J.N. Darby* - Edited by William Kelly, Stow Hill Bible and Tract Depot, Prophetic No.2, Volume 5, p.267.

assembly...are always seen above when the epistles to the assemblies are ended...they are never seen on earth."[698]

In other words, according to Darby, although there is no specific mention of the pretribulation rapture within the Letters to the Seven Churches, the reality of the pretribulation rapture is evidenced by the "fact" that the Church is seen in heaven and not on earth. This "fact" is established in Chapter 4, with the catching up of John[699] and again in Chapter 12, with the catching up of the Man-child.

William Trotter also relies on Revelation 4 to validate the concept of the pretribulation rapture. **Trotter** insists that while, "...the Apocalypse... *makes no historic mention of the fact*, it shows, from the beginning of *chap. iv.*, that the *fact has taken place* ere the scenes it portrays begin to open. The only place the church is seen from chap. iv. to chap. xix.14 is in heaven."[700] **Clarence Larkin,** while commenting on Revelation 4:1, maintains that, "In this 'Rapture' of John we have a *type of the Rapture of the Church*, and it is at this place in the Book that the 'Rapture' of the Church takes place."[701] **E. Schuyler English** contends that, "In Revelation four, the *removal of the Church* to be with the Lord is *indicated*, and in the fourth and fifth chapters it (the Church) is seen *symbolically* in the presence of the Lord."[702] Likewise, **H.A. Ironside**, while commenting on Revelation 4:1 explains that, "...we must understand the rapture of 1Thess.4:16-17, as transpiring between chapter 3 and chapter 4. Of this the rapture of the apostle is *the symbol*."[703] And **Lehman Strauss** claims that, "The open door...is a door of safe deliverance from Great Tribulation."[704]

Clearly, this type of Bible exposition does *not* represent a "literal approach" to the interpretation of the Scriptures as Dispensationalists claim. Yet this is precisely the type

---

[698] *Synopsis of the Books of the Bible* – J.N. Darby, Loizeaux Brothers, Inc. Vol.V, *Colossians - The Revelation*, pp.587-588.

[699] Darby makes this clear when he states, "John is...called up to heaven...The saints then, who will be caught up to meet Christ, are seen only on high here; they belong to heaven, and are no longer dealt with on earth, but have their own place in heaven." *Synopsis of the Books of the Bible* – J.N. Darby, Loizeaux Brothers, Inc., *Colossians - The Revelation*, vol. v, p.589.

[700] *Plain Papers on Prophetic and Other Subjects* - William Trotter, Loizeaux Brothers, n.d., p.432.

[701] *The Book of Revelation* - Clarence Larkin, Rev. Clarence Larkin Estate, 1919, p.33.

[702] *Studies in the Gospel According to Matthew* - E. Schuyler English, Zondervan Publishing House, 1938, p.173.

[703] *Lectures on the Book of Revelation* - H.A. Ironside, Loizeaux Brothers, 1971, p.80.

[704] *The Book of Revelation* - Lehman Strauss, Loizeaux Brothers, 1977, p.84

of imaginative interpretation that is required to support the concept of a pretribulation rapture of the Church! While Dispensationalists admit that the book of Revelation makes *"no mention of the rapture,"* we are nonetheless assured that *"the fact has taken place."* We are guaranteed that the Apostle John is a *"type of the Rapture of the Church"* and that his removal to heaven is the *"symbol"* of the pretribulation rapture. But even some staunch Dispensationalists balk at this excessive spiritualization of the Scriptures. For example, **John Walvoord** honestly admits that, "Although many pretribulationists find in the catching up of John a *symbolic presentation* of the rapture of the church, the *passage obviously falls somewhat short of an actual statement of the rapture.*"[705] With this, we can agree.

9b. Dispensational Argument Two: The Letters to the Seven Churches.

Historically, the letters to the Seven Churches in Revelation 2-3, were addressed to local Churches that existed in western Asia Minor (modern day Turkey) toward the end of the first century. Within these two chapters, the Lord Jesus Christ assesses the spiritual condition of each of these Churches. Today, we can profit from the Lord's evaluation of these Seven Churches by emulating their faithfulness and by avoiding their failures. While Dispensationalists recognize the historic existence of these Seven Churches, as well as the important spiritual lessons that are taught, they generally ignore this important aspect of the Lord's teaching. Instead, Dispensationalists insist that the *primary purpose* of the Lord's messages to these Seven Churches was to present a prophetic outline of Church history for this age.

John Darby confidently asserts; "I cannot doubt then for a moment that...the seven assemblies represent the *history of Christendom*... the seven churches are *successive phases* of the professing assemblies history..."[706] **William Trotter** likewise teaches that, "The seven letters to the churches in Rev. ii., iii... were intended to bear a *prophetic meaning*...Think of the mystical character of the book...How can we think...of limiting the sense of chap. ii., iii. to the application of their statements to the literal seven churches of Asia of that day? or even to this along with the moral application to individuals afterward?"[707] **H.A. Ironside** maintains that, "The seven

---

[705] *The Blessed Hope and the Tribulation* - John F. Walvoord, Zondervan Publishing House, 1976, p.136.
[706] *Synopsis of the Books of the Bible* - J.N. Darby, Loizeaux Brothers, vol.V, pp.562-563.
[707] *Plain Papers on Prophetic and Other Subjects* - Loizeaux Brothers, n.d., William Trotter, pp.308-309.

churches give us a *picture of the whole professing church's history* from the apostolic period to the coming of the Lord Jesus. These two chapters portray the condition of the church on earth, in *seven distinct periods*. The church's history ends at the rapture...that event closes the present dispensation."[708] **A.C. Gaebelein** assures us that, "These messages...had a deep and significant meaning for the different local assemblies. That there are many spiritual lessons written in these messages, is also true. However, all this must take a *secondary place*. The *primary thing is the prophetic interpretation*. The seven churches represent the entire Church on earth...and the conditions of these seven churches *foreshadow the different periods of the Church on earth* from the Apostolic times to the ending days, when the Lord calls His Saints to meet Him in the air."[709] And again, **Gaebelein** confidently declares that, "In the seven messages we learn the beginning, the progress and the end of this present Christian age. It is *the history of Christendom*, the kingdom of the heavens."[710] **Clarence Larkin** contends that, "...chapters two and three, must be a description or *prophetic outline* of the 'Spiritual History' of the Church from the time when John wrote in A.D. 96, down to the taking of the Church, or else we have no prophetic view of the Church...the character of these Seven Churches is descriptive of the Church during *seven periods* of her history..."[711] **Charles Feinberg** teaches that, "In the second and third chapters of the Book of Revelation we have given to us a *marvelously accurate outline of the course of the Church age*..."[712] **E. Schuyler English** claims that, "The *history of the church* is foretold in Revelation 2 and 3..."[713] "...it seems apparent that...these messages are for all churches throughout the full Church age...we have here a *prophetic view of church history*... "[714] And **Dwight Pentecost** affirms this principle when he declares that, "...Revelation two and three *outline the present age* in reference to the program for the church... There is a *prophetic revelation as to the course of the age* in the letters."[715]

Thus, Dispensationalists uniformly maintain that each of the Seven Churches represents a successive "phase" or "period" of Church history, beginning with the apostolic times

[708] *Lectures on the Book of Revelation* - H.A. Ironside, Loizeaux Brothers, 1971, p.32.
[709] *The Revelation* - Arno C. Gaebelein, Loizeaux Brothers, 1961, p.33.
[710] *The Gospel of Matthew* - Arno C. Gaebelein, Loizeaux Brothers, 1982, p.264.
[711] *The Book of Revelation* - Clarence Larkin, Rev. Clarence Larkin Estate, 1919, p.18.
[712] *Premillennialism or Amillennialism?* - Charles Feinberg, Zondervan Publishing House, 1936, p.115.
[713] *Re-Thinking the Rapture* - E. Schuyler English, Loizeaux Brother, 1954, p.92.
[714] *Re-Thinking the Rapture* - E. Schuyler English, Loizeaux Brother, 1954, pp.87.
[715] *Things to Come* - J. Dwight Pentecost, Zondervan Publishing House, 1964, pp.151-152.

and continuing to the end of this age. Furthermore, Dispensationalists insist that any "spiritual lessons" derived from these letters, must take a "secondary place" to the all-important "prophetic interpretation." Dispensationalists interpret this seven-staged prophetic view of Church history as follows:

The Church at Ephesus (Rv.2:1-7).

Darby – "Ephesus...there were works of labor and patience; but the faith, hope and love had in their true energy disappeared...they had left their first love."[716]
Gaebelein -"Ephesus. The apostolic age. The beginning with failure - leaving the first love."[717]
Larkin - "The Church at Ephesus. A Backslidden Church. [718]
Ironside - "Ephesus gives us a picture of the Church as it was in the beginning...yet...we have the evidence of early decline."[719]
Feinberg - "The letter to the church at Ephesus shows the condition of the Church at the end of the apostolic age; she had lost her first love and was growing colder in her orthodoxy."[720]

The Church at Smyrna (Rv.2:8-11).

Darby – "Tribulation and poverty the portion of the assembly..."[721]
Gaebelein -"Smyrna...the enemy revealed." [722]
Larkin - "The Church at Smyrna. A Licentious Church."[723]
Ironside - "Smyrna...the period when the church was crushed beneath the iron heal of pagan Rome."[724]
Feinberg - "The Smyrna church represents the time of the Roman persecutions in the Church."[725]
English - "Smyrna, the suffering church under Roman persecutions..."[726]

[716] *Synopsis of the Books of the Bible* – J.N. Darby, Loizeaux Brothers, Inc., *Colossians - The Revelation*, vol. v, pp.574-575.
[717] *The Gospel of Matthew* - Arno C. Gaebelein, Loizeaux Brothers, 1982, p.264.
[718] *The Book of Revelation* - Clarence Larkin, Rev. Clarence Larkin Estate, 1919, p.18.
[719] *Lectures on the Book of Revelation* - H.A. Ironside, Loizeaux Brothers, 1971, pp.35,39.
[720] *Premillennialism or Amillennialism?* - Charles Feinberg, Zondervan Publishing House, 1936, p.115.
[721] *Synopsis of the Books of the Bible* – J.N. Darby, Loizeaux Brothers, Inc., *Colossians - The Revelation*, vol. v, p.576.
[722] *The Gospel of Matthew* - Arno C. Gaebelein, Loizeaux Brothers, 1982, p.264.
[723] *The Book of Revelation* - Clarence Larkin, Rev. Clarence Larkin Estate, 1919, p.21.
[724] *Lectures on the Book of Revelation* - H.A. Ironside, Loizeaux Brothers, 1971, p.40.
[725] *Premillennialism or Amillennialism?* - Charles Feinberg, Zondervan Publishing House, 1936, p.115.
[726] *Re-Thinking the Rapture* - E. Schuyler English, Loizeaux Brother, 1954, pp.87.

The Church at Pergamos (Rv.2:12-17).

Darby – "Pergamos…seduction by evil teaching within…evil came in – seduction to fall in with the world's ways by evil teaching within."[727]

Gaebelein -"Pergamos...The professing church becomes big, a state institution under Constantine the Great."[728]

Larkin - "The Church at Pergamos. A Licentious Church...the union of Church and State..."[729]

Ironside - "Pergamos...the time when the church was elevated to a place of power...when church and state were united under Constantine and his successors."[730]

Feinberg - "The letter to Pergamos reveals the condition of the Church when it unites with the State..."[731]

English - Pergamos, the worldly church that issued at the conversion of Constantine..."[732]

The Church at Thyatira (Rv.2:18-29).

Darby – "Popery…It is, I have no doubt, the Popery of the middle ages, say to the Reformation; Romanism itself goes on to the end."[733]

Gaebelein -"Thyatira...Rome and her abominations."[734]

Larkin - "The Church at Thyatira...the Papal Church... "[735]

Ironside - "Thyatira...It was in the 7th century that the Bishop of Rome was first recognized as Christ's vicegerent...This was, properly speaking, the beginning of the papacy."[736]

Feinberg - "Thyatira is a church illustrative of the corruption and degeneration that came into the Church when Rome held unrivalled sway during the Middle Ages."[737]

English - Thyatira, when Rome was at its greatest power..."[738]

The Church at Sardis (Rv.3:1-6).

---

[727] *Synopsis of the Books of the Bible* – J.N. Darby, Loizeaux Brothers, Inc., *Colossians - The Revelation*, vol. v, pp.577-578.

[728] *The Gospel of Matthew* - Arno C. Gaebelein, Loizeaux Brothers, 1982, p.264.

[729] *The Book of Revelation* - Clarence Larkin, Rev. Clarence Larkin Estate, 1919, pp.21.

[730] *Lectures on the Book of Revelation* - H.A. Ironside, Loizeaux Brothers, 1971, p.42.

[731] *Premillennialism or Amillennialism?* - Charles Feinberg, Zondervan Publishing House, 1936, p.115.

[732] *Re-Thinking the Rapture* - E. Schuyler English, Loizeaux Brother, 1954, pp.87-88.

[733] *Synopsis of the Books of the Bible* – J.N. Darby, Loizeaux Brothers, Inc., *Colossians - The Revelation*, vol. v, pp.578-579.

[734] *The Gospel of Matthew* - Arno C. Gaebelein, Loizeaux Brothers, 1982, p.264.

[735] *The Book of Revelation* - Clarence Larkin, Rev. Clarence Larkin Estate, 1919, pp.23-24.

[736] *Lectures on the Book of Revelation* - H.A. Ironside, Loizeaux Brothers, 1971, p.49.

[737] *Premillennialism or Amillennialism?* - Charles Feinberg, Zondervan Publishing House, 1936, p.116.

[738] *Re-Thinking the Rapture* - E. Schuyler English, Loizeaux Brother, 1954, pp.87-88.

Darby – "Sardis: a new collateral phase of the assembly's history…Protestantism…I cannot doubt that we have Protestantism here."[739]

Gaebelein - "Sardis - the reformation age."[740]

Larkin - "The Church at Sardis…an excellent type of the Church of the Reformation Period…"[741]

Ironside - "Sardis…the great State-churches of the Reformation, who escaped from Rome, only to fall eventually…into cold lifeless formalism."[742]

Feinberg - "The letter to Sardis discloses the course of the Church during the Reformation period…"[743]

English – "Sardis, the Reformation church…"[744]

The Church at Philadelphia (Rv.3:7-13).

Darby – "Philadelphia as peculiarly associated with Christ Himself…His name openly confessed, the Word kept, the name not denied…He [Christ] lived in the last days of a dispensation…So the saints here…"[745]

Gaebelein -"Philadelphia. The church…the one body of Christ and the removal of the church to be with Him."[746]

Larkin - "The Church at Philadelphia…the evangelistic and missionary…Church…"[747]

Ironside - "Philadelphia…the revival period…those in Protestantism who emphasize the authority of the Word of God."[748]

Feinberg - "Philadelphia represents the presence in the professing church of the true Church."[749]

English – "Philadelphia, the church that returned to the Word of God and found the open door to missionary ministry…"[750]

The Church at Laodicea (Rv.3:14-22).

Darby – "Laodicea: the last state of profession in the assembly…lukewarmness characterizes the last

[739] *Synopsis of the Books of the Bible* – J.N. Darby, Loizeaux Brothers, Inc., *Colossians - The Revelation*, vol. v, pp.579,581.

[740] *The Gospel of Matthew* - Arno C. Gaebelein, Loizeaux Brothers, 1982, p.265.

[741] *The Book of Revelation* - Clarence Larkin, Rev. Clarence Larkin Estate, 1919, p.25.

[742] *Lectures on the Book of Revelation* - H.A. Ironside, Loizeaux Brothers, 1971, p.60.

[743] *Premillennialism or Amillennialism?* - Charles Feinberg, Zondervan Publishing House, 1936, p.116.

[744] *Re-Thinking the Rapture* - E. Schuyler English, Loizeaux Brother, 1954, p.88.

[745] *Synopsis of the Books of the Bible* – J.N. Darby, Loizeaux Brothers, *Colossians - The Revelation*, vol. v, pp.581-582.

[746] *The Gospel of Matthew* - Arno C. Gaebelein, Loizeaux Brothers, 1982, p.265.

[747] *The Book of Revelation* - Clarence Larkin, Rev. Clarence Larkin Estate, 1919, pp.26.

[748] *Lectures on the Book of Revelation* - H.A. Ironside, Loizeaux Brothers, 1971, pp.66,67.

[749] *Premillennialism or Amillennialism?* - Charles Feinberg, Zondervan Publishing House, 1936, p.116.

[750] *Re-Thinking the Rapture* - E. Schuyler English, Loizeaux Brother, 1954, p.88.

state of profession in the assembly...”[751]

Gaebelein -"Laodicea - Judgment. I will spue thee out of my mouth."[752]

Larkin - "The Church at Laodicea. A Lukewarm Church...Our churches today are largely in this 'lukewarm' condition..."[753]

Ironside - "Laodicea...the condition of present-day church affairs...It is the era of democratization, both in the world and the church."[754]

Feinberg - "Laodicea speaks to us of the low spiritual state of the Church in the last days of the present age."[755]

English – "Laodicea, the apostate church of the last days of the age."[756]

Thus, according to Dispensationalists, the primary intent and purpose of these seven letters is to prophetically outline the history of the Church on earth. Dispensationalists contend that *Ephesus* describes the Apostolic era of the Church; *Smyrna* depicts the age of persecution under Imperial Rome; *Pergamos*, reveals the merging of the Church with the secular state under Constantine the Great; *Thyatira*, characterizes the ascendancy of the Papal system; *Sardis* typifies the Protestant Reformation; *Philadelphia* describes the true Bible-believing, missionary Church of the last days just prior to the Tribulation, and *Laodicea* portrays the apostate Church of the last days, which will exist concurrently with the true Church (i.e., Philadelphia).

However, this interpretative approach falls woefully short of taking "every word at its plain, literal, and natural meaning." Clearly, none of these "historical" concepts are legitimately derived from a literal interpretation of the Biblical text. This entire scenario represents a highly imaginative and creative allegorical approach to interpretation reminiscent of the Alexandrian school.[757] Dispensationalists have clearly abandoned their claim to literal interpretation here. They have ignored the plain meaning and obvious application of these letters, insisting instead that they represent a "prophetic outline" of Church history. Yet there is not one statement in any of these verses that

---

[751] *Synopsis of the Books of the Bible* – J.N. Darby, Loizeaux Brothers, Inc., *Colossians - The Revelation*, vol. v, p.585.

[752] *The Gospel of Matthew* - Arno C. Gaebelein, Loizeaux Brothers, 1982, p.265.

[753] *The Book of Revelation* - Clarence Larkin, Rev. Clarence Larkin Estate, 1919, pp.27.

[754] *Lectures on the Book of Revelation* - H.A. Ironside, Loizeaux Brothers, 1971, p.74.

[755] *Premillennialism or Amillennialism?* - Charles Feinberg, Zondervan Publishing House, 1936, p.116.

[756] *Re-Thinking the Rapture* - E. Schuyler English, Loizeaux Brother, 1954, p.88.

[757] The Alexandrian school of interpretation, which was founded in the 2nd century A.D., was known for its allegorical (i.e., non-literal and symbolic) interpretations of the Scriptures. See the *Wycliffe Dictionary of Theology* – Edited by Everett F. Harrison, Geoffrey W. Bromiley and Carl F. Henry, Hendrickson Publishers, 2004, *Alexandria, School Of*, and *Allegory*, pp.35-37.

indicates that they are to be interpreted prophetically. Significantly, these Letters to the Seven Churches do **not** occur in the prophetic section described as "the things which shall take place after these things" (Rv.1:19), but in the section described as, "the things which **are**" - present tense - that is, the actual present state and condition of the Churches when John received his vision. While Dispensationalists recognize this fact, they completely disregard it. For example, **H.A. Ironside** rhetorically asks, "Might it not be that inasmuch as this section of the book presents 'the things which are,' God has been pleased to give us here a prophetic history of the church for the entire dispensation."[758] However, this statement is an obvious contradiction in terms. **Ironside** contends that while the messages to the Seven Churches are described as the "the things which are" they actually depict "the things which shall be hereafter." The fact is that Dispensationalists have abandoned a literal interpretation of Revelation 2-3, for the singular purpose of creating a pretense that allows them to transfer the Lord's promise made to the Church at Philadelphia to the present-day Church. The pivotal verse is Revelation 3:10. Here the Lord promises the Philadelphia Church exemption from an impending "hour of testing." This verse states;

"Because you have kept the word of My perseverance, I also will **keep you from the hour of testing**, that **hour** which is about to come upon the whole world, to **test** those who dwell upon the earth." Revelation 3:10

Dispensationalists claim that the Lord's promise to the Church at Philadelphia prophetically applies to the Church today. They maintain that the Lord's promise to exempt the Church at Philadelphia from an impending "hour of testing" is actually a promise to rapture the Church **before** the beginning of the Great Tribulation.

John Darby is credited with being the first proponent of this view, asserting that, "...He [i.e., Christ] does not make us pass through that hour of temptation which is to sift out those who have their home here, confounding by the power of the enemy and the tribulation of God the men of this world...All this the Philadelphian saint escapes..."[759] Darby's followers have unanimously followed his lead. For example, **Lewis Sperry Chafer** maintains that, "The imminent return of Christ to receive His Church is held

---

[758] *Lectures on Revelation* - H.A. Ironside, Loizeaux Brothers, 1971, p.36.
[759] *The Collected Writings of J.N. Darby* - Edited by William Kelly, Stow Hill Bible and Tract Depot, Prophetic No.2, Volume 5, p.340.

before every believer as a 'blessed hope'...***The determining passage is Revelation 3:10...***" [760] Likewise, **E. Schuyler English** maintains that Revelation 3:10 ranks among "...the ***golden texts*** of those who hold the pretribulation view in regard to the time of the rapture..." [761] While referring specifically to Revelation 3:10, **Henry Thiessen** declares that, "...we have in this text ***a promise that the whole Church will be taken away before the hour of temptation begins*** and not merely an assurance of protection in it." [762] However, in his *Systematic Theology*, **Thiessen** cautiously suggests that, "The promise in Rev.3:10 *seems* to be not merely that God will keep the faithful from temptation, as if to shield them against it, but that he ***will keep them from the hour of trial***, the period as a whole. This *seems* to indicate that the believers will be taken away ***before*** the tribulation begins." [763] Likewise, **Leon Wood** teaches that, "At least ***one passage***, Revelation 3:10, *seems* to say clearly that the Church will not be on earth during the Tribulation." [764] And **John Walvoord** cautiously explains that, "While the rapture of the church is not the subject of the Book of Revelation, there are references that the pretribulationists can ***construe*** as referring to the Rapture." However, he then confidently asserts that, "A ***clear reference*** to the rapture is found in Revelation 3:10-11." [765]

The Dispensational claim that Revelation 3:10 is "a golden text," and "the determining passage" that makes "a clear reference to the rapture," thereby assuring "that the Church will not be on earth during the Tribulation" is predicated upon ***two major assumptions***. Carefully consider the revealing statements of **Henry Thiessen**. While discussing Revelation 3:10, **Thiessen** states;

"***Assuming*** then that the Philadelphia Church represents the Missionary Church and that the 'hour of trial' refers to the future Tribulation, we need to examine the words: 'I will keep thee from the hour of trial.'" [766]

---

[760] *Systematic Theology* - Lewis Sperry Chafer, Kregel Publications, 1993, vol.4, p.369.

[761] *Re-Thinking the Rapture* - E. Schuyler English, Loizeaux Brother, 1954, p.85.

[762] Henry C. Thiessen, as quoted in *Systematic Theology* - Lewis Sperry Chafer, Kregel Publications, 1993, vol.4, p.370.

[763] *Lectures in Systematic Theology* - Henry C. Thiessen, William B. Eerdmans Publishing Co., 1986, p.378.

[764] *Is the Rapture Next?* - Leon J. Wood, Zondervan Publishing House, 1956, p.23.

[765] *The Rapture Question* - John F. Walvoord, Zondervan Publishing House, 1981, p.255.

[766] Henry C. Thiessen, as quoted in *Systematic Theology* - Lewis Sperry Chafer, Kregel Publications, 1993, vol.4, p.369.

Thus, the entire Dispensational argument rests upon two huge assumptions: First, it is *assumed* that the first century Church at Philadelphia symbolically represents the true Church of the last days. Second, it is *assumed* that the phrase, the "hour of trial" refers to the future Great Tribulation. However, Dispensationalists routinely present these two major assumptions as uncontested facts. For example, in his *Systematic Theology*, **Lewis Sperry Chafer** asserts that "It is generally agreed that Philadelphia represents the true Church...It is also conceded that the 'hour of temptation' is a reference to the great tribulation."[767] **Chafer** fails to mention that these "assumptions" are generally accepted facts only within Dispensational circles.

Assumption #1 - The Church at Philadelphia Represents the Modern Day Church.

With respect to the claim that the Church at Philadelphia symbolically represents the true Church of the last days, Dispensationalists provide no textual evidence whatsoever. Instead, they offer only their imaginative claim that these seven letters prophetically reveal the course of this age. But where in the text do we find any reference to the Apostolic era; persecution under Imperial Rome; the secular state under Constantine the Great; the Papal system; the Protestant Reformation; or the missionary Church of the last days? There is not one clear statement to substantiate any of these Dispensational claims. The entire proposition is highly speculative and arbitrary.

Significantly, not one Biblical expositor in the entire history of the Church has recognized these supposed "seven distinct periods" or "phases" of the "whole professing church's history" in Revelation 2-3. Dispensationalists attempt to explain this stunning fact by maintaining that their "prophetic interpretation" was "hidden" from the early Church in order to preserve the Church's incentive to watch for the Lord's "any moment return."

For example, **Clarence Larkin** explains that,

"This interpretation of the 'Messages to the Seven Churches' was *hidden to the early Church*, because time was required for Church history to develop and be written, so a comparison could be made to reveal correspondence. If it had been clearly revealed that the Seven Churches stood for 'Seven Church

---

[767] *Systematic Theology* - Lewis Sperry Chafer, Kregel Publications, 1993, vol.4, p.369.

Periods' that would *have to elapse <u>before</u> Christ could come back*, the incentive to watch would have been absent."[768]

Larkin asserts that the true meaning of Revelation 2-3, was "hidden" from the early Church in order to preserve the all-important Dispensational doctrine of **imminence**.

Carefully consider **Larkin's** explanation. He states that,

"If it had been clearly revealed that the Seven Churches stood for *'Seven Church Periods'* that would *have to elapse before* Christ could come back, the incentive to watch would have been absent."

Larkin recognizes that these seven prophetic periods "*would have to elapse <u>before</u> Christ could come back.*" Remember, Dispensationalists are adamant that there is no event standing between Christ's secret Coming and the pretribulation rapture of the Church.[769] Yet, here we are plainly told that the *entire Church age must intervene <u>before</u> that event can occur!* This contradiction vividly illustrates how the major tenants of Dispensational theology are irreconcilably at odds with each another. In an attempt to offer a satisfactory explanation as to why the prophetic interpretation of the Seven Churches was hidden from prior generations, Dispensationalists inadvertently deny their cardinal doctrine of imminence!

But again, the question begs, "Where is the objective textual evidence that validates the Dispensational assertion that that the Philadelphian Church prophetically represents the Church of the last days? The honest answer is there is no objective evidence whatsoever. The entire proposition is supported solely by assumptions and inferences as **Henry Thiessen** candidly admits, when he states, "*Assuming* then that the Philadelphia Church represents the Missionary Church…"

Assumption #2: The "hour of testing" in Revelation 3:10, refers to the Great Tribulation.

Henry Thiessen further states, "*Assuming* then that the Philadelphia Church represents the Missionary Church and that the **'hour of trial'** refers to the *future* Tribulation, we need to examine

---

[768] *The Book of Revelation* - Clarence Larkin, Rev. Clarence Larkin Estate, 1919, p.18.
[769] See the discussion on the Dispensational doctrine of Imminence in Chapter Four.

the words: 'I will keep thee from the hour of trial.'"[770]

Dispensationalists uniformly point to Revelation 3:10, as conclusive proof of a pretribulation rapture of the Church. The text states:

"Because you have kept the word of My perseverance, I also will keep you from the hour of *testing* [*peirasmos - πειρασμός*], that *hour* which is about to come upon the *whole world* [*oikoumene - οἰκουμένη*], to *test* [*peirazo - πειράζω*] those who dwell upon the earth." (Rv.3:10, emphasis added).

Dispensationalists *assume* that the phrase, "the hour of testing" refers to the future Great Tribulation. They further *assume* that the Lord's promise to keep the Philadelphia Church from that "hour of testing" is a promise to rapture the Church before the beginning of the Tribulation period. For example, **E. Schuyler English** teaches that, "It is very clear that to this church [i.e., Philadelphia] and to those who have ears to hear (vs.13), our Lord gives the promise that He will keep them from the *hour of tribulation* that the whole world will experience, which must quite obviously be the *Tribulation* referred to in Daniel 12, Matthew 24, and Revelation 5-19."[771] Likewise, **Gerald Stanton** asserts that, "It is generally agreed that the *Tribulation* is in view in Revelation 3:10."[772] **John Walvoord** assures us that, "The primary promise to the church of Philadelphia was that they would not enter this hour of trial. Historically, it meant just that. The church of Philadelphia was not to enter the *tribulation period*. By application...*the Philadelphia church, representing the true and faithful church, is promised deliverance before the hour comes*."[773] And **Renald Showers** explains that, "...the *period of testing* to which Jesus referred in Revelation 3:10 is to be identified as the *Tribulation*[774]...Christ will keep or separate the Philadelphia church saints from the period of testing by rapturing them from the earth at His *imminent coming before* the period of testing begins."[775]

[770] Henry C. Thiessen, as quoted by Lewis Sperry Chafer, *Systematic Theology*, Kregel Publications, 1993, vol.4, p.369.
[771] *Re-Thinking the Rapture* - E. Schuyler English, Loizeaux Brother, 1954, p.88.
[772] *Kept From the Hour* - Gerald B. Stanton, Zondervan Publishing House, 1956, p.49.
[773] *The Rapture Question* - John F. Walvoord, Zondervan Publishing House, 1981, pp.66-67.
[774] *Maranatha Our Lord, Come!* - Renald Showers, The Friends of Israel Gospel Ministry, Inc.,1995, p.214.
[775] *Maranatha Our Lord, Come!* - Renald Showers, The Friends of Israel Gospel Ministry, Inc.,1995, p.217.

The Dispensational interpretation of Revelation 3:10, is based upon the **assumption** that the phrase "the hour of testing" is a reference to the future Great Tribulation. **Henry Thiessen** affirms this fact when he states that,

"**Assuming** then that the Philadelphia Church represents the Missionary Church and **that the 'hour of trial' refers to the future Tribulation**, we need to examine the words: 'I will keep thee from the hour of trial.'"[776]

However, the word "testing" (**peirasmos**) is **not** a synonym for the word "tribulation" (**thlipsis**). The word "testing" (**peirasmos**)[777] means to put to the test, to tempt, to try, to prove. However, the word "tribulation" (**thlipsis**)[778] refers to severe suffering, distress, anguish, affliction and persecution. It is significant that the word "tribulation" does **not** occur in Revelation 3:10. If the Lord were actually promising the Church deliverance from the Great Tribulation, we would certainly expect to see the phrase "I will keep you from the hour of **tribulation**" instead of "I will keep you from the hour of **testing**." Especially in light of the fact that the word "tribulation" occurs five other places in the book of Revelation![779]

Revelation 3:10 tells us that a time of "testing" was coming upon the world and that the Christians of Philadelphia were to be preserved. The Lord promised that the Philadelphian believers would be "kept" from "the hour of testing *[peirasmos]*" which was "...about to come upon the **whole world [oikoumene]**[780] **to test [peirazo]**[781] those who dwell upon the earth." (Rv.3:10). The idea is that the Christians at Philadelphia would be proved faithful by this time of testing, whereas, "those who dwell upon the

---

[776] Henry C. Thiessen, as quoted by Lewis Sperry Chafer, *Systematic Theology*, Kregel Publications, 1993, vol.4, p.369.
[777] "peirasmos (πειρασμός)...is used of...trials with a beneficial purpose and effect...of trials or temptations, Divinely permitted or sent..." *An Expository Dictionary of New Testament Words* – W. E. Vine, Thomas Nelson Publishers, Third Printing, n.d,, p.1129.
[778] "thlipsis (θλίψις) primarily means a pressing, pressure...is used of future retributions, in the way of affliction...It is used of the calamities of war...of the distress of woman in child-birth...of the afflictions of Christ...of sufferings in general...See Anguish, Burdened, Distress, Persecution, Tribulation, Trouble." *An Expository Dictionary of New Testament Words* – W. E. Vine, Thomas Nelson Publishers, n.d., Third Printing, p.31.
[779] See Revelation 1:9; 2:9; 2:10; 2:22; 7:14.
[780] "oikoumene (οἰκουμένη), the inhabited earth...is used (a) of the whole inhabited world...(b) of the Roman Empire, the world as viewed by the writer or speaker..." *An Expository Dictionary of New Testament Words* – W. E. Vine, Thomas Nelson Publishers, Third Printing, n.d., p.1246.
[781] "peirazo (πειράζω) signifies...to try...assay...to test, try, prove, in a good sense..." *An Expository Dictionary of New Testament Words* – W. E. Vine, Thomas Nelson Publishers, Third Printing, n.d., p.1128.

earth" (i.e., the unbelievers[782]) would fail the test. Dispensationalists maintain that the phrase, the "whole world" (*oikoumene*) refers to the entire inhabited earth, and therefore must refer to the future Tribulation period. However, this is not necessarily the case. While the phrase the "whole world" (*oikoumene*) can refer to the entire habitable earth, it can also refer to a localized portion of the earth. Thus, the scope of the phrase "the whole world" (*oikoumene*) must be determined by its immediate context. For example, the broader meaning of *oikoumene* is clearly indicated in Matthew 24:14, where the Lord Jesus declares that, "...this gospel of the kingdom shall be preached in the ***whole world [oikoumene]*** for a witness ***to all the nations***, and then the end shall come." (Emphasis added). The phrase "to all the nations" clearly modifies *oikoumene* and confirms that the entire inhabited earth is referred to. However, in Luke 2:1 we are told that, "Now it came about in those days that a decree went out from Caesar Augustus, that a census be taken of all the ***inhabited earth [oikoumene]***."[783] (Emphasis added). Obviously, the term ***oikoumene*** does ***not*** mean that every person on earth was counted in the Imperial Roman census. Rather, the meaning is obviously restricted to that portion of the world under Roman authority.

Likewise, the intended meaning of *oikoumene* in Revelation 3:10 is also restricted in its scope. This is made evident by the immediate context of the verse. The passage is addressed to a literal first century Church located in the city of Philadelphia and there is no textual indication that these words are to be applied prophetically to the Church of the last days. Second, there is no clarifying phrase to indicate that the entire inhabited earth is in view. Thus, "the hour of testing" which was coming upon the "whole world" should be understood to refer to the whole Roman world, of which Philadelphia was a part. There is no indication in the text as to what this time of testing was. It could have been a natural disaster, such as a major earthquake or famine, or perhaps one of the empire-wide persecutions initiated by the Roman government - possibly the Second General Persecution (A.D. 81-96) under Domitian or the Third General Persecution (A.D. 98-117) under Trajan. The text simply does not specify. But to insist, as Dispensationalists do, that this passage is a clear promise that the entire Church will be raptured before the beginning of the Great Tribulation is completely unwarranted.

---

[782] Within the Book of Revelation the phrase, "those who dwell upon the earth," seems to refer specifically to unbelievers. See Revelation 6:10; 8:13; 11:10; 13:8,14; 17:8.

[783] Additional verses that use ***oikoumene*** in the **restricted sense** are: Acts 11:28; 17:6; 19:27; 24:5. Verses that use ***oikoumene*** in the **broad sense** are: Lk.4:5; 21:26; Acts 17:31; Ro.10:18; Heb.1:6; 2:5; Rv.12:9; 16:14.

Chapter Five, Part IV
"Two" First Resurrections

Outline of Chapter Five, Part IV:
1. The First Resurrection Takes Place in Multiple Stages or Phases.
2. The Textual Basis for the Doctrine of Two First Resurrections.
3. The Redefinition of the Word "First."
4. Justification for the Redefinition of the Word "First."
5. The Resurrection in the Old Testament.
6. The Resurrection in the New Testament.

1. The First Resurrection Takes Place in Multiple Stages or Phases.

Dispensationalists teach that there will be "two" resurrections of believers - one *before* the Tribulation and another *after* the Tribulation. They maintain that the resurrection of Christian saints will occur *before* the Tribulation, when Christ comes secretly to rapture the Church. Whereas, the resurrection of Tribulation saints and Old Testament saints will occur *after* the Tribulation when Christ appears in glory.

Revelation 20:4-6 refers to the "first resurrection." The text states;

"And I saw thrones, and they sat upon them, and judgment was given to them. And I *saw* the souls of those who had been beheaded because of the testimony of Jesus and because of the word of God, and those who had not worshipped the beast or his image, and had not received the mark upon their forehead and upon their hand; and they came to life and reigned with Christ for a thousand years. The rest of the dead did not come to life until the thousand years were completed. This is the **first resurrection**. Blessed and holy is the one who has a part in the **first resurrection**; over these the second death has no power, but they will be priests of God and of Christ and will reign with Him for a thousand years." (Revelation 20:4-6; emphasis added).

Revelation 20 clearly describes the "first resurrection" as a post-tribulational event. This fact creates a tremendous problem for the pretribulational rapture theory. The problem, simply stated is this: A pretribulational Coming of Christ to rapture the Church also *requires* a pretribulational resurrection of the righteous saints – this is true because the rapture coincides with the resurrection of the righteous.[784] Thus, if Dispensationalists are to credibly argue for a pretribulational rapture of the Church, they **must** establish a textual basis for a pretribulational resurrection of the Church saints. Dispensationalists meet this demand by resorting to their **doubling methodology**. They simply declare that the "first resurrection" does **not** refer to a single event – rather, they maintain that the phrase "first resurrection" describes a protracted **process** that includes **two** different resurrections, with **two** different groups of believers, occurring at **two** different times.

E. Schuyler English clearly explains the Dispensational position when he states that, "The important thing to discover is whether or not the first resurrection must be a **simultaneous resurrection of all the just at one definite moment**, or whether the first resurrection may be understood to mean the resurrection of **all the just**, to be sure, but in a **series of two or more ascensions.**"[785] Not surprisingly, in the interest of preserving and protecting the doctrine of the pretribulation rapture of the Church, Dispensationalists uniformly teach that "the first resurrection" occurs in a "series of two or more ascensions." They attempt to advance this position by arguing that the phrase, "This is the first resurrection" (Rv.20:5), describes a **process** instead of a **singular event**. For example, **A.C. Gaebelein** declares that, "There is a first resurrection in which **all the saved** have a share, which **begins** when the Lord comes for His Saints and the dead in Christ rise first and we who are alive are caught up together with them to meet the Lord in the air (1Thess.iv:15-17). To this first resurrection belong likewise the martyrs during the great tribulation."[786] In other words, according to **Gaebelein**, the first resurrection "**begins**" with the pretribulational rapture of the Church, and concludes seven years later with the resurrection of the martyrs of the Great Tribulation.

Dispensationalists commonly refer to the "first resurrection" as a process with multiple "stages" or "aspects." For example, **Lehman Strauss** teaches that, "...the 'resurrection of life' does **not occur at one time**. It is in **separate stages at different times.**"[787] **Strauss** also asserts that, "The first resurrection takes place at **different stages**, but it includes **all** who are God's own, raised to eternal life."[788] Likewise, **Leon Wood** teaches

---

[784] See 1Thess.4:13-17.
[785] *Re-Thinking the Rapture* - E. Schuyler English, Loizeaux Brothers, 1954, p.32.
[786] *The Gospel of Matthew* - Arno C. Gaebelein, Loizeaux Brothers, 1961, p.542.
[787] *God's Plan for the Future* - Lehman Strauss, Zondervan Publishing House, 1965, p.90.
[788] *The Book of the Revelation* - Lehman Strauss, Loizeaux Brothers, 1977, p.335.

that, "...there are to be *two aspects* to the resurrection of the righteous: *one before* the tribulation and *one after;* the *first* in connection with the Rapture, and the *second* with the coming in glory."[789] While referring to First Thessalonians 4:16-17, **Wood** further explains that, "This resurrection will include only saints of the church and will be an *aspect* of what is called the 'first resurrection' (Rev.20:5,6)."[790] **Wood** goes on to say that, "Sometime between this exact close of the tribulation and the beginning of the millennial age, *another resurrection of saints* will occur. This will be a resurrection both of *tribulation saints*, whether Jews or Gentiles, who have died during the tribulation period, and also of *Old Testament saints*."[791] And **Dwight Pentecost** contends that, "...the *first resurrection*...is made up of a *number of component parts*...It includes within it *all who, at any time, are raised to eternal life*."[792] Therefore, according to Dispensationalists, the "first resurrection" is not a singular event but a multi-stage process that occurs over a period of many years.

2. The Textual Basis for the Doctrine of "Two" First Resurrections.

Dispensationalists base their assertion that the "first resurrection" is made up of "different aspects" or "stages" on First Corinthians 15:22-24, which states;

"For as in Adam all die, so also in Christ all shall be made alive. But each in his own **order** *[tagma]*: Christ the first fruits, after that those who are Christ's at His **coming** *[parousia]*, then *comes* the end, when He delivers up the kingdom to the God and Father, when he has abolished all rule and all authority and power." (1Cor. 15:22-24; emphasis added).

While commenting on First Corinthians 15:22-24, **Leon Wood** asserts that, "This passage *indicates* there is *an order, a sequence*, in the resurrection activity. That order, as listed here, is first Christ, then those at His coming, and finally those at the end[793]...Not all interpreters agree that this last element refers to another resurrection aspect, but the idea of sequence still remains whether it does or not."[794] **John Walvoord** explains that, "The idea that the first resurrection can be in *more than one stage* is

---

[789] *Is the Rapture Next?* - Leon J. Wood, Zondervan Publishing House, 1956, p.106.
[790] *The Bible and Future Events* - Leon J. Wood, Zondervan Publishing House, 1974, p.31.
[791] *The Bible and Future Events* - Leon J. Wood, Zondervan Publishing House, 1974, p.153.
[792] *Things to Come* - J. Dwight Pentecost, Zondervan Publishing House, 1964, p.397.
[793] *Is the Rapture Next?* - Leon J. Wood, Zondervan Publishing House, 1956, p.114.
[794] *Is the Rapture Next?* - Leon J. Wood, Zondervan Publishing House, 1956, footnote on p.114.

taught in 1Corinthians 15:23, 24. *Three stages (tagma)* of the resurrection of the saints are included: Christ, first; those at His coming, second; and those at the end. While the third resurrection can be debated[795]...this passage clearly distinguishes the resurrection of Christ from the resurrection of the saints and declares that they are *stages*."[796] By "stages" **Walvoord** means, that the resurrection of the righteous consists of multiple resurrections, occurring at different times. For example, **Walvoord** teaches that, "...there is a *series of resurrections* that the Bible presents, namely, Christ's first, then the resurrection of Matthew 27, then the Rapture, and the resurrection of Old Testament saints after the Tribulation."[797] Likewise, **Dwight Pentecost** maintains that, "The order of events in the *first resurrection program* would be: (1) the resurrection of Christ as the beginning of the resurrection program (1Cor.15:23); (2) the resurrection of the church age saints at the rapture (1Thess.4:16); (3) the resurrection of the tribulation period saints (Rev.20:3-5); (4) the resurrection of Old Testament saints (Dan.12:2; Isa.26:19) at the second advent of Christ to the earth; and finally (5) the final resurrection of the unsaved dead (Rev.20:5;, 11-14) at the end of the millennial age. The first *four stages would all be included in the first resurrection* or the resurrection to life..."[798]

However, the entire concept of "different stages" or "a series of resurrections" of the righteous is completely foreign to the text of First Corinthians 15:23-24. The text refers to only two resurrections – Christ's, the first fruits, and those that belong to Christ at His Coming (*parousia*). The fact that Paul distinguishes between the resurrection of Christ and the resurrection of the saints does *not* mean that the resurrection of "those that are Christ's" occurs in "stages." The word "order" (*tagma*,[799]) refers to that which is arranged in a *specific order*, whereas the word "stage," which does *not* occur in the text, refers to a series of individual events which are part of a larger whole. The concept

---

[795] It is hard to imagine how Dispensationalists can legitimately find a "third resurrection" in the phrase, "then comes the end." Consider the comment of A.T. Robertson, referring to 1Cor.15:23, *"Then cometh the end (eita to telos)...the end or consummation of the age or world (Matt. 13:39,49; I Peter 4:7)." Word Pictures in the New Testament* – Archibald Thomas Robertson, Broadman Press, 1931, vol. iv, p.191.

[796] *The Blessed Hope and the Tribulation*- John F. Walvoord, Zondervan Publishing House, 1976, pp.50-51.

[797] *The Rapture Question* - John F. Walvoord, Zondervan Publishing House, 1981 p.208.

[798] *Things to Come* - J. Dwight Pentecost, Zondervan Publishing House, 1964, p.411.

[799] "τάγμα *[tagma]*...anything placed in order; in N.T, order of succession, 1Cor.15:23. *"The Analytical Greek Lexicon Revised* - edited by Harold K. Moulton, Zondervan Publishing House, 1982, p.398. "τάγμα *[tagma]*...that which has been arranged or placed in order; esp. as a military term, a company, troop, division, rank: metaph., 1Cor. 15:23." *A Manual Greek Lexicon of the New Testament* - G. Abbott-Smith, Charles Scribner's Sons, 1953, p.438.

of "stages" is totally absent from the text. Paul is plainly and simply stating the *sequential order* of resurrection.[800] He declares that Jesus Christ is the "first fruits," i.e., the "first-born from the dead" (see Col.1:18; Rv.1:5). The next group to be raised are "those that are Christ's at His coming." The word *tagma* (i.e., order) does not imply multiple resurrections within the group designated as "those that are Christ's." On the contrary, the language that Paul employs excludes the possibility of a partial resurrection of believers. In verse 23, Paul declares that "those that are Christ's," (i.e., *all* the dead that belong to Christ) will rise at His "coming" (*parousia*). Paul's language clearly indicates that the resurrection of the righteous will be a singular event, occurring all at once, encompassing *all* who belong to Christ. Paul underscores this fact in First Thessalonians 3:13, when he prays that the Lord would establish the hearts of the Thessalonian believers "...unblameable in holiness before our God and Father *at the coming* [i.e., *at the parousia*] of our Lord Jesus with *all* His saints." (Emphasis added). When Christ comes, *all* of His saints will be with Him. This fact eliminates any possibility of a Coming of Christ with only *some* of His saints as Dispensationalists maintain. What's more, Paul goes on to say that the event that immediately follows the resurrection of the righteous is "...*the end*, when He [i.e., Christ] delivers up the kingdom to the God and Father." (v.24; emphasis added).

Thus, we are plainly told that the *order of resurrection* begins with Jesus Christ and ends with those that are His. These are the only two groups mentioned. Paul's purpose in First Corinthians 15, is to correct the mistaken belief by some at Corinth that there was no future resurrection of believers (see 1Cor.15:12-19). He accomplishes this by affirming the historical reality of the resurrection of Jesus Christ. Paul characterizes the resurrection of Christ as the "first fruits." Inherent in the term "first fruits" is the idea that Christ's resurrection is the guarantee of the believer's resurrection. Just as the first fruits of the field preceded the full harvest, so the resurrection of Christ precedes the resurrection of His people. Paul's point is that the resurrection of Christ guarantees that *all* those who belong to Him will rise from the dead at His Coming (*parousia*).

---

[800]**Samuel Tregelles** observes that, "1Cor. xv teaches us the *order* of the resurrection: 'Christ the first fruits: afterwards (next in order of succession) they that are Christ's at His coming.' There is no room left for mistake or doubt, unless we depart from the plain words of Scripture." *The First Resurrection* - Samuel P. Tregelles, The Sovereign Grace Advent Testimony, n.d., p.2.

3. The Redefinition of the Word "First."

Dispensationalists attempt to validate their claim that the "first resurrection" is a process that occurs in multiple stages or phases by redefining the word "first." For example, **John Walvoord** explains that, "The problem here is the common misunderstanding of what the word first means. *First does not mean the number one resurrection,* but rather that the resurrection here revealed occurs before the final resurrection in the millennium, mentioned in Revelation 20:12-14. It merely means that the resurrection occurs *first or before* the later resurrection."[801] **Walvoord** further asserts that, "...the term first is used in contrast to the final resurrection mentioned in Revelation 20, the resurrection of the wicked. The resurrection of *all the righteous is first, not in the sense of number one*, but in the sense of being *before* the final resurrection."[802]

Walvoord makes two significant claims. First, he asserts that, "First does *not* mean the *number one resurrection*..." However, it is extremely doubtful that anyone would interpret John's phrase, "this is the first resurrection" to mean, "this is the number one resurrection." Anyone who even casually reads his Bible understands that the resurrection of Jesus Christ was historically the "number one" resurrection from the dead. Contextually, John is clearly referring to the resurrection of the saints in Revelation 20:4-6. The declaration that "this is the first resurrection" refers specifically to those who belong to Christ. The word "first" establishes the fact that there will be no resurrection of any saints before the "first resurrection" which John chronologically places at the post-tribulational advent of Christ. In other words, the first resurrection, which pertains specifically to the saints, will not occur until Christ appears *after* the Tribulation. This is the obvious intent of the phrase "this is the first resurrection." Thus, "the first resurrection" describes a singular event that occurs *after* the Tribulation and *not* a protracted process that begins *before* the Tribulation.

Second, **Walvoord's** contention that, "First merely means that the resurrection occurs *first or before the later resurrection*..." reduces John's use of the word "first" to a mere redundancy and ignores the obvious context of the passage. John makes a clear

---

[801] *The Blessed Hope and the Tribulation* - John F. Walvoord, Zondervan Publishing House, 1976, p.102.
[802] *The Rapture Question* - John F. Walvoord, Zondervan Publishing House, 1979 p.208.

chronological distinction between the resurrection of the saints and the wicked when he says, "The rest of the dead did not come to life until the thousand years were completed." (v.5). Obviously, if the resurrection of the saints occurs 1,000 years prior to the resurrection of the wicked, it will occur "before" the resurrection of the wicked. It is therefore quite evident that John's use of the word "first" is intended to convey more than the fact that the resurrection of the saints will precede the resurrection of the wicked. **Walvoord** further asserts that, "The resurrection of *all the righteous is first*, not in the sense of number one, but in the sense of being *before* the final resurrection." In other words, according to **Walvoord**, the righteous dead will be raised at different times and in various stages or phases and still be considered part of "the first resurrection" because they all will be raised 1,000 years "before" the wicked. However, the fact that something occurs "before" something else does not necessarily make it "first." For example, consider five athletes engaged in a foot race. Only the runner who initially crosses the finish line is described as being the "first." Those that finished 2nd, 3rd, and 4th are not "first" simply because they finished "before" the 5th and final runner. Thus, while four runners finished "before" the 5th and final runner, only the winning runner is "first." Thus, the contention that multiple resurrections, involving different groups of saints, occurring at different times are all "first" is a contradiction in terms that reduces the text of Revelation 20:4-6 to grammatical nonsense.

However, in the interest of protecting the viability of the pretribulation rapture doctrine, Dispensationalists are for the most part united in their insistence that "the first resurrection" is comprised of multiple phases or stages. For example, while discussing the issue of the first resurrection, **Gerald Stanton** fairly represents modern Dispensational thinking when he explains that there are, "...different orders of harvest: Christ...the saints who were raised after His resurrection, the dead in Christ at the rapture...the martyred saints of the Tribulation period; the two witnesses; the Old Testament saints...None of these are in the resurrection of the unjust; therefore, all of them must have a part in the resurrection of the righteous which is termed 'the first resurrection.'"[803] However, **Stanton** then makes a revealing statement when he says, "Admittedly, there is *no clear indication of various stages of resurrection* in the

---

[803] *Kept From the Hour* - Gerald B. Stanton, Zondervan Publishing House, 1956, p.242.

words, 'This is the first resurrection'..."[804] Yet **Stanton** nonetheless insists that, "...*first* is an *order of resurrection* referring to *all* the redeemed..."[805]

Thus, according to Dispensationalists, the phrase "this is the first resurrection" includes all of the righteous dead, who they maintain will be raised in a series of different resurrections at different times. Yet they are all said to be "first" because they will all be raised "before" the final resurrection of the wicked. However, the plain sense of Revelation 20:4-6, as well as common sense do *not* support this imaginative Dispensational interpretation. It is a gross contradiction in terms to argue that multiple resurrections, involving different groups of people, occurring at different times, can all legitimately be referred to as the "first resurrection."

4. Justification for the Redefinition of the Word "First."

Dispensationalists further argue that "the first resurrection" of the saints cannot literally be the first because the resurrection of Jesus Christ precedes this event. For example, while commenting on the meaning of the phrase, "the first resurrection" in Revelation 20:4-6, **John Walvoord** states; "Obviously the resurrection of the saints is *not* the first resurrection to occur in history. While there were numerous restorations[806] of people who had died, including the case of Lazarus, Christ was the first to rise from the dead with a resurrection body." [807] And again, **Walvoord** contends that, "Indeed, everyone has to agree that the resurrection of Jesus Christ Himself is the first resurrection. Any subsequent resurrection could not be resurrection number one."[808]

It is certainly true that Jesus Christ was the very first to rise from the dead in a glorified, resurrected body. However, the Scriptures do *not* refer to the resurrection of Jesus Christ as "the first resurrection." The resurrection of Christ is referred to as being "the first fruits" (1Cor.15:23) and as "the first-born from the dead" (Col.1:18; Rv.1:5). It is the resurrection of the saints that the Scriptures uniquely designate as "the first

---

[804] *Kept From the Hour* - Gerald B. Stanton, Zondervan Publishing House, 1956, p.242.
[805] *Kept From the Hour* - Gerald B. Stanton, Zondervan Publishing House, 1956, p.243.
[806] These miraculous "restorations" to life are recorded in Mt.27:51-53, Lk.8:54; Jn.11:43; Acts 9:40; 20:10 and were all temporary. All of these individuals died again. The term "resurrection" properly refers to the bodily raising of the righteous dead to a glorified, perfect, eternal state of existence. See 1Cor.15:51-55; Phil.3:20-21; 1Jn.3:2.
[807] *The Rapture Question* - John F. Walvoord, Zondervan Publishing House, 1979 p.207.
[808] *The Blessed Hope and the Tribulation* - John F. Walvoord, Zondervan Publishing House, 1976, p.102.

resurrection." The Apostle John was certainly aware of the fact that Jesus Christ was the first to arise from the dead in a glorified state. Thus, his statement "this is the first resurrection" was not intended to mean, "this is resurrection number one" any more than it was intended to describe a resurrection process with multiple stages or phases. Rather, the phrase "this is the first resurrection" is intended to indicate **when the saints** would be resurrected. Thus, the phrase, "this is the first resurrection" (Rv.20:4-5) clearly and unmistakably places the resurrection of **the saints** chronologically **after** the Tribulation, thereby eliminating any possibility of a partial resurrection of the saints before this time.[809]

5. The Resurrection in the Old Testament.

Early Dispensationalists uniformly taught that **both** Old Testament and New Testament saints would be resurrected **before** the beginning of the Tribulation. For example, **William Blackstone**, while referring to 1Corinthians 15:23,[810] explains that, "It seems plain that the resurrection of those 'who are Christ's at His **coming**,' includes **both** those who constitute the **bride,** who are raised at the Rapture when Christ comes into the air; and the **Old Testament saints**..." whereas, according to **Blackstone**, "... those who believe and suffer during the Tribulation...will be raised at the **Revelation** (when Christ comes to the earth), to take part with Him in the millennial kingdom."[811] Likewise, **C.I. Scofield,** in his *Reference Bible*, teaches that, "The 'first resurrection,' that 'unto life,' will occur at the second coming of Christ (1Cor.15.23), the **saints of the O.T. and church ages** meeting Him in the air (1Thess.4.16,17); while the martyrs of the tribulation, who also have part in the first resurrection (Rev.20.4), are raised at the end of the great tribulation."[812]

However, Dispensationalists eventually realized that their linkage of the resurrections of Old Testament and New Testament saints presented a serious problem for the doctrine of the secret pretribulation rapture. The problem was due to the fact that the

---

[809] "With all confidence we may say that God intended to teach in this place, when saying, 'this is the first resurrection,' that He will not raise any of His people with bodies incorruptible prior to the time and development of circumstances here spoken of." *The First Resurrection* - Samuel P. Tregelles, The Sovereign Grace Advent Testimony, n.d., p.2.
[810] 1Cor.15:23 states, "But each in his own order: Christ the first fruits, after that those who are Christ's at His coming."
[811] *Jesus Is Coming* - William E. Blackstone, Kregel Publications, 1989, p.101.
[812] *The Scofield Study Bible* - Oxford University Press, 1909, 1917, 1939, 1945, p.1228.

Old Testament chronologically places the resurrection of Old Testament saints *after* the Tribulation period - *not before*. It is clear from the context of Daniel 12:1-2,13; Isaiah 25:6-8 and Isaiah 26:19-21, that the resurrection of Old Testament saints occurs *after* the Tribulation period and *not before*. Thus, if the Church is raised at the same time as the Old Testament saints, the pretribulation rapture teaching becomes immediately untenable. When Dispensationalists realized this fact they quickly modified their teaching. For example, **Gerald Stanton** explains that, "Darby and his associates, to whom we owe so much, were *not always right*. When they insisted that the resurrection of *Israel's dead* occurs at the *beginning* of the Tribulation, that is, at the same time as that of Church saints, they *were very probably in error...*" **Stanton** then goes on to emphatically state that, "*Darby was wrong* in respect to the time of Israel's resurrection."[813] Some Dispensationalists have attempted to downplay the serious implications and casually brush the entire issue aside. For example, **Lehman Strauss** explains that, "Not all teachers of the Bible are agreed as to the time of the *resurrection of Old Testament saints*. Some believe they are raised when the Church saints are raised at Christ's appearing in the air to raise and rapture the Church; others hold to the view that they are raised at the close of the tribulation. To me this is *not a point of major significance*."[814] Contrary to **Strauss'** claim, this is most definitely a point of major significance because the Apostle Paul unmistakably links the resurrection of the Church with the resurrection of Old Testament saints. Carefully consider the following text:

1Cor.15:51 "Behold, I tell you a mystery; we shall not all sleep, but we shall all be changed, **v.52** in a moment, in the twinkling of an eye, at the last trumpet; for the trumpet shall sound, and the dead will be raised imperishable, and we shall be changed. **v.53** For this perishable must put on the imperishable, and this mortal must put on immortality. **v.54** But **when** this perishable will have put on the imperishable, and this mortal will have put on immortality, **then will come about the saying that is written, 'Death is swallowed up in victory.' v.55 'O death, where is your victory? O death where is your sting?'"** (Emphasis added).

While discussing the resurrection of the Church, Paul refers to Isaiah 25:8,[815]

---

[813] *Kept from the Hour* - Gerald B. Stanton, Zondervan Publishing House, 1956, p.228.

[814] *The Book of the Revelation* - Lehman Strauss, Loizeaux Brothers, 1977, p.335.

[815] Isaiah 25:6-8, "And the LORD of hosts will prepare a lavish banquet for all peoples on this mountain; a banquet of aged wine, choice pieces with marrow, *and* refined, aged wine. (v.7) And on this mountain He will swallow up the covering which is over all peoples, even the veil which is stretched over all nations. (v.8) He will swallow up death for all time, and the Lord GOD will wipe tears away from all faces, and He will remove the reproach of His people from all the earth; for the LORD has spoken."

and Hosea13:14[816] thereby clearly linking the resurrection of the Church with the resurrection of Old Testament saints. According to Paul, the resurrection of the Church coincides with the millennial blessings of Israel. The linkage is undeniable in Isaiah. It is highly significant that Isaiah 25, chronologically places the resurrection of Old Testament saints *after* the Divine judgments associated with the Great Tribulation. These judgments are graphically described in Isaiah 24:1-23. Isaiah 25:6-8 describes the resurrection of Old Testament saints at the commencement of millennial blessings, which clearly begins *after* the Tribulation period. Thus, according to Paul, the resurrection of the Church will coincide with the post-tribulational resurrection and blessings of the Old Testament saints.[817]

For the most part, modern Dispensationalists have acknowledged the fact that Old Testament saints will be raised *after* the Tribulation. For example, **Lewis Sperry Chafer** succinctly states in his *Systematic Theology* that, "In Daniel 12:1-3 we read that, *following* the great tribulation, Daniel's people will be *raised from the dead.*"[818] **John Walvoord** explains that, "Most of the Old Testament passages of which Daniel 12:1-2 is an example do indeed seem to set up a chronology of *Tribulation first, then resurrection of the Old Testament saints*...The best answer...is to concede the point that the resurrection of Old Testament saints is *after* the Tribulation, and to *divorce it completely from the translation and resurrection of the church.*"[819] Thus, in order to preserve the doctrine of a pretribulation rapture, modern Dispensationalists have separated the resurrection of Church saints from Old Testament saints. However, this approach does not solve the immediate problem for Dispensationalists. It merely attempts to ignore the unmistakable linkage that Paul establishes between the resurrections of Old and New Testament saints (1Cor.15:54 cp. Is.25:6-8; 26:19-21; Hos.13:14; Dan.12:1-3, 13; Ro.11:11-15). Dispensationalists offer no textual evidence to substantiate their claim that the resurrections of Old Testament saints and Church saints occur at different times. They offer no reasonable explanation as to why Paul clearly associates the resurrection of the Church with that of Israel. The simple fact of

---

[816] Hosea 13:14, "I will ransom them from the power of Sheol; I will redeem them from death. O death, where are your thorns? O Sheol, where is your sting?" Note that the word "Sheol" generally refers to the abode of the dead or the grave.
[817] Ro.11:11-15, "I say then, they [i.e., the Jews] did not stumble so as to fall...now if their transgression be riches for the world and their failure be riches for the Gentiles, how much more will their fulfillment be...For if their rejection be the reconciliation of the world, what will their acceptance be but **life from the dead**?" (Emphasis added).
[818] *Systematic Theology* - Lewis Sperry Chafer, Kregel Publications, 1993, vol.4, p.23.
[819] *The Rapture Question* - John F. Walvoord, Zondervan Publishing House, 1979 pp.170-171.

the matter is that in order to protect the viability of the pretribulation rapture theory, Dispensationalists have consciously ignored the obvious linkage between the resurrections of Old and New Testament saints. Without any textual justification whatsoever, Dispensationalists have simply "divorced" the resurrections of Church saints from Old Testament saints.

6. The Resurrection in the New Testament

The New Testament clearly links the *resurrection* of the righteous and the *rapture* of the Church with the *Coming* (i.e., *parousia*) of Jesus Christ. Carefully consider the following passages, which associate the *parousia* of Christ with both the *resurrection* and the *rapture* of the Church.

(a) In First Corinthians 15, Paul states that *all* those who belong to Christ will be "made alive" at His "coming [*parousia*]."

"For as in Adam all die, so also in Christ *all shall be made alive*. But each in his own order: Christ the first fruits, after that *those who are Christ's* at His *coming* [*parousia*]." (1Cor.15:22-23, emphasis added).

(b) In First Thessalonians 4, Paul connects the *resurrection* of the saints with the *parousia* of Christ when he states;

"For this we say to you by the word of the Lord, that we who are alive, and remain until the *coming [parousia]* of the Lord, *shall not precede those who have fallen asleep*. For the Lord Himself will descend from heaven...and *the dead in Christ* shall rise first." (1Thess.4:15-16, emphasis added).

Paul is clearly teaching that "those who have fallen asleep" [i.e., those believers who have died[820]] will experience resurrection at "the coming [*parousia*] of Christ" when "the Lord Himself will descend from heaven... and *the dead in Christ* shall rise first." Thus, the resurrection of the saints is unmistakably linked to the *parousia* of Christ.

---

[820] The term "sleep" is sometimes euphemistically used in the New Testament to refer to death (see Jn.11:11-14; 1Cor.11:30; 15:51). It should be noted however, that the word "sleep" refers to the condition of the physical body and *not* the soul which for the believer is present with God at the time of physical death (see 2Cor.5:8; Phil.1:21-24; Rv.6:9-11).

(c) The *rapture* of the Church is clearly linked to the *parousia* of Christ. In First Thessalonians 4:15-17, Paul states;

"For this we say to you by the word of the Lord, that *we who are alive*, and remain until the *coming [parousia]* of the Lord, shall not precede those who have fallen asleep. For the Lord Himself will descend from heaven...Then *we who are alive* and remain shall be *caught up* together with them in the clouds to meet the Lord in the air..." (1Thess.4:15-17, emphasis added).

(d) In Second Thessalonians 2:1, Paul establishes an unmistakable linkage between the *rapture* and the *parousia* of Christ, when he states;

"...with respect to the *coming [parousia]* of our Lord Jesus Christ, and our *gathering together* to Him." (2Thess.2:1, emphasis added).

(e) Again, in 1Cor.15:22-23, 51-52, Paul associates the *rapture* with the *parousia* of Christ when he explains that;

"...in Christ all shall be made alive. But each in his own order: Christ the first fruits, after that those who are Christ's at His *coming [parousia]*... "Behold, I tell you a mystery; we shall not all sleep, but *we shall all be changed*, v.52 *in a moment, in the twinkling of an eye,* at the last trumpet; for the trumpet shall sound, and *the dead will be raised imperishable, and we shall be changed."* (1Cor.15:22-23; 51-52, emphasis added).

(f) The Lord Jesus clearly connects His *parousia* with the *rapture* of His elect when He declares in Matthew 24:27,29, 31;

"...so shall the *coming [parousia]* of the Son of Man be...But immediately *after the tribulation of those days*...He will send forth His angels with a great trumpet and they will *gather together* His elect..." (Matt.24:27, 29, 31 emphasis added).

The following table illustrates the striking parallels between Matthew 24, 1Corinthians 15, 1Thessalonians 4 and 2Thessalonians 2 with respect to the *parousia* of Christ and the *resurrection* and *rapture* of believers.

Matthew 24	1Corinthian 15	1Thessalonians 4	2Thessalonians 2
v.27 "...the *coming [parousia]* of the Son of Man..."	v.23 "...His *coming [parousia]*..."	v.15 "...the *coming [parousia]* of the Lord..."	v.1 "...the *coming [parousia]* of the Lord Jesus..."
v.30 "...they will *see* the Son of Man coming..."		v.16 "For the Lord Himself shall *descend from heaven*..."	v.8 "...the *appearing* of His coming..."
v.30 "...on the *clouds of the sky* ..." 821		v.17 "...in the *clouds*..."	
v.31 "He will send forth His *angels*..."		v.16 "...with the voice of the *archangel*..."	
v.31 "...with a *great trumpet*..."	v.52 "...at the *last trumpet*..."	v.16 "...the *trumpet of God*..."	
v.31 "...His angels will *gather together* His elect..."		v.17 "...we shall always be *with* the Lord."	v.1 "...our *gathering together* to Him."
	v.52 "...the *dead* will be *raised* imperishable..."	v.16 "...the *dead* in Christ *shall rise* first..."	
	v.52 "...we shall be *changed*..."	v.17 "...then we who are alive and remain shall be *caught up*..."822	

---

821 Compare Matthew 26:64 "...I tell you, hereafter you will see the Son of Man sitting at the right hand of power, and coming on the clouds of heaven." Cp. Mk.14:62; Rv.1:7; Dan.7:13-14.

822 The phrase, "caught up...to meet the Lord in the air" (1Thess.4:17) certainly entails a radical change in our state of being (compare 1Cor.15:50-53; Phil.3:20-21; Col.3:4; 1Jn.3:2) and thus parallels 1Cor.15:52.

The Scriptures clearly establish the fact that both the *resurrection* of the saints and the *rapture* of the Church will occur at the *parousia* of Jesus Christ. Thus, the time of the *parousia* becomes the defining element in establishing the time of both the *resurrection* and the *rapture*. The decisive question therefore becomes, "*When* does the *parousia* of the Lord occur - *before* or *after* the Tribulation?" Fortunately, the Scriptures provide a very clear and straightforward answer to this important question.

In Matthew 24, Jesus explicitly states that His Coming (*parousia*) will occur *after* the Tribulation. The Lord Himself declares,

"For just as the lightning comes from the east, and flashes even to the west, so shall the *coming [parousia]* of the Son of Man be...But immediately *after* the tribulation of those days...they will see the Son of Man coming on the clouds of the sky with power and great glory." (Mt.24:27, 29-30, emphasis added).

The Apostle Paul clearly connects the *parousia* of Christ with the destruction of the Antichrist – an event that unquestionably occurs *after* the Tribulation. Paul declares…

"... that lawless one will be revealed whom the Lord will slay with the breath of His mouth and bring to an end by the appearance of His *coming [parousia]*." (2Thess.2:1;8, emphasis added, cp. Rv.19:20).

As demonstrated above, the Scriptures clearly state that both the *resurrection* and the *rapture* of the Church will occur at the *parousia* of Jesus Christ. The Scriptures further declare that the *parousia* will occur *after* the Tribulation. In light of these indisputable Biblical facts, it becomes immediately obvious that if the *resurrection* and the *rapture* occur at the *parousia*, and the *parousia* occurs *after* the Tribulation, then both the *rapture* and *resurrection* must also necessarily occur *after* the Tribulation and *not* before!

Dispensationalists object to this obvious deduction on the basis of two baseless arguments. First they claim that the Gospel narratives must be interpreted "dispensationally."[823] This means that those portions of the Gospels that supposedly apply solely to the Jews must be carefully distinguished from those portions that

---

[823] See Chapter 3, *The Dispensational Hermeneutic*, Number 2, *The Dispensationalizing of the New Testament*, for a discussion of the Dispensational practice of dividing the New Testament into "Jewish" and "Christian" sections.

supposedly apply solely to the Church. Not surprisingly, Dispensationalists argue that all of the prophetic sections rest upon "Jewish ground" and therefore have no direct application to the Church. Thus, the Olivet Discourse, which represents the most comprehensive prophetic teaching given by Christ during His earthly ministry, is said to have no direct application to the Church! Secondly, Dispensationalists assert that the word "*parousia*" has a *double meaning* and is therefore used interchangeably in the New Testament to describe *two different Comings* of Christ - one *before* the Tribulation and one *after* the Tribulation.[824] Dispensationalists then assume that *all* New Testament verses that refer to the Coming of Christ automatically refer to a pretribulational Coming and rapture unless those verses specifically mention events associated with a post-tribulational Coming. For example, while discussing the supposed *double meaning* of the word *parousia*, **John Walvoord**, explains, that;

"...the word [i.e., *parousia*] is used *only of the rapture when it refers to Christ and not to His return to the earth* before the millennium. That it is used frequently of the rapture of the church is clear in the following references (1Cor.15:23; 1Thess.2:19; 4:15; 5:23; 2Thess.2:1(?); James 5:7,8; 2Pt.3:4(?); 1John 2:28)."[825]

Each of these Biblical references cited by **Walvoord** does in fact refer to the *parousia* of Jesus Christ. However, *none of these verses actually describes a pretribulational Coming of Christ*. All of these verses cited by Walvoord are *time-neutral* – they describe neither a pretribulational or post-tribulational Advent.[826] Dispensationalists simply *assume* that these verses are describing a pretribulational Coming and rapture. In other words, according to Dispensationalists, every verse that mentions the Coming of Christ, is automatically *assumed* to refer to a pretribulational Coming of Christ, unless the verse specifically describes events associated with a post-tribulational Coming of Christ. Mark it carefully; the entire argument for the pretribulational rapture rests upon the colossal *assumption* that *all time-neutral* New Testament verses that mention the Coming of Christ automatically refer to a pretribulational Coming – even

---

[824] See Chapter 5, *The Theological Contradictions Created by the Pretribulation Rapture Teaching*, Part II, *Two Second Comings*, Number 1, *Terminology of the Second Coming*, for a detailed discussion of the words *parousia, epiphaneia* and *apokalupsis*.
[825] *New Testament Words for the Lord's Coming* - John F. Walvoord, *Bibliotheca Sacra*, 101:284-289, July 1944, p.285.
[826] Note that while 2Thess.2:1, is itself time-neutral, when it is viewed in the overall context of 2Thessalonians 1:6-10 and 2:1-12, it clearly refers to a post-tribulational Coming of Christ.

though these verses do *not* actually describe a pretribulational Coming![827] This then is the ultimate argument from silence.

However, in order to legitimately maintain their claim that the rapture of the Church is a pretribulational event, Dispensationalists must first establish that Jesus Christ is indeed coming before the Tribulation! They must produce at least one Biblical text that clearly describes a pretribulational Coming of Christ! After all, there are numerous verses that clearly describe the post-tribulational Coming of Christ.[828] Surely there must be one verse in the New Testament that clearly states that Jesus Christ will come before the onset of the Great Tribulation! *Yet, the undeniable fact is that there is not a single verse in the entire New Testament that describes a pretribulational Coming of Jesus Christ for any reason whatsoever - not one!* Furthermore, there is *not* one instance where the words *parousia, epiphaneia* or *apokalupsis* are used to describe a pretribulational Coming of Jesus Christ![829] The entire proposition of a secret, any moment pretribulational Coming, Resurrection and Rapture is a human invention that rests upon nothing more than unsubstantiated assumptions and inferences and *not* the plain, ordinary, literal statements of Scripture!

---

[827] *Time-neutral* verses that describe the Coming (*parousia*) of Christ without indicating either a pretribulational or post-tribulational time-frame are: 1Cor.15:23; 1Thess.2:19; 3:13; 4:15; 5:23; Jas.5:7-8; 2Pt.3:4; 1Jn.2:28. Dispensationalists argue that these *time-neutral* verses depict a secret, any moment pretribulational Coming of Jesus Christ to rapture the Church because they do not mention any other Tribulational events associated with the Coming of Christ.

[828] New Testament verses that clearly describe the *post*-tribulational Advent of Jesus Christ are; Mt.16:27; 24:27-31; 25:31; Mk.8:38; 13:24-27; Lk.9:26; 17:22-24, 26-30; Lk.21:25-27; 2Thess.1:6-10; 2:1-8; 1Pt.4:13; Jude 14-15; Rv.1:7; 6:14-17; 11:15-19; 19:11-16.

[829] The reader is encouraged to closely examine the usage of these words with respect to the Second Advent of Jesus Christ. *Parousia* (Coming) occurs in Mt.24:3,27,37,39; 1Cor.15:23; 1Th.2:19, 3:13, 4:15, 5:23; 2Th.2:1,8; Jas.5:7,8; 2Pt. 3:4; 1Jn.2:28. *Epiphaneia* (Appearing) occurs in 2Th.2:8; 1Tim.6:14; 2Tim.4:1,8; Tit.2:13. *Apokalupsis* (Revelation) occurs in 1Cor.1:7; 2Th.1:7; 1Pt.1:7,13, 4:13 and *Apokalupto* (Revealed) Lk.17:30.

Chapter Five, Part V
"Two" Days of the Lord

Outline for Chapter 5, Part V:
1. The Post-Tribulational Character of the Day of the Lord.
2. Early Dispensationalists Accepted the Post-Tribulational Character of the Day of the Lord.
3. The Realization that the Post-Tribulational Character of the Day of the Lord Jeopardized the Pretribulation Rapture Doctrine.
4. The Dispensational Solution to the Problems Caused by the Post-Tribulational Character of the Day of the Lord.
5. The Unanticipated Contradictions Created by the Dispensational Solution to the Post-Tribulational Character of the Day of the Lord.
6. The Revised Dispensational Solution: "Two" Days of the Lord.
   6a. The Theory of "Two" Days of the Lord Explained.
   6b. The Textual Basis for the Dispensational Doctrine of "Two" Days of the Lord.

1. The Post-Tribulational Character of the Day of the Lord.

The phrase, "the Day of the Lord"[830] refers specifically to the future manifestation of the wrath of God, when at the end of this age, He will enter into judgment with all of the nations of the world.[831] The Scriptures consistently characterize the Day of the Lord as a sudden, cataclysmic time of Divine judgment that brings the present age of man's rebellion to an immediate and decisive end. This "Day" will be preceded by a period of severe tribulation, characterized by the persecution of true believers, unprecedented wars, famines, pestilences and earthquakes,[832] culminating in unparalleled astronomical

---

[830] The Day of the Lord is also referred to as "that day" (Is.2:11), "a day of reckoning" (Is.2:12); "the day of His burning anger" (Is.13:13); "a day of vengeance, a year of recompense" (Is.34:8); "the great and awesome day of the LORD" (Joel 2:31; Mal.4:5); "the great day of the LORD" (Zeph.1:14); "a unique day" (Zech.14:7). The New Testament equivalents are, "His day" (Lk.17:24); "the day of our Lord Jesus Christ" (1Cor.1:8); "the day" (1Cor.3:13); "the day of our Lord Jesus" (2Cor.1:14); "the day of Christ Jesus" and " the day of Christ" (Phil.1:6,10; 2:16); "the day of the Lord" (1Thess.5:2; 2Thess.2:1); "the day of the Lord" and "the day of God" (2Pt.3:10,12).
[831] Isa.2:12-22; 13:6-16; 24:1-6; 17-23; 34:1-6; Joel 2:30-32; 3:1-3, 9-17; Obad.15; Zeph.1:7-18; Zech.12:1-14; 14:1-8. Note that the historical judgments which came upon the "proud and lofty"(Is.2:12), referring to both Israel & Judah (Is.2:1); Babylon (Isa.13); Edom (Is.34:1-8; Obad. 1-21); Israel (Amos 5:18-20); Judah (Joel 2:30-32, 3:1-3: 3:9-17); and Judah and Jerusalem (Zeph.1:1-18, 3:1-11) all transcend the immediate historical setting and prefigure the future final judgment of all the nations at the apocalyptic Day of the Lord at the end of this age.
[832] Mt.24:7,29; Mk.13:8,24-25; Lk.21:10-11,25.

events, cataclysmic geologic upheavals and finally, complete and total darkness.[833] This period of unparalleled suffering will be brought to an abrupt end by the Day of the Lord, when the Lord Jesus Christ will be revealed from heaven in a radiant blaze of Divine glory.[834] Like the lightning flashing from one end of the sky to the other (Mt.24:27; Lk.17:24), every eye will behold Him (Rv.1:7), as He returns with all of the angels of heaven (Mt.25:31) to smite the nations and tread through the winepress of God's fierce wrath (Rv.19:11-15; 14:14-20 cp. Is.63:3).[835] Israel will be delivered (Zech.12:8-14 cp.Rom.11:26-27), the armies of the nations that have gathered against her will be destroyed (Zech.12:1-3 cp. Joel 3:2; 9-14), the nations will be judged (Mt.25:31-33), while those who have believed will be amazed and marvel at the magnificent presence of the Lord of glory (2Thess.1:10)!

2. Early Dispensationalists Accepted the Post-Tribulational Character of the Day of the Lord.

Early Dispensationalists fully accepted the post-tribulational nature of the future Day of the Lord. They uniformly taught that the Day of the Lord would begin *after* the Tribulation when the Lord Jesus Christ visibly returned in power and glory. For example, **William Blackstone** maintained that, "The Revelation[836] ushers in the Day of the Lord." **Blackstone** further explained that, "There is a judgment day coming...This 'day of judgment' is also called 'The day of the Lord,' 'The last day,' and 'The great day.'"[837] **C.I. Scofield** declared that, "The day of Jehovah (called, also, 'that day,' and 'the great day') is that lengthened period of time *beginning* with the return of the Lord in glory..."[838] Likewise, **Lewis Sperry Chafer** taught that, "...the Day of the Lord ...is related to Christ's second advent...this day includes the judgments of God upon the nations and upon Israel and that these judgments *occur at Christ's return*..."[839] And

---

[833] Is.13:10; Joel 2:30-31, 3:15-16; Is.24:1-6;19-21; Rv.6:12-17.
[834] Mt.24:29-31; Mk.13:24-26; Lk.21:25-27; 2Thess.1:6-10; Rv.6:12; Rv.19:11-16.
[835] There is no doubt whatsoever that Jesus Christ administers God's wrath – see Jn.5:22,27; Acts 17:30-31. Also, compare Mt.24:29-31; 2Thess.1:6-10; Rv.11:15-19; 6:12-17; 19:11-18 with Zech.14:1-4 & Is.63:1-6.
[836] Note that early Dispensationalists consistently used the word "Revelation" (*apokalupsis*) to refer to Christ's visible *post-tribulational* appearance. Whereas, the word "Coming (*parousia*) was used to describe Christ's secret pretribulational Coming.
[837] *Jesus is Coming* - William E. Blackstone, Kregel Publications, 1989, pp.79,103.
[838] *The Scofield Study Bible* - C.I. Scofield, Oxford University Press, 1909, 1917, 1939, 1945, p.1349.
[839] *Systematic Theology* - Lewis Sperry Chafer - Kregel Publications, vol.7, p.110.

Louis Talbot insisted that "the day of the Lord...*always* refers to *His visible return in glory* to put an *end to the great tribulation*, and to set up His kingdom."[840]

3. The Realization that the Post-Tribulational Character of the Day of the Lord Jeopardized the Pretribulation Rapture Doctrine.

Modern Dispensational teachers soon recognized that the acceptance of the post-tribulational character of the Day of the Lord by early Dispensational teachers created a serious problem for the pretribulation rapture doctrine. This was due to the fact that Paul's discussion of the rapture in First Thessalonians 4:13-18 immediately transitions into a discussion of the Day of the Lord in First Thessalonians 5:1-11. Clearly, the rapture of the Church and the Day of the Lord are closely linked contextually - the one directly following the other. The obvious conclusion is that these two events find their fulfillment in close proximity to each other.

Referring to the close connection between the rapture in 1Thessalonians 4 and the Day of the Lord in 1Thessalonian 5, **John Walvoord** explains that, "…the implication is that the Rapture and the beginning of the day of the Lord occur at the same time." [841] Likewise, **D. Edmond Hiebert** while commenting on the close connection between 1Thessalonian 4 and 5 observed that, "This paragraph [i.e., 1Thess.5:1-11] is an appropriate companion piece to the preceding [1Thess.4:13-18]. It is the second half of the distinctively eschatological block of material in the epistle." [842]

Thus, early Dispensationalists who accepted the obvious Biblical chronology that portrays the rapture occurring in immediate proximity to the Day of the Lord found it difficult to defend the concept of a rapture occurring some seven years *before* the Day of the Lord. Obviously, if the rapture occurs in close proximity to the Day of the Lord, and the Day of the Lord occurs *after* the Tribulation, there is a strong indication that the rapture must also occur at the end of, or after, the Tribulation. Clearly, this chronology would be fatal to the Dispensational concept of a pretribulation rapture of the Church.

---

[840] *God's Plan of the Ages* - Louis T. Talbot, Louis T. Talbot, 1943, p.138.
[841] *The Rapture Question* - John F. Walvoord, Zondervan Publishing House, 1979, p.213.
[842] *The Thessalonian Epistles* - D. Edmond Hiebert, Moody Press, 1982, p.207.

The contextual relationship between the Coming of Christ, the Day of the Lord and the rapture of the Church is firmly established by 1Thessalonians 4:13-18 and 5:1-11, and is amplified by 2Thessalonians 2:1-2.[843] Look carefully at the text;

"Now we request you, brethren, with regard to the **coming** *[parousia]* of our Lord Jesus Christ, and our **gathering together** *[episunagoge]* to Him, that you may not be quickly shaken from your composure or be disturbed either by a spirit or a message or a letter as if from us, to the effect that the **day of the Lord** has come." (2Thess.2:1-2, emphasis added).

In this passage, Paul clearly links the "coming" or *parousia* of Jesus Christ with the "gathering together" of the Church. The phrase, "our gathering together to Him" is a direct reference to the rapture of the church. The grammatical construction of the phrase "...the coming of our Lord Jesus Christ, and our gathering together to Him" clearly establishes that the "coming" of Christ and the "gathering together" of the saints both occur at the same time.[844] Paul then proceeds to link these two major prophetic events contextually with the Day of the Lord. Paul distinctly associates the *parousia* and the *gathering together* (i.e., *rapture*) with the *Day of the Lord* when he states,

"...with regard to the **coming** of our Lord Jesus Christ, and our **gathering together** to Him...to the effect that the **day of the Lord** has come." (2Thess.2:1-2).

Clearly, within this single sentence, there is a close relationship between the Coming of Christ, the rapture of the Church and the Day of the Lord - especially, in light of the fact that both the Day of the Lord and the gathering of the Church occur at the Coming (i.e., *parousia*) of Jesus Christ![845]

---

[843] While commenting on 2Thess 2:1-2, D. Edmond Hiebert states, "It is a summary statement of the teaching...in 1Thessalonians 4:13-18." *The Thessalonian Epistles* - D. Edmond Hiebert, Moody Press, 1982, p.301.

[844] "The article appears before *parousia* and is not repeated before *episunagoge*, indicating that these are complementary elements in one event." *The Epistles of Paul the Apostle to the Thessalonians* - C.F. Hogg and W.E. Vine, Pickering & Inglis, n.d., p.242. "The two nouns, **coming** (*parousia*) and **being gathered** (*episynagoge*), are governed by the one article and thus depicted as one (complex) event." *1&2 Thessalonians* – David J. Williams, Baker Books, 1992, p.122. "The government of the two nouns under one article makes it clear that one event, viewed under two complementary aspects, is thought of." *The Thessalonian Epistles* - D. Edmond Hiebert, Moody Press, 1982, p.301.

[845] "The 'coming'...and 'gathering' here are grammatically linked, and the use of both terms derives from the sayings of Jesus." *The IVP Bible Background Commentary New Testament* – Craig S. Keener, InterVarsity Press, 1993, p.600.

It is also highly significant that Paul's reference in 2Thessalonians 2:1-2, to the Coming of Christ, the rapture of the Church and the Day of the Lord is bracketed by clear descriptions of the *post*-tribulational appearance of Christ. For example, in chapter one of 2Thessalonians we have a vivid description of the glorious *post*-tribulational Coming of Christ, "...with His mighty angels in flaming fire, dealing out retribution to those who do not know God and to those who do not obey the gospel of our Lord Jesus..." (2Thess.1:6-10). Then immediately following 2Thessalonians 2:1-2, we have a graphic description of the *post*-tribulational Coming of Christ and the subsequent destruction of the Antichrist, "...whom the Lord will slay with the breath of His mouth and bring to an end by the appearance of His coming..." (2Thess.2:8-9).

Yet, modern Dispensationalists routinely ignore the obvious *post*-tribulational context of these passages and insist that the Coming of Christ and the gathering of believers referred to in 2Thessalonians 2:1-2, describes a *pre*tribulational event irrespective of the fact that it is embedded between two unmistakable *post*-tribulational descriptions of the Second Coming of Christ and the associated Day of the Lord. For example, while **John Walvoord** recognizes the post-tribulational context, he denies its significance when he dismissively declares that;

"Second Thessalonians 2 deals with the rapture in verse 1 and with the second coming in verse 8 but this does not make them the same event."[846]

However, Walvoord's assertion is untenable. In 2Thessalonians 2:1-2, Paul clearly links the *parousia* of Christ with the *rapture* of the Church and the ***Day of the Lord***. In verse 8, Paul clearly describes the *parousia* as a *post*-tribulational event. Add to this the fact that the Day of the Lord is uniformly depicted as a *post*-tribulational event throughout Scripture, and the prospect of a *pre*tribulational rapture linked to the *parousia* and the ***Day of the Lord*** is immediately called into serious question. The Dispensational claim that Paul is describing a *pre*tribulational *parousia* of Christ to rapture the Church in verse 1, and a *post*-tribulational *parousia* of Christ in v.8, is contextually indefensible. Both the general and immediate context of Paul's description of the "gathering together" of the saints is clearly and undeniably *post*-tribulational.

---

[846] *The Blessed Hope and the Tribulation* - John F. Walvoord, Zondervan Publishing House, 1976, p.50.

4. The Dispensational Solution to the Problems Caused by the Post-Tribulational Character of the Day of the Lord.

The problem for **modern** Dispensationalists was two-fold. First, there was the problematic teaching of the **early** Dispensationalists who accepted the plain sense of Scripture that clearly places the **start** of the Day of the Lord at the **post**-tribulational **parousia** of Jesus Christ. And second, there was the undeniable connection of the rapture in 1Thessalonians 4:13-18, with the Day of the Lord in 1Thessalonians 5:1-11, as-well-as the obvious post-tribulational context of 2Thessalonians 1:6-10 and 2:1-8.

It was clear to modern Dispensationalists that there was an undeniable contextual relationship between the post-tribulational Coming of Christ, the rapture of the Church and the post-tribulational Day of the Lord. Dispensationalists understood that if the pretribulation rapture theory was to survive, two essential changes had to be made. First, the Day of the Lord could not be understood to mean an apocalyptic day of catastrophic Divine judgment at the end of the tribulation period. And second, the scope of the Day of the Lord would have to be expanded to include the entire 7-year tribulation period. Thus, Dispensationalists decreed that the Day of the Lord would now encompass the entire seven-year Tribulation period and would coincide with a pretribulational rapture of the Church at the beginning of the tribulation, instead of coinciding with a post-tribulational rapture at the end of the Tribulation.

John Walvoord explains the reasoning process when he states;

"The problem left unsolved by the early pretribulationists in their discussion of the day of the Lord has, however, a very simple solution that at one stroke lays to rest the wordy arguments of posttribulationists…The **day of the Lord** as presented in the Old and New Testaments **includes** rather than **follows** the tremendous events of the **tribulation period.**"[847]

Walvoord fairly represent contemporary Dispensational thinking when he argues that the Day of the Lord starts at the **beginning** of the Tribulation, and **not** at the end of the Tribulation period. For example, Dwight Pentecost says, "Thus, it is concluded that the Day of the Lord will **include** the time of the tribulation."[848] And Gerald Stanton asserts

---

[847] *The Rapture Question* - John F. Walvoord, Zondervan Publishing House, 1979, p.175.
[848] *Things to Come* – J. Dwight Pentecost, Zondervan Publishing House, 1964, p.230.

that, "As a period, the Day of the Lord *includes* the Tribulation, and in most texts is synonymous with the Tribulation."[849]

Dispensationalists justify moving the starting point of the Day of the Lord from the visible, glorious Second Coming at the *end* of the Tribulation to a secret, unannounced, any moment Coming at the *beginning* of the Tribulation by asserting that the *entire* seven-year Tribulation period is characterized by Divine wrath. For example, **Gerald Stanton** contends that; "The Tribulation…will be *primarily* and above all else a *period of judgment* from God…"[850] **Lehman Strauss** succinctly states that; "The Tribulation is a *time of wrath*."[851] **Renald Showers** asserts that; "…God's Day of the Lord *wrath* will be poured out throughout the *entire 70th week, even during its first half*."[852] And **John Walvoord** maintains that, "…the divine judgments of God do *not* begin at the end of the Tribulation but certainly *include the entire period* of the Tribulation."[853]

The problem for Dispensationalists is that the Tribulation period is *never* referred to in Scripture as the Day of the Lord. Furthermore, the Day of the Lord is *never* depicted in Scripture as a protracted period of time. Rather, the Day of the Lord is consistently portrayed as a sudden, intense, devastating, time of catastrophic judgment that suddenly and unexpectedly bursts upon the wicked *when* the Lord Jesus Christ is personally and visibly revealed in manifest glory at the *end* of the Tribulation period (see Mt.24:29-31; Rv.19:11-21). The Scriptures declare that the *Day of the Lord*…

- will reveal the *glory, splendor and majesty* of Almighty God in the person of Jesus Christ.[854]
- will be a time of unimaginable *terror* for sinful men.[855]
- will finally *humble the sinful pride of man*.[856]
- will be a time of unprecedented *judgment* upon the nations.[857]

---

[849] *Kept From The Hour* - Gerald B. Stanton, Zondervan Publishing House, 1956, p.81.
[850] *Kept From the Hour* – Gerald B. Stanton, Zondervan Publishing House, 1956, p.34.
[851] *God's Plan for the Future* – Lehman Strauss, Zondervan Publishing House, 1965, p.85.
[852] *Maranatha Our Lord Come!* - Renald E. Showers, The Friends of Israel Gospel Ministry, Inc., 1995, p.16.
[853] *The Rapture Question* - John F. Walvoord, Zondervan Publishing House, 1979, p.223.
[854] Is.2:10,19,21; Mt.16:27; 25:31; Titus 2:13.
[855] Is.2:10,19-21; Is.13:6-9 Zeph.1:17-18; Mal.4:1; 2Thess.1:6-10; Rv.6:15-17.
[856] Is.2:11-12,17; Is.13:12.
[857] Is.34:2; Joel 3:1-2,9-14; Zech.14:1-3; Zech.14:12-13; Mt.25:31-33; Rv.11:17-18; Rv.19:11-16.

- will result in catastrophic *geologic upheavals*.[858]
- will cause unparalleled *astronomical convulsions*.[859]

Are we really to believe the Dispensational assertion that the glory of the Lord, the terror of His presence, the humbling of sinful mankind, the judgment of the nations, the geologic upheavals and astronomical calamities are going to persist for seven continuous years? On the contrary, the clear and unambiguous testimony of the Scriptures declares that *all* of these events associated with the Day of the Lord, will suddenly cascade upon an unbelieving world with terrifying rapidity, *after* the Tribulation, *at* the visible *parousia* of the Lord Jesus Christ.[860]

There is no legitimate textual justification for expanding the scope of the Day of the Lord to include the entire Tribulation period. Nor is there any justification for redefining the essential nature of the Day of the Lord by transforming it from a time of sudden, devastating and decisive judgment into a protracted period of Tribulational calamities, such as wars, famines, earthquakes, plagues and pestilences. While, these Tribulational events may certainly be understood as judgments from God on a rebellious world, it does *not* mean that they are synonymous with the final cataclysmic judgments of the Day of the Lord. Especially in light of the fact that the Scriptures *never* equate the events of the Tribulation period to the judgments of the Day of the Lord.

It is also highly significant that while modern Dispensationalists argue that the entire Tribulation period is characterized by God's wrath, they also inexplicably and paradoxically teach that the first half of the Tribulation period will be a time of "peace."[861] For example, **Leon Wood,** while referring specifically to the "tribulation

---

[858] Is.2:19; Is.13:9,20; Is.24:1,3-4,18-21; Zech.14:4; Rv.11:19; Rv.16:17-20.

[859] Is.13:10,13; Is.34:4; Joel 2:30-31; 3:15-16; Zech.14:6; Mt.24:29; Mk.13:24-26; Lk.21: 25-27; Rv.6:12-14.

[860] See Mt.24:27-31; Mk.13:24-27; Lk.21:25-27; Rv.19:11-21.

[861] Based upon their interpretation of Dan.9:27, modern Dispensationalists maintain that the Tribulation period will be seven years long. They divide these seven years of Tribulation into *two* equal parts of three and a half years each. They maintain that the first half will be peaceful due to a peace covenant between Antichrist and Israel. At the midpoint of the Tribulation week, the Antichrist will break his covenant and the "time of Jacob's trouble" will begin. Thus, the second half of the week will be terrible and horrific for both Israel and the world, and is therefore referred to as the "Great Tribulation."

week," maintains that; "...the week will be divided into a first half of *peace* for Israel and a second half of trouble."[862] **Dwight Pentecost** asserts that; "During the first three and a half years of the tribulation period, Israel will be in her land, and Palestine will be at *peace*."[863] And **John Walvoord** contends that, "The opening hours of the day of the Lord do *not contain great events*. *Gradually* the major events of the day of the Lord unfold, *climaxing* in the terrible judgments with the Great Tribulation..."[864] And again, **Walvoord** further explains that, "...the *Day of the Lord* will begin with what seems to be a *time of peace*. The three and a half years preceding the Great Tribulation will be a *time of relative peace* as compared to a time of war. When the Great Tribulation[865] begins, however, this *time of peace* will abruptly close because the world ruler will break his covenant with Israel..."[866]

Really? The first three and a half years of the Day of the Lord will be a *"time of relative peace?"* This statement represents an astounding contradiction in terms – the events of the Day of the Lord do *not* harmonize with the word "peace." Furthermore, the Scriptures do *not* support the claim that the *"Day of the Lord"* will *"gradually unfold,"* finally *"climaxing"* some seven years after it has begun! There is no possible way that a literal reading of the Biblical passages describing the scope, sequence and nature of the Day of the Lord can be harmonized with this Dispensational scenario. Rather, the Scriptures consistently portray the Day of the Lord as a time of catastrophic judgment that will surprise and terrify the wicked and unbelieving world (Lk.17:26-30 cp. Rv.6:15-17), when the sky is rolled up like a scroll (Rv.6:14 cp. Is.2:10, 19-21) and they behold the Coming of the Lord Jesus Christ with all the angels of heaven (2Thess.1:7-10; Mt.16:27; 25:31). The entire Dispensational scenario is nothing more than a desperate attempt to rescue the pretribulation rapture doctrine from the reality of a post-tribulational Day of the Lord.

Furthermore, the entire Dispensational scheme is refuted by the very words that Dispensationalists use to support it! The Dispensational proposition that the first half of

---

[862] *The Bible and Future Events* – Leon J. Wood, Zondervan Publishing House, 1974, p.60.
[863] *Will Man Survive?* – J. Dwight Pentecost, Zondervan Publishing House, 1980, p.42.
[864] *The Rapture Question* - John F. Walvoord, Zondervan Publishing House, 1979, p.222.
[865] Note that the term *Great Tribulation* is used by Dispensationalists to refer to the *last* three and a half years of the seven year Tribulation period.
[866] *Major Bible Prophecies* – John F. Walvoord, Zondervan Publishing House, 1994, p.416.

the "Tribulation" will be "peaceful" is itself oxymoronic. There is no such thing as a "peaceful" period of "tribulation." The word "tribulation" is *thlipsis*.[867] It denotes severe trials, affliction, anguish and suffering. The word is inconsistent with the concept of "peace," which denotes a state of calm and tranquility, free from conflict and aggression. To describe the first three and a half years of the "Tribulation period" as "a time of relative peace" is an obvious and ridiculous contradiction in terms that completely ignores the literal meaning of the words "peace" and "tribulation." Again, there is no such thing as a peaceful Tribulation! The entire Dispensational argument is both contradictory and ludicrous!

5. The Unanticipated Contradictions Created by the Dispensational Solution to the *Post*-Tribulational Nature of the Day of the Lord.

Early Dispensationalists accepted the fact that the *start* of the Day of the Lord coincided with the *post*-tribulational Coming of Jesus Christ at the very end of the Tribulation. However, modern Dispensationalists eventually realized that acceptance of a *post*-tribulational Day of the Lord seriously jeopardized their argument for a *pre*tribulational rapture. This was due to the close contextual relationship between the *parousia* of Christ, the *rapture* of the Church (1Thess.4:13-18) and the *post*-tribulational *Day of the Lord* depicted in 1Thess.5:1-10 and 2Thess.1:6-10; 2:1-10. Thus, the legitimacy of a *pre*tribulational rapture was called into serious question. However, Dispensationalists attempted to resolve this problem by expanding the scope of the Day of the Lord. Instead of viewing the Day of the Lord as a "unique day" at the end of the Tribulational period (Zech.14:1-8) they argued that the Day of the Lord *included* the entire seven-year Tribulational period. Thus, Dispensationalists arbitrarily moved the *start* of the Day of the Lord from the visible, glorious Second Coming at the *end* of the Tribulation, to a supposed secret, unannounced, Coming at the *beginning* of the Tribulation. While the purpose of this change in the scope of the Day of the Lord was to rescue the concept of the *pre*tribulational rapture, it actually created a serious contradiction.

---

[867] "θλίψις [*thlipsis*]…a pressing, pressing together, pressure…oppression, affliction, tribulation, distress, straits…" *A Greek-English Lexicon of the New Testament* – Joseph Henry Thayer, T&T Clark, 1954, p.291.
Also, "θλίψις…pressure, compression; metaphorically affliction, distress of mind, 2Cor.2:4; distressing circumstances, trial, affliction, Mat.24.9." *The Analytical Greek Lexicon Revised* – Harold K. Moulton, Zondervan Publishing House, 1982, p.195

First, look carefully at **2Thessalonians 2:3-4**, which declares,

"Let no one in any way deceive you, for *it will not come* [i.e., *the Day of the Lord* [868]] unless the apostasy comes **first**, and the man of lawlessness is **revealed**, the son of destruction," (Emphasis added).

This verse clearly states that *two things* must occur **before** the Day of the Lord can come. There must be an "apostasy"[869] and the "man of lawlessness"[870] must be "revealed."[871] The word "apostasy" here denotes a rejection of Christian orthodoxy and the acceptance of false teaching. There is an obvious connection here between the Day of the LORD, the onset of the apostasy and the revealing of the Antichrist whose "signs and false wonders" will deceive those who did not truly believe the truth, but instead "took pleasure in wickedness" (2Thess.2:9-12 cp. Mt.24:24). Paul clearly tells us that this "man of lawlessness" will be "revealed" *when* "...he takes his seat in the temple of God, displaying himself as being God" (v.3-4, cp. Mt.24:15-21, "the abomination of desolation" referred to by Jesus).

---

[868] "Except there come a falling away. Before *except* insert in translation *the day shall not come.* Such ellipses are common in Paul." *Vincent's Word Studies in the New Testament* – Marvin R. Vincent, Hendrickson Publishers, n.d., vol.IV, p.63. Also, "The words in italics, '*it will not be,*' [KJV] are rightly supplied by the translators to complete the sentence which Paul leaves unfinished...The crucial day of the Lord will *not* come 'except the falling away come first, and the man of sin be revealed.'" *The Thessalonian Epistles* - D. Edmond Hiebert, Moody Press, 1982, p.305. And again, "There is an ellipse here...The meaning is clear...The second coming...will *not* take place before certain important things take place...Except the falling away come first...It seems clear that the word here means a religious revolt...And the man of sin be revealed...He seems to be the Antichrist of 1John 2:18...who is doing the work of Satan." *Word Pictures in the New Testament* – Archibald Thomas Robertson, Broadman Press, 1931, vol. IV, p.49-50.

[869] "2Thess.2:3 refers to the anticipated 'apostasy' or 'rebellion' of the last days when many would abandon the faith." *Expository Dictionary of Bible Words* – Stephen D. Renn, Hendrickson Publishers, 2005, p.411. Also, "Christian Greek. Here apostasia is always religious apostasy...St. Paul...taught that before the Lord's Coming there would be an apostasy in conjunction with the manifestation of an evil personage, the Man of Sin (2Th.2:3)." *Christian Words* – Nigel Turner, Thomas Nelson Publishers, 1982, pp.20-21. And again, "ἀποστασία [apostasia]...a falling away, defection, apostasy; in the Bible...from true religion: Acts 21:21; 2Th.2:3." *A Greek-English Lexicon of the New Testament* – Joseph Henry Thayer, T&T Clark, 1954, p.67.

[870] "ἀνομία [anomia]...lawlessness; violation of law." *The Analytical Greek Lexicon Revised* – Harold K. Moulton, Zondervan Publishing House, 1982, p.31. Also, "ἀνομία...the condition of one without law...contempt and violation of law, iniquity, wickedness...Mt.23:28; 24:12; 2Th.2:3." *A Greek-English Lexicon of the New Testament* – Joseph Henry Thayer, T&T Clark, 1954, p.48.

[871] The word *reveal* is; "ἀποκαλύπτω [apokalupto]...uncover; to reveal...to be plainly signified, distinctly declared...to be manifested, appear...2Thess.2:3,6,8." *The Analytical Greek Lexicon Revised* – Harold K. Moulton, Zondervan Publishing House, 1982, p.42. Also, "ἀποκαλύπτω...to uncover, lay open what has been veiled or covered up; to disclose, make bare...to make known, make manifest, disclose what before was unknown...of Antichrist, 2Th.2:3,6,8." *A Greek-English Lexicon of the New Testament* – Joseph Henry Thayer, T&T Clark, 1954, p.62.

The text clearly states that ***before the coming of the Day of the Lord*** there will be first-of-all a wholesale rejection of Christian truth and second, the true character and identity of the Antichrist will be made known to believers when he takes his seat in the temple of God and declares himself to be God. Now then, if the ***start*** of the **Day of the Lord** coincides with the ***beginning*** of the seven-year Tribulation as Dispensationalists maintain, then this necessarily means that the Antichrist will enter the temple of God and declare himself to be "God" ***before the beginning of the Tribulation.*** Dispensationalists attempt to solve this problem by resorting to their failsafe practice of **"doubling"** their way out of difficulty. Dispensationalists simply argue that there is more than one "revealing" of the Antichrist and that the "revealing" referred to by Paul in 2Thessalonians 2:3-4, describes only one of several other "revelations" of the man of sin mentioned in Scripture.

For example, **John Walvoord** maintains that the "man of lawlessness" will;

"...***first be revealed*** as the conqueror of three of the ten countries that had previously been banded together politically. This will occur ***more than seven years before*** the second coming of Christ."[872]

Walvoord further explains that;

"...the man of sin…is ***revealed*** when the seven-year covenant is made with Israel, it may ***not be clear that he is the one described in Scripture as the coming world ruler*** until he breaks his covenant with Israel and begins the Great Tribulation (2Thess.2:3-4)."[873]

In other words, Dispensationalists maintain that while the Antichrist will be "revealed," ***before*** the start of the seven year Tribulation period, no one will actually recognize him as the Antichrist until the middle of the Tribulation, when he takes his seat in the temple of God and displays himself as being God, as described in 2Thessalonians 2:3-4.[874] The problem for Dispensationalists is that the word "reveal" means to disclose, to uncover,

---

[872] *Major Bible Prophecies* – John F. Walvoord, Zondervan Publishing House, 1994, p.322.
[873] *Major Bible Prophecies* – John F. Walvoord, Zondervan Publishing House, 1994, p.417.
[874] Dispensationalists uniformly maintain that the "Great Tribulation," starts in the *middle* of the seven year Tribulation period when the Antichrist seats himself in the rebuilt Temple in Jerusalem, declaring himself to be God, thereby breaking his "peace treaty" with the nation of Israel.

to make apparent, to make known."[875] The Dispensational argument that the Antichrist will be "made known" and at the same time remain "unknown" is both contradictory and nonsensical. When the Antichrist is "revealed" he is made "known" and Paul plainly states in 2Thessalonians 2:1-4, that this "revealing" of the Antichrist occurs **before** the start of the Day of the Lord, **when** he takes his seat in the temple of God and declares himself to be God! Paul's chronology harmonizes perfectly with a post-tribulational view of Scripture that, (a) first sees the start of the Tribulation period, (b) then the revealing of the Antichrist at some time during the Tribulation, and (c) the Second Coming (i.e., the **parousia**) of Jesus Christ at the end of the Tribulation which is referred to as the Day of the LORD.

Thus, in an attempt to rescue the pretribulation rapture doctrine from the obvious post-tribulational context of the Day of the Lord, Dispensationalists have unjustifiably expanded the scope of the Day of the Lord to include the entire seven-year Tribulation period. However, this unwarranted change unintentionally places the apostasy and the revealing of the Antichrist described in 2Thessalonians 2:3-4, **before** the start of the Tribulation itself. This has forced Dispensationalists to resort to their "doubling methodology" by insisting that there are other "revelations" of the "man of lawlessness." [876] However, the multiplication of hypothetical "revealing's" of the Antichrist does **not** solve the dilemma. The real problem for Dispensationalists is that Paul emphatically states that the "man of lawlessness" will be "revealed" **when,** "…he takes his seat in the temple of God, displaying himself as being God" (v.4). Dispensationalists are faced with the troublesome fact that Paul clearly states that the Antichrist will enter the temple of God and declare himself to be God **before** the **start of the Day of the Lord**. Dispensationalists have created an irreconcilable contradiction by asserting that the **start** of the Day of the Lord coincides with the **start** of the Tribulation period, thus placing the revelation of the Antichrist **before** the beginning of the Tribulation! Clearly, this Dispensational scenario is contrary to the plain statements of the Scriptures which unmistakably places the Day of the LORD at the **end** of the Tribulational period and **not** the beginning!

---

[875] See footnote 871 for definition of the word **reveal** (ἀποκαλύπτω - apokalupto).

[876] The Dispensational argument that the Antichrist will be **revealed** – that is "made known," when he conquers three of ten European nations comprising a revived Roman Empire or when he makes a peace covenant with Israel is highly speculative and is clearly at odds with the plain meaning of 2Thessalonians 2:1-4.

Second, look carefully at **Joel 2:30-31**, which declares;

"And I will display wonders in the sky and on the earth, blood, fire, and columns of smoke. The sun will be turned into darkness, and the moon into blood, **before** the great and awesome day of the LORD comes." (Emphasis added).

If the Day of the Lord starts at the beginning of the seven year Tribulation as Dispensationalists assert, then the astronomical disturbances and disorders described by Joel must occur sometime **before** the start of the seven year Tribulation period. But these astronomical signs are clearly depicted in Scripture as **post**-tribulational events that immediately precede the glorious, visible Coming of Jesus Christ **after** the Tribulation. They are never portrayed as **pre**tribulational events![877] Furthermore, the parallel text of Joel 3:12-16 clearly places these astronomical disturbances referred to in Joel 2:30-31, at the **post**-tribulational Day of the Lord. Look carefully at the text;

"Let the nations be aroused and come up to the valley of Jehoshaphat, for there I will sit to judge all the surrounding nations. Put in the sickle, for the harvest is ripe. Come, tread, for the winepress is full; the vats overflow, for their wickedness is great. Multitudes, multitudes in the valley of decision! For the **day of the Lord** is near in the valley of decision. The **sun and moon grow dark, and the stars lose their brightness**. And the Lord roars from Zion and utters His voice from Jerusalem, and the heavens and the earth tremble." Joel 3:12-16 (Emphasis added).

According to Joel, these cataclysmic astronomical events immediately **precede** the start of the Day of the Lord, which according to Joel, is the time when God judges the surrounding nations which have come up against His people, Israel. Joel clearly places this judgment of the nations at the end of the Tribulation – **not** at its beginning.[878] The Dispensational assertion that the Day of the Lord begins at the start of the Tribulation inadvertently places these great astronomical displays and the subsequent judgments at the start of the Tribulation period. This is impossible and only serves to underscore the implausibility of the pretribulation rapture theory as well as the serious contradictions which result when the concept of a secret, pretribulational rapture is forced upon the Scriptures.

Third, look carefully at **Malachi 4:5**, which declares;

---

[877] Look carefully at Mt.24:29; Mk.13:24-26; Lk.21:25-27; Rv.6:12-17.
[878] Compare Joel 2:30-31 and 3:12-16 with Rv.6:12-17; 11:15-18; 19:11-16.

"Behold, I am going to send you Elijah the prophet **before** the coming of the great and terrible day of the LORD. And he will restore the hearts of the fathers to their children, and the hearts of the children to their fathers, lest I come and smite the land with a curse. (Emphasis added).

Dispensationalists commonly teach that one of the two witnesses depicted in Revelation 11:1-13, is Elijah the prophet.[879] Scripture reveals that these two witnesses will prophesy for "twelve hundred and sixty days" (v.3), which is three and a half years.[880] They will have the power to destroy all who would attempt to harm them (v.5), as-well-as to cause severe droughts, to turn water into blood, and to afflict the earth with various and sundry plagues (v.6). They will ultimately be killed by the beast (v.7), their bodies will lie unburied for three-and-a-half days, while the nations rejoice over their demise (v.8). Then, they will miraculously arise from the dead and ascend into heaven while their enemies watch in amazement and fear (vv.11-12).

Dispensationalists maintain that the *Day of the LORD* starts at the *beginning* of the seven year Tribulation period. Malachi 4:5 clearly states that the LORD will send the prophet Elijah "*before* the great and terrible day of the LORD." (Emphasis added). This means that the supernatural judgments wrought by the two witnesses must occur *before* the beginning of the Tribulation period! This of course is untenable.

6. The Revised Dispensational Solution: "Two" Days of the Lord.

In an attempt to rescue the pretribulation rapture doctrine from the obvious post-tribulational context of the Day of the Lord, Dispensationalists initially expanded the

---

[879] For example, "Many expositors believe that one of these two witnesses can be identified with Elijah, here returned to earth at this future time." *The Bible and Future Events* – Leon J. Wood, Zondervan Publishing House, 1974, p.130. And, "Those who hold the view that these will be men who lived previously hold that one of the two witnesses will be Elijah." *Things To Come* – J. Dwight Pentecost, Zondervan Publishing House. 1964, p.306. And, "…it seems more than likely that Elijah is one of the two witnesses." *Revelation: Illustrated and Made Plain* – Tim F. LaHaye, Zondervan Publishing House, 1974, p.206. And again, "Most students…who believe that the two witnesses are persons, are agreed that one of them is Elijah." *The Book of the Revelation* - Lehman Strauss, Loizeaux Brothers, 1977, p.215.

[880] Note that "twelve hundred and sixty days" is equivalent to "forty-two months" or "three and a half years." This is based upon the use of lunar months of 30 days instead of solar months. Thus, 1260 days, divided by 30 days, equals 42 months, divided by 12 months, equals 3.5 years. See Rv.11:2-3 & 13:5. It would also seem that the phrase "a time and times and half a time" (Rv.12:14 cp. Dan.7:25, 12:7) is also equivalent to 3.5 years. Note also that, "The terms for 'month' and 'moon' have the same close connection in the Hebrew language, as in our own and in Indo-European languages generally…" *Dr. William Smith's Dictionary of the Bible* – Baker Book House, 1870 edition reprinted 1971, vol.III, p.2004.

scope of the Day of the Lord to include the entire Tribulation period. However, by moving the start of the Day of the Lord from the *end* of the Tribulation to the *beginning* of the Tribulation, Dispensationalists inadvertently created chronological problems pertaining to the revealing of the Antichrist (2Thess.2:1-4), the onset of the catastrophic end-time celestial signs (Joel 2:30-31; 3:12-16) and the appearance of Elijah the prophet (Mal.4:5). To resolve these glaring contradictions, Dispensationalists have resorted to their most important methodology - the *doubling* of key Bible doctrines.[881] As in so many other instances, when the plain sense of Scripture presents exegetical problems for the all-important pretribulation rapture doctrine, Dispensationalists attempt to escape from the difficulty by simply *doubling* the doctrine in question. Using their *doubling methodology*, Dispensationalists attempt to escape from the "plain, ordinary and literal meaning" of Joel 2:30-31; 3:12-16 and Malachi 4:5, as-well-as the post-tribulational context of 1Thessalonians 5:1-11 and 2Thessalonians 2:1-2, by claiming that there are *two* different and distinct Days of the Lord revealed in Scripture. The *first* "Day" is referred to as the "*broad*" Day of the Lord, which will include the entire seven year Tribulation period. The *second* "Day" is referred to as the "*narrow*" Day of the Lord, which is confined to the very end of the Tribulation when Christ visibly returns in glory and judgment.

Not surprisingly, Dispensationalists contend that the prophecies of both Joel 2:30-31 and 3:12-16, and Malachi 4:5, refer to the "*narrow*" Day of the Lord and *not* to the "*broad*" Day of the Lord. This allows them to defend the pretribulation rapture doctrine by arguing that the prophecies of Joel and Malachi will find their fulfillment *before* the *narrow* Day of the Lord at the *end* of the Tribulation and *not before* the Broad Day of the Lord at the *beginning* of the Tribulation.[882]

Conversely, Dispensationalists assert that Paul's references to the Day of the Lord in 1Thessalonians 5:1-11, and 2Thessalonians 2:1-2, refers to the "*broad*" Day of the Lord and *not* to the "*narrow*" Day of the Lord. Dispensationalists assert that Paul is referring

---

[881] See Chapter 5, Section I, regarding the Dispensational practice of doubling key Bible doctrines in their defense of the pretribulation rapture doctrine.

[882] "...Joel 2:31 refers to the *narrow* Day when Christ comes to earth. It does *not* refer to the *broad Day*...Malachi's great and terrible Day of the Lord is also the *narrow* Day...Malachi indicated that God will send Elijah before the *narrow* Day (4:5), *not* before the *broad* Day..." *Maranatha Our Lord Come!*-Renald E. Showers, The Friends of Israel Gospel Ministry, Inc., 1995, pp.38,40.

to the *pre*tribulational Coming of Christ *before* the start of the *"broad"* Day of the Lord, and *not* to the *post*-tribulational Coming of Christ at the *"narrow"* Day of the Lord.[883] This allows them to readily accept the obvious contextual relationship between the Day of the Lord, the rapture of the Church and the Coming of Christ without forfeiting the concept of a *pre*tribulation rapture.

6a. The Theory of "Two" Days of the Lord Explained.

Renald Showers is one of the primary originators and proponents of this novel new theory. His claim that, "...there will be *two Days of the Lord*"[884] is based upon several significant assumptions. To begin with, **Showers *assumes*** that the Day of the Lord will have a *dual nature*. He states that;

"The Scriptures *indicate* that the future Day of the Lord will have at least a *twofold nature*. First, it will be characterized by *darkness* and a tremendous outpouring of divine wrath upon the world...Second, the Day of the Lord will also be characterized by *light*, an outpouring of divine blessing, and the administration of God's rule."[885]

To substantiate this claim, **Showers** points to Zechariah 14:1-9, observing that,

"...the Prophet Zechariah, after discussing the Day of the Lord (14:1-5)...*indicated* that although the earlier part of 'that day' will be characterized by *darkness*, the latter part will be characterized by *light* (vv.6-7), great blessing (v.8), and God's rule over all the earth (v.9)."[886]

However, a close look at the text of Zechariah 14:1-9 will confirm that Zechariah is clearly referring to a post-tribulational Coming of Jesus Christ and the events that will coincide with that Coming. All of the events referred to by **Showers** are said to occur on "that day" (vv.6,8,9) - that is "that day" when the Lord "...will gather all the nations against Jerusalem to battle..." and "...the LORD will go forth and fight against those nations..." when "...in *that day* His feet will stand upon the Mount of Olives..." (Zech

[883] "...the major subject of 1Thessalonians 5:1-11 is the *broad* Day of the Lord..." And again, "...in 2Thessalonians 2:1-2...Paul...taught the Thessalonians that Christ would come to rapture the church *before*...the *broad* Day of the Lord begins..." *Maranatha Our Lord Come!*-Renald E. Showers, The Friends of Israel Gospel Ministry, Inc., 1995, pp.199, 227-228.
[884] *Maranatha Our Lord Come!*-Renald E. Showers, The Friends of Israel Gospel Ministry, Inc., 1995, p.39.
[885] *Maranatha Our Lord Come!*-Renald E. Showers, The Friends of Israel Gospel Ministry, Inc., 1995, p.32.
[886] *Maranatha Our Lord Come!*-Renald E. Showers, The Friends of Israel Gospel Ministry, Inc., 1995, p.32.

14:1-4). There is no mention, description or indication of "two" different Days of the Lord. There is no mention of a **broad** or **narrow** Day of the Lord. There is only one day depicted - a "unique day" (v.7), which begins with the Advent of Christ (vv.3-4), and results in deliverance and blessing for His people (vv.9-11) and complete destruction and ruin for His enemies (vv.12-13).

Additionally, **Showers** points to Genesis 1:4-6, asserting that,

"Just as each day of creation and the Jewish day consisted of *two phases* - a time of darkness (evening) followed by a time of light (day), Gen.1:4-6 - so the future Day of the Lord will consist of *two phases*, a period of *darkness (judgment)* followed by a period of *light (divine rule and blessing)*."[887]

Thus, **Showers**, *assumes* that because the literal 24-hour day is divided into two parts - night (darkness) and day (light) - the future apocalyptic Day of the Lord will also be divided into two parts - darkness corresponding to Divine judgment and daylight corresponding to Divine blessing. However, this interpretation is far from literal. It is actually completely allegorical. It certainly does not take the words of Scripture at their "plain, literal and ordinary meaning." It is extremely difficult to see how a literal 24-hour day prefigures the future eschatological Day of the Lord, which will be "a unique day" (Zech.14:7) with "none like it" (Jer.30:7). There is absolutely nothing in either the text or the context of Zech.14:1-9 or Genesis 1:4-6 that indicates that the Day of the Lord will have a *"twofold nature"* and therefore *"two distinct phases."* Nor is there anything in these verses that indicates that the literal 24-hour days of Creation prefigure the apocalyptic Day of the Lord. The interpretation rests upon nothing more than unrestrained imagination and unbridled speculation.

Based upon his assumptions that the Day of the Lord will have a *"twofold nature,"* and *"two distinct phases,"* **Showers** then presumes that the Day of the Lord will also have a *"double sense."* He states;

"We have seen that the Day of the Lord will have a *twofold nature* and therefore, *two phases*. In addition...the biblical expression 'the Day of the Lord' has a *double sense (broad and narrow)* in relationship to the future. The *broad sense* refers to an extended period of time involving divine

---

[887]*Maranatha Our Lord Come!*-Renald E. Showers, The Friends of Israel Gospel Ministry, Inc., 1995, p.33.

interventions related at least to the 70th week of Daniel and the thousand year millennium...the **narrow sense** refers to one specific day - the day on which Christ will return to the earth from heaven with His angels."[888]

Showers justifies this assertion by reasoning that;

"Just as the word day in Genesis 1:5 has both a ***broad sense*** (a 24-hour day – 'And the evening and the morning were the first day') and a ***narrow sense*** (the light part of a 24-hour day in contrast with the darkness part – 'And God called the light Day, and the darkness he called Night') - so the expression 'the Day of the Lord' has a ***broad*** and a ***narrow*** sense in relationship to the future."[889]

Showers refers to the "broad sense" as ***the broad Day of the Lord*** and the "narrow sense" as ***the narrow Day of the Lord.***[890]

Showers further explains that;

"There is a genuine sense in which the ***narrow*** Day of the Lord will be a complete Day of the Lord on its own. It will be ***different*** from the ***broad*** Day of the Lord and will take place after a significant part of the broad Day of the Lord has run its course. Thus, there will be ***two Days of the Lord.***"[891]

Showers then contends that;

"The ***broad*** Day of the Lord will start at the beginning of the 70th week of Daniel" and "...will at least cover and include the entire 70th week."[892]

However, according to **Showers**;

"...the ***narrow*** Day is the day of Christ's coming to the earth...the ***narrow*** Day will be the grand climax of the ***judgment phase of the broad day.***"[893]

[888] *Maranatha Our Lord Come!*- Renald E. Showers, The Friends of Israel Gospel Ministry, Inc., 1995, p.35

[889]*Maranatha Our Lord Come!*-Renald E. Showers, The Friends of Israel Gospel Ministry, Inc., 1995, p.35.

[890] See discussion on pages 35-40 in *Maranatha Our Lord Come!* - Renald E. Showers, The Friends of Israel Gospel Ministry, Inc., 1995, p.37.

[891] *Maranatha Our Lord Come!*-Renald E. Showers, The Friends of Israel Gospel Ministry, Inc., 1995, p.39.

[892] *Maranatha Our Lord Come!*-Renald E. Showers, The Friends of Israel Gospel Ministry, Inc., 1995, pp.71,72.

[893] *Maranatha Our Lord Come!*-Renald E. Showers, The Friends of Israel Gospel Ministry, Inc., 1995, p.39.

Thus, according to **Showers**, the *broad* Day of the Lord will begin at the same time as the Tribulation (i.e., the 70th week of Daniel) and continue throughout the entire seven year Tribulation period and then extend into the Millennium, whereas, the *narrow* Day of the Lord will be confined to the very end of the Tribulation period when Christ appears in judgment, bringing the *"judgment phase"* of the *broad* Day of the Lord to a close.

For the sake of clarity, here is a recap of the salient points of **Showers'** mind-numbing teaching.

[1] The Day of the Lord will have a *twofold nature* characterized by *darkness* and *light*.

[2] The *twofold nature* of the Day of the Lord is based upon the observation that a literal 24-hour day has *two phases* - light and darkness. The *darkness phase* corresponds to Divine judgment. The *light phase* corresponds to Divine blessing.

[3] The Day of the Lord also has a *double sense - broad and narrow*.

[4] The *broad* Day of the Lord begins at the same time as the Tribulation. The Tribulation period is referred to as the *darkness phase* or *judgment phase* of the *broad* Day of the Lord.

[5] The *narrow* Day of the Lord refers specifically to the Second Coming of Christ at the end of the Tribulation. The *narrow* Day of the Lord ends the *darkness phase* or *judgment phase* (i.e., the Tribulation period) of the *broad* Day of the Lord.

[6] After the close of the *darkness phase* or *judgment phase* (i.e., the Tribulation period) of the *broad* Day of the Lord, the *light phase* or *blessing phase* (i.e., the Millennium) of the *broad* Day of the Lord begins.

The sole purpose for this incredibly complex and convoluted teaching of *two* Days of the Lord is to rescue the pretribulation rapture teaching from the plain, ordinary and literal statements of Scripture that flatly refute the entire concept of a pretribulational rapture. By *doubling* the Day of the Lord, Dispensationalists attempt to nullify the obvious *post*-tribulational context of 1Thessalonians 5:1-11; 2Thessalonians 2:1-4; Joel 2:30-31; Joel 3:12-16 and Malachi 4:5.

6b. The Textual Basis for the Dispensational Doctrine of *"Two"* Days of the Lord.

The entire Dispensational argument for two Days of the Lord rests upon the assertion that Paul's reference to the Day of the Lord in 1Thessalonians 5:1-2 and 2Thessalonians 2:1-2 refers to a *broad* Day of the Lord. However, the simple fact of the matter is that Paul simply refers to "the day of the Lord" without utilizing the qualifying terms "broad" or "narrow." In other words, there is absolutely no contextual or textual indication that Paul is referring to anything but the *post*-tribulational "Day of the Lord" when the Lord Jesus Christ will be revealed in glory and judgment! Yet, Dispensationalists insist that Paul's reference to "the day of the Lord" must be understood in a "broad" sense. For example, **Renald Showers** claims that,

"...the major subject of 1Thessalonians 5:1-11 is the *broad* Day of the Lord..."[894]

So what exactly is the textual basis for this Dispensational claim that Paul's reference to "the day of the Lord" in 1Thessalonians 5:2 refers to a *broad* Day of the Lord? **Renald Showers** attempts to provide a textual basis for his claim when he rhetorically asks;

"When will the *broad* Day of the Lord begin? A significant passage, 1Thessalonians 5, provides an answer to this question. The Apostle Paul began with a reference to *'the times'* (the spans or periods of time) and *'the seasons'* (the decisive or turning points of time) that God determined to accomplish His purpose for world history. In this way, Paul introduced his major subject of verses 1-11 - the *broad* Day of the Lord, *a significant future span of time* that will include *a major turning point of history* (the destruction of the rule of Satan and rebellious mankind...and the restoration of God's theocratic kingdom rule over the world system)..."[895]

Incredibly, it is from Paul's reference to "the times and the seasons" in 1Thessalonians 5:1, that **Showers** derives the doctrine of *two* Days of the Lord. He does this by equating Paul's phrase, "the times" to "*a significant future span of time*" (i.e., the

---

[894] *Maranatha Our Lord Come!* - Renald E. Showers, The Friends of Israel Gospel Ministry, Inc., 1995, p.199.
[895] *Maranatha Our Lord Come!* - Renald E. Showers, The Friends of Israel Gospel Ministry, Inc., 1995, pp.58-59,

broad Day of the Lord) and the phrase "the seasons" to "*a major turning point of history*" (i.e., the *narrow* Day of the Lord). Thus, according to **Showers**, the textual basis for a *broad* and *narrow* Day of the Lord is derived from the words "times" and "seasons." However, the word "times" (*chronos*), simply refers to the duration or chronological measurement of a period of time, whereas, the word "seasons" (*kairos*), refers to the nature and quality that is characteristic of a period of time.[896]

In First Thessalonians 5:1-2, Paul's purpose is to remind the Thessalonians that they *already knew everything necessary* about the future Day of the Lord. He declares;

"Now as to the *times [chronos – i.e., the duration]* and the *seasons [kairos - i.e., the quality and characteristics]*, brethren, you have *no need of anything to be written to you*. For you yourselves *know full well* that the day of the Lord will come just like a thief in the night..." [897] (Emphasis added).

The Thessalonians had already been instructed as to the "times and the seasons" - that is, they were already aware of *the duration* as well as *the unique quality and characteristics* of the **Day of the Lord**. Paul was therefore, simply reminding them of what they already knew (vv.2-11).[898] Paul was certainly not introducing a new doctrine of two distinct and different Days of the Lord by the phrase "the times and the seasons." The argument that the phrase "the times and the seasons" refers to two different Days of the Lord is completely foreign to the text. The concept is forced upon the text, not fairly

---

[896] "Times (*chronoi*) – the general term for chronological periods...Seasons (*kairoi*) – the opportune times...*Time* denotes quantity; *season* quality." *A Commentary on the Old and New Testaments* – Robert Jamieson, A.R. Fausett, David Brown, Hendrickson Publishers, 1997, vol.3, p.466. "Kairos (καιρὸς)...a period possessed of certain characteristics...Chronos (χρόνος)...denotes a space of time...it implies duration..." *An Expository Dictionary of New Testament Words* – W.E. Vine, Thomas Nelson Publishers, n.d., pp.1004-1005. "καιρὸς [*kairos*]...a limited period of time marked by a suitableness of circumstances, a fitting season." *The Analytical Greek Lexicon Revised* – Harold K. Moulton, Zondervan Publishing House, 1982, pp.208-209. "καιρὸς [*kairos*]...the sense of a fixed and definite period, time, season... χρόνος [*chronos*], time in the sense of duration." *A Manual Greek Lexicon of the New Testament* – G. Abbott-Smith, Charles Scribner's Sons, 1953, p.226. "καιρὸς [*kairos*] is the *suitable* time, χρόνος [*chronos*] the time *measured by duration*." *Vincent's Word Studies in the New Testament* – Marvin R. Vincent, Hendrickson Publishers, n.d., vol. IV, p.43.

[897] "*But of the times and the seasons*; The reference here is to the coming of the Lord Jesus, and to the various events connected with his advent;...*Ye have no need that I write unto you*. That is, they had received all the information on the particular point to which he refers, which was necessary they should have." *Barnes' Notes on the New Testament* – Albert Barnes, Baker Books, 2001, *The First Epistle to the Thessalonians*, p.52.

[898] With respect to the *parousia* of Christ, the gathering together of the saints, the Day of the Lord and the revealing of the Antichrist, consider Paul's statement in 2Thessalonians 2:5, "Do you not remember that while I was still with you, I was telling you these things?"

extracted from it. The text makes no mention of a **broad** or **narrow** Day of the Lord. Neither the concept nor the terminology is present. It is highly significant, that throughout the entire Old Testament, the Day of the Lord is always depicted as a cataclysmic *post*-tribulational event. The Apostle Paul, "a Hebrew of Hebrews" and "as to the Law, a Pharisee" (Phil.3:5), was certainly well-acquainted with these Scriptures and the *post*-tribulational nature of the Day of the Lord. The fact that Paul uses the phrase, "day of the Lord" twice (1Thess.5:2; 2Thess.2:2) without the qualifying terms "**broad**" or "**narrow**" certainly calls the entire scheme of *two* different and distinct Days of the Lord into serious question. Clearly, Paul new of only *one* Day of the Lord – the *one* that coincides with the Second Advent of Jesus Christ *after* the Tribulation.

This Dispensational teaching of *two* Days of the Lord is a new and novel doctrine unknown in the recorded history of the Church. It is a very recent invention designed to preserve and protect the pretribulation rapture doctrine from the "plain, literal and ordinary" meaning of the Scriptures. This complicated and convoluted teaching graphically illustrates the unbelievable lengths to which the proponents of the secret rapture teaching are willing to go in their defense of a doctrine upon which the Scriptures themselves are completely silent!

Conclusion

The New Testament Scriptures do *not* teach a pretribulational Coming of Jesus Christ or a pretribulational rapture of the Church. Dispensationalists have *not* derived their concept of a pretribulation rapture from a literal interpretation of the Biblical text as claimed. Rather, the entire concept is based solely upon imagination, speculation, assumption and inference - *not* the literal statements of Scripture.

The whole pretribulation rapture theory rests upon two preposterous interpretative principles – Inference, and Dispensationalizing the New Testament Scriptures, and one enormous assumption - Imminence.

Inference

The simple fact of the matter is that there is not one New Testament verse that describes a pretribulational *parousia* of Jesus Christ – not one! There is not one New Testament verse that describes a pretribulational rapture of the Church – not one! These two irrefutable facts create a serious problem for the concept of a pretribulational rapture. After all, how do you reasonably promote a doctrine that is never mentioned in Scripture and was unknown for 1,800 years of Church history? The answer: The use of *inference.* The Dispensational argument for the pretribulation rapture is *not* based upon what the Scriptures are plainly and straightforwardly saying. Rather the entire theory is supported and advanced by nothing more than human imagination, speculation and assumption. The entire argument for the pretribulational rapture rests solely upon what Dispensationalists *imagine* the Scriptures are *implying* – *not* what the Scriptures are literally saying!

Dispensationalizing the New Testament Scriptures

While Dispensationalists have no problem advancing doctrines that are never mentioned in Scripture, they frequently find it necessary to explain away what the Scriptures do plainly say and mean. They do this by *"rightly dividing the Word."* This is a euphemistic phrase which refers to the practice of *"dispensationalizing"* the New Testament Scriptures. This is the process whereby Dispensationalists subjectively determine which sections of the New Testament refer to a hypothetical future Jewish remnant and which sections apply to the Church. Dispensationalists defend this startling practice by arguing that large portions of the Gospels and non-Pauline Epistles primarily apply to a future Jewish remnant and therefore have *no direct application* to the Church. This is both an amazing and shocking assertion – but one that is absolutely necessary for the defense of the pretribulation rapture doctrine.

Imminence - An Enormous Assumption

The primary objection raised against the Dispensational proposition of a pretribulational rapture is the fact that there is *not* one New Testament verse that actually describes a pretribulational Coming of Jesus Christ for His Church. The Dispensational response to this significant textual fact is the *assumption of Imminence*. The Dispensational doctrine of Imminence states that the Coming of Jesus Christ to rapture His Church will be a secret, unexpected, unannounced, any moment event. Dispensationalists tacitly argue that the reason why the pretribulational Coming and rapture are *not* specifically mentioned in Scripture is due to the fact that they are secret, unannounced events that could occur at any moment. Thus, the fact that the Scriptures do *not* describe a secret pretribulation rapture, is according to Dispensationalists, proof positive that the rapture will be both secret and pretribulational. This is the ultimate argument from silence!

Doubling Key Bible Doctrines

Dispensationalists have illegitimately forced the concept of a pretribulational rapture upon the Biblical text. Not surprisingly, the proposition that the New Testament teaches an imminent, any moment Coming of Jesus Christ to secretly rapture His Church before the start of the Tribulation period has created numerous textual difficulties for Dispensationalists. Attempts by Dispensationalists to resolve these inconsistencies have in turn led to an incredibly intricate and complex theological system that almost defies understanding. Dispensationalists know no limits in their defense of their all-important pretribulation rapture doctrine. No exegesis is too bizarre - no theory too strange, if the viability of the pretribulation rapture is at risk. Thus, in their development, promotion and defense of the pretribulation rapture doctrine, Dispensationalists have been forced to concoct a disjointed and incoherent end-time scenario that *doubles* numerous key Bible doctrines. This *doubling methodology* is used to resolve numerous textual difficulties created by the pretribulation rapture teaching. For example, in their defense of the pretribulation rapture, Dispensationalists have necessarily divided the people of God into *two* distinct groups – one earthy (the Jews) and the other heavenly (the Church); they have invented *two Second Comings* of Jesus Christ – one before the Tribulation and one after the Tribulation; they have formulated *two different and distinct Gospels* - one declaring God's saving grace, the other declaring political reformation and the establishment of an earthly theocratic kingdom for the Jews; they have devised *two first resurrections* of the righteous – one before the Tribulation for the Church and another after the Tribulation for Israel and the "tribulation saints"; and finally, they have fabricated *two distinct and different Days of the Lord* - one "broad," encompassing the entire Tribulation period and the future Millennium, and the other "narrow," confined to the very end of the Tribulation period when Christ returns in judgment.

Yet, all of these teachings are completely foreign to the plain, simple, straightforward statements of Scripture. Neither the text nor the context of the New Testament suggests *two* different people of God, *two* Second Comings of Jesus Christ, *two* different Gospels, *two* first resurrections or *two* Days of the Lord. None of these teachings are reasonably derived from a literal interpretation of the Scriptures. Rather, they have all been fabricated by Dispensationalists for the singular purpose of rescuing the concept of the secret, any moment pretribulation rapture from the textual problems that the theory itself creates. An honest, reasonable reading of the Scriptures will reveal only *one* Second Coming of Jesus Christ at the end of the Great Tribulation; the preaching of only *one* true Gospel for the salvation of both Jews and Greeks; *one* first resurrection of the righteous dead at the glorious Second Coming of Jesus Christ; and only *one* Day of the Lord, which will commence at the glorious, visible Second Coming of Jesus Christ at the close of the Great Tribulation, when God shall deliver His people, judge the nations and establish His Millennial reign. This then, is the plain, simple, ordinary and literal teaching of the Holy Scriptures that Dispensationalists cannot accept.

Dispensationalists confidently and persuasively offer Christians the comforting promise of exemption from the trials of the Great Tribulation – pleasant and appealing promises that are readily received and embraced by the majority of evangelical Christians in America today. However well intentioned, these Dispensational promises of immunity from suffering are not sanctioned by the Scriptures. Dispensational assurances of escape from the Tribulation are based upon nothing more than an elaborate series of inter-related assumptions, presumptions, analogies, and inferences - *not* the plain, ordinary, literal, straightforward statements of Scripture. Nowhere in the New Testament do we find the promise that Christians are immune from persecution and suffering or that the Church will "escape" the trials of the Great Tribulation via a secret, any moment pretribulation rapture. The entire Dispensational scenario is a cruel fiction that offers a false hope. I realize that this is a disturbing thought for many evangelical Christians. However, as the late **Dr. William J. Erdman**[899] has aptly observed after his careful consideration and subsequent rejection of the any moment rapture theory: *"Better the disappointment of truth than the fair but false promises of error."*[900]

The Scriptures repeatedly warn Christians that persecution is to be expected. Jesus told His disciples, "In the world you have tribulation..." (Jn.16:33). Paul tells believers that it is through "many tribulations that we must enter the kingdom of God" (Acts 14:22) and that we have been called not only to believe in Christ, but "to suffer for His sake" (Phil.1:29). We would do well to remember the example of Jesus Christ (Acts 3:18; Heb.2:10; Heb.5:7-8; Isa.53) - the example of Paul (Acts 20:19-24; 1Cor.4:9-13; 2Cor.4:7-11; 2Cor.11:22-28) - the example of Stephen (Acts 7:59-60) - the example of James (Acts 12:1-2) - and the example of the early Christians (Acts 8:1-2; Rom.8:35-39; Phil.1:29; Heb.10:32-33; 11:37-38; 1Pt.2:20-21; 1Pt.4:12-14,19; 1Pt.5:10).

Dispensationalists understand and accept the fact that Christian can and do suffer. However, they diminish and delimit the significance of these tribulations by claiming that there is an essential difference between *normal* tribulation, which is to be expected, and the *extraordinary* tribulation of the last days. In other words, according to Dispensationalists general tribulation and suffering that is to be expected is somehow less severe than the future tribulation of the last days. However, it is difficult to understand exactly how the persecutions of Imperial Rome; the barbaric Mohammedan invasions of the Middle East and northern Africa; the indescribable cruelty of the Spanish Inquisition; and the brutality of the Papacy's attempts to crush the Reformation, could be less severe for those who suffered and perished than the future persecutions of

---

[899] William Jacob Erdman (1834-1923), was a highly respected and influential Presbyterian minister, and active participant in the early Bible Conference Movement. He was also pastor of the Moody Bible Church and consulting editor for the *Scofield Reference Bible*.
[900] *A Theory Reviewed* - W.J. Erdman, self-published pamphlet, n.d., p.24.

the Antichrist during the Great Tribulation. Exactly how is being killed by the last Antichrist, worse than being killed by former antichrists (1Jn.2:18;22)? How is being beheaded by the last Antichrist worse than being beheaded by Nero? All tribulation, by its very definition is severe! There is no such thing as "mild tribulation." Previous periods of tribulation are limited only in their geographical scope - **not** their intensity. The Great Tribulation will be the worst since man came to be upon the earth (Mt.24:21-22 cp. Dan.12:1) because it will exceed all previous times of persecution in its scope - that is it will engulf the entire world - it will affect all Christians, not just localized groups.

Here then is the perseverance and patience of the saints. Are we mentally and spiritually prepared to drink deeply from the cup of Christ's sufferings? Are we willing, if God so wills, to suffer for truth and righteousness? Do we have the courage to confront evil - to stand steadfast and immovable against satanic deception and lies? Are we willing, if need be, to sacrifice **all** for our Lord and Savior Jesus Christ? (Acts 20:24; Rv.12:11).

Appendix A
Biographical Sketches of Authors Quoted

Blackstone, William Eugene a.k.a. **W.E.B. (1841-1935)** was affiliated with the U.S. Christian Commission during the Civil War. After the war ended he became a successful businessman. Blackstone was also a lay member of the Methodist Episcopal Church and his intense interest in Bible prophecy prompted him to write the best-selling book, *Jesus Is Coming*. This book, which has continuously remained in print since 1878, was instrumental in helping to popularize the secret pretribulational rapture teaching of John Nelson Darby.

Chafer, Lewis Sperry (1871-1952) was a Presbyterian minister, educator and traveling evangelist. He was educated at New Lyme Academy and Oberlin College in Ohio. After his ordination in 1900, Chafer began his ministry as an itinerant evangelist and lecturer. From 1914 to 1923 he taught at the Philadelphia School of the Bible. He was a close friend and associate of C.I. Scofield, who assisted him in establishing the Dallas Theological Seminary in 1924, where Chafer served as president and professor of systematic theology. A prolific author, Chafer's massive, 8-volume work entitled, *Systematic Theology* remains an authoritative source for Dispensational teaching to this day.

DeHaan, Martin R. a.k.a., **M. R. DeHaan (1891-1965)** was a medical doctor turned radio Bible teacher and author. In 1938 Dr. DeHaan began broadcasting from a small radio studio in Grand Rapids, Michigan. His efforts were met with great success and the Radio Bible Class broadcasts were soon heard nationally on hundreds of affiliates.

English, E. Schuyler (1899-1981) was a recognized Biblical scholar. English taught at the Philadelphia School of the Bible from 1935 to1947. He served as president of the school from 1936 to1939. English also served as president of the American Bible Conference Association from 1930-1947. He was the author of numerous commentaries and edited several Christian periodicals, including *Revelation*, *Our Hope*, and the *Pilgrim* and was the acting chairman for *The New Scofield Reference Bible* committee.

Erdman, Charles R. (1866-1960) was the son of William J. Erdmann, a leader in the premillennial movement in the late 19th century. He graduated from Princeton University in 1886 and Princeton Theological Seminary in 1891. He was ordained in 1891 and pastored until 1905, when he became professor of Practical Theology at Princeton Seminary. He presided over the Presbyterian Board of Foreign Missions from 1925 to 1940. Erdman was a prolific writer having authored some 30 Biblical commentaries.

Feinberg, Charles Lee (1909-1995) studied Hebrew prior to his conversion to Christ in 1930. He earned degrees from the Hebrew Institute of Pittsburgh, the University of Pittsburgh, Dallas Theological Seminary, Southern Methodist University and The Johns Hopkins University. Feinberg was an accomplished Hebrew scholar and served on the Scofield Bible revision committee, as well as the Lockman Foundation's translation committee for the New American Standard Bible. Feinberg was also an immensely popular Bible conference speaker, author and seminary professor. He served as professor of Old Testament at the Los Angeles Bible Theological Seminary from 1948 to 1952 and professor of Old Testament at Talbot Theological Seminary from 1952 to 1975.

Gaebelein, Arno Clemens (1860-1945) immigrated to America from Germany in 1879. After being ordained by the Methodist Episcopal Church in 1885, he held numerous pastorates in the eastern U.S. and was without question one of the most successful and influential promoters of Darbyism in America. He wrote numerous books on prophetic subjects, and was a major organizer and promoter of the prophetic Bible conference movement in America. His combined efforts did much to popularize the secret pretribulational rapture theory of John Nelson Darby.

Hiebert, David Edmond (1910-1995) attended Tabor College, John Fletcher College and Southern Baptist Theological Seminary. He pastored several churches and began teaching New Testament Greek at Tabor College in 1942. In 1946 he suffered a complete hearing loss which forced a change in his approach to teaching whereby he had to anticipate student questions. In 1955, Hiebert took a teaching position at the Mennonite Brethren Seminary in Fresno, California where he remained until his retirement in 1985. A highly respected Dispensational scholar, Hiebert authored 17 books and numerous journal articles.

Ironside, Henry Allan a.k.a. **H.A. Ironside (1878-1951)** was a prolific author, popular evangelist, conference speaker, radio teacher and pastor. He was converted at 14 years of age. After his conversion he received Christian instruction at the Salvation Army Training Garrison in Oakland, California. He afterwards spent six years as an officer in the Salvation Army. In 1896, he joined the Plymouth Brethren. The next thirty-four years of his life were spent preaching throughout the U.S. and Canada. He was called to pastor the Moody Memorial Church in Chicago in 1930. He retired from the pastorate in 1948.

Kelly, William (1821-1906) was educated at Downpatrick and at Trinity College Dublin University, Ireland and graduated with honors. Kelly was widely recognized as both a gifted scholar and a godly man. He possessed a personal library of over 15,000 volumes that is said to have weighed some 17 tons. He first met J.N. Darby when he was 24 years old and subsequently joined the Brethren movement. He was a prolific writer, and editor of the periodical *The Bible Treasury*, which published the writings of the leading Brethren expositors of his day. Kelly held the writings of Darby in the highest regard and did everything in his power to increase their circulation. His great love for Darby and his writings no doubt provided the motivation for undertaking the enormous task of editing the 34-volume edition of *The Collected Writings of J.N. Darby*.

Ladd, George Eldon (1911-1982) was a recognized Biblical scholar, holding degrees from Gordon College, Boston University and Harvard University. Ladd was ordained in 1933 into the Northern Baptist Convention. From 1946-1950 he taught New Testament and Greek at Gordon College. In 1950 he assumed the position of Professor of New Testament Exegesis and Theology at the Fuller Theological Seminary in Pasadena, California. He authored several important books dealing with New Testament theology and Bible prophecy. His most important work was *A Theology of the New Testament* which has been in continuous use as a seminary text book since its publication in 1974. As a committed historic premillennialist, Ladd authored *The Blessed Hope* and *The Last Things* – both critical of the pretribulational rapture teaching.

LaHaye, Tim (b.1926) graduated from Bob Jones University and Western Seminary. He pastored the Scott Memorial Church in San Diego, California from 1958 to 1971. In

2002, LaHaye assumed the position of president of the School of Prophecy at Liberty University. LaHaye has written over 50 books, but is best known for his immensely popular *Left Behind* series, which fictionalizes the Dispensational end-time chronology of events. This prophetic series has sold in excess of 65 million copies worldwide. In 2007, Time *Magazine* listed Tim LaHaye as one of the 25 most influential evangelicals in America.

Larkin, Clarence (1850-1924) was a Mechanical Engineer and Architect who left his secular profession at the age of 34, in order to enter the full-time ministry as an American Baptist minister. After thirty years of ministry Larkin undertook the massive project of "illustrating" Dispensational doctrine. Utilizing his draughtsman skills, Larkin produced 90 detailed charts and 15 elaborate cuts that illustrate just about every aspect of Dispensational teaching imaginable. His charts, with explanatory notes were published in book form in 1918 under the title *Dispensational Truth*. This book experienced a wide circulation and did much to spread and popularize Dispensational teaching both in America and abroad.

Mackintosh, Charles Henry a.k.a. **C.H.M. (1820-1896)** was born in County Wicklow, Ireland. Through the letters of his sister and the writings of J.N. Darby, he experienced conversion to Christ when eighteen years old. In 1853 he joined a group of Brethren in Dublin and soon began teaching. He took an active part in a revival that occurred throughout Ireland in 1859 and 1860. His writings played a key role in popularizing Darbyism in late 19th century America.

Newton, Benjamin Wills (1807-1899) was educated at Exeter College, Cambridge. Newton was a respected Bible teacher and leader of the early Brethren movement at Plymouth, England. However, a serious controversy erupted between Newton and John Darby over Darby's new Dispensational approach to Bible interpretation. Newton especially took exception to Darby's "secret" pretribulation rapture theory. Darby and his followers reacted viciously to Newton's criticism. In 1847, they accused Newton of holding a heretical view regarding the Person of Christ. Darby's accusation was based upon implications that were extrapolated from a tract originally written by Newton in 1835. In this tract, Newton had reasoned that Christ was subject to human sufferings, such as pain, hunger, thirst, emotional grief, etc., as a direct result of being born under the federal headship of Adam. The unfounded implication that Darby drew from

Newton's thinking was that if Christ was actually under the federal headship of Adam, then He would also be subject to the imputation of Adam's guilt, as is the rest of humanity. Thus, all of Christ's human sufferings (e.g., pain, hunger, thirst, emotional grieve, etc.) would be obligatory rather than voluntarily. While Newton never intended or anticipated this conclusion, he recognized that others might. Thus, in September of 1847, Newton publicly admitted his error and published a full retraction and apology. In fairness to Newton, I quote from his published "Acknowledgement" to illustrate the true nature of his error. Newton explained;

"My error in this resulted in my holding that the Lord Jesus, while perfectly free from all, even the slightest taint of sin, either original or actual, yet was under Adam, as a federal head, and thus was exposed by His position to the imputation of Adam's guilt, as it is taught respecting mankind in the fifth of Romans. I saw it to be distinctly revealed that the Lord was subject to hunger, thirst, weariness, sorrow, etc., which things we know are the consequences of the Fall; and I erred in attributing His participation in these to a *federal* relationship to Adam...I desire to acknowledge my error in having thus held and taught on this subject; and hereby withdraw all statements of mine, whether in print or in any other form, in which *this error, or any of its fruits* may be found." [901]

 I have burdened the reader with this somewhat lengthy explanation because beginning with John Darby, many Dispensationalists have attempted to discredit the testimony of Mr. Newton by leveling the unfair charge of "heresy" against him. While Newton certainly erred on a fine point of theology, he was never guilty of heresy. On the contrary, a review of his writings unquestionably demonstrates that he was an exceptional and insightful commentator - orthodox in every respect.

Pentecost, J. Dwight (b.1915) holds degrees from Hampden-Sydney College and Dallas Theological Seminary. He has held teaching positions at the Philadelphia Bible Institute and Dallas Theological Seminary. Pentecost is a highly respected and popular pastor, Bible teacher, conference speaker, author and seminary professor. He has authored numerous books on a range of subjects. However, his best-known work is *Things To Come* which comprehensively deals with the subject of Biblical eschatology from the Dispensational perspective.

---

[901] *A History of the Brethren Movement* – F. Roy Coad, Regent College Publishing, The Paternoster Press, 1968, Appendix B, *Statement and Acknowledgement Respecting Certain Doctrinal Errors* - B.W. Newton, p.294. For a more complete discussion of this issue see *A History of the Brethren Movement* – F. Roy Coad, pp.147-152, and *The Origins of the Brethren* – Harold H. Rowdon, Pickering & Inglis Ltd., London, 1967, pp.258-264.

Ryrie, Charles Caldwell (b.1925) is a highly respected Dispensational theologian and Bible commentator. He holds degrees from Haverford College, Dallas Theological Seminary and University of Edinburgh. Ryrie was professor of theology at Dallas Theological Seminary from 1953 until 1958. In 1958 Ryrie was appointed president of the Philadelphia College of the Bible where he served until 1962. In 1962, Ryrie returned to Dallas Theological Seminary as Dean of Doctoral Studies. He retired in 1983.

Scofield, Cyrus Ingerson a.k.a. **C. I. Scofield (1843-1921)** served under General Robert E. Lee during the American Civil War. He practiced law in Kansas and Missouri from 1869 to 1882. In 1882 he was ordained a Congregational minister and pastored the First Church in Dallas, Texas from 1882 to 1895 and the Moody Church in Northfield, Massachusetts from 1895 to 1902. In 1909 he published the *Scofield Reference Bible*, which, more than any other book, popularized the Dispensational interpretation of Scripture and the secret pretribulational rapture.

Showers, Renald is a pastor, author, popular conference speaker and college professor. He holds degrees from Philadelphia Bible Institute, Wheaton College, Dallas Theological Seminary and Grace Theological Seminary. He has taught at Lancaster School of the Bible, the Moody Bible Institute and Philadelphia School of the Bible. Showers was affiliated with The Friends of Israel Gospel Ministry, Inc. and was a faculty member of the Institute of Biblical Studies. Showers has distinguished himself as a highly respected Bible teacher, theologian and able defender of Dispensationalism.

Stanton, Gerald B. (1918-2010) was a graduate of Dallas Theological Seminary and was a popular Bible teacher, author, pastor and conference speaker. He was one of the founding faculty members of Palm Beach Atlantic University, served as professor at Moody Bible Institute and beginning in 1952, he accepted the position of Professor of Systematic Theology at Talbot Theological Seminary. After his retirement, he and his wife taught in numerous Bible colleges and seminaries across Asia.

Strauss, Lehman (1911-1997) was a pastor, college professor, author, radio Bible teacher and conference speaker. He held degrees from Philadelphia School of the Bible and The King's College and was professor of Old Testament at the Philadelphia Bible

Institute. Strauss pastored the Calvary Baptists Church in Bristol, Pennsylvania from 1939 to 1957. He also pastored the High Park Baptist Church in Highland Park, Michigan from 1957 to 1963. Then, in 1963, Strauss retired from the pastoral ministry and began his radio ministry and Bible conference speaking. A prolific writer, Strauss authored some 18 books, the most notable being *The Book of Revelation* and *The Prophecies of Daniel*.

Talbot, Louis T. (1889-1976) was a highly respected and popular conference speaker, radio broadcaster, author, pastor and educator. In 1927 he began a radio ministry which lasted 35 years. Then, in 1932, after several pastorates spanning some 10 years, he was called to the Church of the Open Door in Los Angeles, California, where he remained until 1948. He also served as president of the Bible Institute of Los Angeles (BIOLA) and Chancellor of Talbot Theological Seminary. He retired in 1952 due to poor health.

Thiessen, Henry C. (1883-1947) was a Baptist pastor from 1909 to 1916. From 1916 through 1946 he held professorships at numerous Bible Colleges and Seminaries, including, Fort Wayne Bible College, Northern Baptist Seminary, Evangelical University, Dallas Seminary, and Wheaton College. In 1946 He was named president of the Los Angeles Baptist Seminary. First published in 1945, his *Lectures in Systematic Theology* is still in print and recognized as an excellent introduction to the study of systematic theology and is still widely used in Bible Colleges and Seminaries.

Trotter, William (1818-1865) was converted when he was twelve years old and began to preach at the age of fourteen. By the time Trotter was nineteen years old he was ordained as a minister in the Methodist Church. He later joined the Brethren movement and became a very influential teacher and writer. His works, *Plain Papers on Prophetic Subjects* and *Eight Lectures on Prophecy* were instrumental in popularizing the Dispensational teachings of John Nelson Darby.

Tregelles, Samuel Prideaux (1813-1875) was a close friend of B.W. Newton and played an important part in the Brethren movement at Plymouth. Along with B.W. Newton, Tregelles openly and strongly opposed John Darby's new Dispensational approach to Bible interpretation. Tregelles was a highly respected Biblical scholar with an impressive list of scholarly publications which include, *The Englishman's Greek Concordance* (1839), *The English Hexapla* (1841), *The Englishman's Hebrew and*

Chaldee Concordance (1843), *Lectures on Daniel* (1845-1847), *An English Translation of Gesenius' Hebrew Lexicon* (1847), *Lectures On Historic Evidences Of The Transmission Of The New Testament* (1851), *An Account Of The Printed Text Of The Greek New Testament* (1854), *The Greek New Testament With Ancient Readings in full, and Jerome's Latin Version* (1857-79), *The Hope of Christ's Second Coming* (1864).

Walvoord, John F. (1910-2002), held degrees from Wheaton College, Texas Christian University, Dallas Theological Seminary and Liberty University. Lewis Sperry Chafer took a personal interest in Walvoord, appointing him as his personal assistant and the registrar of the seminary. After Chafer's death in 1952, Walvoord became president of Dallas Seminary where he remained until his retirement in 1986. Walvoord authored over 30 books. He is especially known for his writings on theology and eschatology, and is considered one of the most able proponents and defenders of modern Dispensationalism.

Wood, Leon J. (1918-1977), was a renowned Biblical scholar who authored numerous books on the Old Testament such as *A Commentary on Daniel, Commentaries on Genesis, Israel's United Monarchy* and *The Holy Spirit in the Old Testament*. He was a graduate of Calvin College (AB), Calvin Theological Seminary (Th.M.) and received his Ph.D. from Michigan State University. Wood was Professor of Old Testament and President and Academic Dean at Grand Rapids Bible College and Seminary.

Appendix B
The Eschatology of the Early Church

I. Premillennialism and the Early Church

The belief in a literal one thousand year reign of Christ upon the earth, although not universal, was unquestionably a prominent and widespread belief among the early Christians. **Justin Martyr** (100-165 A.D.) commenting on a future, literal millennium, declared that, "...I and many others are of this opinion, and [believe] that such will take place... For I choose to follow not men or men's doctrines, but God and the doctrines [delivered] by Him... But I and others, who are right-minded Christians on all points, are assured that there will be a resurrection of the dead, and a thousand years in Jerusalem, which will be built, adorned, and enlarged, [as] the prophets Ezekiel and Isaiah and others declare." [902] Thus, Justin affirms that "many" of the "right-minded" Christian believers of his time held to a literal Millennium.

A literal millennial reign of Jesus Christ was clearly taught by the most eminent and influential early Church Fathers. Church historian, **Philip Schaff** has observed that, "The most striking point in the eschatology of the ante-Nicene age is the prominent chiliasm,[903] or millenarianism, that is the belief of a visible reign of Christ in glory on earth with the risen saints for a thousand years... it was indeed not the doctrine of the church embodied in any creed or form of devotion, but a widely current opinion of distinguished teachers, such as Barnabas, Papias, Justin Martyr, Irenaeus, Tertullian, Methodius, and Lactantius; while Caius, Origen, Dionysius the Great, Eusebius (as afterwards Jerome and Agustin) opposed it."[904] While not universal, the belief in a literal Millennium was according to **Schaff**, "a widely current opinion" among the early Church. Likewise, Church historian, **Henry C. Sheldon**, while commenting on the doctrinal beliefs of the early Christians has observed that, "As respects eschatology, millenarian views were more widely prevalent than has been the case at any subsequent

---

[902] *The Ante-Nicene Fathers* - Wm. B. Eerdmans Publishing Company, 1993. *Dialouge With Trypho*, Vol.1, Chap.LXXX, p.239.
[903] "Chiliasm" comes from the Greek χίλια *(chilia)*, which designates the number 1,000. See Rv.20:2-7.
[904] *History of The Christian Church* - Philip Schaff, Wm. B. Eerdmans Publishing Company, 1987, Vol.2, p.614.

era in the history of the Church."[905] Even secular historians have recognized the widespread acceptance of a literal Millennium by the early Christians. In his monumental work, *The Decline and Fall of The Roman Empire*, the humanist historian, **Edward Gibbon**, who was openly hostile towards Christianity, comments, "The ancient and popular doctrine of the Millennium was intimately connected with the second coming of Christ. ...it was inferred that this long period of labour and contention, which was now almost elapsed, would be succeeded by a joyful Sabbath of a thousand years; and Christ, with the triumphant band of saints and the elect who had escaped death, or who had been miraculously revived, would reign upon earth till the time appointed for the last and general resurrection...The assurance of such a Millennium was carefully inculcated by a succession of fathers from Justin Martyr and Irenaeus, who conversed with the immediate disciples of the apostles, down to Lactantius, who was preceptor to the son of Constantine. Though it might not be universally received [i.e., the Millennium], it appears to have been the reigning sentiment of the orthodox believers; and... [to] have contributed, in a very considerable degree, to the progress of the Christian faith."[906]

Premillennialism was unquestionably the predominant eschatological view of the early Church. The overwhelming majority of the early Church Fathers taught a premillennial advent of Christ, followed by a literal earthly reign of one thousand years. This was the common and accepted view of the orthodox believers of the early Church up to the time of Augustine (354-430), whose anti-millenarian views were widely adopted and propagated by the established Church.

II. The Dispensational Doctrine of "Imminence" and the Early Church

The word "imminence" is used by Dispensationalists to refer to the secret, any-moment, pretribulational return of Jesus Christ to raise the Christian dead and rapture His Church *before* the beginning of the Great Tribulation. In a desperate attempt to establish some historical basis for their theology, modern-day Dispensationalists attempt to link their doctrine of "imminence" to the premillennialism of the early Church, by claiming that the early Church also taught the distinctively dispensational doctrine of "imminence."

---

[905] *History of the Christian Church* - Henry C. Sheldon, Hendrickson Publishers, 1994, Vol.1, p.238.
[906] *The History of the Decline & Fall of the Roman Empire* - Edward Gibbon, The George Mace Companies, 1946, Vol.1, p.364.

For example, **John Walvoord** maintains that the pretribulational doctrine of "imminency" was "indicated" and "implied" in the writings of the early Church. **Walvoord** has candidly admitted that, "The expectancy of the Lord's coming was clouded, however, by the belief that the *events of the Tribulation were impending* and that Christ's coming to establish His kingdom was *posttribulational*. Frequently the same writers who *seemed to imply imminency* later detailed events that *must precede* the rapture and the second coming of Christ."[907] In other words, **Walvoord** reluctantly admits that the early Church was post-tribulational, while maintaining that they also held to a "clouded" concept of imminency. For example, **Walvoord** explains that, "The statement...that pretribulationalism was unknown until the nineteenth century is a half-truth. Pretribulationalism as it is known today is comparatively recent, but the *concept* of imminency of the Lord's return - which is the important point - clearly dates to the early church."[908] **Dwight Pentecost** also denies the recent origin of the doctrine of imminence, claiming that, "This doctrine of *imminence*, or 'at any moment coming,' is *not a new doctrine* with Darby, as is sometimes charged, although he did clarify, systematize, and popularize it."[909] **Charles Ryrie** also claims that Dispensationalists, "...maintain that *certain features* of the dispensational system are found in the teaching of the early church."[910] More specifically, **Gerald Stanton** asserts that, "It can likewise be demonstrated that, although the advanced details of a pretribulational theology are *not* found in the ancient church Fathers, belief in an *imminent return* was widely held, and *if imminent, then pretribulational*."[911] **Renald Showers** emphatically declares that, "Believers in the early church held vigorously to belief in the *imminent coming* of Jesus Christ..."[912] And likewise, **Tim LaHaye** categorically states that, "The first-century church believed in the *imminent return* of Christ, possibly during their lifetime."[913]

The Dispensational doctrine of "imminency" or the "any moment coming" is one of the crucial doctrines of Dispensational theology. The doctrine of imminency teaches that

[907] *The Rapture Question* - John F. Walvoord, Zondervan Publishing House, 1981, p.52.
[908] *The Blessed Hope And The Tribulation* - John Walvoord, Zondervan Publishing House, 1976, p.42.
[909] *Things To Come* - J. Dwight Pentecost, Zondervan Publishing House, 1958, p.203.
[910] *Dispensationalism Today* - Charles Caldwell Ryrie, Moody Press, 1965, p.66.
[911] *Kept From The Hour* - Gerald B. Stanton, Zondervan Publishing House, 1956, pp.219-220.
[912] *Maranatha - Our Lord Come!* - Renald Showers, The Friends of Israel Gospel Ministry, Inc., 1995, p.17.
[913] *No Fear Of The Storm* – Tim LaHaye, Multnomah Press, 1992, p.65.

the resurrection of the dead Christian saints and the rapture of the Church will occur secretly, *before* the Great Tribulation, and *without any preceding signs or prophetic warnings*. However, despite the claims of modern Dispensationalists, this signless, unannounced coming of Christ to secretly raise the righteous dead and remove His Church *before* the beginning of the Tribulation was *not* the belief of the early Christians. The early Church did believe that Christ would come within their lifetime, and even that His appearance was near. Dispensationalists readily *assume* that the early Church's belief in a "soon" appearing of Christ is conclusive proof of the existence of the doctrine of "imminency." For example, in an attempt to prove that the doctrine of imminence was held by the early Church, **Gerald Stanton** argues that, "Many authors can be cited to prove that a belief in the *soon return* of Christ existed throughout the first three centuries."[914] However, the early Church's belief in the "soon coming" of Christ is *not* equivalent to a belief in a secret, signless, any moment, pretribulational coming of Christ. The early Church's expectation of a "soon appearing" of Christ was based upon what they thought were the fulfillment of specific prophetic events. While they believed that the Second Advent was near, they also believed that the fulfillment of certain *intervening prophetic events* necessarily *preceded* Christ's Coming. And two critical events that the early Church fully expected to see *before* the Second Coming of Christ was the revealing of the Antichrist and the commencement of the Great Tribulation. Thus, the early Church clearly and unquestionably taught a *post-tribulational rapture* and *not* an "imminent," or "any moment," pretribulational rapture as Dispensationalists commonly claim. As proof of this statement, carefully consider the following testimony from the writings of the early Church Fathers. Please note that for the benefit of the reader, I have taken the liberty of footnoting some of the primary Scripture references that are alluded to in the following quotations.

1. The Didache, also known as *The Teaching of the Twelve Apostles* (c.125 A.D.) contains an exhortation addressed to second century Christians, warning them to prepare themselves for the coming Tribulation and the appearing of the Antichrist.

"For in the last days the false prophets and corrupters shall be multiplied [a]...
and then shall appear the world-deceiver as Son of God, and shall do signs and wonders, and the earth shall be delivered into his hands [b]... then shall the creation of

---

[914] *Kept From The Hour* - Gerald Stanton, Zondervan Publishing House, 1956, p.126.

269

men come into the fire of trial, and many shall be made to stumble and shall perish, but they that endure in their faith shall be saved from under the curse itself. [c] And then shall appear the signs of the truth; [d] first, the sign of an outspreading in heaven; [e] then the sign of the sound of the trumpet; [f] and third, the resurrection of the dead; [g] yet not of all, but as it is said: the Lord shall come and all His saints with Him. [h] Then shall the world see the Lord coming upon the clouds of heaven. [i] " [915]

[a] Mt.24:11; 2Tim.3:1-5. [b] 2Thess.2:9; Rev.13:8. [c] Mt.24:11-13. [d] Mt.24:30. [e] Rv.6:14. [f] Mt.24:31; 1Cor.15:52; 1Thess.4:16. [g] 1Cor.15:20-23, 50-55; 1Thess.4:13-17. [h] 1Thess.3:13; 4:14; Jude 14. [i] Mt.24:30; Rv.1:7.

Note first, that the appearance of the Antichrist and the Great Tribulation *precede* the resurrection of the righteous, which occurs *after* the Tribulation. Second, the "coming" of Christ referred to is His glorious, visible, public appearing *after* the Tribulation, *not* a secret, pretribulational resurrection and rapture *before* the Tribulation.

2. *Constitutions of the Holy Apostles*, were written during the pre-Nicene era (before 325) and compiled c.390.

"For in the last days false prophets shall be multiplied, and as corrupt the word [a]...And then shall appear the deceiver of the world, the enemy of the truth, the prince of lies, whom the Lord Jesus 'shall destroy with the spirit of His mouth, who takes away the wicked with His lips,' [b] and many shall be offended at Him. But they that endure to the end, the same shall be saved. [c] And then shall appear the sign of the Son of man in heaven; [d] and afterwards shall be the voice of a trumpet by the archangel; and in that interval shall be the revival of those that were asleep. [e] And then shall the Lord come, and all His saints with Him, with a great concussion above the clouds, with the angels of His power, in the throne of His kingdom, to condemn the devil, the deceiver of the world, and to render to everyone according to their deeds. [f] " [916]

[a] Mt.24:11,24. [b] 2Thess.2:8. [c] Mt.24:13. [d] Mt.24:30. [e] 1Cor.15:20-23, 50-55; 1Thess.4:13-17. [f] Mt.24:29-31; 16:27.

The sequence of events is undeniably *post-tribulational*. First, notice that the Antichrist is revealed *before* the resurrection of the righteous, and therefore *before* the rapture of

---

[915] *The Ante-Nicene Fathers* - Wm.B. Eerdmans Publishing Co., 1993. *The Teaching of the Twelve Apostles* (also known as *The Didache*), Vol.7, Chap.XVI, p.382.
[916] *The Ante-Nicene Fathers* - Wm.B. Eerdmans Publishing Co., 1993. *Constitutions of the Holy Apostles*, Book VII, Sec.II, Chap.XXXII, Vol.7, p.471.

the Church. Second, the resurrection of the righteous occurs **after** the revealing of the Antichrist and the Tribulation, when Jesus Christ visibly appears in great power and Divine glory.

3. Justin Martyr (c.100-165) was an early Christian evangelist and apologist who contended earnestly against the paganism of Rome. He was martyred for refusing to deny the Name of Jesus Christ.

Referring to the Second Advent of Jesus Christ and the persecution of the Antichrist, Justin declared, "...two advents of Christ have been announced: the one, in which He is set forth as suffering, inglorious, dishonored, and crucified; [a] but the other, in which He shall come from heaven with glory [b], when the man of apostasy, who speaks strange things against the Most High, [c] shall venture to do unlawful deeds on the earth against us the Christians, who having learned the true worship of God [d]... have fled for safety to the God of Jacob and God of Israel [e]..."[917]

[a] Jn.1:29; Phil.2:5-8. [b] Mt.16:27; 25:31. [c] Rv.13:5-6 cp.Dan.7:8,20,25. [d] Jn.4:23-24; Phil.3:3. [e] Heb.6:18.

Justin sees only two comings of Jesus Christ. The first was characterized by suffering that culminated with the Cross, and the second, a glorious appearing **after** the Tribulation at the end of this age. Justin knows nothing of a secret, imminent coming of Christ, located between these two Advents of Christ. Justin describes the Second Advent of Jesus Christ as one continuous, visible and glorious event that will bring the reign of the Antichrist to an end. Also, carefully notice that Justin warns that the Antichrist will persecute "the Christians."

4. Irenaeus (120-202) was the Bishop of Lyons. He vigorously opposed Gnosticism[918] which was making deep inroads into the Church.

"...the prophets announced His two advents: the one indeed, in which He became a man subject to stripes, and knowing what it is to bear infirmity... but the second in which He will come on the clouds, [a] bringing on the day which burns as a furnace [b] and smiting the earth with the word of His mouth, [c] and slaying the impious with the breath of His

---

[917] *The Ante-Nicene Fathers* - Wm.B. Eerdmans Publishing Co., 1993. *Dialogue With Trypho* - Justin Martyr, Vol.1, Chap.CX, pp.253-254.
[918] Generally stated, Gnosticism was the belief that salvation was achieved through secret knowledge.

lips, [d] and having a fan in His hands, and cleansing His floor, and gathering the wheat indeed into His barn, but burning the chaff with unquenchable fire. [e] "[919]

[a] Dan.7:13. [b] Mal.4:1. [c] Rv.19:15. [d] 2Thess.2:8. [e] Mt.3:12; Lk.3:17.

Like Justin, Irenaeus saw only two advents of Jesus Christ: one in humility and suffering, and the other in power and glory that will result in the judgment of the wicked inhabitants of the earth and the deliverance of the righteous. In his explanatory comments regarding the beast of Revelation, Irenaeus declares;

"In a still clearer light has John, in his Apocalypse, indicated to the Lord's disciples what shall happen in the last times, and concerning the ten kings who shall then arise... These have one mind, and give their strength and power to the beast... he who is to come shall slay three, and subject the remainder to his power, and that he shall be himself the eighth among them. And they shall... give their kingdom to the beast, and put the Church to flight. After that they shall be destroyed by the coming of our Lord.[a] "[920]   [a] Rv.17:8-14; cp. Dan.7 & 8.

Here Irenaeus clearly states his belief that the confederation of kings under the control of the Antichrist will "put the Church to flight," after which these persecutors will be "destroyed by the coming of our Lord." Irenaeus clearly and unquestionably places the Church in the Great Tribulation. Irenaeus' belief that the Church would be present on the earth during the reign of the Antichrist is again made evident in his discussion of the mark of the beast in Revelation 13, where he states;

"But he indicates the number of the name now, [a] that when this man comes, we may avoid him, being aware who he is... But when this Antichrist shall have devastated all things in this world, he will reign for three years and six months, [b] and sit in the temple at Jerusalem; [c] and the Lord will come from heaven in the clouds, in the glory of the Father, sending this man and those who follow him into the lake of fire...[d] "[921]

---

[919] *The Ante-Nicene Fathers* - Wm.B. Eerdmans Publishing Co., 1993. *Irenaeus Against All Heresies*, Book IV, Chap.XXXIII, Par.1, Vol.1, p.506.
[920] *The Ante-Nicene Fathers* - Wm.B. Eerdmans Publishing Co., 1993. *Irenaeus Against All Heresies*, Book 5, Chap.XXVI, Par.1, Vol.1, pp.554-555.
[921] *The Ante-Nicene Fathers* - Wm.B. Eerdmans Publishing Co., 1993. *Irenaeus Against All Heresies* - Book 5, Chap.XXX, Par.4, Vol.1, p.560.

ᵃ Rv.13:17-18. ᵇ Rv.13:5. ᶜ 2Thess.2:4. ᵈ Rv.19:20 cp. Dan.7:11.

Irenaeus taught that the Divine purpose for revealing the number of the beast, was so that "when this man comes, *we* may avoid him, being aware who he is." The use of the term "we" is clearly a reference to Christians, of whom Irenaeus was one. Thus, Irenaeus believed that the purpose for the number of the beast, was to enable Christians to identify the Antichrist and thereby avoid him. Also notice that Irenaeus does **not** anticipate a "secret" coming of Jesus Christ prior to the Tribulation. Rather, he sees the Second Coming of Jesus Christ as a visible, glorious event that will occur **after** the Tribulation.

5. Polycrates (130-196) was the bishop of Ephesus. He insisted upon observing Easter on the 14th of Nisan (the Jewish Passover) contending that Jesus died when the Passover lambs were being sacrificed. This eventually resulted in a bitter controversy between the western and eastern churches.

"For in Asia, great luminaries have gone to their rest, who shall rise again in the day of the coming of the Lord, when He cometh with glory from heaven ᵃ and shall raise all the saints.ᵇ " [922] ᵃ Mt.24:30. ᵇ 1Cor.15:20-23, 50-55; 1Thess.4:13-17.

Polycrates makes a clear reference to the glorious post-tribulational advent of Christ. In Matthew 24:30, Jesus declared, "...and they will see the Son of Man coming on the clouds of the sky with power and great glory." Christ is not describing a secret appearing prior to the Great Tribulation, but a glorious, visible manifestation of His presence **after** the Tribulation. Notice carefully, that it is at this glorious, **post-tribulational** coming of Jesus Christ that Polycrates places the resurrection of "all the saints."

6. Hermas (c.160) was the author of *The Shepherd*, an allegory which was widely circulated and read in the early Church.

---

[922] *The Ante-Nicene Fathers* - Wm.B. Eerdmans Publishing Co., 1993. *The Remains of the Second and Third Centuries,* Vol. 8, p.773.

"Stand steadfast, therefore, ye who work righteousness, and doubt not, that your passage may be with the holy angels. Happy ye who endure the Great Tribulation [a] that is coming on, and happy they who shall not deny their own life.[b]" [923]

[a] Mt.24:21. [b] Mt.10:33,39 cp. Mk.8:34-38 cp. Tim.2:12.

The author of *The Shepherd* addresses Christians whom he refers to as those "who work righteousness." He tells them that they will be happy if they successfully **endure** the coming Great Tribulation, and do not deny their life. This is a clear warning against denying Christ, who is the resurrection and the life (Jn.14:6) and who is our life (Col.3:4).

7. Tertullian (145-220) was an early Latin Church Father and Christian apologist who ably defended Christianity against Roman paganism and refuted the heresy of Gnosticism.

Tertullian states that, "In the Revelation of John... the souls of the martyrs are taught to wait [a]... that the city of fornication may receive from the ten kings its deserved doom, [b] and that the beast Antichrist with his false prophet may wage war [c] on the Church of God..." [924] [a] Rv.6:11. [b] Rv.17:1-6 cp. Rv.17:16. [c] Rv.13:7,11-12 cp. Dan.7:21,25.

Tertullian clearly asserts that the Antichrist, along with his false prophet, will "wage war on the Church of God." This necessarily means that the Church will pass through the Great Tribulation, and therefore will **not** be raptured before if commences.

Referring to the resurrection of the righteous, Tertullian declares, "Now the privilege of this favor awaits those who shall at the coming of the Lord be found in the flesh, and who shall, owing to the oppressions of the time of Antichrist, deserve by an instantaneous death, which is accomplished by a sudden change, [a] to become qualified to join the rising saints; as he [Paul] writes to the Thessalonians: 'For this we say unto you by the word of the Lord, that we which are alive and remain unto the coming of the Lord shall not prevent them which are asleep. For the Lord Himself shall descend from

---

[923] *The Ante-Nicene Fathers* - Wm.B. Eerdmans Publishing Co., 1993. *The Pastor of Hermas* - Vision Second, Chap.II, Vol.2, p.11.
[924] *The Ante-Nicene Fathers* - Wm.B. Eerdmans Publishing Co., 1993. *On the Resurrection of the Flesh* - Chap. XXV, Vol.3, p.563.

heaven with a shout, with the voice of the archangel, and with the trump of God: then we too shall ourselves be caught up together with them in the clouds, to meet the Lord in the air: and so shall we ever be with the Lord. [b] '''' [925]   [a] 1Cor.15:51-52. [b] 1Thess.4:15-17.

Carefully note that Tertullian teaches that the New Testament resurrection and rapture passage of First Thessalonians 4:13-17 will be fulfilled at the Second Advent of Christ *after* the Great Tribulation. Tertullian declares that those believers who endure the Tribulation will, "at the coming of the Lord" undergo a "sudden change" and thus "join the rising saints." He then quotes the entire passage of First Thessalonians 4:15-17 as authoritative proof. Tertullian clearly places both the resurrection and the rapture *after* the "oppressions of the time of Antichrist."

8. Hippolytus (170-236) was a contemporary of Cyprian and Tertullian, and a leader in the early Church at Rome. He was banished by Emperor Maximin and died in the mines of Sardinia.

Referring to Revelation 12, Hippolytus declares, "Now, concerning the tribulation of the persecution which is to fall upon the Church from the Adversary, John speaks thus: 'And I saw a great and wondrous sign in heaven; a woman clothed with the sun, and the moon under her feet... and the Dragon was wroth with the woman, and went to make war with the saints of her seed, which keep the commandments of God, and have the testimony of Jesus...[a]' By the 'woman clothed with the sun,' he meant most manifestly the Church endued with the Father's word... 'And the dragon,' he says, 'saw and persecuted the woman which brought forth the man-child. And to the woman were given two wings of the great eagle, that she might fly into the wilderness, where she is nourished for a time, and times, and half a time, from the face of the serpent. [b]' That refers to the one thousand two hundred and threescore days (the half of the week) during which the tyrant is to reign and persecute the Church...." [926]   [a] Rv.12:1-6. [b] Rv.12:13-14.

Hippolytus clearly states that "the Church" will undergo the "tribulation of the persecution" of "the Adversary," and "the serpent," which are clear references to Satan

---

[925] *The Ante-Nicene Fathers* - Wm.B. Eerdmans Publishing Co., 1993. *On the Resurrection of the Flesh* - Chap.XLI, Vol.3, p.575.
[926] *The Ante-Nicene Fathers* - Wm.B. Eerdmans Publishing Co., 1993. *The Extant Works and Fragments of Hippolytus - Treatise on Christ and Antichrist*, Part II, Dogmatical and Historical, Par.60,61, Vol.5, p.216.

who will empower and energize "the tyrant" – i.e., the Antichrist, who will "persecute the Church."

Hippolytus knew nothing of a secret, imminent, any moment rapture of the Church *before* the Tribulation. Rather, he clearly taught that the Second Advent of Jesus Christ would occur *after* the Tribulation, at the visible, glorious appearing of Christ. For example, Hippolytus declared,

"For as two advents of our Lord and Saviour are indicated in the Scriptures, the one being His *first advent* in the flesh, which took place without honour by reason of His being set at nought, as Isaiah spake of Him aforetime, saying, 'We saw Him, and He had no form nor comeliness...[a]' But His *second advent* is announced as glorious, when He shall come from heaven with the host of angels, and the glory of His Father, as the prophet saith, 'Ye shall see the King in glory;' and, 'I saw one like the Son of Man coming with the clouds of heaven; and He came to the Ancient of days, and he was brought to Him.[b]'" [927] [a] Is.53:2-5. [b] Dan.7:13-14.

9. Cyprian (200-258) was the bishop of Carthage in North Africa. He was arrested and tried during the persecution under the Emperor Valerian. Refusing to deny Christ, he was martyred at Utica. Cyprian also clearly taught that the Church would experience the persecution of the Antichrist. Cyprian boldly exclaimed that, "For even Antichrist, when he shall begin to come, shall not enter into the Church because he threatens; neither shall we yield to his arms and violence, because he declares that he will destroy us if we resist." [928]

Clearly, Cyprian fully expected that the Church would see Antichrist revealed, and thus confidently asserts that the Church would not succumb to his threats or violence.

"But how grave is the case of a Christian man, if he, a servant, is unwilling to suffer, when his Master first suffered... if we suffer from the world's hatred, Christ first endured the world's hatred... 'Remember the word that I said unto you, the servant is not

---

[927] *The Ante-Nicene Fathers* - Wm.B. Eerdmans Publishing Co., 1993. *The Extant Works and Fragments of Hippolytus - Treatise on Christ and Antichrist*, Part II, Dogmatical And Historical, Par.44, Vol.5, p.214.
[928] *The Ante-Nicene Fathers* - Wm.B. Eerdmans Publishing Co., 1993. *The Epistles of Cyprian* - Epistle LIV, Par.19, Vol.5, p.346.

greater than his Lord. If they have persecuted Me, they will also persecute you..."[a]' nor let any one of you, beloved brethren, be so terrified by the fear of future persecution, or the coming of the threatening Antichrist, as not to be found armed for all things by the evangelical exhortations and precepts, and by the heavenly warnings. Antichrist is coming, but above him comes Christ also. The enemy goeth about and rageth, but immediately the Lord follows to avenge our sufferings and our wounds." [929] [a] Jn.15:18-20.

Cyprian encourages the early Christians not to fear the threatenings and persecutions of the coming Antichrist. Instead, he encourages them to look forward to the Second Coming of Jesus Christ who will avenge their sufferings.

10. Victorinus (c.300) was Bishop of Poetovio located in Syria. He also died a martyr's death. While Victorinus was a prolific writer, all of his works have unfortunately been lost, with the exception of his commentary on Revelation. Commenting on Revelation, Chapter 7, Victorinus writes,

"'And I saw another angel ascending from the east, having the seal of the living God.[a]' He speaks of Elias the prophet, who is the precursor of the times of Antichrist, [b] for the restoration and establishment of the Churches from the great and intolerable persecution." [930] [a] Rv.7:2. [b] Mal.4:5-6.

Victorinus taught that the prophet Elijah would appear prior to the revealing of the Antichrist in order to spiritually prepare "the Churches" to withstand the coming persecution of the Antichrist.

Before concluding this discussion, there is one other important point that needs to be made with respect to the Dispensational claim that the early Church taught the pretribulational doctrine of "imminence." Dispensationalists maintain that the strongest Biblical evidence for a pretribulational resurrection and rapture of the Church is to be found in First Thessalonians 4:13-18. For example, **John Walvoord** declares that, "Probably the main reason for many pretribulationists' holding to a rapture before the

---

[929] *The Ante-Nicene Fathers* - Wm.B. Eerdmans Publishing Co., 1993. *The Epistles of Cyprian* - Epistle LV, Par.6-7, Vol.5, p.349.
[930] *The Ante-Nicene Fathers* - Wm.B. Eerdmans Publishing Co., 1993. *Commentary on The Apocalypse of The Blessed John* - Victorinus, Vol.7, p.351.

Tribulation is the exhortation of 1Thessalonians 4:18."[931] And again, **Walvoord** stresses that; "Probably more pretribulationists base their conclusion for a pretribulational rapture on 1Thessalonians 4 than any other single passage of Scripture." [932] Likewise, **Gerald Stanton** explains that, "It is recognized by most Bible students that 1Thessalonians 4:13-18 is the primary passage of the Word of God on the subject of the rapture of the Church."[933] **Lehman Strauss**, observes that, "The outstanding prophetic passage in the New Testament which describes in some detail the nature of the Rapture is I Thessalonians 4:13-18... in these six verses the doctrine of the Rapture is stressed with emphasis."[934] While referring to 1Thessalonians 4, **Louis Talbot** asserts that, "In chapter four of this epistle we have one of the clearest of Scripture passages regarding the rapture of the church."[935] And **Renald Showers** maintains that, "First Thessalonians 4:13-18 is the most extensive New Testament passage dealing with the Rapture of the Church."[936]

Modern Dispensationalists first of all claim that the early Church taught the all-important Dispensational doctrine of "imminence" (i.e., a secret, signless, any moment Coming of Christ to rapture the Church). Second, modern Dispensationalists maintain that First Thessalonians 4:13-18 provides the ***primary*** Biblical evidence for an imminent, pretribulational rapture of the Church. It would therefore seem reasonable to expect to find clear evidence for a secret pretribulational resurrection and rapture in early Church writings that refer to First Thessalonians 4:13-18. However, this is ***not*** the case. First Thessalonians 4:13-18, or portions thereof, are referred to in the following Ante-Nicene writers:[937] Tertullian,[938] Cyprian,[939] Origen,[940] Methodius,[941] Clement of Alexandria,[942] The Didache[943] and The Apostolic Constitutions.[944] A careful

---

[931] *The Rapture Question* - John F. Walvoord, Zondervan Publishing House, 1981, p.209.

[932] *The Blessed Hope And The Tribulation* - John F. Walvoord, Zondervan Publishing House, 1976, p.94.

[933] *Kept From The Hour* - Gerald B. Stanton, Zondervan Publishing House, 1956, p.83.

[934] *God's Plan for the Future* - Lehman Strauss, Zondervan Publishing House, 1965, p.85.

[935] *God's Plan of the Ages* - Louis T. Talbot, Louis T. Talbot, 1943, p.138.

[936] *Maranatha - Our Lord Come!* - Renald Showers, The Friends of Israel Gospel Ministry, Inc., 1995, p.198.

[937] *The Ante-Nicene Fathers* - Wm.B. Eerdmans Publishing Co., 1993.

[938] Tertullian: Vol..3, pp.231, 343, 462, 473, 562-563, 575, 590, 713; Vol.4, p.22.

[939] Cyprian: Vol.5, p.548.

[940] Origen: Vol.4, pp.299, 458, 550.

[941] Methodius: Vol.6, p.330.

[942] Clement of Alexandria: Vol.2, p.505.

[943] Didache: Vol.7, p.382.

[944] *Apostolic Constitutions*: Vol.7, p.471.

examination of these occurrences will confirm the fact that neither explicit statements nor the general context of these citations contain any hint whatsoever of the modern doctrine of "imminence." Simply stated, the claim that the early Church held to and taught the modern Dispensational doctrine of "imminence" is historically false.

In conclusion, consider the words of **George Eldon Ladd**, who has observed; "Every church father who deals with the subject expects the church to suffer at the hands of Antichrist. God would purify the Church through suffering, and Christ would save her by His return at the end of the Tribulation when He would destroy Antichrist, deliver His Church, and bring the world to an end and inaugurate His millennial kingdom. The prevailing view is a post-tribulation premillennialism. We can find no trace of pretribulationalism in the early church; and no modern pretribulationalist has successfully proved that this particular doctrine was held by any of the church fathers or students of the Word before the nineteenth century."[945]

And lastly, consider the comments of **Henry W. Frost** - initially an early Dispensationalist and attendee of the early Niagara Bible Conferences of the 1890s. Commenting on the doctrine of the pretribulational rapture, **Frost** contends that, "...the doctrine of a pretribulational resurrection and rapture is a modern interpretation - I am tempted to say, a modern invention. There is not a single proof of such and order of procedure in the Word of God, the two great prophetic passages which deal with the order of events teaching the opposite of this (Matt.24:27-42; II Thess. 2:1-12). Neither is there any such indication in the patristic writings, all of the church fathers - so far as they wrote upon the subject - presenting the fact that the great tribulation was to come and the antichrist was to be revealed *before* the advent of Christ. This explains why the early disciples thought that the Roman persecutions were the prophesied tribulation and the Roman emperor the antichrist. It also explains why succeeding generations of Christians, when great persecutions arose, came to similar conclusions... Throughout the whole of these earlier times, the students of God's Word... held the conviction that the divine order was, first, the great tribulation and the antichrist, and afterwards, the second advent of Christ." [946]

---

[945] *The Blessed Hope* - George Eldon Ladd, Wm.B. Eerdmans Publishing Company, 1956, 1980, p.31.
[946] *The Second Coming of Christ* - Henry W. Frost, Wm.B.Eermans Publishing Company, 1934, p.203.

Appendix C

Did the Early Church Make a Dispensational Distinction Between Israel and the Church?

It is an established historical fact that the theological system of Biblical interpretation known as Dispensationalism is of very recent origin. Dispensationalists admit that modern Dispensational theology is largely the work of John Darby (1800-1882). However, they attempt to mitigate the serious implications of this admission by asserting that the early Church taught certain key elements of Dispensationalism. In an attempt to establish some historical legitimacy for their teaching, Dispensationalists claim that "historical references" and "outlines" of "primitive" Dispensational teachings are to be found in early Church writings. They further maintain that these Dispensational elements were subsequently "lost," and then after some 1,800 years, rediscovered, refined and systematized by John Darby.[947]

For example, consider the theory of **R.A. Huebner**[948] who suggests that the Dispensational doctrine of the imminent pretribulational rapture of the Church was lost almost immediately after the close of the Apostolic era. **Huebner** admits that the writings of the Ante-Nicene Fathers (those writing immediately after the close of the Apostolic era) are post-tribulational. He forthrightly states that,

"The writings of the 'Ante-Nicene fathers' (prior to 325 A.D.) should be classed, in general, as post-tribulational. These men expected Christ to come and set up His 1,000 year kingdom. They expected Antichrist to appear *before* Christ's appearing. They expected to pass through the tribulation. Though they spoke in expectant terms, Antichrist and tribulation, in their view, had to occur first." [949]

---

[947] See Chapter Two, Part 5, The Development of the Pretribulation Rapture Doctrine.

[948] Roy A. Huebner (died February 8, 2008) was a little known Plymouth Brethren preacher and author who maintained that John Darby **rediscovered** the pretribulational rapture teaching as early as 1827. His assertions have been cited by some of the foremost Dispensational teachers and writers in their promotion of the pretribulation rapture doctrine. For example, John Walvoord authoritatively refers to R.A. Huebner in *The Rapture Question* on pages 151-153 and again in *The Blessed Hope and the Tribulation* on pages 44-45. Likewise, Tim LaHaye quotes R.A. Huebner in *No Fear of the Storm* on pages 123,166,168,173.

[949] *The Truth of the Pre-Tribulation Rapture Recovered* - R.A. Huebner, Present Truth Publishers, 1976, p.2.

However, **Huebner** attributes the early Church's post-tribulationalism on their loss of the Apostolic teaching of imminency. **Huebner** theorizes that,

"The apostles had put the saints in an ***expectant posture*** regarding the coming of the Christ to take His saints to be with Himself. This ***expectant posture*** was ***soon lost*** and the parable of the midnight cry (Matt. 25:1-13) depicts this as all the professors of testimony slumbering."[950]

Thus, according to **Huebner** the lack of evidence for a pretribulational rapture within the writings of the early Church, is the result of their losing the "expectant posture" of the Apostle's teaching.

However, **Charles Ryrie** argues that Dispensationalists, "...recognize that as a system dispensationalism was largely formulated by Darby, but outlines of a dispensationalist approach to the Scriptures are found much earlier."[951] And again, **Ryrie** states that, "It is granted by dispensationalists that as a system of theology dispensationalism is recent in origin. But there are historical references to that which eventually was systematized into dispensationalism."[952] In an attempt to demonstrate the historicity of Dispensational theology, Ryrie quotes the Ante-Nicene writers, Justin Martyr (100-165), Irenaeus (120-202), and Clement of Alexandria (150-215). Ryrie effectively demonstrates that these early Church writers recognized different dispensations within Scripture. **Ryrie** then concludes, "It is not suggested nor should it be inferred that these early Church Fathers were dispensationalists in the modern sense of the word. But, it is true that some of them enunciated principles which later developed into dispensationalism, and it may be rightly said that they held to primitive or early dispensational concepts."[953] And specifically what "dispensational concepts" did they hold? **Ryrie** maintains that Justin Martyr "...held a concept of differing programs of God." That Irenaeus "...often spoke of the dispensations of God and especially of the Christian dispensation." And that Clement of Alexandria "...distinguished three patriarchal dispensations (in Adam, Noah, and Abraham) as well as the Mosaic."[954]

---

[950] *The Truth of the Pre-Tribulation Rapture Recovered* - R.A. Huebner, Present Truth Publishers, 1976, p.2.
[951] *Dispensationalism Today* - Charles Caldwell Ryrie, Moody Press, 1970, p.66.
[952] *Dispensationalism Today* - Charles Caldwell Ryrie, Moody Press, 1970, p.67.
[953] *Dispensationalism Today* - Charles Caldwell Ryrie, Moody Press, 1970, p.70.
[954] *Dispensationalism Today* - Charles Caldwell Ryrie, Moody Press, 1970, pp.68-69.

Thus, **Ryrie** establishes the fact that the early Church recognized different dispensations of Divine administrations over the world. But the recognition of different Divine administrations, economies or dispensations is *not* the distinctive characteristic of modern Dispensational theology, nor is it a, "primitive or early dispensational concept." **Ryrie** himself admits that, "...a man can believe in dispensations, and even see them in relation to progressive revelation, *without being a dispensationalist*."[955] The fact is, that the Church has always recognized different economies or dispensations. **Daniel Fuller** correctly observes that, "Almost every Bible student agrees that there are periods in the Bible distinguished by distinct administrations, but this does not mean that everyone is a Dispensationalist."[956] The fact that the early Church recognized different Divine administrations does *not* mean that they taught a "primitive form" of Dispensationalism, any more than it means that Charles Hodge, who recognized four dispensations[957] or Louis Berkhof, who saw two dispensations,[958] taught a "primitive form" of Dispensationalism. It is important to understand, that Darby did not originate the concept of making dispensational distinctions (i.e., recognizing historical divisions and different Divine administrations) within Scripture. Rather, as **Reginald Kimbro** has correctly observed, Darby invented "a new way of viewing these dispensations" and that, "He was not the first to mark dispensations in the Bible. He did bring a *new definition* to what was meant by the dispensational distinctions."[959]

Ryrie further maintains that, "A dispensationalist keeps **Israel and the Church distinct**...This is probably the **most basic theological test** of whether or not a man is a dispensationalist, and undoubtedly the most practical and conclusive. A man who fails to distinguish Israel and the Church will inevitably not hold to dispensational distinctions; and one who does will."[960] Thus, according to **Ryrie**, the essential element of Dispensationalism is the distinction between Israel and the Church. This distinction is prerequisite to all other Dispensational distinctions. If, as **Ryrie** claims, the early

---

[955] *Dispensationalism Today* - Charles Caldwell Ryrie, Moody Press, 1970, p.44.

[956] *The Hermeneutics of Dispensationalism* - Daniel Fuller, Northern Baptist Theological Seminary, Th.D. dissertation, 1957, p.22.

[957] *Systematic Theology* - Charles Hodge, Wm.B. Eerdmans Publishing Co, Vol.2, pp.373-377, where Hodge identifies four dispensations: Adam to Abraham; Abraham to Moses; Moses to Christ; and the Gospel dispensation.

[958] *Systematic Theology* - Louis Berkhof, Wm.B. Eerdmans Publishing Co., 1993. Berkhof refers to, "The Old Testament Dispensation," p.293 and "The New Testament Dispensation," p.299.

[959] *The Gospel According To Dispensationalism* - Reginald C. Kimbro, Wittenburg Publications, 1995, p.23-24.

[960] *Dispensationalism Today* - Charles Caldwell Ryrie, Moody Press, 1970, p.44-45.

Church taught a "primitive" or "undeveloped" form of Dispensationalism, we would naturally expect to find some indication that the early Church made a Dispensational distinction between Israel (Jewish Old Testament believers) and the Church (New Testament believers). However, this is *not* the case. The early Church made *no* such distinction between the redeemed of the Old and New Testaments. Rather, they saw Old and New Testament saints as members of one redeemed body of believers. Consider the testimony of the same three early Church writers that **Ryrie** referred to...

First: **Justin Martyr** (c.100-165) was an early Christian apologist and martyr who saw *no* distinction between Old and New Testament believers, but rather, an essential unity between the two. This accord between Old and New Testament saints is expressed when **Justin** declared that Christians were descended from and were therefore a part of the "spiritual Israel." Justin declared;

"For the true spiritual Israel, and the descendants of Judah, Jacob, Isaac, and Abraham...are we who have been led to God through this crucified Christ..." And again, Justin stated; "And by these words He declares that we, the nations, rejoice with His people, - to wit, Abraham, and Isaac, and Jacob, and the prophets, and in short, all of that people who are well pleasing to God..."[961] Clearly, Justin sees a unity between Old Testament believers and Christians. Justin certainly does not make any sharp dispensational distinctions between Old and New Testament believers.

Likewise, **Irenaeus** (120-202) was the bishop of Lyons and a Christian apologist who refuted Gnosticism. He also saw continuity and unity between Old and New Testament believers. **Irenaeus** stated that, "...God, who introduces, through Jesus Christ, Abraham to the kingdom of heaven, and his seed, that is, the Church, upon which also is conferred the adoption and the inheritance promised to Abraham." And again, speaking of Abraham, Irenaeus asserted; "For his [i.e., Abraham's] seed is the Church, which receives the adoption of God through the Lord, as John the Baptist said: 'For God is able from the stones to raise up children to Abraham.' ...Thus, then, they who are of faith shall be blessed with faithful Abraham, and these are the children of Abraham." [962]

---

[961] *The Ante-Nicene Fathers* - Wm. B. Eerdmans Publishing Co.,1993. Justin Martyr, *Dialogue With Trypho*, Vol.1, Chap.XI, p.200 & Vol.1, Chap.CXXX, p.264.
[962] *The Ante-Nicene Fathers* - Wm. B. Eerdmans Publishing Co.,1993. *Irenaeus Against Heresies* Vol.1, Chap.VII, p.470, Chap.XXXII, p.561.

Like Justin, Irenaeus also sees unity and continuity between Old and New Testament believers, who he describes as descended from Abraham.

Third: **Clement of Alexandria** (150-215) was a Christian philosopher, teacher and presbyter at Alexandria, Egypt, who taught that the true Church was "ancient," and included all of the "just" as "one." Carefully consider Clement's conclusion that; "From what has been said then, it is my opinion that the true Church, that which is really ancient, is one, and that in it those who according to God's purpose are just, are enrolled."[963] Thus, Clement saw all of the just, whether Old or New Testament believers, as a part of the Church, declaring them to be "one."

The topic of the unity and continuity between Old and New Testament believers is not a subject frequently addressed in early Church writings. However, when the subject is touched upon, there is no evidence of any Dispensational dichotomy between Israel and the Church. The early Christians saw the Church as a natural continuation of God's redemptive program and ***not*** a new work that excluded Old Testament believers from "the household of God" which is His Church (1Tim.3:15). After all, the Church does rest upon the foundation of the apostles and **the prophets**, Christ Jesus Himself being the corner stone (Eph.2:19-22, emphasis added).

---

[963] *The Ante-Nicene Fathers* - Wm. B. Eerdmans Publishing Co.,1993. *The Stromata*, Book VII, Chap.XVII, Vol.2, p.555.

Appendix D

Who First Proposed a
Pretribulational Rapture of the Church?

Outline to Appendix D
1. The Historical Background: 1789-1815.
2. Albury: 1826-1830.
3. The Charismata in Scotland and London: 1830-1832.
4. Edward Irving and the Development of Dispensational Theology: 1829-1831.
   a. The *Morning Watch* and the Pretribulation Rapture.
   b. The *Morning Watch* and the Jewish Remnant.
   c. The *Morning Watch* and the Parable of the Ten Virgins.
   d. The *Morning Watch* and the Seven Churches.
   e. The *Morning Watch* and the Two Comings of Christ.
5. John Darby and the Albury Years: 1826-1830
6. Powerscourt: 1831-1833.
7. The Charge of Demonic Origins.
8. Summary
9. Chronology of Key Events.

1. The Historical Background: 1789-1815

The historical forces that gave rise to the doctrine of the secret pretribulation rapture arose in the late seventeen and early eighteen hundreds in Western Europe. Beginning with the French Revolution (1789-1799) and the Napoleonic Wars (1800-1815), civil unrest and military conflicts plagued Europe. As a result, the established political and social institutions of Europe were upset. In England, the forms of worship in the Established Church had devolved into a cold, rote formalism that left many believers spiritually empty and unsatisfied - while a severe cholera epidemic swept through the cities, "unfolding its death-shedding wings over the land."[985] As a direct result of the uncertainty and fear generated by these events, many in England believed that the end of the world was at hand. This conviction led to a renewed interest in the study of unfulfilled Bible prophecy.[986] As a result, two major prophetic conferences were initiated - Albury and Powerscourt - that in turn led to the development and spread of Dispensationalism and the pretribulation rapture doctrine.

2. Albury: 1826-1830

The first of these prophetic meetings were known as the Albury Conferences. They were convened for five consecutive years, from 1826 to 1830, at the estate of Henry Drummond,[987] located in Albury Park, Surrey, England, some thirty miles south of London. Numerous evangelical leaders attended these conferences. Edward Miller, in his *History and Doctrines of Irvingism* lists some 44 participants. One of the most notable attendees was a popular and gifted Scottish Presbyterian minister named Edward Irving.[988] He would prove to be a major contributor to the development of Dispensational doctrine generally and the pretribulation rapture doctrine specifically.

In 1825, Edward Irving was greatly influenced by the teaching of James Hatley Frere (1799-1866). Frere taught a premillennial historicism[989] which immediately captured Irving's imagination.[990] While Frere maintained that Christ would return **before** the millennium, he continued to embrace the Day-Year Theory,[991] which saw the fulfillment of many of the prophecies of Daniel and Revelation in various historical events - especially those of Europe. Then, in 1826, Irving was given a book that would have a major influence on the development of his prophetic views. This book was entitled, *The Coming of the Messiah in Glory and Majesty*. It was written under the pseudonym of Juan Josafat Ben Ezra, who was a Chilean Jesuit priest named Manuel Lacunza (1731-1801). Lacunza adopted a futuristic interpretation of the book of Revelation. Irving was so impressed by the work, that during the summer of 1826, he took leave from his pastoral duties and undertook the daunting task of translating Lacunza's book from Spanish into English.[992] He published his translation of Lacunza's work in 1827 with a lengthy introduction. Henceforth, Irving's ministry was preoccupied with the subject of unfulfilled Bible prophecy. The Rev. James Grant, who was personally acquainted with Irving,[993] commented, "The sensation which he [i.e., Irving] created arose chiefly from his dwelling, in almost every sermon...on his newly adopted belief that **Christ might come** to our world **any day**, and **any hour**...to erect a visible kingdom on earth..."[994]

The first Albury prophetic conference was convened in November of 1826 and lasted for eight days. While premillennial historicism remained the prevailing interpretive view of the participants,[995] Irving's notes of the first meeting clearly reveal the emergence of dispensational concepts and terminology.[996] The second Albury meeting of 1827 seems to have been preoccupied with an attempt to correlate significant current events with specific Bible prophecies.[997] Little is known about the third meeting. However, by the fourth meeting, participants had clearly rejected the post-millennial interpretation of prophecy which was popular at the time. Rather, they now fully expected the re-gathering of the Jews to Palestine; they anticipated an impending Divine judgment upon all of "Christendom;" and they were convinced that a literal earthly Millennium would be inaugurated by the soon appearing of Jesus Christ.[998] The fifth and last Albury meeting was held in July 1830.[999] In response to the news that the gifts of the Spirit had broken out in Scotland, the conference participants passed a resolution declaring, "That it is our duty to pray for the revival of the gifts manifested in the primitive Church; which are wisdom, knowledge, faith, healing, miracles, prophecy, discovery of spirits, kinds of tongues, and interpretation of tongues; and that a responsibility lies on us to inquire into the state of those gifts said to be now present in the west of Scotland."[1000] Irving was keenly interested in the events transpiring in Scotland and actively undertook measures to keep apprised of their developments.

3. The Charismata in Scotland and London: 1830-1832

The first outbreak of tongues occurred on a Sunday evening on March 28, 1830,[1001] in a small town in western Scotland called Fernicarry, located about 15 miles from Port-Glasgow. A young girl named Mary Campbell, a dressmaker by trade and aspiring missionary, was believed to be dying of consumption.[1002] While lying upon her deathbed, accompanied by some relatives and friends, who in anxious anticipation of the restoration of the miraculous "gifts," were praying for Mary's healing. Suddenly, to everyone's amazement, Mary began speaking out loudly in unknown tongues. She continued her ecstatic utterances for over an hour.[1003] Mary believed that she had been gifted with the language of the Pelew Islands of the South Pacific.[1004] While Mary had received the "gift of tongues," she did not at this time receive a physical healing. That event would not occur until after the healing of her friend, Margaret Macdonald, of Port-Glasgow.

The Macdonald's were part of a group that were regularly meeting to pray for the restoration of the supernatural "gifts" of the Spirit. They had been keenly influenced by a sermon preached by Mr. A.J. Scott,[1005] in which he encouraged Christians to actively seek after and expect the restoration of the miraculous gifts of the Spirit.[1006] Margaret Macdonald, who lived with her two brothers and three sisters in Port-Glasgow, fell ill at about the same time as Mary Campbell. One of Margaret's sisters describes the situation in the following words: "For several days Margaret had been so unusually ill that I quite thought her dying...when the power of the Spirit came upon her. She said, 'There will be a mighty baptism of the Spirit this day,' and then broke forth in a most marvelous setting forth of the wonderful work of God; and as if her own weakness had been altogether lost in the strength of the Holy Ghost, continued with little or no intermission for two or three hours in mingled praise, prayer, and exhortation. At dinnertime James and George came home as usual, whom she addressed at great length, concluding with a solemn prayer for James, that he might at that time be endowed with the power of the Holy Ghost. Almost instantly, James calmly said, 'I have got it!'...He then...walked to Margaret's bedside, and addressed her in these words, 'Arise and stand upright.' He repeated the words, took her by the hand, and she arose."[1007]

James then promptly sat down and wrote a letter to Mary Campbell at Fernicarry. Upon receiving the letter, Mary recounted: "I had scarcely read the first page when I became quite overpowered, and laid it aside for a few minutes; but I had no rest in my spirit until I took it up again and began to read. As I read, every word came with power, but when I came to the command to arise, it came home with a power which no words can describe; it was felt to be indeed the voice of Christ; it was such a voice of power as could not be resisted. A mighty power was instantaneously exerted upon me. I first felt as if I had been lifted up from off the earth, and all my diseases taken off me. At the voice of Jesus I was surely made in a moment to stand upon my feet, leap and walk, sing and rejoice.'"[1008] In 1831, Mary was married to a Mr. W. R. Caird, who worked as an office clerk in Edinburgh. The couple soon relocated to London, where they became members of Edward Irving's church.

Soon after Margaret's healing, her brothers, James and George, received the gift of tongues. In a letter dated April 20, 1830, James relates that both he and George received the gift of tongues on Friday, April 16, 1830. James also relates that, "On Saturday, [i.e., April 17, 1830], Mr. C. [i.e., Rev. John McLeod Campbell] came over, and my mouth was again opened. He said, it is written 'pray that ye may interpret;' he accordingly prayed. I was then made to speak in short sentences which George interpreted one by one. The first word of interpretation was 'Behold he cometh - Jesus cometh.'"[1009]

News of the restoration of the "gifts" spread quickly. One of Margaret's sisters writes in a letter dated May 18, 1830, that, "Ever since Margaret was raised and the gift of tongues given, the house has been filled every day with people from all parts of England, Scotland, and Ireland."[1010] This was by no means an exaggeration. The curious were constantly visiting the Macdonald's home in order to observe the new phenomena firsthand. One such visitor was John B. Cardale, along with five companions, who spent some three to four weeks with the Macdonald's. Cardale published the details of his visit in the *Morning Watch*.[1011] Cardale offers an interesting, first-hand look into the events that transpired in Port-Glasgow when he explains that, "The history of one of these meetings is the history of all...the mode of proceeding is for each person who takes a part to first read a Psalm in metre, which is sung by the meeting; then a chapter from the Bible; and then he prays. On this occasion...J. M'D. [i.e., James Macdonald] read and prayed...He then, in the course of prayer...began speaking in an unknown tongue; and after speaking for some time he sung, or rather chanted, in the same tongue...he then...addressed us in English...After he had concluded, a short pause ensued, when suddenly the woman-servant of the M'D's arose and spoke (for a space of probably ten minutes) in an unknown tongue...M. M'D [i.e., Margaret Macdonald] commenced also speaking...in which she gave testimony to the judgments coming on the earth; but also directed the church to the coming of the Lord as her hope of deliverance. When she concluded we left the house."[1012] Cardale went on to report that, "These persons, while uttering the unknown sounds...have every appearance of being under supernatural direction. The manner and voice are different from what they are at other times...their whole deportment gives an impression...that their organs are made use of by supernatural power...I conceive that...the individuals thus gifted are persons living in close communion with God..."[1013]

Not surprisingly, it was John Cardale's wife who first manifested the "gift of tongues" in London. Edward Miller relates that, "At length, on the 30th of April, 1831, the first case occurred in London. Mrs. Cardale spoke with great solemnity in a tongue and

289

prophesied. There were three distinct sentences in an unknown tongue, and three in English. The latter were, 'The Lord will speak to His people - the Lord hasteneth His coming - the Lord cometh.'"[1014] Mr. and Mrs. Cardale soon thereafter joined Irving's church where Mrs. Cardale was immediately received as a gifted prophetess.

In the spring of 1830, Irving dispatched an elder of his church to Scotland to observe and report on the charismata firsthand.[1015] Irving also went to great lengths to insure that he received regular updates of the events in Scotland via the mail.[1016] Irving was captivated by the claims of both Mary and Margaret. He declared that, "Mrs. Caird [Mary Campbell's married name] is a saint of God, and hath the gift of prophecy."[1017] Not surprisingly, when Mary and her husband relocated to London shortly after their marriage, Irving immediately recognized her as a prophetess. Irving was thoroughly convinced that the manifestation of tongues, prophecies and healings represented a genuine work of the Holy Spirit, which, in his opinion, heralded the soon coming of Christ.[1018] In a letter addressed to Dr. Thomas Chalmers,[1019] dated June 2, 1830, Irving declared that, "The substance of Mary Campbell's and Margaret Macdonald's visions or revelations, given in their papers, carry to me a spiritual conviction and a spiritual reproof which I cannot express."[1020]

Regarding the exercise of the charismata within Irving's church, James Grant, who was personally acquainted with Irving, has reported that, "Mr. Irving fully believed that the gifts of working miracles and speaking with tongues were not withdrawn from the Church...I myself have repeatedly heard Miss Hall[1021]...exercise that gift in Mr. Irving's church in Newman Street...the principal communications made by Miss Hall to crowded assemblies related to the personal coming of Christ. I remember being present on one occasion, when in the midst of Mr. Irving's discourse...she arose from her seat, and in tones which no one that heard them ever could forget, shouted aloud, 'He is coming, He is coming, He's coming! Behold, He is at the door. He is here.'"[1022] Irving and his followers were convinced that the Second Coming of Christ was imminent. James Grant, relates that, "The sensation which he [i.e., Edward Irving] created arose chiefly from his dwelling, in almost every sermon...on his newly adopted belief that Christ might come to our world any day, and any hour...to erect a visible kingdom on earth."[1023]

4. Edward Irving and the Development of Dispensational Theology: 1829-1831

Irving played a major role in the development of Dispensational theology - especially the doctrine of the imminent pretribulation rapture. While there is little doubt that Irving was influenced by the free exchange of prophetic ideas at Albury, it appears likely from the historical record, that Irving was the first to publicly advance the proposition of a pretribulational rapture of the Church. B.W. Newton suggests in his reminiscences that Irving first introduced the concept at one of the five Albury Conferences held between 1826 and 1830.[1024] What is certain is that in a sermon dealing with the book of Revelation, preached by Irving before the General Assembly in Edinburgh, in May 1829, Irving makes what can only reasonably be understood as a reference to the pretribulation rapture in language that is consistent with modern Dispensational phraseology, when he declared;

"I believe, though this is not the place to demonstrate it, that the *hope of the Lord's instant coming* shall distinguish all who in that day shall obtain redemption...Now the *very next action* is Christ's coming in the clouds to *gather his people out of the earth before* the vintage of wrath...'Behold I come as a thief: blessed is he that watcheth, and keepeth his garments'...How blessed? by being admitted to that marriage-supper; by being found keeping their garments..." [1025]

In a further exposition of the book of Revelation, published in 1831, Irving declared;

"Neither by my own calculations, nor by the calculations of other men, will I be prevented from desiring my Lord continually, and *expecting him daily*, even as I ever seek to do; and when he saith, 'Behold, I come quickly,' my soul, do thou make answer, 'Even so; come quickly, Lord Jesus.'"[1026]

And again, Irving explained that;

"...the *first resurrection*, and the *change of the living saints* take place <u>*before the in-falling of the judgments upon the nations*</u>, and <u>*before*</u> the sign of the Son of Man appeareth in the heavens...And so *those who are looking for Christ, shall be taken to himself from the judgments to come*. They shall *meet him in the clouds*, where he is in his sign, and there shall they be with him in the clouds...Now if this *removal from the midst of the judgments* be the thing which we have to look for; if *the first resurrection and the changing of the living saints be thus to take place <u>before</u> the great stream of visible judgment comes rolling on;* then *how watchful we should be night and day*, morning watch, noon, and even-tide, to keep our garments, lest we walk naked, and they see our shame; lest we who have been preaching the advent of Christ be *left behind* amongst the foolish virgins, when our *more faithful sisters are admitted to the marriage supper."[1027]*

Irving and the Albury group were convinced that the Coming of Christ and the rapture of the Church were near. They declared that, "...our blessed Lord **will shortly appear**, and that therefore it is the duty of all who so believe to press these considerations on the attention of all men."[1028] In an earnest attempt to fulfill this stated responsibility, Henry Drummond, who convened and hosted the Albury Conferences, funded the publication of *The Morning Watch*, a quarterly journal dedicated to the study of unfulfilled Bible prophecy. The Albury participants, especially Edward Irving, were the primary contributors to its pages.[1029] From its inception in March 1829, *The Morning Watch* presented a **well-developed and mature Dispensational eschatology** to its readers. Consider the following examples from its early pages.

a. *The Morning Watch* and the Pretribulation Rapture

The pretribulation rapture was frequently referred to within the pages of *The Morning Watch*. The English word "rapture," which was adopted from the Latin Vulgate translation, was rarely used. Instead, phrases such as "gathering," "caught up" and "translated" were commonly employed. The primary textual basis relied upon was First Thessalonians 4 and First Corinthians 15. However, Luke 21:36 (i.e., "Watch...praying in order that you may have strength to escape...") was prominent and commonly used to obliquely refer to the pretribulation rapture. Thus, the pretribulation rapture was frequently referred to as an "escape" from the coming tribulation and the ensuing Divine judgments. Additionally, the pretribulation rapture was reserved for those Christians who were faithfully "praying" and "watching" for the Coming of the Lord - thus it appears that the Albury circle advocated a "partial" pretribulation rapture of the saints. Significantly, as late as 1843, John Darby also seems to have advocated a "partial" pretribulational rapture of the Church.[1030] Consider the following examples from the pages of *The Morning Watch*:

(i) *The Morning Watch*, September 1829 - While referring to Revelation 14:14-16 (i.e., the Divine reaping or harvesting of the earth) John Tudor, the editor of *The*

Morning Watch, advocates a partial pretribulation rapture when he warns that some of the "elect" will be left to endure the Tribulation.

"The first-fruits of his [i.e., Christ's] people I therefore believe to be *gathered into the garner at this time of reaping*; and it is for this privilege that I think we are instructed to watch and pray, Luke xxi.36: 'Watch ye therefore, and pray always, that ye may be accounted worthy to *escape all these things* that shall come to pass, and to stand before the Son of Man.' But I wish to be clearly understood as *limiting this privilege to the 'sealed,' thus removed from the 'great tribulation.'* There will still be *elect ones left on the earth*, 'for whose sake the days shall be shortened' (Matt.xxiv.22): these shall be gathered, *partly* during this great tribulation, and *wholly* at Christ's personal coming to destroy his enemies and set up his Millennial kingdom..."[1031]

Tudor postulates a pretribulational gathering of the "sealed" saints who are accounted worthy to "escape" the trials of the Tribulation. Tudor further describes a partial gathering of some during the Tribulation with a complete and final gathering of the elect after the tribulation at Christ's visible Coming.

(ii) *The Morning Watch*, December 1829: In his exposition of the Apocalypse, John Tudor again espouses a pretribulation rapture when he states that God's judgments will "immediately" fall upon "Babylon" (i.e., apostate Christendom) after the "harvest" or translation of the saints.

"On the *translation of the saints*, the dire judgments on Babylon *immediately ensue*...In the harvest *the saints are gathered as wheat into the barn* (Matt.13:30; Rev.xiv.14): *the tares are left* in bundles on the field. Babylon is threshed and burnt as chaff *after* the harvest..."[1032]

(iii) *The Morning Watch*, March 1830 – Edward Irving explains that the faithful saints who are "watching" for the Coming of Christ will be counted "worthy" to "escape" God's judgments via "translation" *before* the impending destruction upon an unfaithful "Christendom." In amazingly typical Dispensational phraseology, Irving bases his promise of "escape" from the coming Tribulation on Luke 21:36, 1Corinthians 15:51-52 and 1Thessalonians 4:15-16, explaining that the promised pretribulational translation is a "...mystery, which had *not* been made known to the church before, and is not to be found explicitly in the Old Testament."

"We have *a promise of escape out of the awful judgment* with which the Gentile church is to be consumed...It is distinctly given to us in the xxist chapter of the Gospel of St. Luke; where we have...*the escape of the last Christians from the destruction of Christendom*...for the times of the Gentiles are now about being accomplished: the time, times and half a time, of the prophet Daniel, are now ended, and we are living on the eve of the time of trouble such as there never was since there was a nation...Watch therefore, and pray always, that ye may be accounted worthy to escape all these things that shall come to pass, and to stand before the Son of Man.' Here we are distinctly taught that *there be some whom God, through watchfulness and constant prayer, intendeth to deliver from those universal judgments* with which Christendom is to be broken to pieces...Now the question is, In what way they shall escape, and at what time we are to look for that escape? With respect to *the manner in which the remnant of the Gentile church shall escape, I think it sufficiently declared in the xvth chap. of the 1st of Corinthians and the ivth of the 1st Thessalonians*: 'Behold, I shew you a mystery: we shall not all sleep, but we shall all be changed, in a moment, in the twinkling of an eye, at the last trump; for the trumpet shall sound, and the dead shall be raised incorruptible, and we shall be changed.' This mystery, which had *not been made known to the church before,* and is *not to be found explicitly in the Old Testament*, is spoken to all believers in Christ, and to them only...This changing of the living and the resurrection of those that sleep in Jesus, take place...*at his appearing*. The other passage, collateral with this, is written 1Thess.iv.15... These two passages [i.e., 1Cor.15 & 1Thess.4] reveal to us that great mystery of the translation of the living saints by an instantaneous transition, from the state of mortality into the state of immortality; and this, and no other, do I believe to be the way of our escape...Now, with respect to the *time at which this translation of the saints taketh place*, it is not to be doubted, as I think, that its time is *before the judgments which fall upon the earth at the coming of the Son of Man and the setting up of his kingdom*...I believe, therefore, in my heart, that *there is close at hand a deliverance of God's faithful ones by translation*; and that now, when we surely see these awful things beginning to come to pass, we ought to be looking up, as our redemption draweth nigh. I know not how soon this is to take place; but my present belief is that *it will take place before the last awful judgment falleth*. I do therefore call upon all who believe in Christ, and hope to be saved through his righteousness, to be upon their watch-towers, *looking out for the sign of his appearing*." [1033]

Note that Irving clearly links the translation (i.e., the rapture) of the saints with the "appearing" of Christ twice.

(iv) *The Morning Watch*, **June 1831** - In an article written anonymously by "FIDUS" (i.e., Latin for true, sure, faithful) reference is again made to a pretribulation rapture of the "watching saints" which will coincide with the resurrection of the "dead in Christ." All others we are told, shall be left to endure the Tribulation.

"I may only mention here, that it is the **great tribulation** from which those dead in Christ, and those who shall then **be alive and looking for him, shall be exempted**, by being **caught up to meet the Lord in the air**, and to serve him in the execution of his wrath; but under which all other men, the blaspheming sinners and **unwatchful saints**, shall suffer - the one being hardened, the other being greatly blessed, through the greatest chastisement of the Lord."[1034]

(v) *The Morning Watch*, **December 1831** - FIDUS again promises believers that they shall be "translated" and thereby "escape" from the coming "desolations" of the "wicked one" (i.e., the Antichrist) during the "universal hour of trial" (i.e., the Tribulation).

"Let us, then, walk with the Lamb whithersoever he goeth; that, being **translated**, we may in the pavilion of God **escape this desolation of the wicked one, and that universal hour of trial**..."[1035]

(vi) *The Morning Watch*, **December 1831** - John Hooper points to Matthew 24:40-41 to support his contention that believers will be "suddenly and unexpectedly...gathered" (i.e., imminently) **before** Christ's "manifestation to the world."

"The Lord will come, it is said, 'as a thief in the night'...The **sudden and unexpected** manner in which God's people will be **gathered** unto himself, **previous** to his **epiphany, or manifestation unto the world**, is thus described: 'In that night, two shall be in one bed; the one shall be taken, and the other left. Two shall be grinding together; the one shall be taken, and the other left. Two shall be in the field; the one shall be taken, and the other left."[1036]

It is interesting to note that Hooper identifies Christ's "epiphany" with His "manifestation unto the world" (i.e., His glorious post-tribulational appearing), thereby reversing the definition of *epiphany* presented by Irving in a March 1830 article (see par.iii, above), as well as an article written by a Mr. T.W.C., in the September 1830 edition of the *Morning Watch* (see par. e., below). This reversal may be due to either confusion or carelessness on Hooper's part. It seems highly doubtful that Hooper was intentionally advocating a position contrary to that of Irving and the *Morning Watch*.

b. The *Morning Watch* and the Jewish Remnant

The Morning Watch, **March 1830** – Edward Irving refers to an unregenerate Jewish Remnant, regathered to their land and living under a "modified form" of the Mosaic Law during the Tribulation, which he describes as the "extirpation" (i.e., the destruction) of the "apostate Gentile church."

"I believe, furthermore, that while this extirpation of the apostate Gentile church is taking place, the Lord shall be gathering the tribes of Israel, and doing before them his mighty acts. I believe that Elias the Tishbite shall be at their head, restoring all things as they were in the days of Moses, and settling them in their own land, to conduct their worship there according to the ordinance prescribed in the last nine chapters of Ezekiel...*the Jews at this time are not converted to Christ, but living under a modified form of the Levitical institution.*"[1037]

c. The *Morning Watch* and the Parable of the Ten Virgins

June 1830 - John B. Cardale's exposition of "The Parable of the Ten Virgins" is interpreted dispensationally to refer to the pretribulational rapture of the "wise" believers and the leaving of the "unwise" to endure the Tribulation.

"...I believe that Jesus Christ, the Son of Man, is coming again...with his saints (the bride) and with his holy angels...And at his coming the dead in Christ will be raised up; and *those alive, and looking for him, as the wise, will be removed, changed, and caught up to meet him in the air; whilst those like the foolish will be left*, too late to be made wise, to deprecate their folly in *the midst of an infidel ungodly world*, and *to feel the full import of trouble such as never was...to try the sons of men.*"[1038]

d. The *Morning Watch* and the Seven Churches

The Morning Watch, **September 1830** - In his exposition of the "Seven Churches of Revelation," FIDUS, in typical Dispensational style, asserts that each of the Seven Churches prophetically represents a historical period of Church history during the present "Gentile dispensation."

"...the seven churches of the Apocalypse...*do cover the whole Gentile dispensation*...
1.The Ephesian church carries us down to the commencement of the great persecution by Nero, in A.D. 64. 2. That of Smyrna represents the church purified by trial at the hands of Rome, till the ascension of Constantine, in 324. 3. The church at Pergamos sets forth the interval between the elevation of Constantine and the rise of the little horn, at the commencement of the 1260 years. 4. The church at Thyatira expresses the testimony of the church against the Papacy during the 1260 years. 5. That of Sardis indicates the state of the church from the end of the 1260 years, until the preparation for the coming of the Lord. 6. The **Philadelphian church** expresses the period of that preparation, until **the Lord come in the air, and be met by his saints changed and risen.** 7. The Laodicean church (the only one yet future) is our sad monitor concerning the history of the church on earth during that

period of great tribulation which shall intervene between the coming of the Lord to the air and the establishment of his throne and rest in Zion."[1039]

e. The *Morning Watch* and the Two Comings of Christ

September 1830 - An article written by "T.W.C." (perhaps T. W. Chevalier, one of the Albury group), maintains that there are two distinct and separate Comings of Christ. The author asserts that the words *epiphaneia* and *parousia* refer to two different Comings and are therefore to be distinguished. The author explains that the rapture will take place at the Appearing (*epiphaneia*) of Christ, which "is the proper object of the believer's love," sometime *before* the Coming (*parousia*) of Christ. The author further declares that "the most important event...that...takes place during the *epiphaneia*, is the resurrection of the dead in Christ, and the...rapture unto the Lord in the air."

"Hence I conclude with perfect confidence that there shall be...a proper ἐπιφάνεια...an EPIPHANEIA, of the Son of Man; *preceding his παρουσία, his advent to the earth, or presence thereon, by a certain period of time* during which all the tribes of the earth shall mourn...For, indeed, it appears that *this 'epiphaneia' of our Saviour (as distinguished, and separate both in time and place, from his awful 'presence'* [964] *to the destruction of the ungodly), is the proper object of the believer's love*...beyond all controversy, the *epiphaneia [i.e., appearing] of our Lord is to be distinguished from his advent, or presence [i.e. parousia]*...so there can be no doubt that he purposes to interrupt his descent or return; remaining for a time in the sky, before he prosecutes his advent to the surface of our planet: and this period (whether it be longer or shorter I cannot tell) is what the Scripture denominates his '*epiphaneia*'...But *the most important event (so accurately timed in the Bible as to leave no doubt that it takes place during the epiphaneia) is the resurrection of the dead in Christ, and the change of both of them and the then living saints, in the act of their ἀπάντησις,* [965] *or rapture unto the Lord in the air.*"[1040]

T.W.C. follows Irving here, who, in an article published in the March 1830 edition of *The Morning Watch*, identified the translation of the saints with the *epiphaneia* [i.e., *appearing*] of Christ. Referring specifically to First Corinthians 15:51-52, Irving stated;

"This changing of the living and the resurrection of those that sleep in Jesus, take place to the very end that they may enter into the kingdom of God, and that they may be like Christ, which we know we

---

[964] The word "presence" is an oblique reference to the post-tribulational "Coming" *[parousia]* of Christ.

[965] The word *apantesis* (ἀπάντησις) properly means "to meet" and not "rapture." The point being made is that the "meeting" with the Lord in the air coincides with the "rapture" of the Church (see 1Thess.4:17).

become at his *appearing*." Irving concludes by admonishing Christians to, "…be upon their watch-towers, looking out for the sign of his *appearing*."[1041]

Irving and his associates uniformly used the word *appearing (epiphaneia)* to refer to the *pre*tribulational rapture and the word *presence* or *coming (parousia)* to refer to the *post*-tribulational appearance of Christ in judgment. However, some years later, John Darby reversed the definitions of these key words. The word *appearing (epiphaneia)* was redefined by Darby to refer to the *appearing* of Christ in judgment *after* the Tribulation and the word *presence* or *coming (parousia)* was redefined to refer to the *Coming* of Christ to rapture His Church *before* the start of the Tribulation. However, Darby's redefinition of the word *parousia* was problematic due to the fact that the word *parousia* is clearly used to describe the *post*-tribulational Coming of Jesus Christ (see Mt.24:27 and 2Thess.2:8). Thus, in an effort to save the concept of the pretribulation rapture, modern Dispensationalists, led by the scholarship of Dallas Seminary, broadened the scope of these two important terms by arguing that the words *epiphaneia* and *parousia* are used interchangeably in the New Testament to refer to *both* the pretribulational and post-tribulational Comings of Christ. Thus, according to modern Dispensationalists, the pre and post-tribulational distinction between these two terms must be determined solely by the "context" of each individual passage.[966]

5. John Darby and the Albury Years: 1826-1830

The events and circumstances of John Darby's life during the Albury years of 1826 through 1830 have a direct bearing upon the discussion about who originated the doctrine of the pretribulation rapture. It is clear that John Darby did not attend any of the Albury Conferences. In 1825 he was appointed deacon in the Established Church in Ireland. Then, in 1826 he was ordained a priest and appointed curate of Calary in County Wicklow, Ireland.[1042] In 1827, Darby was thrown from his horse and sustained a serious injury to his leg that required approximately 15 months of convalescence.[1043] As a result of his injury, Darby took up residence in Dublin with his sister and brother-in-law, Sergeant Pennefather, which lasted well into 1828.[1044] According to Darby, it was at this time that he experienced spiritual conversion to Christ. Darby stated that, "I

---

[966] See Chapter Five, Part II, Number 1, "Terminology of the Second Coming," for a discussion of the Dispensational claim that the words *parousia* and *epiphaneia* have a dual meaning in the New Testament.

am daily more struck with the connection of the great principles on which my mind was exercised by and with God, *when I found salvation and peace*...in **1827**...but *the church and redemption I did not know till the time I have spoken of*; but eight years before, universal sorrow and sin pressed upon my spirit." And again, Darby recalled that, "...in Dublin, Ireland, **1827-1828**...I had *found peace to my own soul by finding my oneness with Christ*, that it was no longer myself as in the flesh before God, but that I was in Christ, accepted in the Beloved, and sitting in heavenly places with Him."[1045]

It was also at this same time that Darby became acquainted with some of the early Brethren in Dublin[1046] as well as Francis William Newman,[1047] who had been called as tutor to Sergeant Pennefather's household in the autumn of 1827.[1048] Early in 1828, while Darby was still convalescing in Dublin, J.G. Bellett, a close friend of Darby's, visited London and became acquainted with "...those who were warm and alive on prophetic truth, having had their minds freshly illuminated by it." Bellett wrote to Darby from London, and upon his return to Dublin, personally related to Darby what he had seen and heard, finding that, "his [i.e., Darby's] mind and soul had traveled rapidly in the direction which had thus been given to it."[1049] It is possible and even probable that Bellett's reference to "those who were warm and alive on prophetic truth" was an oblique reference to Irving, who at the time was one of the most well-known preachers in London. What is certain is that by 1829, Darby was well acquainted with the prophetic teachings of both Irving and the *Morning Watch*. This is made evident by an article written by Darby from Dublin in 1829, wherein he repeatedly refers to Irving and the *Morning Watch* as he takes issue with some obscure points of Bible interpretation advanced by Irving.[1050]

Towards the end of 1828, F.W. Newman departed from Pennefather's household and returned to Oxford.[1051] Then, in the summer of 1830, Newman invited Darby to visit Oxford, where he met Newman's friends, Benjamin Wills Newton and George Vicesimus Wigram,[1052] where, according to Professor Stokes,[1053] Darby "...exercised for a time a tremendous influence."[1054] In very close proximity to Darby's visit to Oxford, the news of the outbreak of the charismata in Scotland was received at Oxford. The report that tongues, prophecy and healings had been manifested in Scotland caused a great stir among the faculty and students.[1055] At Newton's suggestion, both Darby and Wigram traveled to Scotland to investigate the authenticity of these supposed manifestation of the Spirit.[1056]

Darby visited the Macdonald's house in Port-Glasgow and witnessed the exercise of the "gifts" firsthand in 1830.[1057] He later published an account of his visit to Scotland to correct statements that Newman made in his book *Phases of Faith*.[1058] Darby began his rebuttal by declaring that, "Mr. Newman is not quite right in his account of the report of the 'Irish Clergyman,' [note: this is the title by which Newman referred to Darby[1059]] or at least of what the 'Irish Clergyman' saw and heard. There was a pretended interpretation. Two brothers, respectable ship-builders at Port-Glasgow, of the name of M'D - [i.e., Macdonald], and their sister, were the chief persons who spoke, with a Gaelic maid-servant, in the tongues, and a Mrs. J, - in English. J. M'D - [i.e., James Macdonald] spoke on the occasion alluded to, for about a quarter of an hour, with great energy and fluency, in a semi-Latin sounding speech - then sung a hymn in the same. Having finished, he knelt down and prayed there might be interpretation; as God had given one gift, that he would add the other. His sister got up at the opposite side of the room, and professed to give the interpretation, - but it was a string of texts on overcoming, and no hymn, and one; if not more, of the texts was quoted wrongly... Previous to the time of exercising the gifts, they read, sung psalms, and prayed...This being finished, the 'Irish Clergyman' was going away, when another said to him, 'Don't go, the best part is probably to come yet,' so he staid, and heard what has just been related. He was courteously admitted, as one not believing, who came to see what was the real truth of the case...The M'D-s. [i.e., the Macdonald's] were, in ordinary life, quite sober men, and he believes, most blameless. Their names were so public, that there is no indelicacy in alluding to them, but the 'Irish Clergyman' did not think they had that kind of peace and deliverance from legal thoughts, which is the sign, in another way, of the Spirit's power." [1060]

By 1829, Darby seems to have adopted a premillennial view of Scripture with a definite Dispensational slant. However, there is no indication of a pretribulation rapture at this time. He refers to the millennium as "a restoration of Paradise under the Second Adam"[1061] - to the "Jewish and Gentile dispensations" as the "hinge upon which the subject and understanding of Scriptures turns"[1062] - the establishment of Christ's earthly kingdom and the restoration of the Jews to their land[1063] - the motivation to missions, which the premillennial perspective encourages[1064] - but he is completely silent about a pretribulational, escape, removal, translation or rapture of the Church. In an article written by Darby entitled, *On Days Signifying Years in Prophetic Language*, published by the *Christian Herald* in 1830, Darby makes it plain that he had *not* yet fully embraced a futuristic premillennial interpretation of Scripture. Rather he advocated a premillennial historicism, which equated the prophecies about the Antichrist and the predicted persecution of the saints described in the books of Daniel and Revelation directly to the Papacy. Darby referred to a "long continuance of time" and "long continuance period" that would result in the "wearing out of the saints"- no doubt an oblique reference to the then popular historicist Day-Year Theory, which interpreted the 1260 days of Daniel and Revelation as 1260 years. For example, Darby states:

"Let us now consider the symbols in Daniel...As to 'time, times, and dividing of a time,'...we have three times and a half, or 1260 days, ascribed to the little horn which rose up...amongst, the three horns (of which *I believe there has never been any doubt in applying it to Papal power*)...he is to make war with the saints and to prevail against them, wearing them out - a statement which I do *not* find applicable to the *final apostasy*. Here then we have evidence of this expression being used as a *symbol*...of some *long continuance of time, during which there is a prevailing power wearing out the saints of the Most High*...We have therefore again, *the term of days used for a long continuous period*..." [1065] Darby goes on to explain, "We may now proceed to the passages in the Revelation...The next is, that the holy city should be given to the Gentiles 42 months (the well-known period of 1260 days, a *symbolical prophecy*, and containing in the term evidence of some *unliteral* meaning)...Now in chapter 13 we have *a beast* who continues precisely the same period, recognized to be in power (under the form of the ten horns being crowned, i.e., the Roman Empire in its divided state) by the northern nations under the *papacy*, as may be plainly seen in chapter 17."[1066]

6. Powerscourt: 1831-1833

The second series of prophetic conferences were known as the Powerscourt Conferences. They were held at the estate of Lady Theodosia Powerscourt, located in county Wicklow, Ireland. She has been described as, "young, attractive, widowed, and very pious."[1067] The Countess of Powerscourt was also very interested in the study of unfulfilled Bible prophecy.[1068] When visiting London, she would frequently make arrangements to hear Edward Irving preach.[1069] Lady Theodosia was also personally acquainted with Henry Drummond, and attended at least some of the Albury Conferences.[1070] She was so impressed that she determined to duplicate them at Powerscourt. The Powerscourt Conferences were convened for three consecutive years, beginning in 1831 and ending in 1833.[1071] The most respected clergyman from England, Scotland and Ireland were invited. Each conference lasted approximately one week, with the Rev. Robert Daly, the Rector of Powerscourt, presiding. Topics of discussion revolved around unfulfilled Bible prophecy. Each day's discussion was divided into morning and evening sessions, which were begun and ended with prayer[1072]. The proceedings were not restricted to religious leaders, for according to the eye-witness testimony of Mrs. Hamilton Madden "...all the neighborhood were invited to hear them twice a day."[1073] Additionally, under the direction of the Rev. Robert Daly, Lady Powerscourt also hosted bi-weekly Bible studies every second Tuesday evening at her estate. These studies also focused on the study of unfulfilled Bible prophecy and were also open to the residents of Wicklow.

John Darby actively participated in all three of the Powerscourt Conferences. The First Powerscourt Conference was held October 4th thru the 7th, 1831. Details of the discussions are vague. Generally, the participants discussed whether they were living in the "last days" and if so, they sought to determine if the saints were destined to suffer. The question of whether the 1260 days should be interpreted literally as days, or symbolically as years was debated and the prophetic events that were believed to precede the Second Coming were discussed.[1074]

The second Powerscourt Conference was held September 24th through the 28th, 1832, and covered a broad range of topics. In a letter to the *Christian Herald*, John Darby outlined the proceedings as follows:

"Monday Evening, Six o'clock, September 24th, 1832 - An examination into the quotations given in the New Testament from the Old, with their connections and explanations, viz.: - Matt.1:23, Is.vii.14; Mt.ii.15, Hos., xi.1..."
"Tuesday. - The Prophetical character of each book in the Bible; including the three great feasts of the Jews, the blessings pronounced on Jacob's sons, the Parables in the Gospel, and the Epistles to the Seven Churches in Revelation."
"Wednesday. - "Should we expect a personal Antichrist? If so, to whom will he be revealed? Are there to be one or two evil powers in the world at that time? Is there any uniform sense for the word Saint in the Prophetic, or New Testament scripture? By what covenant did the Jews, and shall the Jews, hold the land?"
"Thursday. - An inquiry into, and a connection between Daniel and the Apocalypse."
"Friday. - What light does scripture throw on present events, and their moral character? What is the next to be looked for and expected? Is there a prospect of a revival of

Apostolic churches before the coming of Christ? What [are] the duties arising out of present events? To what time, and to what class of persons do 1Tim.iv.; 2Tim.iii.; Jude; Matt.xxiv.23,24; and 2Peter iii. refer?"[1075]

J. B. Stoney, a Brethren participant in the conferences, maintained that Irvingites were present at one of the Powerscourt conferences.[1076] Based upon the recollection of Mrs. Hamilton Madden, Edward Irving attended the second Powerscourt Conference.[1077] It was at this conference, according to Darby, that the restoration of the miraculous sign "gifts" were introduced into the discussion - a topic near and dear to Irving's heart. Darby relates that, "There was but one individual who introduced anything which could have given pain to any on these subjects; and that was a reference to the reception of 'the gifts' and the principles connected with it. Little, however, was said upon it; and while the principles were calmly inquired into by a few, it did not, I think, affect the meeting, otherwise to direct the earnest desires and prayers of many, for the more abundant presence of that Holy Ghost, by which alone, error can be brought to light, and the believer guided into all truth. On the whole, this part of the meeting was, perhaps, the most practically profitable, from the elucidation of the doctrine of the Holy Spirit causally drawn from it..." [1078]

The third Powerscourt conference began on Monday, September 23rd and concluded on Saturday, September 28th, 1833.[1079] The most notable among the many attendees, were John Nelson Darby, Benjamin Wills Newton (the leader of the Brethren at Plymouth), George Muller and Henry Craik (the leaders of the Brethren at Bristol).[1080] It is apparent from entries in Henry Craik's diary, that one of the major topics of discussion was the perceived distinction between Jewish and the Christian dispensations.[1081] According to Brethren historian Harold Rowdon, it was this distinction between dispensations that Darby used to introduce the concept of a pretribulation rapture of the Church into the prophetic discussions at the conference. **Rowdon** states that at Powerscourt, Darby introduced his belief that, "...the era of the Christian Church is to be distinguished from all that has gone before and all that will follow. The Christian dispensation (i.e. the administration of God's purposes during the Christian era) was therefore distinguished from the Jewish dispensation on the one hand and the future dispensation on the other." **Rowdon** then observes that; "This distinction was the means by which Darby related the idea of the rapture of the Church to the unfulfilled prophecies of Scripture."[1082] Historian **Ernest Sandeen** agrees, stating that, "Darby introduced into discussion at

Powerscourt the ideas of a secret rapture of the church and of a parenthesis in prophetic fulfillment between the sixty-ninth and seventieth weeks of Daniel."[1083] It is highly probable, that it is this 1833 Powerscourt conference that **H.A. Ironside** is referring to when he claimed that, "It was in these meetings that the precious truth of the rapture of the Church was brought to light...The views brought out at Powerscourt castle not only largely formed the views of Brethren elsewhere, but as years went on obtained wide publication in denominational circles..."[1084]

However, contrary to **Ironside's** claim, the secret pretribulation rapture "was brought to light" at least *four years before* Darby's introduction of the topic at Powerscourt. As previously demonstrated, Edward Irving advocated a pretribulation rapture in May 1829 and *The Morning Watch* began heralding the pretribulation rapture in September 1829. Also, in 1831, Wigram rented a vacant chapel in Plymouth, where Captain Percy Francis Hall regularly preached, attracting large crowds. According to B.W. Newton, Captain Hall, "was greatly drawn to Irvingism" and prayed for the restoration of the miraculous sign gifts at Plymouth.[1085] Not surprisingly, Newton also relates that on the second Sunday that meetings were held in the rented chapel in late 1831, Captain Hall preached on the topic of the "Secret Rapture."[1086]

Although Darby introduced the topic of the pretribulational rapture into the discussion at the 1833 Powerscourt Conference, his views on prophecy were still in their formative stages and still lacked certainty and maturity. Referring specifically to Darby's prophetic opinions at the time of Powerscourt, **Harold Rowdon** cautions that, "...it should not be concluded that these ideas were fully developed as early as **1833**."[1087] Similarly, historian **Ernest Sandeen** says, "Darby held an open mind on both of these subjects [i.e., the secret rapture and the parenthesis theory] as late as **1843**."[1088] Likewise, with respect to Darby's position on the secret rapture **Harold Rowdon** relates that, "Even as late as **1843**, Darby's mind was not fully made up."[1089] Darby's uncertainty is made apparent by a series of letters that were exchanged between himself and **B.W. Newton** in **1840 or 1841**. **Newton** wrote; "I believe that it is essential to the existence of Prophecy about the Church that there should be intervening events foretold. You on the contrary say there can be no intervening events for the Church's expectation and refuse to receive any thought from Scripture inconsistent with this main principle." **Newton** went on to say that in his judgment he believed that **Darby's** approach to prophetic interpretation, "...would destroy Christianity if carried out."[1090]

In his response to Newton, **Darby** revealed serious reservations as to the validity of the pretribulation rapture theory, when he confessed, "As to any secret coming I have no conviction about it and the proofs to me are certainly very feeble and vague."[1091]

7. The Charge That the Pretribulation Rapture Doctrine Had Demonic Origins

Opponents of the pretribulation rapture theory have frequently charged that the doctrine had demonic origins. It is asserted that the teaching that the church would escape from the coming Tribulation was first revealed through a prophetic utterance made in Edward Irving's church in London. The source of this allegation seems to be the highly respected and renowned Bible scholar, Samuel P. Tregelles.[1092] In his book, *The Hope of Christ's Second Coming*, **Tregelles** states in a footnote that;

"I am not aware that there was any definite teaching that there would be a secret rapture of the Church at a secret coming, until this was given forth as an 'utterance' in Mr. Irving's Church, from what was there received as being the voice of the Spirit. But whether any one ever asserted such a thing or not, it was from that supposed revelation that the modern doctrine and modern phraseology respecting it arose. It came not from Holy Scripture, but from that which falsely pretended to be the Spirit of God..."[1093]

Likewise, **Robert Cameron**,[1094] who was very active in the premillennial movement in America in the late 1800s and early 1900s, has charged that;

"The mention of this view, so far as I can ascertain, during the whole period of Christian history, was in the church of Edward Irving, in London, in the later part of 1831 and the early part of 1832...for the first time in the whole history of the Christian church, the new and strange doctrine that the church should be translated secretly, and before the great tribulation, was made known...not by Mr. Irving alone, but by those who 'spoke in the power,' as they called the testimony of these deceiving spirits, professing to be the Spirit of God." [1095]

It is evident however, from historical evidence that both Tregelles and Cameron were mistaken as to the origin of the pretribulation rapture teaching. However, they were certainly correct in asserting that the doctrine of the Lord's imminent, pretribulational Coming was the predominant subject matter of the tongues and prophecies in Edward Irving's church. The close relationship between the manifestation of the miraculous "gifts" and the doctrine of the secret Coming of Christ is undeniable. Consider the statement of Robert Baxter, who was a recognized prophet and Apostle within Irving's church. **Baxter** stated that;

"One circumstance of these manifestations cannot but force itself upon observation; that is, *the continual use which was made of the doctrine of the second advent of our Lord*. This was the *leading theme of the utterances*. The *nearness* of it, its *suddenness*, and the fearful judgments which would accompany it, were the *continual arguments* which were used to excite our minds, and stimulate our decision; as well as to support us under difficulties, and to induce us to lay all other things aside to further the work."[1096]

While the close relationship between the charismata and the secret, pretribulational Coming of Christ is undeniable, it does not necessarily follow that the doctrine of the secret rapture originated via these prophetic utterances. In fact, the historical evidence indicates that the doctrine of the secret pretribulation rapture originated well *before* the first prophecies were uttered within Irving's church.

More recently, Dave MacPherson, who has conducted extensive historical research in an attempt to discover the origin of the pretribulation rapture doctrine, has concluded that a young Scottish girl, estimated to be about 15 years old, was the first to declare that the saints would be raptured before the onset of the Great Tribulation. **MacPherson** maintains that his research demonstrates that, "...Margaret Macdonald had a private revelation in Port Glasgow, Scotland, in the early part of 1830[1097] that a select group of Christians would be caught up to meet Christ in the air *before* the days of Antichrist."[1098] According to MacPherson, Miss Macdonald claimed that she had received a Divine revelation of the soon, pretribulational Coming of Christ. MacPherson bases his conclusion on a letter written by Margaret that recounted the contents of her vision, in which she declared that;

"...I heard the trump of God in my ears so loud that all other sounds were lost. Indeed I heard unutterable things: the sound of the trumpet seemed to wax louder and louder as if that moment the Lord was to have been revealed...I saw the Lord coming in the glory of his Father and of all the holy angels...I was desiring so much the speedy arrival of the day of the Lord..."[1099]

While Miss Macdonald's testimony hints at an imminent pretribulation rapture, it fails to clearly assert it. Thus, MacPherson's contention that Margaret Macdonald was the first to articulate a pretribulation rapture relies primarily upon Dr. Robert Norton's[1100] assessment of Margaret's vision. **Norton**, who chronicled the Pentecostal experiences of Margaret Macdonald and her brothers, James and George, explained that;

"Marvelous light was shed upon Scripture, and especially on the doctrine of the second Advent...by Miss M.M - [i.e., Margaret Macdonald]...here we **first see** the distinction between that final stage of the Lord's coming, when every eye shall see Him, and His **prior appearing** in glory to them that look for Him."[1101]

Dr. Norton clearly attributed the Dispensational concept of dividing the Second Coming of Christ into two stages (i.e., one before the tribulation and one after the tribulation) to Margaret Macdonald. Furthermore, Dr. Norton states that this was the "*first*" time that this "*distinction*" was made. However, Dr. Norton was mistaken. Margaret Macdonald was *not* the first to divide the second Coming of Christ into two distinct stages or phases and thereby advocate a pretribulation rapture of the Church. Rather, the historical evidence establishes that Edward Irving and the Albury group had made this distinction as early as 1829.[1102]

It is true that the imminent Coming of Christ was a common theme of the prophetic utterances in both Scotland and London. It is also true that the pretribulation rapture teaching quickly became the predominant subject of the prophecies and utterances within Edward Irving's church in London. However, it also becomes evident from the historical evidence that the concept of the pretribulation rapture was *adopted* by the prophets and prophetesses within Irving's church, and not *originated* by them. This fact is underscored by the declarations of Robert Baxter, who was one of the leading prophets within Irving's church.[1103] For example, while under the control of "the power," Baxter relates that he uttered a prophecy predicting *when* the pretribulation rapture of the Church would take place. This prophecy was delivered on January 14, 1832, when Baxter and a group of young men affiliated with an outreach ministry within Irving's church were visiting Irving's home. **Baxter** recounts that he suddenly came under the power of the Spirit and for the space of some two hours began "preaching in the Spirit." He explains that it was revealed that, "...we were commanded to count the days, one thousand three score and two hundred - 1260 - the days appointed for testimony, at the end of which the saints of the Lord should go up to meet the Lord in the air, and evermore be with the Lord."[1104] To clarify what he meant by the "going up of the saints,"[1105] **Baxter** went on to explain that;

"An opinion had been advanced in some of Mr. Irving's *writings*, that *before* the second coming of Christ, and *before* the setting in upon the world of the 'days of vengeance,' emphatically so called in the Scriptures, the saints would be caught up to heaven like Enoch and Elijah; and would be thus saved from the destruction of this world, as Noah was saved in the ark, and as Lot was saved from Sodom."[1106]

Clearly, Baxter was already well aware of Irving's pretribulational teachings prior to his "revelation" in 1832, and either consciously or unconsciously incorporated them into his utterances. Interestingly, Baxter explained that he found it difficult to accept Irving's teaching that the Church would escape from the coming Tribulation by means of a pretribulation rapture. Rather, he was convinced that the Church would find "refuge" in "some earthly sanctuary" until the Lord returned after the Tribulation. However, **Baxter** relates that he experienced a "sudden change of opinion" when;

"...the passages in Matt.xxiv, 'Two shall be in the field, one shall be taken, and the other left; two women shall be grinding at the mill, one shall be taken, and the other left,' were brought to me in the power, accompanied with the sudden conviction I have before described - 'This is the translation of the saints, whilst the rest of the world are left in their usual occupations.' Another passage was also brought to me - Luke xxi.36. 'Watch ye, therefore, and pray always, that ye may be accounted worthy to escape all these things that shall come to pass, and to stand before the Son of Man,' - accompanied by the same overpowering conviction, 'This is from the days of vengeance, and the standing before the Son, is for those who are counted worthy to be translated.'"[1107]

Baxter's prophecy of the coming pretribulation rapture was repeated on numerous occasions. He relates that;

"The prophecy of the 1260 days testimony and going up of the saints, set forth a period of three years and a half, from the time of its delivery, up to the translation of the saints. The words of the prophecy were most distinct, to count from that day (viz. 14th January, 1832) 1260 days, and three days and a half; (Rev.xi.11) and on innumerable other occasions, by exposition and by prophecy, was the same thing again and again declared, and most largely opened."[1108]

Baxter's prophecy left him open to the charge that he was attempting to predict, what Christ Himself said was unpredictable - the day He would return (see Mark 13:32 - i.e.,

308

that no man knows the day or the hour of Christ's return). However, in anticipation of such criticism, **Edward Irving** explained in a letter dated January 27th, 1832, that;

"He [i.e. Robert Baxter] said in the Spirit that the two orders of witnesses were now present in the church, the 1260 days of witnessing are begun, and that within three and a half years, the saints will be taken up, according to the 12th chapter of the Apocalypse. (This is not to date the Lord's *coming*, which is some time *after* His saints are with Him.) Edwd. Irving"[1109]

Thus, Irving defended Baxter against the charge of predicting the time of Christ return, by separating the rapture from the Coming. However, by April 1832, only one year after his first contact with Irving's church, Baxter experienced serious reservations about the legitimacy of the "gifts." His doubts began when a friend accused Irving of teaching that Christ possessed a "sinful nature." Baxter was shocked by the accusation but remained confident that his friend was mistaken about Irving and gave the matter no further thought. However, shortly thereafter, Baxter received a letter from a member of Irving's church. The letter referred to Irving's exposition of Romans 8, in which he taught that the Lord, in His humanity, struggled against a "carnal mind" and had "the law of sin to contend with." The correspondent was troubled by these assertions and sought Baxter's opinion. Then, a few days later, a visiting clergyman called upon Baxter at his residence and gave him a book written by Irving that confirmed that Irving did in fact teach that the "law of sin" was indeed present within the person of Jesus Christ. Baxter stated that "...I not only found, on further reading of his work, that his views were unsound on the human nature of our Lord, but that he was also still more unsound on the doctrines concerning holiness; he rejecting the imputation of the righteousness of Christ, and holding a perfect holiness in the flesh."[1110]

Baxter then resolved to address Irving directly. He explained that, "...in much heaviness, I sat down to write to Mr. Irving, stating fully his error in conceiving the law of sin to be in the flesh of Jesus; and stating also what I conceived to be the truth concerning our holiness."[1111] **Irving** responded to Baxter's inquiry in a letter dated April 21, 1832, in which he unflinchingly declared; "Concerning the flesh of Christ...I believe it to have been no better than our flesh, as to its passive qualities or properties, as a creature thing...Christ had the motions of the flesh...the law of the flesh was there all present: but whereas in us it is set on fire by an evil life, in him it was, by a holy life, put down..."[1112] Irving's response delivered a "great blow" to Baxter, calling into serious doubt the legitimacy of the "gifts." **Baxter** reasoned; "Here I saw doctrines, which I could never have believed Mr. Irving held, not only avowed by him, but sustained and enforced by the utterance, in power, of those who were deemed the gifted persons."[1113] A crisis of conscience immediately ensued. **Baxter** resolved: "...I could not for a moment doubt the erroneousness of Mr. Irving's views. I was then, of necessity, compelled to conclude the utterances which supported those views were not of the Spirit of God. Upon this, doubt arose in my own mind...whether the whole work were not of Satan...I was convinced it must be a work of Satan, who, as an angel of light, was permitted for a time to deceive us."[1114]

Thus, in May of 1832, **Baxter** traveled to London to personally inform Mr. Irving that he was convinced "...that we had all been speaking by a lying spirit, and not by the Spirit of the Lord."[1115] **Baxter** concluded that, "...such is the cunning craftiness of the enemy, that if we put ourselves under his power, by giving heed to seducing spirits, our eyes are blinded by him, and our minds are darkened by him, until we are, both blind and foolish beyond belief."[1116]

8. Summary

As previously mentioned, during the early 1800s, there was a resurgence of interest in unfulfilled Bible prophecy sparked by the fear and uncertainty generated by the political and social unrest within Europe. Many Christians were convinced that the Second Coming of Christ was very near. This led to a renewed interest in and study of the prophetic Scriptures in an attempt to discern "the signs of the times." Many new ideas and approaches to prophetic interpretation were advanced. Most significantly, post-millennialism was abandoned in favor of premillennialism - the historicist Day-Year Theory was exchanged for a futuristic view of prophecy - and soon thereafter, the theory of the pretribulation rapture was heralded by Irving and *The Morning Watch*. These new prophetic ideas were quickly disseminated via books, periodicals, sermons and personal conversations.

For example, we know for certain that Captain Hall, a popular Brethren preacher at Plymouth was greatly influenced by Irving's doctrines.[1117] Irving may also have had a significant influence on the prophetic ideas of J.G. Bellett when he traveled to London in 1828 and was introduced to new prophetic ideas there.[1118] Bellett certainly exercised a profound influence over John Darby when he returned from London and shared his new prophetic ideas with Darby.[1119] We also know for certain that by 1829, Darby was well aware of both Irving's and *The Morning Watch's* Dispensational teachings.[1120] Lady Powerscourt was well acquainted with both Henry Drummond and Edward Irving, having attended at least some of the Albury Conferences.[1121] Likewise, the Countess made it a point to hear Irving preach whenever she traveled to London.[1122] She also entertained Irving and his family in 1830, when they visited Ireland.[1123] Significantly, Lady Powerscourt was also well acquainted with John Darby. Darby attended all three of the Powerscourt Conferences. By the third conference in 1833, Lady Powerscourt was engaged to marry Darby, although the engagement was ultimately called off.[1124] It would be hard to imagine that Lady Powerscourt never discussed Irving's prophetic views with Darby.

The timing and sequence of the historical events in conjunction with the complex chain of human interactions strongly suggest that Darby was dependent upon Irving and the *Morning Watch* for much of his Dispensational system. The learned Professor George Stokes, who was a contemporary of John Darby, emphatically states that Darby derived his prophetic views directly from Edward Irving.[1125] The historical evidence seems to validate this claim. Any attempts to argue that Darby was unaware of Irving's views regarding the pretribulation rapture theory are simply untenable. While the seminal idea may have originated elsewhere, the historical record confirms that Edward Irving, along with the Albury group, originated, developed and propagated the concept of the pretribulation rapture well before John Darby publicly advocated it at Powerscourt in 1833.

Both Irving and Darby possessed strong and persuasive personalities. The influence that they exerted over their contemporaries, especially with regard to prophetic interpretation, is incalculable. However, due to Irving's untimely death in 1834, his contribution to prophetic study quickly faded into obscurity. Darby became the driving force behind the new pretribulation rapture theory, and was therefore, credited with originating it by succeeding generations. The fact that Darby claimed in later years to have discovered the theory gave credence to the prevailing opinion that he was the originator - especially in light of the fact that he spent his entire life refining and popularizing the theory. Thus, most Dispensationalists, who know little about the historical development of this doctrine, have unhesitatingly accepted Darby's claim to originality - a claim that the historical record certainly calls into serious question.

9. Timeline of Key Events Related to the Development of the Pretribulation Rapture Doctrine

Below is the sequence of events, listed in chronological order, which pertain to the development of the secret pretribulation rapture doctrine.

1825 – Edward Irving was introduced to the study of unfulfilled Bible prophecy by James Hatley Frere. Irving adopts a premillennial historicist view of prophecy.

1825 – John Darby appointed deacon in the Irish Church.

1826 - Darby ordained a priest and appointed curate of Calary in County Wicklow, Ireland.

1826 - Irving translates Lacunza's *The Coming of the Messiah in Glory and Majesty*.

1826 - November - The first Albury Conference articulates distinctive Dispensational concepts and terminology.

1827 - The second Albury Conference attempts to correlate current events with unfulfilled Bible prophecy.

1827-1828 - Darby is injured in a horse accident; convalesces at his sister's home in Dublin. Meets Francis Newman and early Brethren leaders.

1827-1828 - Darby experiences personal conversion to Christ.[1126]

1828 - J. G. Bellett visits London and is introduced to "those who were warm and alive on prophetic truth."[1127] (Irvingites?) Upon his return to Dublin, Bellett informs Darby of all that he heard.

1828 - The third Albury Conference is convened – particulars discussed are unknown.

1829 - March - Henry Drummond funds the publication of *The Morning Watch*, a quarterly journal dedicated to explaining prophetic truth. From its inception, the journal presented a well-developed and mature Dispensational eschatology.

1829 - May - Irving preaches a sermon before the General Assembly in Edinburgh, advocating a pretribulation rapture.[1128]

1829 - The fourth Albury Conference anticipates the regathering of the Jews to Palestine; impending judgment upon apostate Christendom; the establishment of an earthly Millennium. B.W. Newton's reminiscences suggest that Irving introduced the pretribulation rapture theory at one of the Albury Conferences. If so, it seems probable that it was at this fourth conference.

1829 - September - John Tudor advocates a pretribulation rapture in *The Morning Watch*.[1129]

1829 - December - John Tudor again advocates a pretribulation rapture in *The Morning Watch*.[1130]

1830 - March (?) - Margaret Macdonald of Glasgow is miraculously healed when her brother James commands her to arise from her sick-bed.

1830 - March 28th – Fernicary, Scotland: Mary Campbell speaks in tongues. Shortly thereafter, Mary receives a letter from James Macdonald which initiates her miraculous healing.

1830 - Irving takes measures to be kept appraised of the manifestation of the "gifts" in Port-Glasgow via mail and first hand reports from friends.

1830 - March - Irving advocates a pretribulation rapture in *The Morning Watch*.[1131]

1830 - March - In *The Morning Watch*, Irving describes an unregenerate Jewish remnant that will exist in the last days.[1132]

1830 - April 16th - James and George Macdonald speak in tongues.

1830 - June - J.B. Cardale in *The Morning Watch* advocates a pretribulation rapture based upon his interpretation of the Parable of the Ten Virgins.[1133]

1830 - July - The fifth Albury Conference - Participants issue a call to pray for the restoration of the miraculous sign gifts as manifested in the early Church.

1830 - August or September[1134] - Darby is invited to Oxford by Francis Newman, where he meets B.W. Newton and George V. Wigram.

1830 - Darby & Wigram visit Port-Glasgow to evaluate "the gifts."[1135]

1830 - September - In *The Morning Watch,* "FIDUS" interprets the *Letters to the Seven Churches* (Rv.2-3) as a prophetic outline of Church history.[1136]

1830 - September - *The Morning Watch* divides the Advent of Christ into two distinct phases by making a distinction between the words, **epiphaneia** (the pre-tribulation **appearance** of Christ) and **parousia** (the glorious visible **Coming** of Christ to earth).[1137]

1830 – December - Darby publishes an article in the *Christian Herald* that advocates the historicist Day-Year Theory.[1138]

1831 – Edward Irving publishes an *Exposition of the Book of Revelation in a*

Series of Lectures that expresses well-developed Dispensational concepts.[1139]

1831 - April 30th - Mrs. John B. Cardale is the first to manifest the gift of tongues in London. Shortly thereafter she joins Irving's church and is recognized as a "prophetess."[1140]

1831 - May - The gifts of tongues and prophecy begin to be exercised in the early morning prayer meetings at Irving's church. Then sometime between August 1831 and January 1832, Irving allows these gifts to be used in the Sunday morning church services.[1141]

1831 - June - In *The Morning Watch*, "FIDUS" advocates a pretribulation rapture.[1142]

1831 - October 4-7 - The first Powerscourt Conference. Questions explored: "Are these the last days?" "Will the saints suffer?" "Are the 1260 days literal or symbolic?" "What prophetic events precede the Coming of Christ?"[1143]

1831 – (The latter part of) Captain Percy Francis Hall preaches on the pretribulation rapture at Plymouth.[1144]

1831 – (The latter part of) - Darby visits Newton at his home in Plymouth.[1145]

1832 - January 14th - Robert Baxter prophesies that the pretribulation rapture would take place in 1260 days from Jan.14, 1832.[1146]

1832 - January 27th - Irving defends Baxter's prediction of the rapture of the Church "within 1260 days" based on the argument that the Advent of Christ would be in two distinct phases. Irving explained, "This is *not* the date of the Lord's *coming*, which is sometime *after* His saints are with Him."[1147] In other words, Baxter was predicting the *Appearing* of Christ (*epiphaneia*) and *not* the *Coming* (*parousia*) of Christ.

1832 – April 21st – Robert Baxter is shocked and dismayed to learn that Edward Irving maintained that the principle of sin was present in the flesh of Christ.

1832 - May - Baxter informs Irving that he was convinced that all of the "prophets" within Irving's church were being deceived by "a lying spirit."[1148]

1832 - September - The second Powerscourt Conference: Explored the prophetic character of each of the books of the Bible; discussed whether the Antichrist would be a literal person and the connection between Daniel and Revelation; analyzed current events in the light of the prophetic Scriptures in an attempt to determine what events should be expected next. According to Mrs. Madden, Irving attended this conference.[1149]

1832 or 1833 - Mr. T. Tweedy helps Darby resolve a "difficulty" which he encountered with the secret pretribulation rapture theory by suggesting that 2Thessalonians 2:1-2, offered "decisive proof from Scripture" for a pretribulation rapture.[1150] In a letter to B.W. Newton, Darby introduces the concept of "dispensationalizing" New Testament verses that do not harmonize with the secret pretribulation rapture theory.[1151]

1833 - March 13th - Edward Irving is excommunicated by the Church of Scotland for denying the impeccability of Christ - Irving held the heretical view that, "the flesh of Christ...to have been no better than our flesh..."[1152]

1833 - The third Powerscourt Conference: John Darby introduces the concept of the secret pretribulational rapture in conjunction with a discussion about the supposed differences between the Jewish and Christian dispensations.[1153]

1834 - December 7th - Edward Irving dies at 42 years of age.

1840 or 1841 - In a letter to B.W. Newton, Darby expresses uncertainty about the validity of the secret pretribulation rapture.[1154]

1843 - Darby advocates a partial pretribulation rapture.[1155]

1850 - Darby claims that he discovered the pretribulation rapture in 1830, while studying 2Thessalonians 2.[1156]

1882 – John Darby dies.

END-NOTES TO APPENDIX D

[985] *Edward Irving: An Ecclesiastical and Literary Biography* - Washington Wilks, William Freeman, London, 1854, p.206.

[986] "The events transacting on the continent and at home - a revolutionary dynasty on the throne of France; Belgium struggling to break its unnatural bond with Holland, and Poland to get from under the foot of Russia; a fierce political agitation shaking the most ancient institutions of England; and cholera, for the first time, unfolding its death-shedding wings over the land; everywhere change, strife, and terror..." *Edward Irving: An Ecclesiastical and Literary Biography* - Washington Wilks, William Freeman, London, 1854, p.206. And also, "The impulse came eventually, strange to say, from the outburst of the forces of evil. The startling violence of the French Revolution...the old barriers of society were overthrown...fundamental and widespreading changes were introduced...These events had hardly passed by when the career of the first Napoleon appeared, like the passage of a brilliant meteor in the heavens, and amazed and perplexed the minds of men...alarm and dissatisfaction with the system of religion then prevailing were greatly increased...The customs and forms inherited from previous generations had hardened into a stiff, artificial conventionalism...One of the early consequences, therefore, of this uneasy desire for change was an eager study of Holy Scripture... And as men were then looking forward, the study of prophecy in particular attracted a great deal of attention." *The History and Doctrines of Irvingism* - Edward Miller, C. Kegan Paul & Co., London, 1878, vol.1, pp.7-9

[987] Henry Drummond (1786-1860) was a wealthy banker and member of Parliament. He financed the publication of the prophetic quarterly journal *The Morning Watch*. This quarterly became the official organ of the Catholic Apostolic Church, which traces its origin to Edward Irving, Henry Drummond, Mr. Taplin and John B. Cardale in 1832. Their goal was to duplicate what they perceived to be the purity and simplicity of worship of the early Church as depicted in the book of Acts.

[988] Edward Irving was an extremely popular preacher. His short-lived career began as the assistant to the renowned Rev. Thomas Chalmers in Glasgow, Scotland in 1819. In July of 1822, Irving assumed the pastorate of the Caledonian Chapel in Hatton Garden, London. A gifted orator, he soon attracted huge crowds. However, his ministry was wrought with controversy over his questionable views concerning the nature of Jesus Christ. Irving denied the doctrine of impeccability, teaching that Christ possessed a sinful human nature. According to Irving, Christ remained sinless in practice due to the restraining influence of the Holy Spirit and not because He had a sinless nature. As a result, Irving was deposed from his pastorate by the Presbytery of London in May, 1832. The Presbytery of Annan excommunicated him from the Presbyterian Church on March 13, 1833, finding him guilty of heresy. Irving died on December 7, 1834, at 42 years of age.

[989] Historicism: The Historicist sees the fulfillment of the prophecies of the book of Revelation primarily in the events of European history. The Futurist sees the prophecies of the book of Revelation fulfilled during the future Tribulation period.

[990] Mrs. Margaret Oliphant observed that it was, "Mr. Hatley Frere, who, according to his own testimony, was the first to turn Irving's thoughts towards prophecy." In a letter written to Hatley Frere, Irving declared, "...I waited upon you and offered myself as your pupil, to be instructed in prophecy according to your ideas thereof...I am forever beholden to you, most dear and worthy friend..." *The Life of Edward Irving* - Mrs. Margaret Oliphant, Hurst and Blackett, London, 1862, vol.1, pp. 226,396.

[991] The Day-Year Theory: Generally speaking, prophecies pertaining to the Antichrist were applied to the Papacy of Rome. The 1260 days (i.e., 3 1/2 years, 42 months, time and times and half a times) of Daniel and Revelation were interpreted as 1260 years.

[992] *The Roots of Fundamentalism* - Ernest R. Sandeen, The University of Chicago Press, 1970, p.17.

[993] "...it was my privilege to be personally acquainted with Mr. Irving..." *The Plymouth Brethren: Their History and Heresies* - James Grant, William Macintosh, London, 1875, p.1.

[994] *The Plymouth Brethren: Their History and Heresies* - James Grant, William Macintosh, London, 1875, p.2. Also, Professor Stokes has observed that, "His [i.e., Edward Irving's] teaching which was closely modeled upon the style of the old Hebrew prophets, dealt very largely with the subject of unfulfilled prophecy and the speedy manifestation of the Second Advent of Christ." *The Contemporary Review* - Volume XLVIII. July-December, 1885, *John Nelson Darby*, George T. Stokes, p.543.

[995] The fourth conference resolved: "That a great period of 1260 years commenced in the reign of Justinian, and terminated at the French Revolution, and that the vials of the Apocalypse began then to be poured out; that our blessed Lord will shortly appear, and that therefore it is the duty of all who so believe to press these considerations on the attention of all men." *Dialogues on Prophecy* by Henry Drummond, as quoted in *The History and Doctrines of Irvingism* - Edward Miller, C. Kegan Paul & Co., London, 1878, vol.1, p.45.

[996] Regarding the first Albury Conference of 1826: Irving relates that, "We believed in common that the present form of the dispensation of the gospel was a time commensurate with the times of the Gentiles, which are again commensurate with the period of Jerusalem's being trodden underfoot, and the Jews' dispersion; that the restoration of the Jews would introduce a new era into the Church and the world, which might be called the universal dispensation of the benefits of Christ's death, while this is the dispensation to the Church only, which is few compared with the whole. That the conclusion of the later in great judgments, and the commencement of the former in great mercies, was hard at hand, yea, even at the very door; all being agreed that the 1260 and 1290 days of Daniel were accomplished, and the remaining 45 begun, at the conclusion of which the blessedness will be fully arrived." *The History and Doctrines of Irvingism* - Edward Miller, C. Kegan Paul & Co., London, 1878, vol.1, pp.38-39.

[997] Regarding the second Albury Conference: "The second meeting, in 1827...The interpretations of prophecy appear now to have taken a more definite turn, and to have been carried onwards from merely general notions about the return of the Jews to Jerusalem, and the approaching coming of the Lord for His millennial reign on earth, to a detailed application of the 'times and the seasons' of the current period. The Apocalyptic Vial was supposed to have been poured out on Rome in A.D. 1798; and it was concluded that the coming of the Lord would take place in 1847...It is striking to see the stress then laid upon passing events...a war with Turkey seemed to the council to denote the near approach of the end. Indeed, the sixth vial was supposed to foreshadow the fall of the Ottoman Empire... [and a political speech which warned that conflict

of opinions and opposing principles might] become the groundwork of a general war, was eagerly seized upon as indicating the nearness of the battle of Armageddon. It was thought that there would soon be a general apostasy of the Church, and that the Jews would be the instruments of Almighty God's displeasure." *The History and Doctrines of Irvingism* - Edward Miller, C. Kegan Paul & Co., London, 1878, vol.1, pp.41-42,43. However, not all of the Conference participants agreed with this approach, which attempted to equate unfulfilled Bible prophecies to current events. Rev. Robert Story of Rosneath remarked that many of the Conference participants were attempting "to ascertain the mind of God regarding the things that shall shortly come to pass." Story's perception was that, "...in any answer one may be certain either prophecy would be twisted to meet fact, or fact would be mutilated to fit prophecy..." *Memoir of the Life of the Rev. Robert Story* - Robert Herbert Story, Macmillan and Co., 1862, p.103.

[998] The fourth Albury Conference concluded, 1. "That the present Christian dispensation is not to pass insensibly into the millennial state by gradual increase of the preaching of the gospel; but that it is to be terminated by judgments, ending in the destruction of this visible Church and polity, in the same manner as the Jewish dispensation has been terminated." 2. "That during the time that these judgments are falling upon Christendom, the Jews will be restored to their own land." 3. "That the judgments will fall principally, if not exclusively, upon Christendom, and begin with that part of the Church of God which has been most highly favoured, and is therefore most deeply responsible." 4. "That the termination of these judgments is to be succeeded by that period of universal blessedness to all mankind, and even to the beasts, which is commonly called the millennium." 5. "That a great period of 1260 years commenced in the reign of Justinian, and terminated at the French Revolution, and that the vials of the Apocalypse began then to be poured out; that our blessed Lord will shortly appear, and that therefore it is the duty of all who so believe to press these considerations on the attention of all men." *Dialogues on Prophecy* by Henry Drummond, as quoted in *The History and Doctrines of Irvingism* - Edward Miller, C. Kegan Paul & Co., London, 1878, vol.1, pp.44-45.

[999] *The Origins of the Brethren* - Harold H. Rowdon, Pickering & Inglis Ltd., 1967, p.10.

[1000] *The History and Doctrines of Irvingism* - Edward Miller, C. Kegan Paul & Co., London, 1878, vol.1, p.46.

[1001] "Mary Campbell was the first person to speak with unknown tongues (on Sunday evening, March 28, 1830)." *The Incredible Cover-Up* - Dave MacPherson, Alpha Omega Publishing Company, 1975, p.54. Also, "One Sunday evening in the end of March 1830, as Mary lay in weakness upon a sofa...she broke forth, speaking in an unknown tongue, in loud ecstatic utterances, for more than an hour." *Letters of Thomas Erskine of Linlathen* - Edited by William Hanna, David Douglas, Edinburgh, 1884, Chapter VII, The Spiritual Gifts - Letters from 1830-1835, p.129. Also, "On a Sunday evening in the month of March, Mary, in the presence of a few friends, began to utter sounds to them incomprehensible, and believed by her to be a tongue such as of old might have been spoken on the day of Pentecost, or among the Christians of Corinth. This was the first manifestation of the restored 'gift.' - for such it was imagined to be..." *Memoir of the Life of the Rev. Robert Story* - Robert Herbert Story, Macmillan and Co., 1862, p.204.

[1002] "Mary Campbell who intended to exchange her occupation of dressmaking for missionary life...was confined to her room, and was supposed to be on the verge of the disease, a species of consumption...*The History and Doctrines of Irvingism* - Edward Miller, M.A., C. Kegan Paul & Co., London, 1878, vol.1, p.52.

[1003] "One Sunday evening in the end of March 1830, as Mary lay in weakness upon a sofa, suffering apparently under the same disease which carried her sister [i.e., Isabella Campbell] to the grave, whilst those around her were praying for the restoration of the gifts bestowed upon the primitive Church, suddenly, as if possessed by a superhuman strength, she broke forth, speaking in an unknown tongue, in loud ecstatic utterances, for more than an hour." *Letters of Thomas Erskine of Linlathen* - Edited by William Hanna, David Douglas, Edinburgh, 1884, Chapter VII, The Spiritual Gifts - Letters from 1830-1835, p.129.

[1004] "The tongue itself was supposed by Mary Campbell, who was the first to exercise it, and apparently by all who believed in the reality of the gift at that time, to be in truth a language...Mary Campbell herself expressed her conviction that the tongue given to her was that of the Pelew Islands..." *The Life of Edward Irving* - Margaret Oliphant, Hurst & Blackett, 1862, vol. II, p.147,206. Also, "By and by she [i.e., Mary Campbell] announced that she believed it to be the language of a group of islands in the Southern Pacific Ocean..." *Memoir of the Life of the Rev. Robert Story* - Robert Herbert Story, Macmillan and Co., 1862, p.204.

[1005] Mr. A.J. Scott later became Professor Scott, of Owens College, Manchester. *Memoir of the Life of the Rev. Robert Story* - Robert Herbert Story, Macmillan and Co., 1862, p.152.

[1006] "...a company of devout persons at the dull little town of Port-Glasgow...were daily meeting to unite in prayer for a special outpouring of the Holy Spirit. Among these was a pious family named M'Donald, consisting of two brothers and three sisters...These good people, along with others, had been led to pray for and to expect the restoration of 'spiritual gifts' to the Church, by a sermon on the nature of the '*Charismata*' of the Corinthians, preached by Mr. A.J. Scott." *Memoir of the Life of the Rev. Robert Story* - Robert Herbert Story, Macmillan and Co., 1862, p.205.

[1007] *Letters of Thomas Erskine of Linlathen* - Edited by William Hanna, David Douglas, Edinburgh, 1884, Chapter VII, The Spiritual Gifts - Letters from 1830-1835, pp.130-131, as quoted from *Memoirs of James and George Macdonald of Port-Glasgow* - Robert Norton, John F. Shaw, London, 1840, pp.107-108.

[1008] *Letters of Thomas Erskine of Linlathen* - Edited by William Hanna, David Douglas, Edinburgh, 1884, Chapter VII, The Spiritual Gifts - Letters from 1830-1835, pp.131-132, as quoted in *A Vindication of the Religion of the Land* - Rev. A. Robertson, pp.251-254.

[1009] *The Incredible Cover-Up* - Dave MacPherson, Alpha Omega Publishing Company, 1975, p.54, as quoted from *Memoirs of James and George Macdonald of Port-Glasgow* - Robert Norton, John F. Shaw, London, 1840, p.111.

[1010] *Letters of Thomas Erskine of Linlathen* - Edited by William Hanna, David Douglas, Edinburgh, 1884, Chapter VII, The Spiritual Gifts - Letters from 1830-1835, p.133.

[1011] *The Morning Watch* , Volume II - 1830, *On the Extraordinary Manifestations in Port-Glasgow,* John B. Cardale, pp.869-870.

[1012] *The Morning Watch* , Volume II - 1830, *On the Extraordinary Manifestations in Port-Glasgow,* John B. Cardale, pp.870-871.

[1013] *The Morning Watch* , Volume II - 1830, *On the Extraordinary Manifestations in Port -Glasgow,* John B. Cardale, pp.872-873.

[1014] *The History and Doctrines of Irvingism* - Edward Miller, M.A., C. Kegan Paul & Co., London, 1878, vol.1, p.66.

[1015] "When, therefore, in the spring of 1830, he [i.e., Irving] heard of Scottish women speaking as did the Twelve on the day of Pentecost...He dispatched an elder to inquire into the thing, who brought back a good report, and found the tongues of flame sitting on his own wife and daughters." *Edward Irving: An Ecclesiastical and Literary Biography* - Washington Wilks, William Freeman, London, 1854, p.204.

[1016] "When these extraordinary events became known they reached the ear of Irving by many means. One of his deacons belonged to a family in the district, who sent full and frequent accounts. Others of his closest friends - Mr. Story, in whose parish the wonder had first arisen, and Mr. Campbell, whose teaching had helped inspire it...one of the immediate circle around him [i.e. Irving], an Englishman and a lawyer, went down to Port-Glasgow to examine the report." *The Life of Edward Irving* - Margaret Oliphant, Hurst & Blackett, 1862, vol. II, p.134.

[1017] *The Life of Edward Irving* - Margaret Oliphant, Hurst & Blackett, 1862, vol. II, p.235.

[1018] Irving declared: "I believe the Holy Ghost is as mighty in the Church, and, but for our unbelief, would be as apparent, as ever He was. I pray you to be upon your guard against speaking evil of any mighty work which you may hear of in the Church; for in the last days God will pour out His Spirit upon all flesh." *The Life of Edward Irving* - Margaret Oliphant, Hurst & Blackett, 1862, vol. II, p.142.

[1019] Thomas Chalmers was the minister of St. John's Church in Glasgow, Scotland, which boasted some 10,000 attendees. From about 1819 to 1822, Irving served as pastoral assistant to Chalmers.

[1020] *The Life of Edward Irving* - Margaret Oliphant, Hurst & Blackett, 1862, vol. II, p.139.

[1021] Miss Hall was one of the recognized prophetesses within Edward Irving's church. Miller lists the first prophets and prophetesses as, "...Mr. Taplin...Miss Emily Cardale [the sister of John Cardale], Mrs. Caird [Mary Campbell's married name], Miss Hall, Miss Smith. Mrs. Cardale [the wife of John Cardale], and Mr. Baxter." *The History and Doctrines of Irvingism* - Edward Miller, C. Kegan Paul & Co., London, 1878, vol.1, pp.71-72.

[1022] *The Plymouth Brethren: Their History and Heresies* - James Grant, William Macintosh, London, 1875, p.3.

[1023] *The Plymouth Brethren: Their History and Heresies* - James Grant, William Macintosh, London, 1875, p.2. Also, "The burden of the prophetic utterances was the speedy coming of the Lord to set up his kingdom in the earth, the judgments about to fall upon Christendom, the sorrow of God over his scattered flock, his love which still lingered and longed to save, the humiliation and glory of Christ, and the necessity of a work to recovery and rebuilding in the church to prepare his way." *Bibliotheca Sacra & Theological Review*, Vol. XXIII, 1866, *The Catholic Apostolic Church* - pp.124-125. Also, regarding the early Irvingite movement - "...all the arrangements in it were originally made upon the assumption, that the then generation would witness the Lord's return to His Church. " *The History and Doctrines of Irvingism* - Edward Miller, C. Kegan Paul & Co., London, 1878, vol.1, p.319. And again, "The Coming of the Lord is expected by these people to take place before the great outburst of Antichrist." *The History and Doctrines of Irvingism* - Edward Miller, C. Kegan Paul & Co., 1878, vol.2. p.5.

[1024] "The exact origin of the teaching of the 'Secret Rapture' is obscure, but in some recorded but unpublished reminiscences, B.W. Newton, the prophetic teacher who was so prominent in the early Brethren movement, suggests that Irving introduced it at one of the Albury conferences. Newton was at Oxford at the time, and although he did not attend the conferences, so far as we know, a friend with whom he was in close touch at Oxford, Dr. William Marsh, did attend the Albury conferences; so Newton's reminiscence may not be unfounded." *Prophetic Developments* - F. Roy Coad, C.B.R.F. Occasional Paper Number 2 (Pinner, Middlesex, 1966), p.17. Note also that it was the fourth Albury Conference that declared, "...*our blessed Lord will shortly appear*, and that therefore it is the duty of all who so believe to press these considerations on the attention of all men." *Dialogues on Prophecy* by Henry Drummond, as quoted in *The History and Doctrines of Irvingism* - Edward Miller, C. Kegan Paul & Co., London, 1878, vol.1, pp.44-45.

[1025] *Lectures on the Book of Revelation – as (in substance) preached in Edinburgh during the General Assembly, in May 1829* - Edward Irving, Baldwin and Cradock, London, 1829, Lecture I., pp.89-90.

[1026] *Exposition of the Book of Revelation in a Series of Lectures* - Edward Irving, Baldwin and Cradock, 1831, vol.III, p.1233. Consider some similar statements made by Irving in this exposition; [1] "There is a season and a time, during which the saints are **not upon earth, but in the heavens**…being invested in rule and authority with Christ…they **come with Christ**, in order to execute the vengence written: during which **hour of temptation** they are **not upon the earth, but in heaven**…" p.1025. [2] "The promise of the Spirit to the church [i.e., Philadelphia, Rv.3:7-13], and therewith to all churches…that they shall have their abode in the temple of God, and in the New Jerusalem, the city of his God…To these poor and weak brethren he promiseth the seal of his Father's name upon their forehead, that they may be **delivered out of the midst of the judgments which are to come upon the earth**." p.1054-1055. [3] "These Philadelphians…Christ greatly commendeth their patience in keeping his word when all the earth was forsaking it, and promiseth them **immunity from the hour of tribulation** which is coming to try **all** the people upon the face of the **whole earth**. This is…the day of **Christ's appearing**, from the evils of which, these virgins and faithful servants shall be **preserved by being taken into that New Jerusalem**." p.1105.

[1027] *Exposition of the Book of Revelation in a Series of Lectures* - Edward Irving, Baldwin and Cradock, 1831, pp.165-166.

[1028] *Dialogues on Prophecy* by Henry Drummond, as quoted in *The History and Doctrines of Irvingism* - Edward Miller, C. Kegan Paul & Co., London, 1878, vol.1, pp.44-45.

[1029] Regarding the *Morning Watch*, Edward Miller observed that, "…at the expense of Henry Drummond, *The Morning Watch*, a quarterly periodical upon prophecy, was started. The first number, which owed a large part of its letter-press to the pen of Irving, came out in March 1829. It was regularly continued till June, 1833…The editor was Mr. John Tudor, described by Irving as 'very learned, modest, and devout.' Thus the prophetical views of the Albury party were steadily disseminated through their recognized organ, which ambitiously claimed a place amongst the first quarterlies of the day." *The History and Doctrines of Irvingism* - Edward Miller, C. Kegan Paul & Co., London, 1878, vol.1, pp.45-46.

[1030] In a letter dated 1843, Darby makes an allusion to the rapture of the saints that echoes Irving's and *The Morning Watch's* position of a partial rapture of just the "faithful" and "watchful" saints. Darby explained, "I find many more classes of saints and glory in the Apocalypse than heretofore, though all blessed. It may be **some will pass through**, but I am more than ever confirmed that it is not presented to our faith, but the contrary, and that **the faithful will be kept from it**. If **some pass through it**, it would make a difficulty for those who could not separate the signs of special blessing there, from the evidence of greater faithfulness which made us escape it." *Letters of J.N.D.*, Volume One, 1832-1868, Stow Hill Bible and Tract Depot, London, n.d., p.58.

[1031] *The Morning Watch* - Volume I, *On the Structure of the Apocalypse* (September 1829) - John Tudor, p.308.

[1032] *The Morning Watch* - Volume I, 1830, *On the Interpretation of the Apocalypse* (December 1829) - John Tudor, p.574.

[1033] The extended quotation is: "We have **a promise of escape** out of the awful judgment with which the Gentile church is to be consumed, no less than had the Jews. It is distinctly given to us in the xxist chapter of the Gospel of St. Luke; where we have, in the same discourse, both the **escape** of the first Christians from Jerusalem, and the **escape** of the last Christians from the destruction of Christendom. After foreshowing to his apostles and disciples what trials should befall them, the Lord thus advertiseth them of Jerusalem's destruction, and of the manner of their deliverance out of it (ver.20): 'When ye shall see Jerusalem compassed with armies, then know that the desolation thereof is nigh. Then let them which are in Judea flee to the mountains; and let them which are in the midst of it depart out; and let not them that are in the countries enter thereinto. For these be the days of vengeance, that all things which are written may be fulfilled. But woe unto them that are with child, and to them that give suck, in those days! for there shall be great distress in the land, and wrath to this people; and they shall fall by the edge of the sword, and be led captive into all the nations; and Jerusalem shall be trodden down of the Gentiles, until the times of the Gentiles be fulfilled.' Such are the warning and instruction given to the disciples; and the remainder of the chapter contains the warning and instruction given to us, upon whom the ends of the world are come: for the times of the Gentiles are now about being accomplished: the time, times and half a time, of the prophet Daniel, are now ended, and we are living on the eve of the time of trouble such as there never was since there was a nation. The warning to us begins: 'And there shall be signs in the sun, and in the moon, and in the stars; and upon the earth, distress of the nations, with perplexity; the sea and waves roaring; men's hearts failing them for fear, and for looking after those things which are coming on the earth; for the powers of heaven shall be shaken: and then shall they see the Son of Man coming in a cloud with power and great glory...When ye see these things come to pass, know ye that the kingdom of God is nigh at hand...Take heed to yourselves, lest at any time your hearts be overcharged with surfeiting, and drunkenness, and cares of this life, and that day come upon you unawares; for as a snare it shall come upon all them that dwell upon the face of the whole earth. Watch therefore, and pray always, that ye may be accounted worthy to **escape all these things that shall come to pass, and to stand before the Son of Man.'** Here we are distinctly taught that there be some whom God, through watchfulness and constant prayer, intendeth to deliver from those universal judgments with which Christendom is to be broken to pieces...Now the question is, In what way they shall **escape**, and at what time we are to look for that **escape**? With respect to the manner in which the **remnant of the Gentile church shall escape**, I think it sufficiently declared in the xvth chap. of the 1st of Corinthians and the ivth of the 1st Thessalonians: 'Behold, I shew you a mystery: we shall not all sleep, but we shall all be changed, in a moment, in the twinkling of an eye, at the last trump; for the trumpet shall sound, and the dead shall be raised incorruptible, and we shall be changed.' This mystery, which had not been made known to the church before, and is not to be found explicitly in the Old Testament, is spoken to all believers in Christ, and to them only...This changing of the living and the resurrection of those that sleep in Jesus, take place to the very end that they may enter into the kingdom of God, and that they may be like Christ, which we know we become at his appearing. The other passage, collateral with this, is written 1Thess.iv.15. 'For this we say unto you by the word of the Lord, that we which are alive, and remain until the coming of the Lord, shall not prevent them which are asleep. For the Lord himself shall descend from heaven, with a shout, with the voice of the archangel, and with the trump of God: and the dead in Christ shall rise first: then we, which are alive and remain, shall be caught up together with them in the clouds, to meet the Lord in the air: and so shall we ever be with the Lord.' These two passages [i.e., 1Cor.15 & 1Thess.4] reveal to us that great mystery of the translation of the living saints by an instantaneous transition, from the state of mortality into the state of immortality; and this, and no other, do I believe to be the way of our **escape**...Now, **with respect to the time at which this translation of the saints taketh place, it is not to be doubted, as I think, that its time is before the judgments which fall upon the earth** at the coming of the Son of Man and the setting up of his kingdom...I believe, therefore, in my heart, that **there is close at hand a deliverance of God's faithful ones by translation;** and that now, when we surely see these awful things beginning to come to pass, we ought to be looking up, as our redemption draweth nigh. I know not how soon this is to take place; but my present belief is that it will take place before the last awful judgment falleth. I do therefore call upon all who believe in Christ, and hope to be saved through his righteousness, to be upon their watch-towers, looking out for the sign of his appearing. *The Morning Watch*, Volume II, 1831, *Signs of the Times and the Characteristics of the Church* (March 1830), Edward Irving, pp.156-160.

[1034] *The Morning Watch*, Vol.III, 1831, *Commentary on the Seven Apocalyptic Churches* (June 1831) - FIDUS, p.284.

[1035] *The Morning Watch*, Vol.IV, 1832, *Commentary on the Seven Apocalyptic Epistles* (December 1831), FIDUS, p.264.

[1036] *The Morning Watch*, Vol.IV, 1832, *The Church's Expectation*, (December 1831), John Hooper, p.325.

[1037] *The Morning Watch*, Volume II, 1831, *Signs of the Times and the Characteristics of the Church* (March 1830) - Edward Irving, p.162.

[1038] *The Morning Watch*, Volume II, 1831, *On the Parable of the Ten Virgins* - (June 1830), John B. Cardale, p.367.

[1039] *The Morning Watch*, Volume II, 1831, *Commentary on the Epistles to the Seven Churches in the Apocalypse* (September 1830), FIDUS, p.510.

[1040] *The Morning Watch*, Volume II, 1831, *On the Epiphany of Our Lord Jesus Christ and the Gathering of His Elect* (September 1830) - T.W.C., pp.587,588,589, 590.

[1041] *The Morning Watch*, Volume II, 1831, *Signs of the Times and the Characteristics of the Church* (March 1830), Edward Irving, pp.157,160.

[1042] *The Origins of the Brethren* - Harold H. Rowdon, Pickering & Inglis, Ltd., London, 1967, p.44.

[1043] Darby explained in a letter, "An accident happened which laid me aside for a time; my horse was frightened and had thrown me against a door-post." *Letters of J.N.D.* - Volume Three, 1879-1882, Stow Hill Bible and Tract Depot, n.d., p. 298.

[1044] "...1827...After he [Darby] had been for two-and-a-half years in his curacy, he was thrown by his horse against a doorpost, and forced to remain in convalescence for some time - it was undoubtedly this accident that had brought him to the home of his brother-in-law [i.e., Sergeant Pennefather] at the time of F.W. Newman's arrival..." *A History of the Brethren Movement* - F. Roy Coad, Regent College Publishing, 2001, p.27.

[1045] The extended quotations of Darby's spiritual conversion are as follows: "I am daily more struck with the connection of the great principles on which my mind was exercised by and with God, **when I found salvation and peace**, and the questions agitated and agitating the world at the present day: the absolute, divine authority and certainty of the Word, as a divine link between us and God, if everything (church and world); personal assurance of salvation in a new condition by being in Christ; the church as His body; Christ coming to receive us to Himself; and collaterally with that, the setting up of a new earthly dispensation, from Isaiah xxxii. (more particularly the end); all this was when laid aside at E.P.'s **in 1827**; the house character of the assembly on earth (not the fact of the presence of the Spirit) was subsequently. It was a vague fact which received form in my mind long after, that there must be a wholly new order of things, if God was to have His way, and the craving of the heart after it I had felt long before; **but the church and redemption I did not know till the time I have spoken of**; but eight years before, universal sorrow and sin pressed upon my spirit." "Guelph, February 10th, 1863" *Letters of J.N.D.* - Volume One, 1832-1868, Stow Hill Bible and Tract Depot, London, n.d., pp.344-345.

And also, "We began to meet in Dublin, Ireland, **1827-1828...I had found peace to my own soul by finding my oneness with Christ,** that it was no longer myself as in the flesh before God, but that I was in Christ, accepted in the Beloved, and sitting in heavenly places with Him. This led me directly to the apprehension of what the true church of God was, those that were united to Christ in heaven...The coming of the Lord was the other truth which was brought to my mind from the word, as that which, if sitting in heavenly places in Christ, was alone to be waited for, that I might sit in heavenly places with Him. Isaiah xxxii. brought me the earthly consequences of the same truth, though other passages might seem perhaps more striking to me now: but I saw an evident change of dispensation in that chapter, when the Spirit would be poured out on the Jewish nation, and a king reign in righteousness...New York 1868" *Letters of J.N.D.* - Volume One, 1832-1868, Stow Hill Bible and Tract Depot, London, n.d., pp.515-516.

And once again, "An accident happened which laid me aside for a time; my horse was frightened and had thrown me against a door-post. During my solitude, conflicting thoughts increased; **but much exercise of soul had the effect of causing the scriptures to gain complete ascendancy over me...It then became clear to me that the church of God, as He considers it, was composed only of those who were so united with Christ,** whereas Christendom as seen externally, was really the world, and could not be considered as 'the church'...At the same time, I saw that the Christian, having his place in Christ in heaven, has nothing to wait for save the coming of the Saviour, in order to be set, in fact, in the glory which is already his portion 'in Christ.'...At that time I had to use crutches when moving about, so that I had no longer any opportunity for making known my convictions in public; moreover, as the state of my health did not allow me to attend worship, I was compelled to stay away...In my retreat, the 32nd chapter of Isaiah taught me clearly, on God's behalf, that there was still an economy to come, of His ordering; a state of things in no way established as yet. The consciousness of my union with Christ had given me the present heavenly portion of the glory. Whereas this chapter clearly sets forth the corresponding earthly part. I was not able to put these things in their respective places or arrange them in order, as I can now; but the truths themselves were then revealed of God, through the action of His Spirit, by reading His word. What was to be done? I saw in that word the coming of Christ to take the church to himself in glory. **I saw there the cross, the divine basis of salvation,** which should impress its own character on the Christian and on the church in view of the Lord's coming; and also meanwhile the Holy Spirit was given to be the source of the unity of the church, as well as the spring of its activity, and indeed of all the Christian energy." *Letters of J.N.D. - Volume Three, 1879-1882*, Stow Hill Bible and Tract Depot, n.d., pp. 298-299.

Note: Some Dispensationalists have asserted that Darby developed the pretribulation rapture theory in or around 1827. They base this assertion upon Darby's allusions to the Second Coming of Christ within the text of his personal testimony as cited above. However, Darby's realization of the reality of the return of Christ to establish the millennium was not a new idea at this time in history. Many evangelicals at this time expected the soon, premillennial coming of Christ - without postulating a pretribulation rapture scenario. Darby's statements certainly lack any specific reference to a pretribulation rapture. Darby's recollections seem to be very broad generalizations of what he began to see and understand from his reading of the Word of God from a position of true faith. Furthermore, Darby testifies that his understanding of these concepts was initially limited and took many years to fully mature. Also, it seems extremely difficult to accept the reasonableness of the notion that at the time of Darby's conversion to Christ, he suddenly understood the scope and sequence of Dispensational doctrine. Additionally, the earliest date in which Darby publicly acknowledged the pretribulation rapture theory is 1833, at the third Powerscourt Conference. Thus, Tim LaHaye's statement on this subject seems well beyond any sensible possibility: "[Darby]...had come to accept the imminent return of Christ and the separation of the church and Israel between 1826 and 1827...it took several years to make definitive all of his doctrines, but the awareness of the coming of Christ at any moment was one of his earliest positions." *No Fear of the Storm* - Tim LaHaye, Multnomah Press Books, 1992, p.166.

[1046] *The Origins of the Brethren* - Harold H. Rowdon, Pickering & Inglis, Ltd., London, 1967, p.46.
Some of the early Brethren in Dublin were Francis Hutchinson, Dr. Edward Cronin and J.G. Bellett.

[1047] Re: Francis William Newman - "He took a 'double first' at Oxford, became Fellow of Balliol, and was afterwards Professor of Latin at University College, London, and finally Professor of Political Economy at Oxford..." *A History of the Plymouth Brethren* - William Blair Neatby, Hodder and Stoughton, London, 1902, p.45.

[1048] *The Origins of the Brethren* - Harold H. Rowdon, Pickering & Inglis, Ltd., London, 1967, p.62.

[1049] *Interesting Reminiscences* - J.G. Bellett, p.3, as quoted by *The Origins of the Brethren* - Harold H. Rowdon, Pickering & Inglis, Ltd., London, 1967, p.50. Also, "The study of unfulfilled prophecy was a prominent feature of the movement [i.e., Brethrenism] from the first; or perhaps it would be more correct to say that it was one of the main foundations of the whole system. Bellett had his interest in the subject greatly enlarged during a visit to London in the beginning of 1828, of which he communicated the results to Darby, only to find that Darby's 'mind and soul had traveled rapidly' in the same direction." *A History of the Plymouth Brethren* - William Blair Neatby, Hodder and Stoughton, London, 1902, p.12.

[1050] *The Collected Writings of J.N. Darby* - Edited by William Kelly, Kingston Bible Trust, n.d., *Reflections Upon the Prophetic Inquiry and the Views Advanced In It* - Dublin, 1829, Volume 2, Prophetic No.1, pp.8, 19,20,32,33,42.

[1051] *The Origins of the Brethren* - Harold H. Rowdon, Pickering & Inglis, Ltd., London, 1967, p.63.

[1052] *The Origins of the Brethren* - Harold H. Rowdon, Pickering & Inglis, Ltd., London, 1967, p.65.
See also, The Roots of Fundamentalism - Ernest R. Sandeen, The University of Chicago Press, 1970, p.30.

[1053] George Thomas Stokes, B.A., M.A., B.D., D.D. (1843-1898) was the highly educated Professor of Ecclesiastical History at Trinity College, Dublin and a prolific author who specialized in the ecclesiastical history of Ireland, and western Europe. He also served as the vicar of All Saints Church in Newtown Park in Dublin.

[1054] "Newman...introduced Darby to Oxford in the year 1830, where he exercised for the time a tremendous influence." *The Contemporary Review* - Volume XLVIII. July-December, 1885, *John Nelson Darby*, October, 1885, George T. Stokes, p.546.

[1055] *The Origins of the Brethren* - Harold H. Rowdon, Pickering & Inglis, Ltd., London, 1967, p.66.

[1056] *The Origins of the Brethren* - Harold H. Rowdon, Pickering & Inglis, Ltd., London, 1967, p.66.

[1057] Darby stated that, "Mr. Newman [i.e., F.W. Newman, who referred to Darby as the "Irish Clergyman"] is not quite right in his account of the report of the 'Irish Clergyman," or at least of what the 'Irish Clergyman' saw and heard. There was a pretended interpretation. Two brothers, respectable ship-builders at Port-Glasgow, of the name of M'D - [i.e., Macdonald], and their sister, were the chief persons who spoke, with a Gaelic maid-servant, in the tongues, and a Mrs. J, - in English. J. M'D - [i.e., James Macdonald] spoke on the occasion alluded to, for about a quarter of an hour, with great energy and fluency, in a semi-Latin sounding speech - then sung a hymn in the same. Having finished, he knelt down and prayed there might be interpretation; as God had given one gift, that he would add the other. His sister got up at the opposite side of the room, and professed to give the interpretation, - but it was a string of texts on overcoming, and no hymn, and one; if not more, of the texts was quoted wrongly...Previous to the time of exercising the gifts, they read, sung psalms, and prayed...This being finished, the 'Irish Clergyman' was going away, when another said to him, 'Don't go, the best part is probably to come yet,' so he staid, and heard what has just been related. He was courteously admitted, as one not believing, who came to see what was the real truth of the case...The M'D-s. [i.e., the Macdonald's] were, in ordinary life, quite sober men, and he believes, most blameless. Their names were so public, that there is no indelicacy in alluding to them, but the 'Irish Clergyman' did not think they had that kind of peace and deliverance from legal thoughts, which is the sign, in another way, of the Spirit's power."*The Irrationalism of Infidelity Being a Reply to Phases of Faith* - John Nelson Darby, Groombridge and Sons, London, 1853, pp.301-302.

[1058] Newman stated: "So long ago as is 1830, when the Irving 'miracles' commenced in Scotland, my particular attention had been turned to this subject, and the Irvingite exposition of the Pauline phenomena appeared to me so correct that I was vehemently predisposed to believe the miraculous tongues. But my friend 'the Irish clergyman' wrote me a full account of what he heard with his own ears, which was to the effect that none of the sounds, vowels or consonants, were foreign; that the strange words were moulded after the Latin grammar, ending in -abus, -obus, - ebat, -avi, etc., so as to denote poverty of invention rather than spiritual agency; and that there was no interpretation." *Phases of Faith* - Francis William Newman, Watts & Co., London, 1907, p.89.

[1059] Professor Stokes explained that, "...the Irish clergyman (the name by which he [i.e., Newman] always designates Mr. Darby)..." *The Contemporary Review* - Volume XLVIII. July-December, 1885, *John Nelson Darby*, October, 1885, George T. Stokes, p.546.

[1060] *The Irrationalism of Infidelity Being a Reply to Phases of Faith* - John Nelson Darby, Groombridge and Sons, London, 1853, pp.301-302.

[1061] "In a word, the millennium may be considered as a restoration of Paradise under the Second Adam..." *The Collected Writings of J.N. Darby* - Edited by William Kelly, Kingston Bible Trust, n.d., *Reflections Upon the Prophetic Inquiry and the Views Advanced In It* - Dublin, 1829, Volume 2, Prophetic No.1, p.24.

[1062] "...the Jewish and Gentile dispensations - the hinge upon which the subject and understanding of Scriptures turns" *The Collected Writings of J.N. Darby* - Edited by William Kelly, Kingston Bible Trust, n.d., *Reflections Upon the Prophetic Inquiry and the Views Advanced In It* - Dublin, 1829, Volume 2, Prophetic No.1, p.18.

[1063] "I believe that Christ also...has a distinct kingdom from the Father...for the removal of evil...the Jews being restored, the temporal promises being ever theirs, not the Gentiles; but that these shall enjoy the common blessing with them..." *The Collected Writings of J.N. Darby* - Edited by William Kelly, Kingston Bible Trust, n.d., *Reflections Upon the Prophetic Inquiry and the Views Advanced In It* - Dublin, 1829, Volume 2, Prophetic No.1, p.23.

[1064] "For no strong motive for missionary exertion exists with antimillenarians, as with those who believe God's judgments are presently coming; for that belief urges them to special labour for the gathering in of God's elect...before the scourge sweeps the earth to preserve them that believed." *The Collected Writings of J.N. Darby* - Edited by William Kelly, Kingston Bible Trust, n.d., *Reflections Upon the Prophetic Inquiry and the Views Advanced In It* - Dublin, 1829, Volume 2, Prophetic No.1, p.25.

[1065] *The Collected Writings of J.N. Darby* - Edited by William Kelly, Kingston Bible Trust, n.d., *On Days Signifying Years in Prophetic Language* - Dublin, 1829, Volume 2, Prophetic No.1, pp.38-39.

[1066] *The Collected Writings of J.N. Darby* - Edited by William Kelly, Kingston Bible Trust, n.d., *On Days Signifying Years in Prophetic Language* - Dublin, 1829, Volume 2, Prophetic No.1, pp.39-40.

[1067] "...Lady Theodosia Powerscourt - young, attractive, widowed, and very pious - had visited Henry Drummond at Albury and entertained Edward Irving when he visited Dublin on a preaching tour." *The Roots of Fundamentalism* - Ernest R. Sandeen, The University of Chicago Press, 1970, p.34.

[1068] "...Lady Powerscourt...was very fond of the study of prophecy; she had evening meetings every second Tuesday for the purpose at Powerscourt House..." *Personal Recollections of the Right Rev. Robert Daly, D.D.* - Hamilton Madden, Dublin, 1872, p.18.

[1069] Re: Lady Powerscourt: "She had, during her visits to London about this time, gone frequently to hear Mr. Irving, and (though not agreeing with him in his more peculiar views) had entered warmly, and even enthusiastically, into his desire for the study of prophecy." *Memoir of the Late Right Rev. Robert Daly* - Mrs. Hamilton Madden, James Nisbet & Co., London, 1875, p.149.

[1070] "An interesting account is given in the *Memoir of the Rev. Edward Irving* of some meetings which were held in the year 1826, at Albury, the seat of Henry Drummond, Esq. Lady Powerscourt was present at these meetings, as appears from a letter to Mr. Daly, of which the following is an extract: - 'I am going to the prophets' meeting at Mr. Drummond's...No arguments are to me stronger than yours, so much so that I always conclude I have strong grounds for an opinion if it is not shaken by your arguments to the contrary.'" *Memoir of the Late Right Rev. Robert Daly* - Mrs. Hamilton Madden, James Nisbet & Co., London, 1875, pp.149-150. Professor George Stokes states that, "Among the devout and honorable women who attended the Albury conferences in great numbers, was the Countess of Powerscourt." *The Contemporary Review* - Volume XLVIII. July-December, 1885, *John Nelson Darby*, October, 1885, George T. Stokes, p.543. Brethren historian William Neatby states that, "At these meetings Edward Irving took part, and to Albury Irvingism traces its rise. Lady Powerscourt attended these conferences, and was so delighted with them that she established a similar series of meetings at

Powerscourt House near Bray, in the county of Wicklow..." *A History of the Plymouth Brethren* - William Blair Neatby - Hodder & Stoughton, 1902, p.38.

[1071] The first Powerscourt Conference was held October 4th to 7th, 1831; the second Powerscourt Conference was held September 24th to 28th, 1832; the third Powerscourt Conference was held September 23rd to 28th, 1833.

[1072] RE: Powerscourt Conferences: "...she [i.e., Lady Powerscourt] invited to her house the most remarkable men, of whatever Christian denomination they might be, who were interested in the study of prophecy, from all parts of England, Scotland, and Ireland, and entertained them at her house for a week; during which time meetings were held morning and evening, to which everyone in the neighborhood was invited, Mr. Daly took the chair, and they were conducted uniformly on his part in a spirit of Christian love, and in a very judicious manner. A subject was arranged for consideration for each day, and a copy of the paper which contained them given to each person. The meetings were begun and concluded with prayer." *Memoir of the Late Right Rev. Robert Daly* - Mrs. Hamilton Madden, James Nisbet & Co., London, 1875, pp.149-150.

[1073] RE: The Powerscourt Conferences - "...the 'discussions'...were held for three or four consecutive summers by Lady Powerscourt, when she had her house filled with the most eminent divines of every denomination, in England, Scotland, and Ireland; topics were arranged for discussion, chiefly on prophetical subjects; and all the neighbourhood were invited to hear them twice a day." *Personal Recollections of the Right Rev. Robert Daly, D.D.* - Mrs. Hamilton Madden, Dublin, 1872, p.18.

[1074] *The Origins of the Brethren* - Harold H. Rowdon, Pickering & Inglis Ltd., 1967, p.88.

[1075] *Letters of J.N.D.*, Volume One, 1832-1868, pp.6-7.

[1076] "It was reported by J.B. Stoney, one of the Brethren, that Irvingites were present at one of the conferences." *The Origins of the Brethren* - Harold H. Rowdon, Pickering & Inglis Ltd., 1967, p.87.

[1077] Mrs. Madden preserved a speech which she said was delivered by Edward Irving at the second Powerscourt Conference in October, 1832, wherein Irving stated, "...I think it best to ask one of my brethren to entreat the Lord's pardon and forgiveness for all the evil that has crept in amongst us, through our defilement and infirmity...that though there may have been error brought forward, the Lord may be pleased to lead us into all truth...in the various observations which have been made, (this evening particularly), there have been great differences of opinion upon what appear to be fundamental point of doctrine, to pray that we may be enabled to exercise towards each other a spirit of love, and of interest for one another. For myself, I earnestly desire to ask that all should remember me as a Christian friend, and especially where they think I have erred..." *Personal Recollections of the Right Rev. Robert Daly, D.D.* - Mrs. Hamilton Madden, Dublin, 1872, p.19. Mrs. Madden also recalled that Rev. Daly, who presided over the Powerscourt Conferences, had a strong dislike for Mr. Irving's teaching. She explains that, "These discussions were held annually at Powerscourt House for three or four years. They were much enjoyed by many, but they became latterly a source of great anxiety to Mr. Daly, who felt that he was set as a watchman over the souls of his parishioners, and feared lest the many strange doctrines which were propounded then might disturb the simplicity of their faith, and alienate them from their scriptural Church. Unfortunately these students of prophecy (although the interest they felt in that study was shared by him) held, and brought forward, on other subjects very erroneous opinions. Amongst these was the celebrated and truly pious though mistaken man, Edward Irving. Mr. Daly's opinion concerning the doctrines held by the Irvingite party is expressed in a letter to a Christian friend: - 'My dear Miss P., ...I feel a great deal for the state the Lord's Church is in, yet I cannot think that really Christian people will be long left in the fundamental errors of Irvingism...pretensions to gifts...they denied the imputed righteousness of Christ...As a body they have departed from the gospel of Christ." *Memoir of the Late Right Rev. Robert Daly* - Mrs. Hamilton Madden, James Nisbet & Co., London, 1875, pp.149-150.

[1078] *Letters of J.N.D. Volume One, 1832-1868* - Stow Hill Bible and Tract Depot, London, n.d., p.5. Also, an entry in the Diary of the Rev. Peter Roe, regarding the second Powerscourt Conference states, "1832, Sept. 29th - Spent from Tuesday morning to Friday evening at the Meeting at Powerscourt House, for the consideration of prophetical subjects: and upon the whole it was unprofitable. Many of the subjects were evidently difficult to be understood. The most extravagant assertions were made, and dogmas quite opposed to each other maintained with the greatest pertinacity. The duty of seeking for miraculous gifts was strongly insisted upon! Oh, what a fool is man!" *Memoir of the Life of the Late Rev. Peter Roe* - Samuel Madden, William Curray, Jun. and Company, Dublin, 1842, p.445.

[1079] *The Origins of the Brethren* - Harold H. Rowdon, Pickering & Inglis Ltd., 1967, p.96.

[1080] *A History of the Brethren Movement* - F. Roy Coad, Regent College Publishing, 1968, p.109 and *The Origins of the Brethren* - Harold H. Rowdon, Pickering & Inglis Ltd., 1967, p.96.

[1081] Re: Henry Craik's diary entries from the third Powerscourt Conference:
"Monday, 23rd September, 1833 - Arrived at Powerscourt...In the evening, we considered the difference between the Everlasting Covenant and the Covenant of the Lord. Tuesday, 24th September, 1833 - Is the visible Christian Church founded on the basis of the Jewish? What is the nature of the ministry and ordinances of the former? Are the promises to either, or both, conditional? Wednesday, 25th September, 1833 - The analogy between the close of this dispensation and the former. What is mystic Babylon? Is the call out to her to be a Divine set period, or is it a perpetual call? Thursday, 26th September, 1833 - What is the connection between the present and the future dispensation? Friday, 27th September, 1833 - The Temptations of Satan." *Passages from the Diary and Letters of Henry Craik* - Edited by W. Elfe Tayler, J. F. Shaw & Co., London, 1866, pp.168-169.

[1082] *The Origins of the Brethren* - Harold H. Rowdon, Pickering & Inglis Ltd., 1967, p.97.

[1083] *The Roots of Fundamentalism* - Ernest R. Sandeen, The University of Chicago Press, 1970, p.38.

[1084] *A Historical Sketch Of The Brethren Movement* - H.A. Ironside, Loizeaux Brothers, 1985, p.23.

[1085] *The Origins of the Brethren* - Harold H. Rowdon, Pickering & Inglis, Ltd., London, 1967, p.78.

[1086] *The Origins of the Brethren* - Harold H. Rowdon, Pickering & Inglis, Ltd., London, 1967, p.82, per the *Fry MS.*, pp.250; cf. p.237.

[1087] *The Origins of the Brethren* - Harold H. Rowdon, Pickering & Inglis Ltd., 1967, p.97.

[1088] *The Roots of Fundamentalism* - Ernest R. Sandeen, The University of Chicago Press, 1970, p.38.

[1089] *The Origins of the Brethren* - Harold H. Rowdon, Pickering & Inglis Ltd., 1967, p.235, fn.57.

[1090] *The Origins of the Brethren* - Harold H. Rowdon, Pickering & Inglis Ltd., 1967, p.233, as quoted from the *Fry Letters*, 1845, Folio 1.

[1091] *The Origins of the Brethren* - Harold H. Rowdon, Pickering & Inglis Ltd., 1967, p.233, as quoted from the *Fry Letters*, 1845, Folio 1.

[1092] Samuel Tregelles was associated with the Brethren movement beginning in 1835. By his own testimony, his knowledge of events prior to that were received second hand, and thus he seems to have been legitimately mistaken as to the origin of the pretribulation rapture. Tregelles stated, "I know something of the early days of the Brethren in this and other places...I was associated with the Christians meeting here [i.e., Plymouth], when they were about eighty in number in the early part of 1835: from those who were then united in fellowship I received much information as to what had taken place during the four previous years..." *Three Letters* - S.P. Tregelles, Houlston & Sons, London, 1894, pp.4-5.

1093 *The Hope of Christ's Second Coming* - Samuel P. Tregelles, The Sovereign Grace Advent Testimony, 1860 edition reprinted, n.d., p.35.

1094 Robert Cameron's conclusions were based solely upon Robert Baxter's personal account of the events that transpired in Edward Irving's church from 1830 to 1832, which Baxter published in *A Narrative of Facts* in 1834.

1095 *To the Friends of Prophetic Truth* - Robert Cameron, *Watchword and Truth*, August 1902, Vol. XXIV, No.8, pp.235,236.

1096 *Narrative of Facts* - Robert Baxter, James Nisbet, London, 1834, p.142.

1097 MacPherson maintains that, "...Margaret had her pre-trib revelation on some particular evening between February 1 and April 14." *The Incredible Cover-Up* - Dave MacPherson, Alpha Omega Publishing Company, 1975, p.54.

1098 *The Incredible Cover-Up* - Dave MacPherson, Alpha Omega Publishing Company, 1975, p.93.

1099 *The Incredible Cover-Up* - Dave MacPherson, Alpha Omega Publishing Company, 1975, pp.49-52, as quoted from *Memoirs of James and George Macdonald of Port-Glasgow* - Robert Norton, John F. Shaw, London, 1840, pp.101-107.

1100 Robert Norton was a medical doctor who, in 1830 traveled from London to Scotland to personally investigate the charismata. He subsequently became acquainted with the Macdonald's and was convinced that the manifestations represented a true restoration of the miraculous sign gifts. He wrote several books that chronicled the unfolding of events in Scotland. Thereafter, he studied for the ministry and was ordained in the Church of England. However, in 1854 he left the Established Church and joined the Catholic Apostolic Church at Albury where he remained until 1862. He died in London in 1883. See *The Incredible Cover-Up* - Dave MacPherson, Alpha Omega Publishing Company, 1975, pp.38-43.

1101 *The Incredible Cover-Up* - Dave MacPherson, Alpha Omega Publishing Company, 1975, p.37, as quoted from *The Restoration of Apostles and Prophets; in the Catholic Apostolic Church* - Robert Norton, 1861, p.15.

1102 See section "**4. Edward Irving and the Development of Dispensational Theology: 1829-1831**" in **Appendix D, pp.291-298.**

1103 "Mr. Baxter was a prolific deliverer of prophecies...he predicted 'that God had cut short the present appointment for ordaining ministers by the laying on of hands by succession from the Apostles...that in 1260 days from January 14th, 1832, the Lord Jesus would come again in glory; the living saints would be caught up to meet Him, and the dead saints would be raised; that the man of sin should be Louis Napoleon, who would overthrow the Protestant Church, and the Papacy, and then stand forth, exercising all the mighty power and working of evil spirits, and claiming and receiving for himself the worship of all nations, as the Christ of God come again upon the earth to establish His kingdom.'" *The History and Doctrines of Irvingism* - Edward Miller, London, 1878, vol.1, p.79. Also, "The writers of the *Church's Broken Unity*, p.259, reckon up forty-three prophecies of Mr. Baxter which were signally unfulfilled, besides others." *The History and Doctrines of Irvingism* - Edward Miller, London, 1878, vol.1, p.81 footnote.

1104 *Narrative of Facts* - Robert Baxter, James Nisbet, London, 1834, pp.16-17.

[1105] *Narrative of Facts* - Robert Baxter, James Nisbet, London, 1834, p.17.

[1106] *Narrative of Facts* - Robert Baxter, James Nisbet, London, 1834, p.17.

[1107] *Narrative of Facts* - Robert Baxter, James Nisbet, London, 1834, pp.17-18

[1108] *Narrative of Facts* - Robert Baxter, James Nisbet, London, 1834, pp.18-19.

[1109] *The Life of Edward Irving* - Margaret Oliphant, Hurst & Blackett, 1862, vol. II, p.235.

[1110] *Narrative of Facts* - Robert Baxter, James Nisbet, London, 1834, pp.100-102. Irving stated: "And in the face of all these certainties, if a man will say that his [i.e. Christ's] flesh was not sinful flesh as ours is, with the same dispositions, and propensities, and wants, and afflictions, then, I say, God hath sent that man strong delusions that he should believe a lie."

[1111] *Narrative of Facts* - Robert Baxter, James Nisbet, London, 1834, p.102.

[1112] *Narrative of Facts* - Robert Baxter, James Nisbet, London, 1834, p.107.

[1113] *Narrative of Facts* - Robert Baxter, James Nisbet, London, 1834, p.108.

[1114] *Narrative of Facts* - Robert Baxter, James Nisbet, London, 1834, pp.116-118.

[1115] *Narrative of Facts* - Robert Baxter, James Nisbet, London, 1834, p.118.

[1116] *Narrative of Facts* - Robert Baxter, James Nisbet, London, 1834, p.28.

[1117] "...Captain Hall [Percy Francis] was greatly drawn to Irvingism..." *The Origins of the Brethren* - Harold H. Rowdon, Pickering & Inglis Ltd., 1967, p.78.

[1118] "Bellett had his interest in the subject [i.e., Bible prophecy] greatly enlarged during a visit to London in the beginning of 1828..." *A History of the Plymouth Brethren* - William Blair Neatby, Hodder and Stoughton, London, 1902, p.12. See also, *The Origins of the Brethren* - Harold H. Rowdon, Pickering & Inglis Ltd., 1967, p.50.

[1119] "Bellett had his interest in the subject [i.e., Bible prophecy] greatly enlarged during a visit to London in the beginning of 1828, of which he communicated the results to Darby, only to find that Darby's 'mind and soul had traveled rapidly' in the same direction." *A History of the Plymouth Brethren* - William Blair Neatby, Hodder and Stoughton, London, 1902, p.12. See also, *The Origins of the Brethren* - Harold H. Rowdon, Pickering & Inglis Ltd., 1967, p.50.

[1120] See *The Collected Writings of J.N. Darby* - Edited by William Kelly, Kingston Bible Trust, n.d., *Reflections Upon the Prophetic Inquiry and the Views Advanced In It* - Dublin, 1829, Volume 2, Prophetic No.1, wherein Darby makes numerous references to both Edward Irving and *The Morning Watch*. For example, see pp.8,19,20,32,33,42.

[1121] *Memoir of the Late Right Rev. Robert Daly* - Mrs. Hamilton Madden, James Nisbet & Co., London, 1875, pp.149-150.

[1122] "...Lady Theodosia Powerscourt...had visited Henry Drummond at Albury and entertained Edward Irving when he visited Dublin on a preaching tour." *The Roots of Fundamentalism* - Ernest R. Sandeen, The University of Chicago Press, 1970, p.34. Also, "While visiting London, Lady Powerscourt went to hear Edward Irving and evidently attended the 1826 Albury Park Conference for the study of prophecy." *Origins of the Brethren* - Harold H. Rowdon, Pickering & Inglis, Ltd., London, 1967, p.86.

[1123] "Edward Irving visited Ireland during September, 1830, and stayed with Lady Powerscourt." *Origins of the Brethren* - Harold H. Rowdon, Pickering & Inglis, Ltd., London, 1967, p.86.

[1124] "...Darby had thoughts of marrying her [Lady Powerscourt], but was advised against it by those whom he consulted, on the ground that marriage would hamper his itinerant ministry." *Origins of the Brethren* - Harold H. Rowdon, Pickering & Inglis, Ltd., London, 1967, p.86. Also, "Darby threw himself wholeheartedly into this fervour of prophetic expectation and discussion...It is said that at this time he was contemplating marriage to the widowed Lady Powerscourt: but that the engagement was broken off by mutual agreement when his commitment to a traveling ministry became obvious." *A History of the Brethren Movement* - F. Roy Coad, Regent College Publishing, 2001, p.109.

[1125] **"From Irving, then, Darby derived his prophetical system**, which became one of the most prominent features of his system, and one of the rocks, too, on which the system was rent asunder." *The Contemporary Review* - Volume XLVIII. July-December, 1885, *John Nelson Darby*, October, 1885, George T. Stokes, p.545. Note also, that Brethren historian F. Roy Coad, while referring to "Irvingism," has stated that, "...Darby had **adopted**, the doctrine of the 'secret rapture of the saints." *A History of the Brethren Movement* - F. Roy Coad, Regent College Publishing, 2001, p.128.

[1126] In a letter dated 1863, Darby stated; "I am daily more struck with the connection of the great principles on which my mind was exercised by and with God, **when I found salvation and peace**, and the questions agitated and agitating the world at the present day: the absolute, divine authority and certainty of the Word, as a divine link between us and God, if everything (church and world); **personal assurance of salvation in a new condition by being in Christ; the church as His body; Christ coming to receive us to Himself; and collaterally with that, the setting up of a new earthly dispensation, from Isaiah xxxii.** (more particularly the end); all this was when laid aside at E.P.'s in **1827**; the house character of the assembly on earth (not the fact of the presence of the Spirit) was subsequently. It was a vague fact which received form in my mind long after, that there must be a wholly new order of things, if God was to have His way, and the craving of the heart after it I had felt long before; but the church and *redemption I did not know till the time I have spoken of*; but eight years before, universal sorrow and sin pressed upon my spirit." "Guelph, February 10th, 1863" *Letters of J.N.D.* - Volume One, 1832-1868, Stow Hill Bible and Tract Depot, London, n.d., pp.344-345. And again in a letter dated 1868, Darby explained; "We began to meet in Dublin, Ireland, **1827-1828...I had found peace to my own soul by finding my oneness with Christ, that it was no longer myself as in the flesh before God, but that I was in Christ, accepted in the Beloved, and sitting in heavenly places with Him.** This led me directly to the apprehension of what the true church of God was, those that were united to Christ in heaven...The coming of the Lord was the other truth which was brought to my mind from the word, as that which, if sitting in heavenly places in Christ, was alone to be waited for, that I might sit in heavenly places with Him. Isaiah xxxii. brought me the earthly consequences of the same truth, though other passages might seem perhaps more striking to me now: but I saw an evident change of dispensation in that chapter, when the Spirit would be poured out on the Jewish nation, and a king reign in righteousness...New York 1868" *Letters of J.N.D.* - Volume One, 1832-1868, Stow Hill Bible and Tract Depot, London, n.d., pp.515-516.

[1127] J.G. Bellett, *Interesting Reminiscences*, p.3, as quoted in *The Origins of the Brethren* - Harold Rowdon, Pickering & Inglis, Ltd., London, 1967, p.50.

[1128] *Lectures on the Book of Revelation* - Edward Irving, Baldwin and Cradock, London, 1829, Lecture I., pp.89-90.

[1129] *The Morning Watch* -Volume I, 1830, *On the Structure of the Apocalypse* (September 1829) - John Tudor, p.308.

[1130] *The Morning Watch* - Volume I, 1830, *On the Interpretation of the Apocalypse* (December 1829) - John Tudor, p.574.

[1131] *The Morning Watch*, Volume II, 1831, *Signs of the Times and the Characteristics of the Church* (March 1830), Edward Irving, pp.156-160.

[1132] *The Morning Watch*, Volume II, 1831, *Signs of the Times and the Characteristics of the Church* (March 1830) - Edward Irving, p.162.

[1133] *The Morning Watch*, Volume II, 1831, *On the Parable of the Ten Virgins* - John B. Cardale, (June 1830), p.367.

[1134] Rowdon records that; "Darby dated the visit after July 1830." *Interesting Reminiscences*, p.14."Newton affirmed that Darby first visited Oxford a few weeks before news came of the manifestation of extraordinary gifts of the Spirit." *Fry MS*, pp.234, 236, as referenced in *The Origins of the Brethren* - Harold H. Rowdon, Pickering & Inglis, Ltd., London, 1967, pp.71-72, fn 67. "...Newman was able to persuade Darby to visit Oxford, where he arrived in the earlier part of 1830." fn states, "the early summer months of 1830." *A History of the Brethren Movement* - F. Roy Coad, Regent College Publishing, 2001, p.59. Neatby assigns the time of Darby's visit to Oxford as, "August or early September, 1830." *A History of the Plymouth Brethren* - William Blair Neatby, Hodder and Stoughton, London, 1902, fn. 1, p.50.

[1135] *The Origins of the Brethren* - Harold H. Rowdon, Pickering & Inglis, Ltd., London, 1967, p.66.

[1136] *The Morning Watch* , Volume II, 1831,*Commentary on the Epistles to the Seven Churches in the Apocalypse* (September 1830), p.510.

[1137] *The Morning Watch* , Volume II, 1831,*On the Epiphany of Our Lord Jesus Christ and the Gathering of His Elect* (September 1830) - T.W.C., pp.587,588,589,590.

[1138] *The Collected Writings of J.N. Darby* - Edited by William Kelly, Kingston Bible Trust, n.d., *On Days Signifying Years in Prophetic Language*, Volume 2, Prophetic No.1, pp.38-40.

[1139] *Exposition of the Book of Revelation in a Series of Lectures* - Edward Irving, Baldwin and Cradock, 1831, vol.III. Dispensational concepts advanced by Irving in this exposition include the following: [1] "There is a season and a time, during which the saints are *not upon earth, but in the heavens*...being invested in rule and authority with Christ...they *come with Christ*, in order to execute the vengeance written: during which *hour of temptation* they are *not upon the earth, but in heaven*..." p.1025. [2] "The promise of the Spirit to the church [i.e., Philadelphia, Rv.3:7-13], and therewith to all churches...that they shall have their abode in the temple of God, and in the New Jerusalem, the city of his God...To these poor and weak brethren he promiseth the seal of his Father's name upon their forehead, that they may be *delivered out of the midst of the judgments which are to come upon the earth*." p.1054-1055. [3] "These Philadelphians...Christ greatly commendeth their patience in keeping his word when all the earth was forsaking it, and promiseth them *immunity from the hour of tribulation* which is coming to try *all* the people upon the face of the *whole earth*. This is...the day of *Christ's appearing*, from the evils of which, these virgins and faithful servants shall be *preserved by being taken into that New Jerusalem*." p.1105.

[1140] *The Origins of the Brethren* – Harold Rowdon, Pickering & Inglis Ltd., 1967, p.67 and *The Incredible Cover-Up* – Dave MacPherson, Alpha Omega Publishing Co., 1975, pp.28, 34.

[1141] *Narrative of Facts* - Robert Baxter, James Nisbet, London, 1834, pp.11-12. It would appear that the early morning prayer meetings, which began in May 1831, continued on as usual, even after the charismata were allowed to be exercised in the Sunday public worship services sometime between August 1831, and January 1832.

[1142] *The Morning Watch*, Vol.III, 1831, *Commentary on the Seven Apocalyptic Churches* (June 1831) - FIDUS, p.284.

[1143] *The Origins of the Brethren* - Harold H. Rowdon, Pickering & Inglis Ltd., 1967, p.88.

[1144] "According to Newton, on the second Sunday that the chapel at Plymouth was used, Hall preached on the theme of the 'Secret Rapture.'" *The Origins of the Brethren* - Harold H. Rowdon, Pickering & Inglis, Ltd., London, 1967, p.82, per the *Fry MS.*, p.250; cf. p.237. Captain Percy Hall's preaching no doubt occurred in later 1831 when Hall, Newton, Darby and Wigram "took decisive steps" to "launch the Brethren movement at Plymouth." See "*The Origins of the Brethren* - Harold H. Rowdon, p.74.

[1145] Regarding the Brethren assembly, Darby stated: "It did not begin at Plymouth till 1832, where I went at Mr. Newton's request, then a fellow of Exeter College, Oxford." *Letters of J.N.D.* , 1832-1868, Stow Hill Bible and Tract Depot, n.d., Volume One, p.515. Rowdon states: "The latter part of 1831...Newton...invited Darby to his home in Plymouth..." *The Origins of the Brethren* - Harold H. Rowdon, Pickering & Inglis, Ltd., London, 1967, p.74.

[1146] *Narrative of Facts* - Robert Baxter, James Nisbet, London, 1834, pp.16-19.

[1147] *The Life of Edward Irving* - Margaret Oliphant, Hurst & Blackett, 1862, vol. II, p.235.

[1148] Baxter told Irving, "...that we had all been speaking by a lying spirit, and not by the Spirit of the Lord." *Narrative of Facts* - Robert Baxter, James Nisbet, London, 1834, p.118.

[1149] *Memoir of the Late Right Rev. Robert Daly* - Mrs. Hamilton Madden, James Nisbet & Co., London, 1875, pp.149-150.

[1150] Referring specifically to the origin of the pretribulation rapture doctrine, William Kelly explains that, "Now it so happens that, during a visit to Plymouth in the summer of 1845, Mr. B. W. Newton told me that, many years before, Mr. Darby wrote to him a letter in which he said that a suggestion was made to him by Mr. Tweedy (a spiritual man and most devoted ex-clergyman among the Irish Brethren), which to his mind quite cleared up the difficulty previously felt on this very question...It was new however to hear that Mr. Tweedy, who died full of blessed labours in Demerara, was the one who first suggested, as decisive proof from Scripture, 2 Thess.ii.1,2."*The Rapture of the Saints: Who Suggested It, Or Rather on What Scripture?* - William Kelly, T. Weston, 1905, p.8.

[1151] B.W. Newton explained that, "At last Darby wrote from Cork, saying he had discovered a method of reconciling the whole dispute, and would tell me when he came. When he did, it turned out to be **the 'Jewish Interpretation.' The Gospel of Matthew was not teaching Church Truth, but Kingdom Truth,** and so on. He explained it to me and I said, 'Darby, if you admit that distinction you virtually give up Christianity.' Well, they kept on at that until they worked out the result, as we know it. **The Secret Rapture was bad enough, but this was worse.**" *Prophetic Developments with a Particular Reference to the Early Brethren Movement* - F. Roy Coad, C.B.R.F. Occasional Paper Number 2 (Pinner, Middlesex, 1966), p.24, as quoted from the *Fry Manuscript* located in the Christian Brethren Archive at John Rylands University Library at Manchester, England.

[1152] *Narrative of Facts* - Robert Baxter, James Nisbet, London, 1834, p.107.

[1153] *The Origins of the Brethren* - Harold H. Rowdon, Pickering & Inglis, Ltd., London, 1967, pp.96-97. See also, *The Roots of Fundamentalism* - Ernest R. Sandeen, The University of Chicago Press, 1970, p.38.

[1154] In a letter to B. W. Newton, Darby expressed reservations about the pretribulation rapture theory, when he confessed, **"As to any secret coming I have no conviction about it and the proofs to me are certainly very feeble and vague."** *The Origins of the Brethren* - Harold H. Rowdon, Pickering & Inglis Ltd., 1967, p.233, as quoted from the *Fry Letters*, 1845, Folio 1.

[1155] In a letter dated 1843, Darby makes an allusion to the rapture of the saints that seems to echo Irving's and the *The Morning Watch's* position of a partial rapture comprising only the "faithful" and "watchful" saints. Darby explained, "I find many more classes of saints and glory in the Apocalypse than heretofore, though all blessed. It may be some will pass through, but I am more than ever confirmed that it is not presented to our faith, but the contrary, and that the faithful will be kept from it. If some pass through it, it would make a difficulty for those who could not separate the signs of special blessing there, from the evidence of greater faithfulness which made us escape it." *Letters of J.N.D.*, Volume One, 1832-1868, Stow Hill Bible and Tract Depot, London, n.d., p.58. With respect to the partial rapture position of the Morning Watch, see *On the Structure of the Apocalypse* (September 1829) - John Tudor, *The Morning Watch,* London, 1830, Volume I, p.308; *The Morning Watch*, Volume II, 1831, *Signs of the Times and the Characteristics of the Church* (March 1830), Edward Irving, pp.156-160 and *The Morning Watch*, Vol.III, 1831, *Commentary on the Seven Apocalyptic Churches* (June 1831) - FIDUS, p.284.

[1156] While referring specifically to 2Thess.2:-1-3, Darby writes in the year 1850, "It is this passage which, twenty years ago, made me understand the rapture of the saints before - perhaps a considerable time before - the day of the Lord (that is, before the judgment of the living)." *The Collected Writings of J.N. Darby – Examination of Mr. Gaussen's Daniel the Prophet* - Edited by William Kelly, vol. 11, Prophetic No.4, n.d., p.67. See also *The Rapture of the Saints: Who Suggested It, Or Rather on What Scripture?* - William Kelly, T. Weston, 1905, p.5-6.

Bibliography

A Commentary on the Old and New Testaments – Robert Jamieson, A.R. Fausset, David Brown, Hendrickson Publishers, 1997. No Copyright.

A Companion to the New Scofield Reference Bible - E. Schuyler English, Oxford University Press Inc., New York. Copyright 1972.

A History of the Brethren Movement - F. Roy Coad, Regent College Publishing, 5800 University Blvd., Vancouver, B.C. Canada V6T 2E4. Copyright 1968, by Paternoster Press. Reprinted 2001.

A History of the Plymouth Brethren - William Blair Neatby, Hodder and Stoughton, London, 1902. No Copyright.

A Historical Sketch of the Brethren Movement - H.A. Ironside, Loizeaux Brothers Inc. Copyright 1985.

A Manual Greek Lexicon of the New Testament – G. Abbott-Smith, Charles Scribner's Sons. Copyright 1953.

A Theory Reviewed - Rev. William J. Erdman, D.D., self published, n.d. No Copyright.

AMG's Annotated Strong's Dictionaries - James Strong, edited by Warren Baker and Spiros Zodhiates, AMG Publishers. Copyright 2009.

An Expository Dictionary of New Testament Words – W.E. Vine, Thomas Nelson Publishers, Third Printing, n.d. No Copyright.

Backgrounds To Dispensationalism - Clarence B. Bass, Wm. B. Eerdmans Publishing Co., Grand Rapids, Michigan. Copyright 1960.

Basic Theology - Charles C. Ryrie, Victor Books. Copyright 1986.

Barnes' Notes on the New Testament – *The First Epistle to the Thessalonians* - Albert Barnes, Baker Books, 2001. No Copyright.

Bibliotheca Sacra, 101:284-89, July 1944. *New Testament Words for the Lord's Coming* - John F. Walvoord. Copyright 1944.

Christian Words - Nigel Turner, Thomas Nelson Publishers, Nashville, Tennessee. Copyright 1981 by T. & T. Clark, Ltd.

Crucial Questions About the Kingdom of God - George Eldon Ladd, Wm.B. Eerdmans Publishing Co., Grand Rapids Michigan. Copyright 1952, 1968.

Daniel's Great Prophecy - Nathaniel West, The Hope of Israel Movement, 128 Second Street, New York City. Copyright 1898, by Rev. Nathaniel West, D.D.

Dictionary of Theological Terms – Alan Cairns, Ambassador Emerald International. Copyright 2002.

Dispensationalism - Lewis Sperry Chafer, Copyright 1936, by Dallas Seminary. Copyright 1951 by Lewis Sperry Chafer. Published by Dallas Seminary Press, n.d.

Dispensational Truth - Clarence Larkin, Published by Rev. Clarence Larkin, Glenside, PA. Copyright 1918. Revised & Enlarged Edition Copyright 1920.

Dispensationalism in America - C. Norman Kraus, John Knox Press. Copyright 1958 by C.D. Deans, Richmond, Virginia.

Dispensationalism Today - Charles Caldwell Ryrie, Moody Press. Copyright 1965, by The Moody Bible Institute of Chicago, Sixth Printing, 1970.

Edward Irving: An Ecclesiastical and Literary Biography - Washington Wilks, William Freeman, London, 1854. No Copyright.

Exposition of the Book of Revelation in a Series of Lectures - Edward Irving, Baldwin and Cradock, 1831, vol.III. No Copyright.

Expository Dictionary of Bible Words - Stephen D. Renn, Editor, Hendrickson Publishers. Copyright 2005.

Five Letters – Benjamin Wills Newton, Houlston and Sons, London, 1877. No Copyright.

God's Plan for the Ages - Louis T. Talbot. Published by Louis T. Talbot. Copyright 1936, 1943.

God's Plan for the Future - Lehman Strauss, Zondervan Publishing House, Grand Rapids, Michigan. Copyright 1965.

History of The Christian Church - Philip Schaff, Wm. B. Eerdmans Publishing Company, Vol., 2, 1987. Copyright by Charles Scribner's Sons, 1910.

History of the Christian Church, Vol.1 - Henry C. Sheldon, Hendrickson Publishers. Copyright 1994.

In the Heavenlies - H.A. Ironside, Loizeaux Brothers, 1937. No Copyright.

Is the Rapture Next? - Leon J. Wood, Zondervan Publishing House, Grand Rapids, Michigan. Copyright 1956.

Israel My Glory - May/June 2007, *Why Study Biblical Prophecy?*- Renald Showers. Copyright 2007.

Jesus Is Coming - William E. Blackstone, Kregel Publications, Grand Rapids, Michigan. Copyright 1989. Originally published by Fleming H. Revell. Copyright 1898, 1908, 1932.

John Nelson Darby – W. G. Turner, C. A. Hammond, 11 Little Britain E.C. I, London, 1944. No Copyright.

Kept From The Hour - Gerald Stanton, Zondervan Publishing House, Grand Rapids, Michigan. Copyright 1956.

Lectures in Systematic Theology – Henry C. Thiessen, William B. Eerdmans Publishing Company, Grand Rapids, Michigan, Copyright 1949, 1977, 1979.

Lectures on the Book of Revelation – *as (in substance) preached in Edinburgh during the General Assembly, in May 1829* - Edward Irving, Baldwin and Cradock, London, 1829. No Copyright.

Lectures on the Gospel of Matthew - William Kelly, Loizeaux Brothers, 1943. No Copyright.

Lectures on the Second Coming – William Kelly, Believer's Bookshelf, 138 Twelfth Street, Sunbury, PA 17801, 1970. No Copyright.

Lectures on the Book of Revelation, H.A. Ironside Loizeaux Brothers, Inc. Neptune, New Jersey, 1920, 1971. No Copyright.

Letters of J.N.D. - Volume 1, 1832-1868, Stow Hill Bible and Tract Depot, n.d. No Copyright.
Letters of J.N.D. – Volume III, 1879-1882, Stow Hill Bible and Tract Depot, n.d. No Copyright.

Letters of Thomas Erskine of Linlathen - Edited by William Hanna, David Douglas, Edinburgh, 1884, Chapter VII, The Spiritual Gifts - Letters from 1830-1835. No Copyright.

Light From the Ancient East – Adolf Deissman, Hendrickson Publishers, 1995. No Copyright.

Major Bible Prophecies - John F. Walvoord, Harper Paperbacks, Harper Collins Publishers, 1994. Copyright 1991 by John F. Walvoord.

Maranatha – James H. Brooks, Fleming H. Revell Company, n.d., No Copyright.

Maranatha – Our Lord, Come! Renald E. Showers, The Friends of Israel Gospel Ministry, Inc., P.O. Box 908, Bellmawr, New Jersey, 08099. Copyright 1995.

Memoir of the Late Right Rev. Robert Daly - Mrs. Hamilton Madden, James Nisbet & Co., London, 1875. No Copyright.

Memoir of the Life of the Rev. Robert Story - Robert Herbert Story, Macmillan and Co., 1862. No Copyright.

Narrative of Facts - Robert Baxter, James Nisbet, London, 1834. No Copyright.

Moody: His Words, Works and Workers – Dwight Lyman Moody, edited by W.H. Daniels, Nelson & Phillips, 1877. No Copyright.

Moody Monthy –
- Nov., 1942 – *The Story of the Scofield Reference Bible, Part II, A Brief Biographical Sketch*, Arno C. Gaebelein. Copyright 1942.
- Feb., 1943 - *Story of the Scofield Reference Bible, Part V – The Work Begun in 1902, Published in 1909* - A.C. Gaebelein. Copyright 1943.

No Fear of the Storm - Tim LaHaye, Copyright 1992 by Tim LaHaye, Multnomah Press Books, Questar Publishers, Inc., P.O. Box 1720, Sisters, Oregon, 97759.

Not Wrath…But Rapture, H. A. Ironside, Loizeaux Brothers, Inc. Neptune, New Jersey, n.d. No Copyright.

Papers On The Lord's Coming - C.H.M. [Charles H. Mackintosh], Loizeaux Brothers Publishers, n.d. No Copyright.

Passages from the Diary and Letters of Henry Craik - Edited by W. Elfe Tayler, J. F. Shaw & Co., London, 1866. No Copyright.

Personal Recollections of the Right Rev. Robert Daly, D.D. - Hamilton Madden, Dublin, 1872. No Copyright.

Phases of Faith - Francis William Newman, Humanities Press, Leicester University Press, 1970. No Copyright.

Plain Papers on Prophetic and Other Subjects, William Trotter, Loizeaux Brothers, Bible Truth Depot, New York, n.d. No Copyright.

Plymouth-Brethrenism: A Refutation of its Principles and Doctrines - Rev. Thomas Croskery, William Mullan & Son, London & Belfast, 1879. No Copyright.

Premillennialism or Amillennialism? - Charles Feinberg, Zondervan Publishing House. Copyright 1936.

Prophecy Made Plain – Dr. C .I. Scofield, The Gospel Hour, Inc., Oliver B. Greene, Director, Box 2024, Greenville, South Carolina. Copyright, 1967.

Prophetic Developments with a Particular Reference to the Early Brethren Movement
F. Roy Coad, C.B.R.F. Occasional Paper Number 2 (Pinner, Middlesex, 1966). Copyright 1966 by F.R. Coad.

Re-Thinking the Rapture - E. Schuyler English, Loizeaux Brothers, Neptune, New Jersey. Copyright 1954, by E. Schuyler English.

Rightly Dividing the Word of Truth – C.I. Scofield, Loizeaux Brothers, 1896.
No Copyright.

Scofield Bible Correspondence Course, Vol.1, Old Testament - C.I. Scofield, Moody Bible Institute of Chicago. Copyright 1907 by C.I. Scofield.

Scofield Bible Correspondence Course, Volume III, The Gospels and Acts - C.I. Scofield. Moody Bible Institute, Correspondence School, 820 North LaSalle Street, Chicago, Illinios. Copyright 1959, 1966.

Scofield Bible Correspondence Course, Volume IV, The Epistles and the Revelation – C. I. Scofield, Moody Bible Institute. Copyright 1960, 1975.

Scofield Bible Correspondence Course, Volume V, Twenty-Six Great Words of Scripture – C. I. Scofield, Moody Bible Institute, Correspondence School, 820 North LaSalle Street, Chicago, Illinois 60610. Copyright 1960.

Studies in the Gospel According to Matthew - E. Schuyler English, Zondervan Publishing House. Copyright 1935, by Fleming H. Revell Company. Copyright assigned to E. Schuyler English 1938.

Scriptural Truth About the Lord's Return - Robert Cameron, Fleming H. Revell Company. Copyright 1922.

Smith's Dictionary of the Bible – William Smith, edited by H.B. Hackett, 5 volumes, 1870 edition reprinted by Baker Book House, 1971. No Copyright.

Synopsis of the Books of the Bible - J.N. Darby, Loizeaux Brothers, 1950. No Copyright.

Systematic Theology - Lewis Sperry Chafer. Copyright 1948, 1976, by Dallas Theological Seminary. Published by Kregel, Inc., 1993.

Thayer's Greek English Lexicon of the New Testament – Joseph H. Thayer, Hendrickson Publishers, reprinted1896 edition 2005. T&T Clark, Edinburgh, 1901 fourth edition reprinted 1953.

The Ante-Nicene Fathers - Wm. B. Eerdmans Publishing Company, Grand Rapids, Michigan, 1993. No Copyright.
- *The Teaching of the Twelve Apostles* (also known as *The Didache*), Chap.XVI, Vol.7.
- *Constitutions of the Holy Apostles*, Book VII, Sec.II, Chap.XXXII, Vol.7.
- *Dialogue With Trypho*, Chap. CX, Vol.1.
- *Dialogue With Trypho*, Chap.XI, Chap.CXXX, Vol.1.
- *Irenaeus Against Heresies*, Book IV, Chap.XXXIII, Par.1, Vol.1.
- *Irenaeus Against Heresies*, Book V, Chap.XXVI, Par.1, Vol.1.
- *Irenaeus Against Heresies* - Book V, Chap.XXX, Par.4, Vol.1.
- *Irenaeus Against Heresies,* Chap.VII, Chap.XXXII, Vol.1.
- *The Stromata*, Book VII, Chap.XVII, Vol.2
- *The Remains of the Second and Third Centuries,*Vol. 8.
- *The Pastor of Hermas* - Vision Second, Chap.II, Vol.2.

- *On the Resurrection of the Flesh* - Chap. XXV, Vol.3.
- *On the Resurrection of the Flesh* - Chap.XLI, Vol.3.
- *The Extant Works and Fragments of Hippolytus - Treatise on Christ and Antichrist*, Part II, Par.44, 60,61, Vol.5.
- *The Epistles of Cyprian* - Epistle LIV, Par.19, Vol.5; Epistle LV, Par.6-7, Vol.5.
- *Commentary on The Apocalypse of The Blessed John* - Victorinus, Vol.7.
- *The Divine Institutes* - Lactantius, Book VII, Chap.XVII, XX, Vol.7.

The Analytical Greek Lexicon Revised 1978 Edition – Harold K. Moulton, Zondervan Publishing House. Copyright 1978, reprinted 1982.

The Bible and Future Events - Leon J. Wood, The Zondervan Publishing House, Grand Rapids, Michigan. Copyright 1973, 1974.

The Blessed Hope – George Eldon Ladd, Wm.B. Eerdmans Publishing Company, Grand Rapids, Michigan. Copyright 1956, 1980.

The Blessed Hope and the Tribulation - John F. Walvoord, Zondervan Publishing House, Grand Rapids, Michigan. Copyright 1976.

The Book of Revelation - Clarence Larkin, Rev. Clarence Larkin Estate, P.O. Box 334, Glenside, PA 19038. Copyright 1919 by Clarence Larkin.

The Book of the Revelation - Lehman Strauss. Reprinted 1977, by Loizeaux Brothers, Neptune, New Jersey. Copyright by Lehman Strauss 1964.

The Collected Writings of J.N. Darby - Edited by William Kelly, Stow Hill and Tract Depot, n.d., Vol.2, Prophetic No.1; Vol.11, Prophetic No.4. No Copyright.

The Contemporary Review - Volume XLVIII. July-December, 1885, *John Nelson Darby*, George T. Stokes. No Copyright.

The Decline and Fall of the Roman Empire – Edward Gibbon, The George Mace Companies, Vol. 1, 1946. No Copyright.

The First Resurrection - Samuel P. Tregelles, The Sovereign Grace Advent Testimony, n.d. No Copyright.

The End of This Present World – Lehman Strauss, Zondervan Publishing House, Grand Rapids, Michigan. Copyright 1967.

The Epistles of Paul to the Thessalonians – Charles R. Erdman, The Westminster Press, Copyright 1935, by Charles R. Erdman.

The Gospel According To Dispensationalism – Reginald C. Kimbro, Wittenburg Publications, 136 Main Street, Toronto, Canada M4E 2V8. Copyright 1995.

The Gospel of Matthew - A.C. Gaebelein, Copyright 1910, by A.C. Gaebelein. Published 1961 by Loizeaux Brothers, Inc., Fifth Printing, April 1982.

The Great Parenthesis - H.A. Ironside, Zondervan Publishing House, Grand Rapids, Michigan. Copyright MCMXLIII (1943).

The Hermeneutics of Dispensationalism, Daniel Payton Fuller. Doctoral Dissertation, Northern Baptist Theological Seminary, Chicago, Illinois, May 1957. Copyright 1966.

The History and Doctrines of Irvingism - Edward Miller, C. Kegan Paul & Co., London, 1878. No Copyright.

The History of the Brethren - Napoleon Noel, Edited by William F. Knapp, 120 West Maple Ave., Denver, Colorado. Copyright 1936, by W. F. Knapp.

The History and Teaching of the Plymouth Brethren – J.S. Teulon, Society for Promoting Christian Knowledge, London, 1883. No Copyright.

The Hope of Christ's Second Coming - Samuel P. Tregelles, The Sovereign Grace Advent Testimony, 1860 edition reprinted, n.d. No Copyright.

The Incredible Cover-Up - Dave MacPherson, Alpha Omega Publishing Company. Copyright 1975.

The International Standard Bible Encyclopedia – James Orr, Editor, Hendrickson Publishers, 2002. Copyright by Wm.B.Eerdmans Publishing Co., 1939, 1956.

The Irrationalism of Infidelity Being a Reply to Phases of Faith - John Nelson Darby, Groombridge and Sons, London, 1853. No Copyright.

The IVP Bible Background Commentary New Testament – Craig S. Keener, InterVarsity Press, Copyright 1993.

The Life of Edward Irving - Mrs. Margaret Oliphant, Hurst and Blackett, London, 1862. No Copyright.

The Morning Watch, Volume I, 1830, *On the Structure of the Apocalypse* (September 1829), John Tudor. No Copyright.

The Morning Watch, Volume I, 1830, *On the Interpretation of the Apocalypse* (December 1829), John Tudor. No Copyright.

The Morning Watch , Volume II - 1830, *On the Extraordinary Manifestations in Port Glasgow,* John B. Cardale. No Copyright.

The Morning Watch, Volume II, 1831, *Signs of the Times and the Characteristics of the Church* (March 1830), Edward Irving. No Copyright.

The Morning Watch, Volume II, 1831, *On the Parable of the Ten Virgins* (June 1830), John B. Cardale. No Copyright.

The Morning Watch, Volume II, 1831,*Commentary on the Epistles to the Seven Churches in the Apocalypse* (September 1830), FIDUS. No Copyright.

The Morning Watch, Volume II, 1831,*On the Epiphany of Our Lord Jesus Christ and the Gathering of His Elect* (September 1830) - T.W.C. No Copyright.

The Morning Watch, Vol.III, 1831, *Commentary on the Seven Apocalyptic Churches* (June 1831), FIDUS. No Copyright.

The Morning Watch, Vol.IV, 1832, *Commentary on the Seven Apocalyptic Epistles* (December 1831), FIDUS. No Copyright.

The Morning Watch, Vol.IV, 1832, *The Church's Expectation*, (December 1831), John Hooper. No Copyright.

The Origins of the Brethren - Harold H. Rowdon, Pickering & Inglis Ltd., London. Copyright 1967 by Harold H. Rowdon.

The Plymouth Brethren: Their History and Heresies - James Grant, William Macintosh, London, 1875. No Copyright.

The Rapture: Pre-Mid-Post-Tribulational? - Richard R. Reiter, Zondervan Publishing House. Copyright 1984.

The Rapture of the Saints: Who Suggested It, Or Rather on What Scripture? - William Kelly, T. Weston, 1905. No Copyright.

The Rapture Question - John F. Walvoord, Copyright 1957 by Dunham Publishing Company. Copyright 1979 by Zondervan. Twenty-Third Zondervan Printing, November 1981.

The Return of Christ - Charles R. Erdman, George H. Doran Company, New York. Copyright 1922.

The Revelation - Arno C. Gaebelein, Loizeaux Brothers, Inc., 1961. No Copyright.

The Revelation of Christ to His Servants of Things That Are, and Things That Shall Be – F.W. Grant, Loizeaux Brothers, Bible Truth Depot, n.d. Reprinted by Forgotten Books, FB&c LTD., Dalton House, 60 Windsor Ave., London, SW192RR. Copyright 2015.

The Roots of Fundamentalism - Earnest R. Sandeen, The University of Chicago Press. Copyright 1970 by The University of Chicago.

The Second Advent Not Secret But In Manifest Glory – Benjamin Wills Newton, Houlston and Sons, London, 1877. No Copyright.

The Second Coming of Christ - Henry W. Frost, D.D., Wm.B. Eerdmans Publishing Company, Grand Rapids, Michigan, Copyright 1934.

The Secret Rapture - M.R. De Hann, The Radio Bible Class, P.O. Box 22, Grand Rapids, Mich., n.d., No Copyright.

The Scofield Study Bible – Edited by C.I. Scofield, Oxford University Press, Inc., New York. Copyright 1909, 1917, 1939, 1945.

The Story of the Scofield Reference Bible – Frank E. Gaebelein, Oxford University Press, Copyright 1959.

The Thessalonian Epistles - D. Edmond Hiebert, Moody Press, 1982. Copyright 1971 by Moody Bible Institute of Chicago.

The Truth of the Pre-Tribulation Rapture Recovered - R.A. Huebner, Present Truth Publishers, P.O. Box414, Millington, NJ 07946, 1976. No Copyright.

The Zondervan Pictorial Encyclopedia of the Bible – Merril C. Tenney, General Editor, The Zondervan Corporation, Copyright 1975, 1976.

Theological Lexicon of the New Testament – Ceslas Spicq, translated and edited by James D. Ernest, Hendrickson Publishers. Copyright 1994.

There Really Is A Difference – Renald E. Showers, The Friends of Israel Gospel Ministry, Inc., Bellmawr, New Jersey, Copyright 1990, Eighth Printing, 2002.

Things To Come – J. Dwight Pentecost, Academie Books, Zondervan Publishing House, Grand Rapids, Michigan. Copyright 1958 by Dunham Publishing Company. First Grand Rapids Printing 1964.

Three Letters - S.P. Tregelles, Houlston & Sons, London, 1894. No Copyright.

Thru the Bible with J. Vernon McGee - J. Vernon McGee, Thru the Bible Radio, P.O. Box 7100, Pasadena, CA 91109. Copyright 1983 by J. Vernon McGee.

Training God's Army – Virginia Lieson Brereton, Indiana University Press. Copyright 1990.

Tribulation Till Translation - George L. Rose, Rose Publishing Company, 1231-B East Harvard Street, Glendale, California. Copyright 1943 by George L. Rose.

Vincent's Word Studies in the New Testament – Marvin R. Vincent, Hendrickson Publishers, n.d. No Copyright.

Watchword and Truth - *To the Friends of Prophetic Truth* - Robert Cameron, Vol. XXIV, May 1902, No.5; August 1902, No.8. No Copyright.

Will Man Survive? - J. Dwight Pentecost, Copyright 1971 by Moody Bible Institute of Chicago. Assigned to J. Dwight Pentecost 1980. Zondervan Books edition published, 1980.

Will the Church Pass Through the Great Tribulation? C.I. Scofield, Philadelphia School of the Bible, Inc. Copyright 1917.

Word Pictures in the New Testament, Archibald Thomas Robertson, Broadman Press, Nashville Tennessee. Copyright, 1931 by the Sunday School Board of the Sothern Baptist Convention.